Advanced Concepts, Methods, and Applications in Semantic Computing

Olawande Daramola
Cape Peninsula University of Technology, South Africa

Thomas Moser
St. Pölten University of Applied Sciences, Austria

A volume in the Advances in Computational
Intelligence and Robotics (ACIR) Book Series

Published in the United States of America by
IGI Global
Engineering Science Reference (an imprint of IGI Global)
701 E. Chocolate Avenue
Hershey PA, USA 17033
Tel: 717-533-8845
Fax: 717-533-8661
E-mail: cust@igi-global.com
Web site: http://www.igi-global.com

Library of Congress Cataloging-in-Publication Data

Names: Daramola, Olawande, 1973- editor. | Moser, Thomas, 1981- editor.
Title: Advanced concepts, methods, and applications in semantic computing /
  Olawande Daramola and Thomas Moser, editors.
Description: Hershey, PA : Engineering Science Reference, [2021] | Includes
  bibliographical references and index. | Summary: "The book provides a
  sound theoretical foundation for the application of semantic methods,
  concepts, technologies for practical problem solving offering original
  research on advanced concepts, methods, algorithms, technologies, and
  applications of semantic computing in real-world situations"-- Provided
  by publisher.
Identifiers: LCCN 2020026769 (print) | LCCN 2020026770 (ebook) | ISBN
  9781799866978 (h/c) | ISBN 9781799866985 (s/c) | ISBN 9781799866992
  (ebook)
Subjects: LCSH: Semantic computing.
Classification: LCC QA76.5913 .A38 2021 (print) | LCC QA76.5913 (ebook) |
  DDC 006--dc23
LC record available at https://lccn.loc.gov/2020026769
LC ebook record available at https://lccn.loc.gov/2020026770

This book is published in the IGI Global book series Advances in Computational Intelligence and Robotics (ACIR) (ISSN: 2327-0411; eISSN: 2327-042X)

British Cataloguing in Publication Data
A Cataloguing in Publication record for this book is available from the British Library.

For electronic access to this publication, please contact: eresources@igi-global.com.

Advances in Computational Intelligence and Robotics (ACIR) Book Series

Ivan Giannoccaro
University of Salento, Italy

ISSN:2327-0411
EISSN:2327-042X

MISSION

While intelligence is traditionally a term applied to humans and human cognition, technology has progressed in such a way to allow for the development of intelligent systems able to simulate many human traits. With this new era of simulated and artificial intelligence, much research is needed in order to continue to advance the field and also to evaluate the ethical and societal concerns of the existence of artificial life and machine learning.

The **Advances in Computational Intelligence and Robotics (ACIR) Book Series** encourages scholarly discourse on all topics pertaining to evolutionary computing, artificial life, computational intelligence, machine learning, and robotics. ACIR presents the latest research being conducted on diverse topics in intelligence technologies with the goal of advancing knowledge and applications in this rapidly evolving field.

COVERAGE

- Cognitive Informatics
- Automated Reasoning
- Intelligent control
- Brain Simulation
- Synthetic Emotions
- Cyborgs
- Machine Learning
- Computer Vision
- Adaptive and Complex Systems
- Algorithmic Learning

Titles in this Series

For a list of additional titles in this series, please visit: www.igi-global.com/book-series

Handbook of Research on Deep Learning-Based Image Analysis Under Constrained and Unconstrained Environments
Alex Noel Joseph Raj (Shantou University, China) Vijayalakshmi G. V. Mahesh (BMS Institute of Technology and Management, India) and Ruban Nersisson (Vellore Institute of Technology, India)
Engineering Science Reference • © 2021 • 381pp • H/C (ISBN: 9781799866909) • US $295.00

AI Tools and Electronic Virtual Assistants for Improved Business Performance
Christian Graham (University of Maine, USA)
Business Science Reference • © 2021 • 300pp • H/C (ISBN: 9781799838418) • US $245.00

Applications of Artificial Intelligence for Smart Technology
P. Swarnalatha (Vellore Institute of Technology, Vellore, India) and S. Prabu (Vellore Institute of Technology, Vellore, India)
Engineering Science Reference • © 2021 • 330pp • H/C (ISBN: 9781799833352) • US $215.00

Resource Optimization Using Swarm Intelligence and the IoT
Vicente García Díaz (University of Oviedo, Spain) Pramod Singh Rathore (ACERC, Delhi, India) Abhishek Kumar (ACERC, Delhi, India) and Rashmi Agrawal (Manav Rachna University, India)
Engineering Science Reference • © 2021 • 300pp • H/C (ISBN: 9781799850953) • US $225.00

Deep Learning Applications and Intelligent Decision Making in Engineering
Karthikrajan Senthilnathan (Revoltaxe India Pvt Ltd, Chennai, India) Balamurugan Shanmugam (Quants IS & CS, India) Dinesh Goyal (Poornima Institute of Engineering and Technology, India) Iyswarya Annapoorani (VIT University, India) and Ravi Samikannu (Botswana International University of Science and Technology, Botswana)
Engineering Science Reference • © 2021 • 332pp • H/C (ISBN: 9781799821083) • US $245.00

Handbook of Research on Natural Language Processing and Smart Service Systems
Rodolfo Abraham Pazos-Rangel (Tecnológico Nacional de México, Mexico & Instituto Tecnológico de Ciudad Madero, Mexico) Rogelio Florencia-Juarez (Universidad Autónoma de Ciudad Juárez, Mexico) Mario Andrés Paredes-Valverde (Tecnológico Nacional de México, Mexico & Instituto Tecnológico de Orizaba, Mexico) and Gilberto Rivera (Universidad Autónoma de Ciudad Juárez, Mexico)
Engineering Science Reference • © 2021 • 554pp • H/C (ISBN: 9781799847304) • US $295.00

701 East Chocolate Avenue, Hershey, PA 17033, USA
Tel: 717-533-8845 x100 • Fax: 717-533-8661
E-Mail: cust@igi-global.com • www.igi-global.com

Table of Contents

Preface...xii

Acknowledgment..xvi

Section 1
Background, Concepts, and Methods

Chapter 1
An Overview and Technological Background of Semantic Technologies............................1
Reinaldo Padilha França, State University of Campinas (UNICAMP), Brazil
Ana Carolina Borges Monteiro, State University of Campinas (UNICAMP), Brazil
Rangel Arthur, Faculty of Technology (FT), State University of Campinas (UNICAMP), Brazil
Yuzo Iano, State University of Campinas (UNICAMP), Brazil

Chapter 2
The Impact of Deep Learning on the Semantic Machine Learning Representation............22
Abdul Kader Saiod, Nelson Mandela University (NMU), South Africa
Darelle van Greunen, Nelson Mandela University (NMU), South Africa

Chapter 3
Semantic and Blockchain Technology...50
Aswini R., IFET College of Engineering, India
Padmapriya N., IFET College of Engineering, India

Chapter 4
Structuring Abstraction to Achieve Ontology Modularisation...72
Zubeida Khan, Council for Scientific and Industrial Research, Pretoria, South Africa
C. Maria Keet, Department of Computer Science, University of Cape Town, South Africa

Chapter 5
Integrating Semantic Acquaintance for Sentiment Analysis 93
Neha Gupta, Manav Rachna International Institute of Research and Studies, Faridabad, India
Rashmi Agrawal, Manav Rachna International Institute of Research and Studies, Faridabad, India

Chapter 6
A Review of the IoT-Based Pervasive Computing Architecture for Microservices in
Manufacturing Supply Chain Management 113
 Kamalendu Pal, City, University of London, UK

Section 2
Applications

Chapter 7
Semantic Medical Image Analysis: An Alternative to Cross-Domain Transfer Learning 128
 Joy Nkechinyere Olawuyi, Adeyemi College of Education, Nigeria
 Bernard Ijesunor Akhigbe, Department of Computer Science & Engineering, Obafemi
  Awolowo University, Nigeria
 Babajide Samuel Afolabi, Obafemi Awolowo University, Nigeria
 Attoh Okine, University of Delaware, USA

Chapter 8
Creation of Value-Added Services by Retrieving Information From Linked and Open Data
Portals 147
 Antonio Sarasa-Cabezuelo, Universidad Complutense de Madrid, Spain

Chapter 9
NreASAM: Towards an Ontology-Based Model for Authentication and Auto-Grading Online
Submission of Psychomotor Assessments 166
 A. Kayode Adesemowo, Nelson Mandela University, South Africa
 Oluwasefunmi 'Tale Arogundade, Federal University of Agriculture, Abeokuta, Nigeria

Chapter 10
UcEF for Semantic IR: An Integrated Context-Based Web Analytics Method 190
 Bernard Ijesunor Akhigbe, Department of Computer Science & Engineering, Obafemi
  Awolowo University, Nigeria

Chapter 11
A Framework to Data Integration for an Internet of Things Supporting Manufacturing Supply
Chain Operation 218
 Kamalendu Pal, City, University of London, UK

Chapter 12
Towards Semantic Data Integration in Resource-Limited Settings for Decision Support on Gait-
Related Diseases 236
 Olawande Daramola, Cape Peninsula University of Technology, South Africa
 Thomas Moser, St. Pölten University of Applied Sciences, Austria

Compilation of References 257

About the Contributors 290

Index 295

Detailed Table of Contents

Preface xii

Acknowledgment xvi

Section 1
Background, Concepts, and Methods

Chapter 1
An Overview and Technological Background of Semantic Technologies 1
> *Reinaldo Padilha França, State University of Campinas (UNICAMP), Brazil*
> *Ana Carolina Borges Monteiro, State University of Campinas (UNICAMP), Brazil*
> *Rangel Arthur, Faculty of Technology (FT), State University of Campinas (UNICAMP), Brazil*
> *Yuzo Iano, State University of Campinas (UNICAMP), Brazil*

The Semantic Web concept is an extension of the web obtained by adding semantics to the current data representation format. It is considered a network of correlating meanings. It is the result of a combination of web-based conceptions and technologies and knowledge representation. Since the internet has gone through many changes and steps in its web versions 1.0, 2.0, and Web 3.0, this last call of smart web, the concept of Web 3.0, is to be associated with the Semantic Web, since technological advances have allowed the internet to be present beyond the devices that were made exactly with the intention of receiving the connection, not limited to computers or smartphones since it has the concept of reading, writing, and execution off-screen, performed by machines. Therefore, this chapter aims to provide an updated review of Semantic Web and its technologies showing its technological origins and approaching its success relationship with a concise bibliographic background, categorizing and synthesizing the potential of technologies.

Chapter 2
The Impact of Deep Learning on the Semantic Machine Learning Representation 22
> *Abdul Kader Saiod, Nelson Mandela University (NMU), South Africa*
> *Darelle van Greunen, Nelson Mandela University (NMU), South Africa*

Deep learning (DL) is one of the core subsets of the semantic machine learning representations (SMLR) that impact on discovering multiple processing layers of non-linear big data (BD) transformations with high levels of abstraction concepts. The SMLR can unravel the concealed explanation characteristics and modifications of the heterogeneous data sources that are intertwined for further artificial intelligence (AI) implementations. Deep learning impacts high-level abstractions in data by deploying hierarchical architectures. It is practically challenging to model big data representations, which impacts on data and knowledge-based representations. Encouraged by deep learning, the formal knowledge representation has the potential to influence the SMLR process. Deep learning architecture is capable of modelling efficient big data representations for further artificial intelligence and SMLR tasks. This chapter focuses on how deep learning impacts on defining deep transfer learning, category, and works based on the techniques used on semantic machine learning representations.

Chapter 3

Semantic and Blockchain Technology 50

Aswini R., IFET College of Engineering, India
Padmapriya N., IFET College of Engineering, India

Blockchain is a distributed ledger with the ability of keeping up the uprightness of exchanges by decentralizing the record among participating clients. The key advancement is that it enables its users to exchange resources over the internet without the requirement for a centralised third party. Also, each 'block' is exceptionally associated with the past blocks by means of digital signature which implies that creation a change to a record without exasperating the previous records in the chain is beyond the realm of imagination, in this way rendering the data tamper-proof. A semantic layer based upon a blockchain framework would join the advantages of adaptable administration disclosure and approval by consensus. This chapter examines the engineering supporting the blockchain and portrays in detail how the information distribution is done, the structure of the block itself, the job of the block header, the block identifier, and the idea of the Genesis block.

Chapter 4

Structuring Abstraction to Achieve Ontology Modularisation 72

Zubeida Khan, Council for Scientific and Industrial Research, Pretoria, South Africa
C. Maria Keet, Department of Computer Science, University of Cape Town, South Africa

Large and complex ontologies lead to usage difficulties, thereby hampering the ontology developers' tasks. Ontology modules have been proposed as a possible solution, which is supported by some algorithms and tools. However, the majority of types of modules, including those based on abstraction, still rely on manual methods for modularisation. Toward filling this gap in modularisation techniques, the authors systematised abstractions and selected five types of abstractions relevant for modularisation for which they created novel algorithms, implemented them, and wrapped them in a GUI, called NOMSA, to facilitate their use by ontology developers. The algorithms were evaluated quantitatively by assessing the quality of the generated modules. The quality of a module is measured by comparing it to the benchmark metrics from an existing framework for ontology modularisation. The results show that the module's quality ranges between average to good, whilst also eliminating manual intervention.

Chapter 5

Integrating Semantic Acquaintance for Sentiment Analysis 93

Neha Gupta, Manav Rachna International Institute of Research and Studies, Faridabad, India
Rashmi Agrawal, Manav Rachna International Institute of Research and Studies, Faridabad, India

The use of emerging digital information has become significant and exponential, as well as the boom of social media (forms, blogs, and social networks). Sentiment analysis concerns the statistical analysis of the views expressed in written texts. In appropriate evaluations of the emotional context, semantics plays an important role. The analysis is generally done from two viewpoints: how semantics are coded in sentimental instruments, such as lexicon, corporate, and ontological, and how automated systems determine feelings on social data. Two approaches to evaluate sentiments are commonly adopted (i.e., approaches focused on machine learning algorithms and semantic approaches). The precise testing in this area was increased by the already advanced semantic technology. This chapter focuses on semantic guidance-based sentiment analysis approaches. The Twitter/Facebook data will provide a semantically enhanced technique for annotation of sentiment polarity.

Chapter 6

A Review of the IoT-Based Pervasive Computing Architecture for Microservices in
Manufacturing Supply Chain Management 113
  Kamalendu Pal, City, University of London, UK

Supply chain coordination needs resource and information sharing between business partners. Recent advances in information and communication technology (ICT) enables the evolution of the supply chain industry to meet the new requirements of information sharing architectures due to globalization of supply chain operations. The advent of the internet of things (IoT) technology has since seen a growing interest in architectural design and adaptive frameworks to promote the connection between heterogenous IoT devices and IoT-based information systems. The most widely preferred software architecture in IoT is the semantic web-based service-oriented architecture (SOA), which aims to provide a loosely coupled systems to leverage the use of IoT services at the middle-ware layer to minimise system integration problems. This chapter reviews existing architectural frameworks for integrating IoT devices and identifies the key areas that require further research for industrial information service improvements. Finally, several future research directions in microservice systems are discussed.

Section 2
Applications

Chapter 7

Semantic Medical Image Analysis: An Alternative to Cross-Domain Transfer Learning 128
  Joy Nkechinyere Olawuyi, Adeyemi College of Education, Nigeria
  Bernard Ijesunor Akhigbe, Department of Computer Science & Engineering, Obafemi
    Awolowo University, Nigeria
  Babajide Samuel Afolabi, Obafemi Awolowo University, Nigeria
  Attoh Okine, University of Delaware, USA

The recent advancement in imaging technology, together with the hierarchical feature representation capability of deep learning models, has led to the popularization of deep learning models. Thus, research tends towards the use of deep neural networks as against the hand-crafted machine learning algorithms for solving computational problems involving medical images analysis. This limitation has led to the use of features extracted from non-medical data for training models for medical image analysis, considered optimal for practical implementation in clinical setting because medical images contain semantic contents that are different from that of natural images. Therefore, there is need for an alternative to cross-domain feature-learning. Hence, this chapter discusses the possible ways of harnessing domain-specific features which have semantic contents for development of deep learning models.

Chapter 8
Creation of Value-Added Services by Retrieving Information From Linked and Open Data
Portals 147
    Antonio Sarasa-Cabezuelo, Universidad Complutense de Madrid, Spain

In recent decades, different initiatives have emerged in public and private institutions with the aim of offering free access to the data generated in their activity to anyone. In particular, there are two types of initiatives: open data portals and linked data portals. Open data portals are characterized in that it offers access to its content in the form of a REST-type web services API that acts as a query language. On the other hand, linked data portals are characterized in that its data is represented using ontologies encoded by RDF triplets of the subject-predicate-object style forming a knowledge graph. This chapter presents a set of value-added service creation cases using the information stored in open data and linked data repositories. The objective is to show the possibilities offered by the exploitation of these repositories in various fields such as education, tourism, or services such as the search for taxis at an airport.

Chapter 9
NreASAM: Towards an Ontology-Based Model for Authentication and Auto-Grading Online
Submission of Psychomotor Assessments 166
    A. Kayode Adesemowo, Nelson Mandela University, South Africa
    Oluwasefunmi 'Tale Arogundade, Federal University of Agriculture, Abeokuta, Nigeria

Core and integral to the fourth industrial revolution, knowledge economy, and beyond is information and communication technology (ICT); more so, during and post the novel coronavirus pandemic. Yet, there exists a skills gap in ICT networking and networks engineering. Not only do students perceive ICT networking to be difficult to comprehend, lecturers and institutions grapple with the adequacy of ICT networking equipment. Real-life simulators, like the Cisco Packet Tracer, hold the promise of alternate teaching opportunities and evidenced-based environments for (higher-order) assessment. Research in the last decade on ontology for assessments have focused on taxonomy and multiple-choice questions and auto-generation and marking of assessments. This chapter extends the body of knowledge through its ontology-based model for enabling and auto-assessing performance-based and/or pseudo-psychomotor assessment. The auto-grading online submission system assists with authenticity and enables authentic and/or sustainable assessments.

Chapter 10
UcEF for Semantic IR: An Integrated Context-Based Web Analytics Method 190
    Bernard Ijesunor Akhigbe, Department of Computer Science & Engineering, Obafemi
    Awolowo University, Nigeria

At present, keyword-based techniques allow information retrieval (IR) but are unable to capture the conceptualizations in users' information needs and contents. The response to this has been semantic search computing with commendable success. Surprisingly, it is still difficult to evaluate Semantic IR (SIR) and understand the user contexts. The absence of a standardized cognitive user-centred evaluative paradigm (CUcEP) further exacerbates these challenges. This chapter provides the state-of-the-art on IR and SIR evaluation and a systematic review of contexts. Appropriate user-centred theories and the proposed evaluative framework with its integrated-context, web analytic conception, and related data analytic technique are presented. A descriptive approach is adopted, with the conclusion that multiple contexts are essential in SIR evaluation since "searching by meaning" is a multi-dimensional cognitive conception, hence the need to consider the impact of context dynamicity. Finally, the foregrounded semantic items will be applied to standardize the CUcEP in future.

Chapter 11

A Framework to Data Integration for an Internet of Things Supporting Manufacturing Supply
Chain Operation 218
Kamalendu Pal, City, University of London, UK

With the usage of the technologies like the internet of things (IoT) and Semantic Web service spanning across the spectrum of manufacturing, production, and distribution, typical supply chain management (SCM) systems depend on a multitude of services for operation purpose. The unprecedented growth of valuable data produced by decentralised information systems along the global manufacturing supply chain has led to a persuasive appeal for a semantic approach to integrating distributed data facilities in the field of collaborating logistic services. This technology combines a set of new mechanisms with grounded knowledge representation techniques to address the needs of formal information modelling and reasoning for web-based services. This chapter describes a framework, apparel business decentralised data integration (ABDDI), which exploits knowledge representation techniques and languages (e.g., description logics – DLs) to annotate relevant business activities. Finally, a simple business case is presented to demonstrate the framework's semantic similarity assessment functionality.

Chapter 12

Towards Semantic Data Integration in Resource-Limited Settings for Decision Support on Gait-
Related Diseases 236
Olawande Daramola, Cape Peninsula University of Technology, South Africa
Thomas Moser, St. Pölten University of Applied Sciences, Austria

Resource-limited settings (RLS) are characterised by lack of access to adequate resources such as ICT infrastructure, qualified medical personnel, healthcare facilities, and affordable healthcare for common people. The potential for the application of AI and clinical decision support systems in RLS are limited due to these challenges. Towards the improvement of the status quo, this chapter presents the conceptual design of a framework for the semantic integration of health data from multiple sources to facilitate decision support for the diagnosis and treatment of gait-related diseases in RLS. The authors describe how the framework can leverage ontologies and knowledge graphs for semantic data integration to achieve this. The plausibility of the proposed framework and the general imperatives for its practical realisation are also presented.

Compilation of References 257

About the Contributors 290

Index 295

Preface

Semantic computing (SC) is particularly critical for the development of semantic systems and applications that must utilize semantic analysis, semantic description, semantic interfaces, and semantic integration of data and services to deliver their objectives. SC also has enormous capabilities to enhance the efficiency and throughput of systems that are based on key emerging concepts and technologies such as mobile computing, Internet of things (IoT), semantic web, linked data, knowledge graphs, cloud computing, and blockchain technology. Thus, an edited collection of original research that expounds advanced concepts, methods, algorithms, technologies, and applications of semantic computing for solving challenges in real-world domains is vital.

The book provides a sound theoretical foundation for the application of semantic methods, concepts, technologies for practical problem solving. It offers a comprehensive and reliable resource for students, researchers, and professionals in the field of semantic computing on how semantic-oriented approaches can be used to aid new emergent technologies.

The target audience of this book are professionals and researchers working in the field of semantic computing in various disciplines, e.g., software engineering, systems engineering, knowledge engineering, electronic commerce, computer science, and information technology. Moreover, the book will enable students and upcoming researchers in the various aspects of semantic computing to gain improved expertise, knowledge, and insight on how to tackle real-world problems by using advanced semantic-based concepts, methods, and technologies.

A total of 23 experts from 8 countries contributed to the book as authors. The book is structured into two sections. The first section of the book contains six chapters related to background, concepts and methods of Semantic Computing, including deep learning, blockchain technology, sentiment analysis and much more.

The first chapter, "An Overview and Technological Background of Semantic Technologies," by Reinaldo Padilha França, Ana Carolina Borges Monteiro, Rangel Arthur, and Yuzo Iano, aims to provide an updated overview of the Semantic Web and its technologies, showing and approaching its technological origins, with a concise bibliographic background, categorizing and synthesizing the potential of technologies. It is based on the research of scientific papers and books that address the theme of the present work, exploring mainly a brief historical overview and applicability of techniques related to Semantic Technology of the past five years. The major finding of the chapter is that the central goal of Semantic Technologies is knowledge, which is a living, organic being that branches into books, newspapers, libraries, research centers, businesses, government institutions, just as in the gigantic arena of user-generated content and on the social networks.

Chapter 2, "The Impact of Deep Learning on the Semantic Machine Learning Representation," by Abdul Kader Saiod and Darelle van Greunen, presents a comprehensive review of the impact of Deep Learning on the Semantic Machine Learning representation scheme, analyzing the existing Deep Learning literature including the impact of data quality. Key findings of the chapter are that Semanticists will have to take into consideration Deep Learning for efficient implementation. Deep Learning will need to be conducted thoroughly by technology concerns. Both technologies can accomplish extensive results if they cooperate.

Chapter 3, "Semantic and Blockchain Technology," by Aswini Raja and N. Padma Priya, focuses on Semantic Blockchain, i.e., the utilization of Semantic web principles on blockchain based frameworks. A semantic layer based upon a blockchain framework would join the advantages of adaptable administration disclosure and approval by consensus. This chapter examines the engineering supporting the blockchain and portrays in detail how the information distribution is done, the structure of the block itself, the job of the block header, the block identifier, and the idea of the Genesis block. Key findings of the chapter are that Blockchain won't improve individuals, yet it may make a portion of the safeguards fundamental in individuals' everyday lives faster, less expensive, progressively secure and increasingly straightforward.

Chapter 4, "Structuring Abstraction to Achieve Ontology Modularization," by Zubeida Khan and C. Maria Keet, presents modularization techniques for structuring ontologies into modules. It systematized abstractions and selected five types of abstractions relevant for modularization for which novel algorithms were created, implemented and wrapped it in a GUI, called NOMSA, to facilitate their use by ontology developers. The algorithms are evaluated quantitatively by assessing the quality of the generated modules. The quality of a module is measured by comparing it to the benchmark metrics from an existing framework for ontology modularization. The results show that module's quality ranges between average to good, whilst also eliminating manual intervention

Chapter 5, "Integrating Semantic Acquaintance for Sentiment Analysis," by Neha Gupta and Rashmi Agrawal, discusses the concepts related to sentiment analysis and the importance of semantic in sentiment analysis. Sentiment analysis is generally done from two viewpoints: how semantics are coded in sentimental instruments, such as lexicon, corporate and ontological, and how automated systems determine feelings on social data. In the chapter, the focus lies on semantic guidance-based sentiment analysis approaches. A key contribution of the chapter is case study related to the sentiment analysis on the protests for CAA and NRC in India during December 2019. Sentiment analysis techniques have been applied on twitter data to know the opinions of the people of the country on the issue of the protests.

Chapter 6, "A Review of the IoT-Based Pervasive Computing Architecture for Microservices in Manufacturing Supply Chain Management," by Kamalendu Pal, reviews existing architectural frameworks for integrating IoT devices and identifies the key areas that require further research for industrial information service improvements. As has been stated in the chapter, there are lot of issues and challenges that limit the effectiveness and performance of the paradigm Internet of things and people (IoT-P), particularly those related to the IoT reference architectures used that usually focus on sensors and network aspects, neglecting the application domain, information presentation aspects, and other relevant features of IoT-P. In future all these issues will be considered to propose a software architecture, which will help the manufacturing industry automation purpose.

The second section of the book contains six chapters that focused on the application of semantic technologies in various fields of practical applications.

Chapter 7, "Semantic Medical Image Analysis: An Alternative to Cross-Domain Transfer Learning," by Joy Olawuyi, Bernard Akhigbe, Babajide Afolabi, and Attoh Okine, presents the application of semantic annotations that are derived from domain-specific features in the design of deep learning models that are used for medical image analysis. The concept was presented as a viable alternative to cross-domain feature learning which involves the use of non-medical data for training of machine learning models for medical image analysis. The authors observed that although cross-domain feature learning is being increasingly adopted now, it has inherent limitations that makes semantic image analysis necessary. The chapter offers the application of semantic-based methods to enhance the performance of deep learning models for medical image analysis.

Chapter 8, "Creation of Value-Added Services by Retrieving Information From Linked and Open Data Portals," by Antonio Sarasa-Cabezuolo, discusses how information retrieved from linked open data can be leveraged to create value-added services in some selected real-world domains. The chapter presents the analysis of some possible applications of the exploitation of information from open and linked data portals in different fields: education, tourism and customer-oriented services in transportation, and health with all uses cases related to the region of Madrid in Spain. The chapter provides useful insight on how freely available data in open repositories and linked open data can be reused through the application of semantic technologies such as SPARQL or web services to facilitate enhanced services in real-world domains.

Chapter 9, "NreASAM Ontology-Based Model for Authentication and Auto-Grading Online Submission of Psychomotor Assessments," by Kayode Adesemowo and Oluwasefunmi 'Tale Arogundade, describes the design, development and evaluation of an ontology-based model for enabling and auto-assessing performance-based and/or pseudo-psychomotor assessment. The proposed system has an auto-grading online submission system that assist with authenticity and enables authentic and/or sustainable assessments of students in an ICT Networking subject in a university. The chapter offers a demonstration of a plausible application of semantic technologies to aid e-education, which is particularly relevant at a time when there is increased shift towards online learning due to pandemic situations such as COVID-19 that restricts physical interactions.

Chapter 10, "UcEF for Semantic IR: An Integrated Context-Based Web Analytics Method," by Bernard Akhigbe, highlights the need for a Contextual approach to the within the both the non-cognitive and Cognitive Context of IR Evaluation (CCoIRE) that will promote the association of Users Information Need (UIN) with semantic concepts to represent real users. This form of cognitive-based approach to the semantic description of terms to aid the retrieval of ambiguous terms based on relevance as a departure from the traditional IR topic and key-word based approaches. To realize this, the author proposed a novel, User-centered Evaluative Framework (UcEF) that is obtained from a synergy of cognitive and measurement theories to replace the usual system-centric evaluative methodology with user-centricity. The UcEF is designed to use its potentials from context dynamicity to guide stakeholders on the inclusion of users' usage experiences as key elements from users' context during an evaluation exercise. It will also guide on the means to formulate Key Performance Indexes (KPIs) using the Web Analytics Method (WAM) to avoid going off the limit. The chapter provides valuable perspective, and a new approach on the evaluation of semantic information retrieval systems.

Chapter 11, "A Framework to Data Integration for an Internet of Things Supporting Manufacturing Supply Chain Operation," by Kamalendu Pal, describes the Apparel Business Decentralized Data Integration (ABDDI) framework that exploits knowledge representation techniques and languages (e.g. Description Logics – DLs) to annotate relevant business activities. It does this by leveraging the massive growth of data that are regularly produced by decentralized systems within the global manufacturing supply chain in order to support diverse types of services within the supply chain management (SCM) systems. The chapter concludes with an illustration of the framework by using a simple business case to provide insight on the applicability of the Internet of Things (IoT) and Semantic Web to supply chain management.

Chapter 12, "Towards Semantic Data Integration in Resource-Limited Settings for Decision Support on Gait-Related Diseases," by Olawande Daramola and Thomas Moser, discusses the potential of the use semantic technologies and semantic-based system architecture to facilitate the integration of health data from multiple sources in resource limited settings to enhance the quality of decision support in rural healthcare. The chapter describes how the use of semantic technologies such as ontologies and knowledge graph can support the diagnosis and treatment of gait-related diseases in resource-limited settings where challenges such as shortage of qualified personnel, infrastructure, ready access to medical devices, and healthcare by common people exist. The conceptual design and potential use cases of the proposed solution were presented to provide insight on the plausible application of semantic technologies to aid rural healthcare in poor countries and resource-limited settings.

The book provides a comprehensive and reliable resource for students, researchers, and professionals in the field of semantic computing on how semantic-oriented approaches can be used to aid new emergent technologies. It is expected to provide a better understanding of semantic technologies developments, applications, trends and solutions. Moreover, the book will introduce students and upcoming researchers in the various aspects of semantic computing and help to gain improved expertise, knowledge, and insight on how to tackle real-world problems by using semantic-based concepts, methods, and technologies.

Acknowledgment

This book project was partly supported by the Centre for International Cooperation & Mobility (ICM) of the Austrian Agency for International Cooperation in Education and Research (OeAD-GmbH) under Grant No. ZA 10/2019. It was also partly supported by the National Research Foundation of South Africa under Grant No. STGR 180414320796.

Section 1
Background, Concepts, and Methods

Chapter 1
An Overview and Technological Background of Semantic Technologies

Reinaldo Padilha França

State University of Campinas (UNICAMP), Brazil

Ana Carolina Borges Monteiro

State University of Campinas (UNICAMP), Brazil

Rangel Arthur

Faculty of Technology (FT), State University of Campinas (UNICAMP), Brazil

Yuzo Iano

State University of Campinas (UNICAMP), Brazil

ABSTRACT

The Semantic Web concept is an extension of the web obtained by adding semantics to the current data representation format. It is considered a network of correlating meanings. It is the result of a combination of web-based conceptions and technologies and knowledge representation. Since the internet has gone through many changes and steps in its web versions 1.0, 2.0, and Web 3.0, this last call of smart web, the concept of Web 3.0, is to be associated with the Semantic Web, since technological advances have allowed the internet to be present beyond the devices that were made exactly with the intention of receiving the connection, not limited to computers or smartphones since it has the concept of reading, writing, and execution off-screen, performed by machines. Therefore, this chapter aims to provide an updated review of Semantic Web and its technologies showing its technological origins and approaching its success relationship with a concise bibliographic background, categorizing and synthesizing the potential of technologies.

DOI: 10.4018/978-1-7998-6697-8.ch001

INTRODUCTION

It is believed that in the future there will be no barriers, where the knowledge will be available any-where, regardless of language, geographical location, social level, or intellectual ability. Technology will be responsible for the legacy that people (users) will leave for future generations and for the change in social, economic, and environmental relationships that the world needs so much. The main question for the future is not about the best man or the best technology, nor even which of the two can perform a particular task with the greatest excellence; the main question is what is the best form of cooperation between people and technology (Biundo & Wendemuth, 2017; Sheridan, 2016; Ying, 2017).

In the current scenario where the written media is moving, where the amount of information is copi-ous, in the form of texts, photographs, videos, it becomes necessary to have at hand any kind of tool that helps to catalog. At the same step that effective research of all this huge wealth of multimedia content allows professionals not to get lost in long tedious processes, and can perform tasks as efficiently as possible. In this sense, all solutions based on semantic enrichment technologies that arise oriented to the said tasks of cataloging, processing and analyzing information are of particular importance, so that the means do not lose efficiency, buried by such level of information. These technologies offer a whole range of possibilities for professionals, so that they can make the most of dynamic content, and all with less time spent (Bolívar, 2018).

A digital memory common to humanity is in the process of being formed. However, the exploitation of this memory is limited by problems of semantic opacity, difficulty in establishing classification systems and due to linguistic and cultural fragmentation, since it involves questions of languages, ontologies, storage, and retrieval of information/knowledge. These semantic technologies aim to provide additional intelligence to all processes that are performed in the media, including self-cataloging, enrichment, research, and content retrieval. These features include diffuse searches, natural language queries, or multilingual searching, among others. A whole range of tools that facilitate and improve the daily work of both documentation and writing staff, always for the sake of effectiveness and accuracy (Horrocks et al, 2016; Gyrard et al, 2017; Monteiro et al, 2019).

Semantic technology is the foundation for Web 3.0, also known as Semantic Web. Just as social networking paved the way for Web 2.0, semantic technology will enable Web 3.0. However, there is a fundamental difference between these two "revolutions". Semantics can be applied to any type of text and will revolutionize the way that is interacted with information stored on the Internet or in any application. Semantic technology will enable Web 3.0, but applies to any other information process, whether on the web or in a personal document folder. True semantic technology is a fundamental piece of artificial intel-ligence and allows the user to extract or produce knowledge from any text-based information. The idea is basically to assign meaning to content on the Internet, no longer searching for information in isolation or keywords, but in a way that the web can build a more elaborate response from various relationships (Gretzel, 2015; Algosaibi et al, 2015; Hiremath & Kenchakkanavar, 2016).

One of the great motivations that promoted the growth of this theme was the growth and extension of the Web beyond traditional computers. At the time it was created, its purpose was primarily to display documents, with any page of content, linked together manually. Today, what it's seen is a huge field through which the Internet has expanded. Most everyday devices have network access, whether pocket-sized or attached to other functional objects. The Internet is ubiquitous. As such, it is not too difficult to note that the governing standard for the beginning of the Web no longer applies today. Several different media, contexts, and needs have emerged, leading to conclude that the creation of a new form of Web is inevitable (Oldenziel, 2006; Fillmore & Baker, 2010).

Cognitive Computing refers to the ability of automated systems to deal with awareness, criticism, logic, attention, modes of reasoning. Semantic Computing facilitates and automates the cognitive processes involved in defining, modeling, translating, transforming, and querying the deep meanings of words, phrases, and concepts. The machines started collecting data and turning it into information. Cognitive computing goes beyond that, transform this information into knowledge, but machines will never have a mind of their own (Hurwitz et al, 2015; Hwang & Chen, 2017).

Semantic Computing is natural language processing, the heart of Cognitive Computing. Data scientists use Cognitive Computing tools - natural language processing, pattern recognition, and machine learning - to extract the semantics implicit in unstructured content sources. Extracted entities, relationships, facts, feelings, and other artifacts are used to form Semantic Web constructs, such as RDF ontologies (Resource Description Framework), that drive the creation of indexes, tags, annotations, and other metadata. Cognition, the rational thinking machine, is empty without semantics. For the big data analytics industry, if the Semantic Web is not brought to the center of this new era, in-depth research on cognitive computing will be counterproductive (Sheu et al, 2009; Pradhan et al, 2016).

The implementation of semantic features does not yet follow a defined structure. As it is not known what the future holds, it is not yet known which approach will be used for Semantic Web, as some experts are considering adapting existing resources such as the use of tags in HTML documents. Still considering ontologies, which are widely used in artificial intelligence technologies as one of the ways to represent knowledge about the world or some part of it. The Semantic Web, or Web 3.0, can be seen as a private wizard. The idea is that this large network, or even your browser, helps the user with their problems (Lilleberg et al, 2015).

This chapter is motivated to provide a scientific contribution related to an overview and current discussion about the essentiality of Semantic Technologies, addressing their key points and their importance, which are a complex and heterogeneous concept which derives technology's potential.

Therefore, this chapter aims to provide an updated overview of semantic technology, showing and approaching a concise bibliographic background, categorizing, and synthesizing the potential of technology.

METHODOLOGY

This study was based on the research of scientific papers and books that address the theme of the present work, exploring mainly a brief historical overview and applicability of techniques related to **Semantic Technology**. These papers were analyzed based on the publication date of fewer than **5** years, with emphasis on publications and indexing in renowned databases, such as IEEE and Google Scholar. Evaluating that this research work is an overview, it is not a meta-analysis, which depends on the systematic accumulation of information, with practically the majority of research on a given subject, with the establishment of procedures that guide the synthesis of these studies produced in a given research area, which is not the focus of this study.

Web 3.0

Since the emergence of the first version of the Web, early in the first-generation Internet, simplistic search engines, and e-mail, revolutionary concepts naturally come to those who have been dependent on libraries, post offices, and phones for a lifetime. The World Wide Web (WWW) became popular worldwide and evolved in a nanosecond of history, compared to the penetration time of most other human inventions, considered as Web 1.0, its virtue being the democratization of access to information, presenting data and information. Predominantly static, characterized by allowing little or no interaction, user interaction with comments or manipulating, and creating simple content. This web 1.0 technologies are still used for displaying content such as laws and manuals on pages. But concerning this slice of history, it was marked by centralized production of content, such as news portals and also content directories, where the user was responsible for browsing and locating relevant content on his own, something very similar to the broadcasting model of the media industry such as TVs, radios, newspapers, and magazines, where there is predominantly passive action in a process where few is produced and many is consumed (Hiremath & Kenchakkanavar, 2016; Berners-Lee & Fischetti, 2001; Choudhury, 2014).

Web 2.0 was the era of social computing, cross-checking, communication and collaboration, real-time virtual chats and friendship networks, contributions to Wikipedia, and virtual worlds, and even democratization of content production. Having a contrast to its version 1.0, its generated content is predominantly by its users in a process where many produce and all consume, in platforms of user-generated content are in social networks, video streaming platforms, blogs, among others. In this version, the user is no longer just a consumer and becomes a producer or co-producer as search engines become more advanced and proliferate as there is no more room for directory link lists, given the immense volume of content (Mahdisoltani et al, 2015; Hiremath & Kenchakkanavar, 2016; Shuen, 2018; Allen, 2017; Kollmann et al, 2016).

Thus and in this scenario where every day the volume of data and information on the Internet grows exponentially, appearing a multitude of new websites, images, and videos, coupled with the huge and growing amount of information constantly being made available on the network, the current big challenge is to extract what is relevant to people's work and daily life, thus emerging Web 3.0, showing valuable tools, serving for better organization of information, to organize and make even smarter use of the Web. knowledge already available online. In Web 3.0 there is software that learns from content collected on the Internet, analyzing its popularity and reaching conclusions, without the need for people to refine search terms, being able to do it alone, approaching the world of Artificial Intelligence. Web 3.0 brings together the virtues of its 1.0 and 2.0 versions with machine intelligence additions where they unite with users in content production and action making the Internet infrastructure from supporting to leading content generation, and processes. In these scenarios, Web 3.0 services join professional users and producers in actively creating knowledge, and coupled with today's high processing power, it is able to bring high value-added services and products, be it to businesses and people, because of its assertiveness and high personalization, promoting the democratization of action and knowledge (Hiremath & Kenchakkanavar, 2016; Reis, 2016; Rudman & Bruwer, 2016; Ragnedda & Destefanis, 2019).

Since Web 2.0 has established itself in the lives of people who daily attend social networks, the next step in this technological evolution in a world where machines are getting closer and closer to the universe of artificial intelligence, comes to Web 3.0, where the difference between its predecessor is between having someone who just lists all the restaurants one can go to for lunch, having no prior knowledge of whether these restaurants are open or if they will still serve food. In contrast, in the newer and more current scenario, it facilitates and suggests exactly where a user can go eating, knowing the geographical location, what time is most convenient for him, and what gastronomic preferences. That is, the difference between versions 2.0 and 3.0 is between getting a list of answers and a concrete, personalized solution to a question, that is, profoundly the difference between syntax and semantics (Newman et al, 2016; Shivalingaiah & Naik, 2008).

Web 3.0 introduces a different perspective on how to use the Internet, since unlike the previous version, where the user has active participation, in 3.0 version the focus is on technologies that allow customizing the user experience. Considering a change of one paradigm in which the user was accustomed, concerning the interconnection of networks that foster socialization, reaching a paradigm where the content that is produced becomes meaningful. And there is an approximation to the world of artificial intelligence where the machine learns from the user. Instead of simply entering keywords into a search engine to search for a particular subject and get thousands of pages indexed in the past paradigm, arriving at this new paradigm where the user only gets a concrete and personalized response that satisfies their needs. Thus, Web 3.0 is the vision of an era when search engines are not simply about collecting and presenting data that is scattered across the Internet, but is capable of processing that information and producing concrete answers (Hiremath & Kenchakkanavar, 2016; Hendler, 2009).

Web 3.0 emerges gradually, pointing to significant changes in the way as is used the Web, since it is the continuity of the Web as is known, from version 1.0 to 2.0, moving towards a more dynamic environment where Knowledge in action can accelerate business exponentially in virtually every area, from retail to applied molecular medicine, from individual companies to large corporations, culminating in the approach of the world of artificial intelligence, making the distinction between researching a search engine with numerous results and a unique one tailored and customized to the user. Some examples of Web 3.0 applications are in the Wolfram Alpha search engine, and may be considered one of the first milestones of this new Web. As long as the site returns a response, where the system processes responses by collecting data from multiple pages and bases containing only information relevant to that particular question. Still considering Apple Siri can also summarize vast amounts of information on knowledge and useful actions; Google Squared, while still in its experimental phase, has the same goal of answering concrete questions from users, filtering and interpreting results, extracting information from the web, and presenting data in a structured form in tables. It is important to highlight that knowledge is the justified and contextualized information capable of making change, which can be translated as action capacity, in this context the Web begins to bring knowledge capable of promoting large scale changes, leading to organizations, companies, and people, the democratization of the ability to act and knowledge to a much greater extent than compared to what was achieved with versions 1.0 and 2.0 (Hiremath & Kenchakkanavar, 2016; Erragcha & Romdhane, 2014; Metz, 2007; Rudman & Bruwer, 2016).

Semantic Web

Semantics is the branch of linguistics that studies the meaning of words. In the semantic web, content is overvalued and isolated data is transformed into information that generates broad knowledge about any subject or Internet user, this data in the form of codes and symbols of all kinds, such as age, gender, photos, messages, frequency in a site, delivers personalized results according to characteristics, creating a reflection of online behavior (Ristoski & Paulheim, 2016; Gyrard et al, 2017).

Web 3.0 and the semantic web are not synonymous, Semantic Web is just an extension of Web 3.0 that allows users to share content across application and website boundaries, through which it is possible to produce accurate results that are processed by the use of specific software and computer languages to produce more content that machines can use and reach conclusions, not merely keyword-based results. In this context with properly organized information facilitates the creation of these smarter and more agile search systems and robots, coupled with the Semantic Web, machines will understand this information and thus can assist people in everyday tasks as long as our current web, It is a web that only humans understand precisely the information available. In its previous versions, it was extremely complex on the Web to make a system to sensibly read and understand any information, today this scenario is different, since web pages are being created semantically, which no longer searches for such complex information from search robots (Solanki & Dongaonkar, 2017; Choudhury, 2014; Kollmann et al, 2016).

In today's modern scenario, web pages are built on language such as HTML/JavaScript/PHP that present information requested from a database. HyperText Markup Language (HTML) is the main markup language used in website construction, consisting of a set of tags that make up the formatting commands of the language. It can have attributes, values, and inherited architecture, which allows formatting, allowing browsers to interpret the page. However, browsers only limit the interpretation of tags without knowing what content is associated with them, and there is no meaning between them that makes it difficult for them to understand the content (Biega et al, 2013; Krause, 2016; Collins, 2017; Jackson, 2016).

The Resource Description Framework (RDF) helps to organize information and the Ontology Web Language (OWL) it's allowed to represent, relate and manipulate this information, helping the semantic web to make the machines understand the information that a page presents and the relationship that comes to have more information (Ma & Yan, 2016; Tawfeq & Mohammed, 2015; Faheem et al, 2018; Carroll et al, 2016).

RDF is a standardized web data exchange model that facilitates information fusion by allowing programs and websites to exchange data, through which everything is considered as a resource, identified through a unique identifier called Uniform Resource Identifier (URI). The most common format for a URI that can extract knowledge is the traditional Uniform Resource Locator (URL) used to locate a particular page on the Internet. Using schemes allows page designers to use a collection of vocabularies to integrate HTML tags with RDF schemes to add information to page content (Faheem et al, 2018; Carroll et al, 2016; Sauermann et al, 2007).

By adding the OWL language it is possible to define and instantiate ontologies, which is relative to the ability to describe the genres of identities existing in the world and how they relate to each other, and may include descriptions of classes and subclasses, properties, instances of classes and relationships between these instances. Extensible Markup Language (XML) allows users to add arbitrary structure to their documents, but it says nothing about what structures mean, it allows everyone to create their own tags, hidden labels such as labels, annotations on web pages, or sections of text on a page, just as scripts can make use of these tags in sophisticated ways. Since tags are the most correct way to make a page semantic, it is they that will define what type of information is in a particular part of the page displayed, it is what searchers read. The use of the semantic web search results make it more relevant and may even be considered "smart". Nowadays the Internet is moving towards something that will be increasingly directed to the user, providing value-added services. United with the semantic web has been developing as time goes by, since the chance of making mistakes is much smaller, which makes the results more relevant and consequently making possible purchases for the client sites to be made more often. The Semantic Web incorporates meaning into web information, providing an environment where machines and users work together, with each type of information properly identified, making it easy for systems to find more accurate information on a given subject (Carvalho et al 2017, Bohring & Auer, 2015; Varghese et al, 2015; Zan et al, 2017).

Semantic Technology

Nowadays, the Internet is a space where information is found from all over the world through various sources, some reliable, some not, together with the growth of this communication network, the proportions of its scope and all its facilities for access and publication of information, the volume of data became unmanageable. Within this context, the semantic web has emerged as a solution for organizing this current online information network, but it is also about the future of the rethought Internet in a different way than it is known. Seen as an innovation that is organizing information on the Internet and thereby revolutionizing the delivery of content to the user (Comer, 2018; Mossberger et al, 2007).

To cite the example of social networks, the semantic web is already present allowing to aggregate various data between communities such as blogs, Facebook, Instagram, and others, all enriching the possibilities of searching for information. Since the main goal of the semantic web is not to train machines to behave like people, but to develop technologies and languages that make information readable to machines. This purpose involves the development of technological models that allow the global sharing of machine-assisted knowledge, ranging from the integration of XML languages or technologies, RDF, metadata architectures, ontologies, computational agents, among others, favoring the creation of Web services ensure the interoperability and cooperation of these technologies (Golbeck, 2006; Varde et al, 2010; Nasution et al, 2016, Wang et al, 2015; Brambilla et al, 2017; Seyler et al, 2018).

In this scenario, metadata is complementary data that "talks" about the original data, meaning that data referring to other data added by technological tools, seek convergence to the content searched on the web. They are, in essence, data about data, is possible to understand them as an aggregate of small information for a given base. Its use includes possibilities for linking main data, such as a photo, for example, are metadata examples with dimensions, resolution, creation date, and sometimes even location of the scene (Fugazza et al, 2016; Casanovas et al, 2016; Jiang et al, 2016).

Also, in these scenarios, several technologies were proposed in order to make the semantic web viable. In this sense, the W3C (World Wide Web Consortium) consortium was created, where standards are defined for semantic applications that result in a web where machines can infer information regardless of format (text, image, and sound), and is one of the major efforts focused on standardizing data description nomenclatures. At the web development level, HTML is the first layer of client-side development, with three where the first is information-related, which is the HTML that will display it on the page. The second is CSS, which formats this HTML so that it is readable, usable, and beautiful in appearance. And the third that defines the behavior of these elements, which are basically found by Javascript and Ajax. With the advent of the semantic web, W3C is studying new ways to insert meaning into HTML. Currently, only the basics are done. In earlier versions of HTML there were no tags with proper semantics, so developers ended up using simple tags for all situations, and creating their own naming patterns through the id or class attributes (Daoust, 2018; Seltzer, 2016).

In HTML5 several semantic tags were created to tell user agents which content is being inserted into each of the page divisions, organizing and standardizing development. The HTML5 specification brings many new elements to web developers, making it easier to manipulate the elements, enabling the developer to modify the characteristics of objects in a non-intrusive manner, making it transparent to the end-user while still allowing the structure of an object to be described web document with standardized semantics, the biggest evolution of this version is in its semantics. Unfortunately, the adoption of HTML 5 is not that simple, since depending on the browser there may be a lack of compatibility with the new features (Silva, 2018).

However, when dealing with the semantic web, large amounts of information are questioned, where much of this information contains sensitive data, and security issues of such data must be raised. Since current Web 3.0 technologies facilitate information aggregation and sharing, however, the ability to adequately secure the information that is shared is lacking, even considering that these technologies have flaws in information access control, whether related to access to information made available in RDF documents either through OWL. How much ontologies need to be protected as it deals with sensitive information about a particular subject or user. These points reveal a clear breach of the privacy of the average user, not facing this problem literally as a matter of privacy, since some laws deal with it, but more important is the ease of access to information that the use of semantics abides by. Because when using an e-commerce website to purchase products, in addition to specific searches being carried out on that site, it may simultaneously spy on other searches performed elsewhere and take advantage of this information to suggest products to purchase without having been searched (Horrocks et al, 2016; Oldenziel, 2006).

As far as social media information processing machines do not really understand how people perceive and interpret other people, concerning the likes that are shared, it is not actually possible to create objective and concrete boundaries between personal tastes that are shared by others people, in short, friendships themselves have very complex pillars that cannot be interpreted correctly by a search engine, relating that with current technology "a non-human medium will never be the ultimate manager of human interaction". Thus, the implementation of semantic technology is underway, but it may still take some time for all web users to use it correctly. When effectively implemented, all information present on the Internet will be like a great encyclopedia, with easily accessible content, and quick summaries, and the information will be as meaningful to people as it is to machines, making for a much more friendly dialogue (Brambilla et al, 2017; Nasution et al, 2016).

LITERATURE REVIEW OF USE SEMANTIC WEB TECHNOLOGY

In 2019 the expansion of social use within web applications was studied by providing a set of social media that allowed users to freely contribute and interact with each other, bundled with e-learning systems that greatly benefited from the concepts of the social web and emerging technologies of web semantics, where students and teachers live and interact primarily in the world of Web 2.0 and social networks, since web semantics, in particular, provides machine-understandable content to help develop collaborative services, and an interactive method is developed that provided students in the same virtual learning community with the best strategies, with relevant resources that met their needs (Freire et al, 2019).

In 2018, the emerging dynamics of social networks for meaningful learning and the appropriation of Web 3.0 were analyzed, taking responsibility for knowledge management so that these contents allow the generation of meaningful knowledge in the creation of critical knowledge. Where researchers concluded that due to the influence of Information and Communication Technologies (ICT) and electronic devices, higher education institutions can expand education through these technological resources related to social networks, contributing to the preparation of critical participants for society (Vogt et al, 2018).

Also, in 2018 a prototype of a semantic version of a semantic web content management system that is controlled by a set of source code ontologies, working in conjunction with a Java-based middleware and Semantic Programming Ontology (SPrO) was introduced. Which interprets the descriptions contained in the source code ontologies, dynamically decoding, allowing the generation of instance-based semantic morphological descriptions by filling in input forms (Sein-Echaluce et al, 2018).

As early as 2018 it was seen that active learning promotes knowledge creation as a learning strategy for co-working and individual students, where a technological framework based on Web 3.0 was developed and tested in the which all resources generated by students and teachers are organized and classified employing an ontology that can be transferred to other disciplines. And a semantic search system that operates through inferences between the elements of ontologies was also developed, which resulted in an ontology better access to the knowledge created, as well as improved resource search capabilities (Ouf et al, 2018).

In 2017, current approaches to e-learning were studied and applied to students in the learning process, since the e-learning ecosystem needs to merge the concept of personalization, related to the semantic personalization of the learning environment, based on ontology playing a role in building the smart e-learning ecosystem. Where a smart e-learning ecosystem framework was proposed and implemented using an ontology, promoting the creation of four separate ontologies for the complete personalized learning package comprised of student model and all components of the learning process (learning objects, learning activities, and teaching methods) (Russo, 2017).

Also, in 2017, it was studied that Web 3.0 was signed by a series of technical innovations, resulting in a new concept of knowledge sharing, being analyzed the affinity networks related to the theme "città di Chieti". Which are the discussion movements created by the network and understand how the social sciences can study their social form, content, and function (Ristoski & Paulheim, 2017).

In 2016 it was researched that data mining and knowledge discovery in databases (KDD) is a research field concerned with obtaining top-level information from data, performing knowledge-intensive tasks, and generally benefiting from the use of data additional knowledge from various sources combining Semantic Web data. This provided a comprehensive overview of these approaches at different stages of the knowledge discovery process, showing how Linked Open Data can be used at various stages to create content-based recommendation systems, provided the full potential of the Semantic Web and Linked Open Data for data mining and KDD still needs to be unlocked (Noskova et al, 2016).

Still, in 2016 it was studied that Web 3.0 creates the potential for the implementation of new teaching strategies by bringing new forms of teachers' professional pedagogical activities, where new educational practices require awareness of new networking opportunities and acceptance and understanding of new strategies. Where the movement towards student needs regarding the design of an educational information environment and student perception through this informational environment was emphasized (Rodriguez-Mier et al, 2016).

An Integrated Semantic Web Service Discovery was presented in 2015, which performed a theoretical analysis of the composition of graph-based services in terms of dependence on service discovery, allowing the generation of a graph-based composition that contains the set of services that are semantically relevant to an input and output request, yet include an ideal composition search algorithm that was able to extract the best composition from the graph, minimizing the length and number of services, providing information on how integrated composition systems can be designed to perform well in real-world web scenarios. Also, in 2015 was studied the dramatic growth of Internet and multimedia applications, linked to the concept of smart web or web 3.0 offers users the opportunity to share information in order to reach a wider audience and provide that audience with very accessible accessibility and interpretation with legacy image search systems that rely on text annotations, such as keywords and captions to retrieve images. Yet these systems suffer from the high cost of manual text annotations and language problems, considering that to solve these problems, an image recovery and management technique has been introduced considering the actual content of the image and is not dependent on the associated metadata (Irtaza et al, 2015).

Semantic Web and Applications

It is clear that the Web is currently flooded with data and that this volume only grows with each passing day, but it is also a fact that this data does not have a clear and established meaning, which makes it impossible to use in an integrated way without conflicts. Where the determining meaning and the possibility of converting this data into information usable by anyone operator, whether this machine or human, is the major goal of the Semantic Web. Being seen as the Web in operation in the future, where machines can understand the meaning of data the same way humans do, acting on it, processing repetitive tasks, and providing concrete insights to users in various fields. The term Semantic Web is like an "umbrella" of techniques, patterns, and concepts, not just an intrinsic set of frameworks and languages to use (Bernstein et al, 2016; Berners-Lee et al, 2001; Shadbolt et al, 2006).

The Semantic Web is also referred to as a web of connected data relying on an abundance of evolving technology resources extracting value from that data, where many technology giants are already striving to bring this reality forward by developing new standards that allow mature technologies to benefit simply for that purpose. Where this effort is not recent, it has long focused on developing vocabularies related to tags that machines understand through Linked Data Vocabularies, and can offer an organic growth ecosystem that offers a wide variety of resource description vocabularies. Which form ontologies designed to provide precise meanings for specific subjects, ensuring interoperability between semantic databases, thereby enabling data crossover and proving exchanges between dynamic data streams with less effort (Wood et al, 2014; Bizer, 2009; Vandenbussche et al, 2017).

Applications for these technologies can be found in an "intuitive search" that enables the Internet to "interpret" a user's browsing to the point of delivering accurate and accurate search results. In the same way, that semantic search is one of the features of Web 3.0, considered as custom searches. Something that today's top search engines have become central to the current human digital experience, with search engine ranking algorithms increasingly optimized for the user experience by targeting the most suitable search pages, but with the Semantic Web's biggest advent, instead of pointing to potential search solutions, a prompt response will be delivered (Solanki & Dongaonkar, 2016; Hendler, 2009; Hiremath & Kenchakkanavar, 2016).

Voice assistants are other mechanisms that explore the concepts of Web 3.0, which are software that learn to recognize the voice of device owners through interaction by interaction, update themselves through known information, making their navigation easier, more dynamic. However, although they are in a process of learning and evolution, they are still not able to meet all user demands, but the tendency is that this ability is continually developed over time (Dominic et al, 2016).

Three-dimensional graphics are fundamental visual elements for the user experience as high-quality images and videos help a website visitor better understand their content, even more so when it comes to e-commerce, whose e-commerce Operations depend on the consumer's understanding of the product. With the advent of Web 3.0 along with the advances of virtual and augmented reality, it is possible to use devices to get a three-dimensional view of exposed items. In the example of a museum site, 3D imaging technology, visitors can take virtual tours, observing every detail of the environment as if it were physically present (Nayak et al, 2012; Sołtysik-Piorunkiewicz, 2015).

Cryptocurrency is a reality so that in the future financial transactions can increasingly be made through encrypted, secure, instant, and independent transactions. Where through the use of Blockchain technology, digital wallets have very transparently recorded information related to the amount, receipt, payment, timing of the transaction, ensuring the authenticity and legitimacy of the transfers. Just as data security is and will increasingly be one of the main concerns of the modern Internet user, as Web 3.0's intended functionality addresses this issue, since messaging applications will increasingly be present, one of the solutions proposed by Web 3.0 is the decentralization of user data, which can be achieved using Blockchain technology (Vasek, 2015; Murugesan, 2009; Pilkington, 2016; Zheng et al, 2017).

In this context, the evolution of the Internet is the transformation into a more humane and less technically rigid environment, becoming increasingly "smart" and more intuitive, where all trends point to a new era adapted to the user's reality. Having one of the biggest challenges when it comes to web evolution is behavioral identification, segmentation, that is, making the online universe "hear" better what the user wants, understanding their browsing attitudes, being a challenge to build of this behavioral relationship, since there is no online and offline world, but a world that is made up of people (Griffiths et al, 2016; Lynch, 2016).

DISCUSSION

The faster spread of the Internet and new information technologies have had a more significant impact on human relations. As technology has evolved, the amount of data and information that has been circulating is very large. It grows over the years, with a plethora of new websites, images, and videos, as well as billions of documents that make up the World Wide Web and the links that link them. However, a combination of new factors and new technologies now emerging on the horizon promises to further subvert and revolutionize these structures, where scientists, researchers, and business groups are finding new forms of human intelligence mining, targeted at Web 3.0. Since with so much information available, the big challenge and focus are knowing how to extract what's relevant to the business and everyday life.

Situated at the confluence of artificial intelligence, augmented reality, 5G Internet, virtual reality, the increasingly popular and cheap microprocessors, and sensors as well as the interconnection of a multitude of devices, called IoT (Internet of Things). The advent of technologies each secure data storage and encryption, enabling Web 3.0 to be able to juxtapose data layers from the so-called "real" world to the so-called "virtual" world, essentially becoming a space web. However, despite the efforts and development of these new technologies, there is still no clear consensus on a definition of Web 3.0, but basically, it can be treated as a computational environment that exists in a three-dimensional space, containing a hybrid of virtual and realities that generates the possibility of connecting billions of network devices by extracting value and inferring accurate answers.

On this horizon, a glimpse of a future is allowed where more powerful systems can act as personal consultants in areas as diverse as a virtual educational consultancy with the Internet helping a high school student and identifying the right college course through their skills to financial planning by mapping a retirement plan for a couple, or even the best travel package financial plan for a couple who went on vacation, since through Web 3.0 and the new technological tools through it will be possible to create new spaces and environments of work and leisure.

Since virtual reality glasses will be allowed a more enhanced virtual immersion experience being transported to this new computing environment in three dimensions, as in the example of the museum mentioned above, having data and information exchange through sensors, being stored and encrypted surely. Considering that through encryption there will be more identity verification and certification tools using blockchain technology, already seen as successful with cryptocurrencies. But new protocols need to be developed specifically for Web 3.0, since if TCP/IP is currently the foundation of network architecture, new models should be created in the future, with a focus on maintaining interaction and security of all these new virtual environments.

Highlighting the potential for human knowledge mining is an extraordinarily lucrative example, since with current technology it is already possible to systematically exploit human knowledge and decisions about what is relevant to order search results. Where even more in the future the Saint Grail for semantic web developers will be to build a system that will make it possible to give a complete and reasonable answer to the simple question.

In the business field, the use of this new medium can make business easier as it will provide more direct contact with customers, helping to gain new ones and qualifying their already established database, as sites giving way to small web systems will further result in increased interactivity.

Just as a wide range of organizations across industries are integrating semantic standards into their information systems with a focus on structuring and managing this dispersed knowledge. Creating online applications that collaborate in new ways with other organizations, making better decisions, and reducing costs information technology (IT) infrastructure and resulting in the drive to develop and sell new customized products and services.

However today and shortly it is still unlikely that there will be complete artificial intelligence systems, but one certainty is that the Internet will produce a growing cascade of useful intelligence-based systems from commercial efforts that will exploit it further, with obvious candidates. Specific areas such as travel sites and restaurant reviews and custom product developers will benefit even more from Web 3.0, revolving around the potential of user services, intelligent searchers interpreting questions, even through social networks, databases, and turning attention to the corporate sector innovations.

TRENDS

A normal and natural thing on the Internet today focused on social networks that have emerged opinion-makers, where many people seek to have their place in the sun being recognized in cyberspace. Factor derived from the evolution of human thinking which turned the virtual into a necessity for real life, as can be seen drawing a historical line, where people started watching, started collaborating, and currently want to highlight (Comer, 2018).

Closer relationships between brands and consumers increasingly seeking maximum interaction between real and virtual are points of web 2.0, while web 3.0 tends to organize this massive amount of information produced in the virtual environment and use it. More cleverly seeking to overcome the barriers between real and virtual, since it tends to unite the characteristics of the Internet of yesterday and today by adding elements of artificial intelligence. The continuing present collaboration between man and machine, building a promising future for a digital experience without power centralization, freer, and safer. One of the important points related to Web 3.0 is data security with the unregulated exploitation of user information by technology giants representing an excessive centralization of digital power (Marchand & Raymond, 2015; Prabhu, 2017).

With this horizon, users' freedom will increase, as they will no longer be so easily achieved by Digital Marketing efforts, as long as users, using technologies such as encryption, tend to have full control over their data, meaning that instead of companies customizing their experiences, users go hand in hand with artificial intelligence to shape their own navigation. Search engines will be much more accurate and the data generated by everyone will be available on Web 3.0. Searchers will be intelligent systems, a kind of personal consultant, through more powerful languages, neural networks, and genetic algorithms. Whereby machines will be able to refine searches by crossing data, locking dialogues with each other, and offering them under a custom interface or specific to each user. Web 3.0 will be able to give answers like a counselor, crosschecking information, answering concrete questions, establishing values, and ratings (Ferrari, 2016; Rudman et al, 2016).

As is expected more and more concepts such as Web 3.0, Internet semantics, big data, and voice and image processing programs tend to converge at one point, so that in the next few years all these concepts will be increasingly dependent on each other. Importantly, many advances made in the areas of technology and engineering are later used in other areas. Thus, the development and implementation of these concepts are expected to positively impact human health on environmental, agricultural, and human health issues. Based on this, is expected technology to bring direct benefits to both the planet and the human quality of life (Irtaza et al, 2005; Feussner et al, 2017; Estrela et al 2018).

CONCLUSION

The Internet has revolutionized humanity's lifestyle, and the web has seen the distances that prevented communication between people and the barriers to accessing information diminishing. If through web 1.0 it allowed humans to access data stored on machines and its version 2.0 enabled contact and sharing of data between people, web 3.0 is one that allows computers to access data from other computers, i.e., where machines talk to people to make sense of large amounts of data. It is intended to organize the data already available on the Internet in a broader, intelligent and integrated way, creating an environment with which the insertion of new data in the virtual world will no longer be made by the computer keyboard only, but by the convergence of media and technologies that will be used at the same time.

Thus, the semantic web is not separate, but an extension of the current one in which information takes on a well-defined specific meaning, allowing computers and people to work cooperatively. Where since HTML and the web made all documents online like a huge book, data representation and inference models like RDF and Schema will be able to transform all data around the world into a single database. Along with the vocabularies chosen to define the level of relationship between the data, which in practice will result in data interoperability creating a new form of integration and use of documents, files, and services that are part of everyday life. So, semantics will create a break from what is currently differentiated as web access and local access, and in this new scenario, there will be a constant and increasingly natural gift of artificial intelligence.

The Semantic Web, which is nothing more than a computer at a level where the machine itself begins to interact with another machine, which reaches a level of intelligence and begins to talk to each other exchange information. It provided that morphological variations, synonyms with correct meanings, generalizations, links between concepts, links between knowledge and questions in natural language, with the ability to indicate the most relevant phrases, customization, and organic progress, ability to operate are considered without using statistics, user behavior, and other artificial means, still having the ability to detect their own performance. Through it, access to knowledge will be further democratized by imposing common standards for data coding and query, allowing to maximize the value of data through reuse, while reducing technology spending on system integration costs.

Finally, the central goal is knowledge, which is a living, organic being that branches into books, newspapers, libraries, research centers, businesses, government institutions, just as in the gigantic arena of user-generated content and on the social networks. Where this universe of intrinsic specificities and peculiarities to each of these segments requires a broad portfolio of technologies to standardize the interrelationships of your data. It requires a technology that is intelligent and cannot be clogged with trillions of data, but having the ability to process it, having the ability to infer essential truths and deduce implications.

REFERENCES

Algosaibi, A. A., Albahli, S., & Melton, A. (2015). World Wide Web: A survey of its development and possible future trends. In *The 16th International Conference on Internet Computing and Big Data-ICOMP* (Vol. 15, pp. 79-84). Academic Press.

Allen, M. (2017). Web 2.0: An argument against convergence. In *Media Convergence and Deconvergence* (pp. 177–196). Palgrave Macmillan. doi:10.1007/978-3-319-51289-1_9

Berners-Lee, T., & Fischetti, M. (2001). *Weaving the Web: The original design and ultimate destiny of the World Wide Web by its inventor*. DIANE Publishing Company.

Berners-Lee, T., Hendler, J., & Lassila, O. (2001). The semantic web. *Scientific American, 284*(5), 28–37. doi:10.1038cientificamerican0501-34 PMID:11341160

Bernstein, A., Hendler, J., & Noy, N. (2016). A new look at the semantic web. *Communications of the ACM, 59*(9), 1–5. doi:10.1145/2890489

Biega, J., Kuzey, E., & Suchanek, F. M. (2013, May). Inside YAGO2s: a transparent information extraction architecture. In *Proceedings of the 22nd International Conference on World Wide Web* (pp. 325-328). 10.1145/2487788.2487935

Biundo, S., & Wendemuth, A. (Eds.). (2017). *Companion technology: a paradigm shift in human-technology interaction*. Springer. doi:10.1007/978-3-319-43665-4

Bizer, C. (2009). The emerging web of linked data. *IEEE Intelligent Systems, 24*(5), 87–92. doi:10.1109/MIS.2009.102

Bohring, H., & Auer, S. (2015). Mapping XML to OWL ontologies. In *Marktplatz Internet: Von e-Learning bis e-Payment, 13*. Leipziger Informatik-Tage (LIT 2005).

Bolívar, M. P. R. (2018). *Smart Technologies for Smart Governments*. Springer. doi:10.1007/978-3-319-58577-2

Brambilla, M., Ceri, S., Della Valle, E., Volonterio, R., & Acero Salazar, F. X. (2017). Extracting emerging knowledge from social media. In *Proceedings of the 26th International Conference on World Wide Web* (pp. 795-804). International World Wide Web Conferences Steering Committee. 10.1145/3038912.3052697

Carroll, J., Herman, I., & Patel-Schneider, P. F. (2015). *OWL 2 web ontology language RDF-based semantics*. W3C Recommendation.

Carvalho, R. N., Laskey, K. B., & Costa, P. C. (2017). PR-OWL–a language for defining probabilistic ontologies. *International Journal of Approximate Reasoning, 91*, 56–79. doi:10.1016/j.ijar.2017.08.011

Casanovas, P., Palmirani, M., Peroni, S., van Engers, T., & Vitali, F. (2016). Semantic web for the legal domain: The next step. *Semantic Web, 7*(3), 213–227. doi:10.3233/SW-160224

Choudhury, N. (2014). World wide web and its journey from web 1.0 to web 4.0. *International Journal of Computer Science and Information Technologies, 5*(6), 8096–8100.

Collins, M. J. (2017). Hypertext Markup Language. In Pro HTML5 with CSS, JavaScript, and Multimedia (pp. 3-14). Apress. doi:10.1007/978-1-4842-2463-2_1

Comer, D. E. (2018). *The Internet book: everything you need to know about computer networking and how the Internet works*. Chapman and Hall/CRC. doi:10.1201/9780429447358

Daoust, F. (2018). Report from the World Wide Web Consortium. *SMPTE Motion Imaging Journal, 127*(8), 72–73. doi:10.5594/JMI.2018.2850378

Dominic, M., Francis, S., & Pilomenraj, A. (2014). E-learning in web 3.0. *International Journal of Modern Education and Computer Science, 6*(2), 8–14. doi:10.5815/ijmecs.2014.02.02

Erragcha, N., & Romdhane, R. (2014). New faces of marketing in the era of the web: From marketing 1.0 to marketing 3.0. *Journal of Research in Marketing, 2*(2), 137–142. doi:10.17722/jorm.v2i2.46

Estrela, V. V., Monteiro, A. C. B., França, R. P., Iano, Y., Khelassi, A., & Razmjooy, N. (2018). Health 4.0: Applications, management, technologies and review. *Medical Technologies Journal, 2*(4), 262–276.

Faheem, M., Sattar, H., Bajwa, I. S., & Akbar, W. (2018). Relational Database to Resource Description Framework and Its Schema. In *International Conference on Intelligent Technologies and Applications* (pp. 604-617). Springer.

Ferrari, S. (2016). Marketing Strategies in The Age of Web 3.0. In Mobile Computing and Wireless Networks: Concepts, Methodologies, Tools, and Applications (pp. 2132-2149). IGI Global.

Feussner, H., Ostler, D., Kranzfelder, M., Kohn, N., Koller, S., Wilhelm, D., & Schneider, A. (2017). Surgery 4.0. In *Health 4.0: How Virtualization and Big Data are Revolutionizing Healthcare* (pp. 91–107). Springer. doi:10.1007/978-3-319-47617-9_5

Fillmore, C. J., & Baker, C. (2010). A-frames approach to semantic analysis. In The Oxford handbook of linguistic analysis. OUP.

Freire, R., Díaz, J., & Vera, N. (2019). Redes sociales para el aprendizaje significativo: apropiación tecnológica de la web 3.0. In *Conference Proceedings* (*Vol. 3*, No. 1, pp. 160-172). Academic Press.

Fugazza, C., Pepe, M., Oggioni, A., Tagliolato, P., & Carrara, P. (2016). Streamlining geospatial metadata in the Semantic Web. *IOP Conference Series. Earth and Environmental Science*, *34*(1), 012009. doi:10.1088/1755-1315/34/1/012009

Golbeck, J. (2006). Combining provenance with trust in social networks for semantic web content filtering. In *International Provenance and Annotation Workshop* (pp. 101-108). Springer. 10.1007/11890850_12

Gretzel, U. (2015). 9 Web 2.0 and 3.0. *Tongxin Jishu*, *5*, 181. doi:10.1515/9783110271355-011

Griffiths, M. D., Kuss, D. J., Billieux, J., & Pontes, H. M. (2016). The evolution of Internet addiction: A global perspective. *Addictive Behaviors*, *53*, 193–195. doi:10.1016/j.addbeh.2015.11.001 PMID:26562678

Gyrard, A., Patel, P., Datta, S. K., & Ali, M. I. (2017). Semantic web meets internet of things and web of things. In *Proceedings of the 26th International Conference on World Wide Web Companion* (pp. 917-920). International World Wide Web Conferences Steering Committee. 10.1145/3041021.3051100

Hendler, J. (2009). Web 3.0 Emerging. *Computer*, *42*(1), 111–113. doi:10.1109/MC.2009.30

Hiremath, B. K., & Kenchakkanavar, A. Y. (2016). An alteration of the web 1.0, web 2.0 and web 3.0: A comparative study. *Imperial Journal of Interdisciplinary Research*, *2*(4), 705–710.

Horrocks, I., Giese, M., Kharlamov, E., & Waaler, A. (2016). Using semantic technology to tame the data variety challenge. *IEEE Internet Computing*, *20*(6), 62–66. doi:10.1109/MIC.2016.121

Hurwitz, J., Kaufman, M., Bowles, A., Nugent, A., Kobielus, J. G., & Kowolenko, M. D. (2015). *Cognitive computing and big data analytics*. John Wiley & Sons.

Hwang, K., & Chen, M. (2017). *Big-data analytics for cloud, IoT, and cognitive computing*. John Wiley & Sons.

Irtaza, A., Jaffar, M. A., & Muhammad, M. S. (2015). Content-based image retrieval in a web 3.0 environment. *Multimedia Tools and Applications*, *74*(14), 5055–5072. doi:10.100711042-013-1679-2

Irtaza, A., Jaffar, M. A., & Muhammad, M. S. (2015). Content-based image retrieval in a web 3.0 environment. *Multimedia Tools and Applications*, *74*(14), 5055–5072. doi:10.100711042-013-1679-2

Jackson, W. (2016). HTML5 History: The Past and Future of HTML Markup. In HTML5 Quick Markup Reference (pp. 1-4). Apress.

Jiang, G., Evans, J., Endle, C. M., Solbrig, H. R., & Chute, C. G. (2016). Using Semantic Web technologies for the generation of domain-specific templates to support clinical study metadata standards. *Journal of Biomedical Semantics*, *7*(1), 10. doi:10.118613326-016-0053-5 PMID:26949508

Khaled, A., Ouchani, S., & Chohra, C. (2019). Recommendations-based on semantic analysis of social networks in learning environments. *Computers in Human Behavior*, *101*, 435–449. doi:10.1016/j.chb.2018.08.051

Kollmann, T., Lomberg, C., & Peschl, A. (2016). Web 1.0, Web 2.0, and Web 3.0: The development of e-business. In *Encyclopedia of e-commerce development, implementation, and management* (pp. 1139–1148). IGI Global. doi:10.4018/978-1-4666-9787-4.ch081

Krause, J. (2016). HTML: Hypertext Markup Language. In Introducing Web Development (pp. 39-63). Apress.

Lilleberg, J., Zhu, Y., & Zhang, Y. (2015). Support vector machines and word2vec for text classification with semantic features. In *2015 IEEE 14th International Conference on Cognitive Informatics & Cognitive Computing (ICCI* CC)* (pp. 136-140). IEEE. 10.1109/ICCI-CC.2015.7259377

Lynch, M. P. (2016). *The Internet of Us: Knowing more and understanding less in the age of big data.* WW Norton & Company.

Ma, Z., & Yan, L. (2016). A review of RDF storage in NoSQL databases. In *Managing Big Data in Cloud Computing Environments* (pp. 210–229). IGI Global. doi:10.4018/978-1-4666-9834-5.ch009

Mahdisoltani, F., Biega, J., & Suchanek, F. M. (2013, January). *Yago3: A knowledge base from multilingual Wikipedias.* Academic Press.

Marchand, M., & Raymond, L. (2015). Characterizing the IT Artefact through Plato's Ontology: Performance Measurement Systems in the Web 3.0 Era. In Artificial Intelligence Technologies and the Evolution of Web 3.0 (pp. 325-350). IGI Global.

Metz, C. (2007). Web 3.0. *Pc Magazine, 26*(7/8), 74–79.

Monteiro, A. C. B., Iano, Y., França, R. P., & Razmjooy, N. (2019). WT-MO Algorithm: Automated Hematological Software Based on the Watershed Transform for Blood Cell Count. In Applications of Image Processing and Soft Computing Systems in Agriculture (pp. 39-79). IGI Global.

Mossberger, K., Tolbert, C. J., & McNeal, R. S. (2007). *Digital citizenship: The Internet, society, and participation.* MIT Press. doi:10.7551/mitpress/7428.001.0001

Murugesan, S. (Ed.). (2009). *Handbook of Research on Web 2.0, 3.0, and X. 0: Technologies, Business, and Social Applications: Technologies, Business, and Social Applications.* IGI Global.

Nasution, M. K., Noah, S. A. M., & Saad, S. (2016). *Social network extraction: Superficial method and information retrieval.* arXiv preprint arXiv:1601.02904.

Nayak, R., Senellart, P., Suchanek, F. M., & Varde, A. S. (2013). Discovering interesting information with advances in web technology. *SIGKDD Explorations, 14*(2), 63–81. doi:10.1145/2481244.2481255

Newman, R., Chang, V., Walters, R. J., & Wills, G. B. (2016). Web 2.0—The past and the future. *International Journal of Information Management, 36*(4), 591–598. doi:10.1016/j.ijinfomgt.2016.03.010

Noskova, T., Pavlova, T., & Iakovleva, O. (2016). Web 3.0 technologies and transformation of pedagogical activities. In Mobile Computing and Wireless Networks: Concepts, Methodologies, Tools, and Applications (pp. 728-748). IGI Global.

Oldenziel, R. (2006). Introduction: Signifying semantics for a history of technology. *Technology and Culture, 47*(3), 477–485. doi:10.1353/tech.2006.0194

Ouf, S., Ellatif, M. A., Salama, S. E., & Helmy, Y. (2018). A proposed paradigm for smart learning environment based on semantic web. *Computers in Human Behavior, 72,* 796–818. doi:10.1016/j.chb.2016.08.030

Pilkington, M. (2016). 11 Blockchain technology: principles and applications. *Research handbook on digital transformations*, 225.

Prabhu, D. (2017). *Application of web 2.0 and web 3.0: an overview*. LAP LAMBERT Academic Publishing.

Pradhan, A. M., & Varde, A. S. (2016, October). Ontology-based meta knowledge extraction with semantic web tools for ubiquitous computing. In *2016 IEEE 7th Annual Ubiquitous Computing, Electronics & Mobile Communication Conference (UEMCON)* (pp. 1-6). IEEE.

Ragnedda, M., & Destefanis, G. (Eds.). (2019). *Blockchain and Web 3.0: Social, Economic, and Technological Challenges*. Routledge. doi:10.4324/9780429029530

Reis, R. L. D. P. (2016). *O jornalismo em Portugal e os desafios da Web 3.0* (Doctoral dissertation).

Ristoski, P., & Paulheim, H. (2016). Semantic Web in data mining and knowledge discovery: A comprehensive survey. *Journal of Web Semantics*, *36*, 1–22. doi:10.1016/j.websem.2016.01.001

Ristoski, P., & Paulheim, H. (2017). Semantic Web in data mining and knowledge discovery: A comprehensive survey. *Journal of Web Semantics*, *36*, 1–22. doi:10.1016/j.websem.2016.01.001

Rodriguez-Mier, P., Pedrinaci, C., Lama, M., & Mucientes, M. (2016). An integrated semantic web service discovery and composition framework. *IEEE Transactions on Services Computing*, *9*(4), 537–550. doi:10.1109/TSC.2015.2402679

Rudman, R., & Bruwer, R. (2016). Defining Web 3.0: Opportunities and challenges. *The Electronic Library*, *34*(1), 132–154. doi:10.1108/EL-08-2014-0140

Russo, V. (2017). Urban media activism in web 3.0. Case analysis: the city of Chieti. In *Recent Trends in Social Systems: Quantitative Theories and Quantitative Models* (pp. 303–313). Springer. doi:10.1007/978-3-319-40585-8_27

Sauermann, L., Cyganiak, R., & Völkel, M. (2007). *Cool URIs for the semantic web*. Academic Press.

Sein-Echaluce, M. L., Fidalgo-Blanco, Á., & Esteban-Escaño, J. (2018). Technological ecosystems and ontologies for an educational model based on Web 3.0. *Universal Access in the Information Society*, *18*(3), 645–658. doi:10.100710209-019-00684-9

Seltzer, W. (2016). World Wide Web Consortium (W3C) standards for the open web platform. *Open Source, Open Standards, Open Minds Conference Proceedings*.

Seyler, D., Dembelova, T., Del Corro, L., Hoffart, J., & Weikum, G. (2018, July). A study of the importance of external knowledge in the named entity recognition task. In *Proceedings of the 56th Annual Meeting of the Association for Computational Linguistics* (vol. 2, pp. 241-246). 10.18653/v1/P18-2039

Shadbolt, N., Berners-Lee, T., & Hall, W. (2006). The semantic web revisited. *IEEE Intelligent Systems*, *21*(3), 96–101. doi:10.1109/MIS.2006.62

Sheridan, T. B. (2016). Human-robot interaction: Status and challenges. *Human Factors*, *58*(4), 525–532. doi:10.1177/0018720816644364 PMID:27098262

Sheu, P. C. Y., Wang, S., Wang, Q., Hao, K., & Paul, R. (2009). Semantic computing, cloud computing, and semantic search engine. In *2009 IEEE International Conference on Semantic Computing* (pp. 654-657). IEEE. 10.1109/ICSC.2009.51

Shivalingaiah, D., & Naik, U. (2008). *Comparative study of web 1.0, web 2.0 and web 3.0*. Academic Press.

Shuen, A. (2018). *Web 2.0: A Strategy Guide: Business thinking and strategies behind successful Web 2.0 implementations*. O'Reilly Media.

Silva, M. S. (2018). *Fundamentos de HTML5 e CSS3*. Novatec Editora.

Solanki, M. R., & Dongaonkar, A. (2016). A Journey of human comfort: Web 1.0 to web 4.0. *International Journal of Research and Scientific Innovation, 3*(IX), 75–78.

Sołtysik-Piorunkiewicz, A. (2015). The evaluation method of Web 2.0/3.0 usability in e-health knowledge management system. *Online Journal of Applied Knowledge Management, A Publication of the International Institute for Applied Knowledge Management, 3*(2).

Tawfeq, J. F., & Mohammed, S. M. (2015). Resource Description Framework Schemas for E-Library. *Journal of Madenat Alelem College, 7*(2), 27–35.

Vandenbussche, P. Y., Atemezing, G. A., Poveda-Villalón, M., & Vatant, B. (2017). Linked Open Vocabularies (LOV): A gateway to reusable semantic vocabularies on the Web. *Semantic Web, 8*(3), 437–452. doi:10.3233/SW-160213

Varde, A., Rundensteiner, E., & Fahrenholz, S. (2010). XML based markup languages for specific domains. In *Web-based Support Systems* (pp. 215–238). Springer. doi:10.1007/978-1-84882-628-1_11

Varghese, A., Varde, A. S., Peng, J., & Fitzpatrick, E. (2015). A framework for collocation error correction in web pages and text documents. *SIGKDD Explorations, 17*(1), 14–23. doi:10.1145/2830544.2830548

Vasek, M. (2015). *The age of cryptocurrency*. Academic Press.

Vogt, L., Baum, R., Köhler, C., Meid, S., Quast, B., & Grobe, P. (2018). Using Semantic Programming for Developing a Web Content Management System for Semantic Phenotype Data. In *International Conference on Data Integration in the Life Sciences* (pp. 200-206). Springer.

Wang, P., Xu, B., Wu, Y., & Zhou, X. (2015). Link prediction in social networks: The state-of-the-art. *Science China. Information Sciences, 58*(1), 1–38. doi:10.100711432-014-5237-y

Wood, D., Zaidman, M., Ruth, L., & Hausenblas, M. (2014). *Linked Data*. Manning Publications Co.

Ying, J. (2017). *U.S. Patent Application No. 29/556,275*. Washington, DC: US Patent Office.

Zan, T., Pacheco, H., Ko, H. S., & Hu, Z. (2017). BiFluX: A Bidirectional Functional Update Language for XML. *Information and Media Technologies, 12*, 1–23.

Zheng, Z., Xie, S., Dai, H., Chen, X., & Wang, H. (2017). An overview of blockchain technology: Architecture, consensus, and future trends. In *2017 IEEE International Congress on Big Data (BigData Congress)* (pp. 557-564). IEEE.

ADDITIONAL READING

Albukhitan, S., Alnazer, A., & Helmy, T. (2020). Framework of Semantic Annotation of Arabic Document using Deep Learning. *Procedia Computer Science*, *170*, 989–994. doi:10.1016/j.procs.2020.03.096

Asfand-E-Yar, M., & Ali, R. (2020). Semantic Integration of Heterogeneous Databases of Same Domain Using Ontology. *IEEE Access: Practical Innovations, Open Solutions*, *8*, 77903–77919. doi:10.1109/ACCESS.2020.2988685

Augello, A., Infantino, I., Pilato, G., & Vella, F. (2020). Sensing the Web for Induction of Association Rules and their Composition through Ensemble Techniques. *Procedia Computer Science*, *169*, 851–859. doi:10.1016/j.procs.2020.02.152

d'Amato, C. (2020). Machine learning for the semantic web: Lessons learnt and next research directions. Semantic Web, (Preprint), 1-9.

Dridi, A., Sassi, S., Chbeir, R., & Faïz, S. (2020). A Flexible Semantic Integration Framework for Fully-integrated EHR based on FHIR Standard. In ICAART (2) (pp. 684-691). doi:10.5220/0008981506840691

Hitzler, P., Bianchi, F., Ebrahimi, M., & Sarker, M. K. (2020). Neural-symbolic integration and the Semantic Web. *Semantic Web*, *11*(1), 3–11. doi:10.3233/SW-190368

Liu, D., Etudo, U., & Yoon, V. (2020). X-IM Framework to Overcome Semantic Heterogeneity Across XBRL Filings. *Journal of the Association for Information Systems*, *21*(4), 4. doi:10.17705/1jais.00626

Lu, W., Wang, P., Ma, X., Xu, W., & Chen, C. (2020). Enrich cross-lingual entity links for online wikis via multi-modal semantic matching. *Information Processing & Management*, *57*(5), 102271. doi:10.1016/j.ipm.2020.102271

Lu, W., Zhang, X., Lu, H., & Li, F. (2020). Deep hierarchical encoding model for sentence semantic matching. *Journal of Visual Communication and Image Representation*, *71*, 102794. doi:10.1016/j.jvcir.2020.102794

Nugroho, I. M. R. A., & Sentana, I. W. B. (2020). Query Rewriting with Thesaurus-Based for Handling Semantic Heterogeneity in Database Integration. *Knowledge Engineering and Data Science*, *3*(1), 11–18. doi:10.17977/um018v3i12020p11-18

Pacha, S., Murugan, S. R., & Sethukarasi, R. (2020). Semantic annotation of summarized sensor data stream for effective query processing. *The Journal of Supercomputing*, *76*(6), 4017–4039. doi:10.100711227-017-2183-7

Perez, N., Accuosto, P., Bravo, À., Cuadros, M., Martínez-Garcia, E., Saggion, H., & Rigau, G. (2020). Cross-lingual semantic annotation of biomedical literature: Experiments in Spanish and English. *Bioinformatics (Oxford, England)*, *36*(6), 1872–1880. PMID:31730202

Rastogi, M., Afshan Ali, S., Rawat, M., Vig, L., Agarwal, P., Shroff, G., & Srinivasan, A. (2020). Information Extraction From Document Images via FCA-Based Template Detection and Knowledge Graph Rule Induction. In *Proceedings of the IEEE/CVF Conference on Computer Vision and Pattern Recognition Workshops* (pp. 558-559).

Rinaldi, A. M., Russo, C., & Madani, K. (2020). A Semantic Matching Strategy for Very Large Knowledge Bases Integration. *International Journal of Information Technology and Web Engineering, 15*(2), 1–29. doi:10.4018/IJITWE.2020040101

Zhang, L., Wang, T., Liu, Y., & Duan, Q. (2020). A semi-structured information semantic annotation method for Web pages. *Neural Computing & Applications, 32*(11), 6491–6501. doi:10.100700521-018-03999-5

KEY TERMS AND DEFINITIONS

Cognitive Computing: It refers to the ability of automated systems to deal with awareness, criticism, logic, attention, modes of reasoning. It facilitates and automates the cognitive processes involved in defining, modeling, translating, transforming, and querying the deep meanings of words, phrases, and concepts.

Semantic Computing: It is natural language processing, the heart of Cognitive Computing, i.e., tools for natural language processing, pattern recognition, and machine learning, with a purpose to extract the semantics implicit in unstructured content sources.

Semantic Web: Is where content is overvalued and isolated data is transformed into information that generates broad knowledge about any subject or Internet user, this data in the form of codes and symbols of all kinds, such as age, gender, photos, messages, frequency in a site, delivers personalized results according to characteristics, creating a reflection of online behavior.

Web 3.0: It learns from content collected on the Internet, analyzing its popularity, and reaching conclusions, without the need for people to refine search terms, being able to do it alone. It brings together the virtues of its 1.0 and 2.0 versions with machine intelligence additions where they unite with users in content production and action making the Internet infrastructure from supporting to leading content generation, and processes.

Chapter 2
The Impact of Deep Learning on the Semantic Machine Learning Representation

Abdul Kader Saiod
Nelson Mandela University (NMU), South Africa

Darelle van Greunen
Nelson Mandela University (NMU), South Africa

ABSTRACT

Deep learning (DL) is one of the core subsets of the semantic machine learning representations (SMLR) that impact on discovering multiple processing layers of non-linear big data (BD) transformations with high levels of abstraction concepts. The SMLR can unravel the concealed explanation characteristics and modifications of the heterogeneous data sources that are intertwined for further artificial intelligence (AI) implementations. Deep learning impacts high-level abstractions in data by deploying hierarchical architectures. It is practically challenging to model big data representations, which impacts on data and knowledge-based representations. Encouraged by deep learning, the formal knowledge representation has the potential to influence the SMLR process. Deep learning architecture is capable of modelling efficient big data representations for further artificial intelligence and SMLR tasks. This chapter focuses on how deep learning impacts on defining deep transfer learning, category, and works based on the techniques used on semantic machine learning representations.

INTRODUCTION

Semantic Machine Learning and Deep Learning share the goal of composing artificial intelligence that simulates human possibilities such as indexing, validating, prognosticating and reasoning. Both fields have been impacting data and knowledge analysis considerably as well as their associated abstract representations (Dagmar *et al.* 2019). Deep Learning is an essential part of the Semantic Machine Learning Representations that perceives to experience high-level abstractions in big data by implementing

DOI: 10.4018/978-1-7998-6697-8.ch002

hierarchical frameworks. Therefore, Deep Learning discovers an intricate Big Data structure using the backpropagation algorithm to specify internal logic to manipulate each computational model of the operation. Artificial Intelligence domains are challenging the traditional approaches to exploit structured knowledge to improve potential decision-making process performances. Deep Learning is an emerging approach and has been widely implemented in semantic artificial intelligence (Bordes *et al.* 2012) as well as in knowledge transfer (Yue-ting *et al.* 2017), linguistic data processing (Gemma 2020), computer visualisation (Alejandra *et al.* 2019) and many more. Artificial Intelligence is frequently aimed at representing the high-level human cognitive capabilities, such as making decisions, inferences and validations. On the other hand, knowledge-based representations facilitate logic reapplication and the sharing of inappropriate subsist semantic resources. Deep Learning is implemented to integrate big data representations, that transformations with multi-layer data processing algorithms. Today, such algorithms are well considered in the field of machine learning, where they have been successfully implemented to numerous real-world issues. With the challenges outlined, how can Deep Learning be implemented to address some important aspects such as semantic indexing, data tagging, searching, extracting complex patterns from Big Data, fast information retrieval and simplifying discriminative tasks in the SMLR process? Deep learning with semantic knowledge-based representation enhances the reapplication and sharing of knowledge in appropriate subsisting existing ontologies, which are divided into two nodes: decreasing the domain workload to reducing the processing time and enabling interoperability to provide a comprehensive process with other similar systems.

CONTEXT

The aim of Deep Learning is to builds a persuasive instance for vindicating potential relationship between ontological linguistics and connectionism. This chapter will investigate further arguments and impacts extending them to the Semantic Machine Learning Representations in terms of improving data quality issues. The predominant features of DL in some of its breakthroughs in linguistic value processing have come from incorporating appropriation and terminologies from SMLR. Unfortunately, linguistic semantics has, to date, been much less influenced by DL research (Christopher *et al.* 2018). According to Lewis (1970), "To say what a meaning IS, we may first ask what a meaning DOES, and then find something that does that". Machine learning is based on learning functions and classifiers to assemble and accumulate data, so the data quality standard that is implemented should be comprehensive. DL and Semantic terminologies share the motivation of implementing artificial intelligence that simulates our capabilities such as indexing, validating, formalising, defining, establishing and acquiring. Both terminologies have been concluding information and knowledge-based exploration considerably the related abstract affirmation to improve the Data Quality (DQ) issue. "All progress is born of inquiry. Doubt is often better than overconfidence, for it leads to inquiry and inquiry leads to the invention" is a famous Hudson Maxim in the context of which the significance of research can well be understood. This inquisitiveness is the mother of all knowledge and the method, which man employs for obtaining the knowledge of whatever the unknown, can be termed as research (Kothari 2004). Collected data were subjected to descriptive statistical and inferential statistical analysis, measurement modelling and structural equation modelling to provide the objectives formulated by this study. Matching is a process of finding alignment between sets of correspondences with a semantic verification output of the matching process (Hiba *et al.* 2020). This merging is a process of creating a new set of possibly overlapping data. However, this study aims to determine the best illustrate object to find a semantically fundamental equivalent motive in DL impacts in SMLR to address DQ issues. This provides a strong theoretical and practical framework to work with heterogeneous, complex, conflicting and automatic consensus methods for big data. This means that each information amalgamated data associated with a distinguishable adumbration characteristic. Therefore, conflict may happen on EHRs integration, if a diverse amalgamated data associated with the same apprehension in the diverse systems (Saiod *et al.* 2017). The technical level of the integration system, including the semantic level, should be modelled in such a way that the data will not miss during the data exchange between the system and business placing.

DEEP LEARNING CONCERNED

Deep Learning is becoming most commonly used in artificial intelligence. Today, with the massive size of data processing, the potential of big data offers great opportunities in the various sectors (Chen *et al.* 2014, Wu *et al.* 2014). Hierarchical Deep Neural Networks (DNNs) have proven interoperability in Natural Language Processing (NLP) and DL is starting to demonstrate a principle role in big data integration problems. Machine learning is a part of artificial intelligence which is generally aimed at replacing human intervention. But the Deep Learning algorithm and method are significantly dependent on scientists and researchers, according to organisational needs. It is very similar to converting the human brain into a system process for decision making. Most of the traditional methods develop a linear algorithm but deep learning applies a multiple neurons method to handle complex and big data from diverse heterogeneous sources using a nonlinear algorithm (Renguang *et al.* 2019). Deep Learning has been widely implemented in big data platforms such as robotic, automatic and natural language processing etc. The Deep Learning algorithm is capable of processing the optimal features efficiently by using the security domain knowledge base automatically (Shadi *et al.* 2019). Due to the scalability, Deep Learning handles data efficiently and accurately. Deep Learning can be used in a developed powerful sequential algorithm to perform a historical knowledge interaction. The scalable feature makes it possible to combine multiple algorithms to develop a hybrid method of integrating complex data from diverse heterogeneous sources.

SEMANTIC MACHINE LEARNING REPRESENTATIONS

Semantic Machine Learning Representation is an artificial intelligence algorithm based on technological and organisational measures that impact the entire data lifecycle. Semantic Machine Learning combines thoroughly appropriate algorithms and components that handle the most general issues such as classification and guidance in a highly precise manner. Existing literature shows that there are currently several techniques being proposed to developed artificial intelligence which historically has faced database management systems (Saiod *et al.* 2019a). After a deep analysis of several cutting-edge commercial solutions available on the software market and an intensive review of literature, it appears artificial intelligence is often inoperable due to the inconsistent or low-quality data. A semantic knowledge-base is implemented on the principle of a semantically enhanced artificial intelligence architecture, which provides means for a more automated DQ management. Machine learning is classified into three sections, as below:

1. Data collection;
2. Develop a knowledge base;
3. Reapplying existing logic to develop future predictions;

Several dimension matrixes for determining Data Redundancy (DR) are available for narrative text. Sequence classification methods, such as the one proposed by Zhang *et al.* (2011) are, "accurate yet expensive due to the high complexity of string alignment even when optimised". The lower DR dimension metric introduces collective words, apprehension or significant coincidence bigrams. Although semantic similarity could be determined by using these methods, they do not provide particular vindication for copy-paste performances that can regenerate the entire contexts.

The majority of bioinformatics semantic similarity algorithms are founded on detruncating inconsequential smaller substrings to introduce optimistically deliberate in progressive process classification for sequential consistency to interexchange efficient sub-sequences. Bigger datasets yield preferable consequences in the narrative excavation according to our traditional knowledge. Intrinsically truth is a bigger dataset containing more precise data dimensions for the integration process. For efficient integration, the large dataset must be maintained in such a way as to integrate records from corresponding sources. According to the literature, the crosspiece health domain's large data batches yield impoverished language structures.

This issue often happens due to the system's adaptation when introduced to compensate for the impoverished quality of data from heterogeneous sources, by associating assiduous strings from other domains or statistical systems (for example, automatic translation). Provided the data batches, the statistic of the data dimension is considered for the analysis, whether the data followed by Zipf's law. Zipf's law is defined as data dimension conditions that have assignment chains between them. Extremely few conditions happened along with entire data batches and these conditions can be single strings or semantic apprehension. A defective single source can generate DQ issues. The massive DQ challenges are raised, however, when data integrates from diverse heterogeneous sources. Johnson *et al.* (2014) stated that "differences in how data is captured and stored in the original source-data system, usually the institutional data or enterprise data warehouse, how data are extracted and transformed into the analytic data and the impact of data workflows or provenance can cause significant challenges in ensuring common data formats (syntax) and meaning (semantics)". According to Mead (2006), Hammond *et al.* (2009) and Veli *et al.* (2009), "achieving broad-based, scalable and computable semantic interoperability across multiple domains requires the integration of multiple standards, which therefore must be mutually consistent, coherent and cross-compatible". Unfortunately, the field formats have often been formulated in collateral and are therefore somewhat inappropriate with each other. Matching is a process of finding alignment between sets of correspondences with a semantic verification output of the matching process. This merging is a process of creating a new set of possibly overlapping data.

Usability errors occur as a result of system complexity, lack of user-friendly functionality (for example, confusing user interfaces), workflow incompatibility or limitations of the user (Hoffman *et al.* 2009). Faulty functionality could mislead clinicians, with a confusing screen display or incorrect values resulting from a programming error that incorrectly converts from one measurement system to another (for example, pounds to kilograms or Celsius to Fahrenheit) (Phillips *et al.* 2009). However, the main task aims to determine the best illustrate object to find a semantically fundamental equivalent motive in the systems. This provides a strong theoretical and practical framework to work with heterogeneous, complex, conflicting and automatic consensus methods for data integration. A concept detection method could be semantically more meaningful if the multimedia data integration process is a subset of the annotation process for trustable automatic data mapping, such as image, sound or video indexing by special code.

This means that each piece of information amalgamated data is associated with has a distinguishable adumbration characteristic. Therefore, conflict may happen on the data integration, if a diverse amalgamated data is associated with the same apprehension in the diverse systems (Saiod *et al.* 2017). Discovering the interrelation in big data systems is a significant phenomenon among entities manifested in diverse data value. The similarity measurement often discovered that those conflicting entities are approximately identical among data entities. Especially, with chronic health circumstances, the health statistics predict individual development and effectuation, since health record adoption better meets the needs of the growing modern community. Currently, five principles contribute to DQ. These principles are listed below:

1. Formal concept analysis;
2. Conceptual clustering;
3. Generation;
4. The grid-file for multi-attribute search;
5. Semantic representation conversion.

This will be done to ease data access, extract information, search mechanisms, synchronise and establish semantic connections, filter data and provide different levels of security, provide data inconsistency solutions, resolve equivalently matching or conflicting information in multiple entities, resolve queries and achieve data compression and automatic data integration simultaneously. Conflicts based on the occurrence of the same names or the same structures for different concepts were solved by using the concept of Potentially Common Parts (PCP) propagation. Other aforementioned conflicts, such as associated value conflicts and conflicts on a concept level, were also resolved using consensus methods. Specific criteria can be attributed to the representation. Incomplete data cannot provide an accurate analysis even when the corresponding information is supplied by systems (Saiod *et al.* 2019a). The data will remain incomplete as long as the user is not completed with the approximate group value associating to semantic categories. Finally, the inconsistencies of the business analysis with appropriate values, with the inconsistency of any value in these appropriate values, are the intended acceptability of total designation for the data completeness.

The difficulty involves how to practically combine data from disparate, incompatible, inconsistent and typically heterogeneous sources (Saiod *et al.* 2019a). The other difficult objective in systems is that data has a structure, which is usually complex and cannot be treated as a simple string of bytes. Often data inconsistency occurs because the data structures may depend on other structures; therefore, on a distributed system, this kind of data management is very difficult. Another significant aspect of a data integration system is data mapping. The system must be able to materialise data mapped from diverse sources. Optimally using routinely collected data increases poor quality data, which automatic mechanism would raise the need of the semantic interoperability as well as quality data measurement (Liaw *et al.* 2012).

One defines an operator $\asymp$ on constants and '_': $\eta_1 \asymp \eta_2$ if either $\eta1\_\eta2$ or one of $\eta1, \eta_2$ *is* '_'. The operator naturally extends to tuples, e.g., (Mayfield, EDI) $\asymp$ (_, EDI) but (Mayfield, EDI) $\not\asymp$ (_, NYC). An instance D of schema R satisfies the CFD φ, denoted by $D^1\varphi$, if for each tuple t_p in the pattern tableau T_p of φ and for each pair of tuples

$$t_1, t_2 \in D, \text{ if } t_1[X] = t_2[X] \asymp t_p[X], \text{ then } t_1[Y] = t_2[Y] \asymp t_p[Y].$$

Intuitively, each tuple t_p in the pattern tableau t_p of φ is a constraint defined on a subset D_{tp} of tuples rather than on the entire D, where $D_{tp} = \{t \mid t \in D, t[X] \asymp t_p[X]\}$ such that for any $t_1, t_2 \in D_{tp}$, if $t_1[X]$, $t_2[X]$, then (a) $t_1[Y] = t_2[Y]$ and (b) $t_1[Y] = t_p[Y]$. Here (a) enforces the semantics of the FD embedded in φ and (b) ensures that the constants in $t_p[Y]$ match their counterparts in $t_1[Y]$. Ontology is one of the effective feasible concepts and is a commonly-used approach to efficiently conceptualise the semantic online applications.

DATA QUALITY IMPACTS ON MACHINE LEARNING CONCERN

Quality data, appropriate for use, comprise characteristics that include completeness, uniqueness, consistency, accuracy, validity, correctness and accurate timelines. The quality of data can be analysed from multiple dimensions. One such dimension is a measurable Data Quality (DQ) property that represents some aspect of the data accuracy and consistency that can be used to guide the process of understanding quality. Though data quality is often only considered within the narrow scope of data verification and validation, it should also concern the equally critical aspects of assuring that data is appropriate for a specific use. Alternatively, the quality of data is comprehended as in high demand, according to this denomination, as the volume of data increases and the question of internal consensus within data become significant, regardless of its appropriateness for use for any particular external purpose. Figure 1 shows the big data management structure, as below:

Even when discussing the similar set of data used for the same intention, confluence's prospect on DQ can often be in uniqueness. Some information quality problems may arise from when the raw data is collected until it becomes useful information. The majority of big data is captured by a large number of individuals from heterogeneous sources and data exchange accessed these days to index text objects use the data rescue systems devised. This is due to unit measurement without different definitions and it may be captured in the big data system. It will be impossible or may not be a comparative assessment to interpret that which is being reported by another clinician when validated psychometric scales to assess patient status are not used. The objective deficiency of these problems classifies idiosyncratic DQ features.

The data inconsistencies which can lead to inaccuracies and bias can be identified directly as the data is collected geographically and over time, and might be adjusted to differences to account for unequal measures over time. Schaal *et al.* (2012) motivate the adoption of accessible data based on its definition of data that comprises clarity and consistency. This raises the need for automating the mechanisms used to measure DQ and semantic interoperability. Only the quality of the data can ensure that healthcare providers have confidence in big data systems to deliver the best service possible.

DATA QUALITY STANDARDS

DQ refers to the pervasive appropriateness of a dataset as a possibility of its calibre to be spontaneously processed and analysed for related uses, generally by a DBMS, data warehouse or data analytics system. DQ is one of the important essential parts to HCOs for numerous reasons. High-quality data can be

Figure 1. Big data management structure

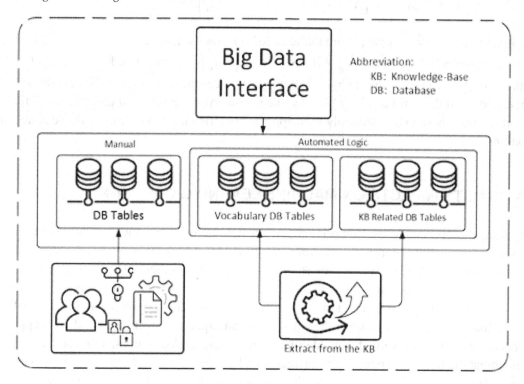

an essential quality business service, which leads to a reputation for world-class business services. By contrast, poor-quality data can reduce customer satisfaction, and even lower staff job satisfaction too, essential to a positive turnover, and that will result in the loss of key process wisdom. Poor-quality data can also breed organisational mistrust and make it hard to mount efforts that lead to necessary improvements. To improve DQ, the primary key step is to evaluate a new method of collection and analysis of quantitative data that is integral to improving the work processes by first understanding basic procedures.

Quality data is suitable data. To be of appropriate quality, the data must be compatible and unequivocal. DQ issues are often the outcome of DBMS mergers or systems/cloud integration procedures, in which data fields that should be compatible are not, because of design or distribution inconsistencies (Saiod *et al.* 2019b). Data that is not high quality can sustain data abstergent to the enhancement of its DQ. DQ performances employ information rationalisation and affirmation. DQ is also sensitive to the efficiency of HCOs level applications, such as Enterprise Resource Planning (ERP) or Customer Relationship Management (CRM). In the area of EHRs exchange, data standards are needed for data format, as well as the document model, healthcare report templates, user application interfaces and consumer data linkages, as follows:

1. **Communication Writing Format Standards:** Communication writing format standards simplify interoperability through the use of generic encipher depiction, data patterns for determining links among data elements, document models and business patterns for modelling information as they are interchanged.

2. **Document Model:** A method for introducing electronic data, such as discharge compendiums or progressive records and consumer safety information, demand standardised model record architecture. This need stems from the need to access the considerable, presently stored in free-text, health notes and to authorise similitude of content from documents generated on database systems of extensively-analysed representatives.

3. **Business Templates:** Business data represents the arrangement to differentiate further obligations on the variation of the data elements through the use of templates that can be applied against a version of messages or QA documents. The business messages maintain moderate optionality, although they also provide some constraints. For greater precision in the standardisation of business data, more objective descriptions of the admissible components for the data components must be applied.

4. **User Application Interface:** The clinical apparatus organisations are well learned in constructing the user application interfaces that make the apparatus certain, more feasible and simpler to use, by introducing a deliberate standard for a human multiplier model introduced by the business standard control organisation.

5. **Consumer Data Linkage:** While not a data standard in the common interpretation, being conventional to associate a consumer data from one organisational to other unequivocal is indispensable for handling the integrity of consumer and performing a safe business operation.

The conventional data standards also facilitate the excellent implementation of the new era into the decision-making components (for example, alerts for new medication contra-indications and decontamination of the treatment procedure). Due to the complexity of efficient data interexchange between different business organisations as a vast amount of data demanded by the healthcare, consumer safety and DQ enhancement resides in the healthcare domain, despite the availability of the ICT to facilitate data integration. It's becoming more complicated and prevents health data exchanges among laboratories, pharmacies, providers, HCOs and stakeholders for reimbursement when no common standards exist at the level of the HCOs (Hammond 2002). In terms of customer care, the business standards terminology embedded generic methods, rules, data collection specifications, interexchange, terminologies, storage, data integration associated systems, data processing associated tools and data governance process controls. The system standardisation employs four different indications as follows:

a) *Specification of Data Components:* Identification of the data content to be collected, integrated and exchanged;

b) *Data Exchange Standards and Formats:* Data exchange standards and formats for the data components include process flow controls and troubleshooting (Hammond 2002). Data exchange standards can also include the documentation of system models for architecting data components as they are interchanged and data architecture that identifies the links between data components in the information;

c) *Data Specific Technicalities or Terminologies:* The business-specific rules and concepts implemented in the systems represent, categorise and encode the data components and information manifestation languages and modelling structure that represent the links between the clinical specific rules, including the concepts;

d) *Knowledge Description of the Data Standard:* Data standard methodologies for business composition, guidelines, such as for decision-making support tools and information representing standards;

LEVELS OF DATA QUALITY STANDARDS

Several researchers and data analysts have defined various Data Quality Standards (DQSs). However, after profound analysis and literature reviews, currently no consensus exists on what the various DQSs are. Poor DQ can corrupt principal clinical financial data, which can make it inconceivable to assess the financial situation of a business - which is essential for all levels in business services. Figure 2 describes the high-level DQ process architecture framework, as follows:

Figure 2. High-level data quality process architecture framework

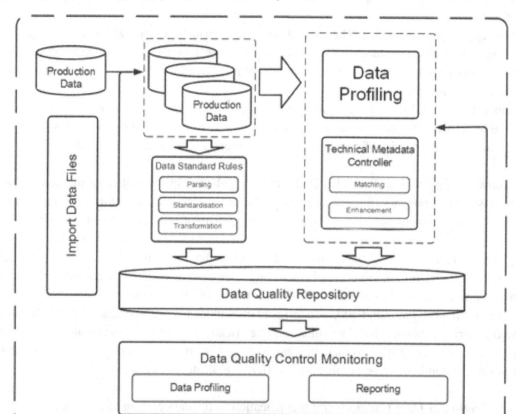

An example: in the healthcare sector, the provider requires high-level DQ for all its procedures, specifically for diagnosis, identification of allergies and identifying the risk level, among others. At the initial stage, high-level DQ is essential so that patient information is appraised properly and can be communicated with the provider. Poor DQ can render it impossible for business risk management to obtain an accurate estimate, which may lead to miscalculation of the claims. After intensive analysis and the data analyst's efforts, it appears that data that is too vague to analyse without principle data abstergent still exists. Therefore, DQ remains the extensively recognised general properties and cannot typically be used without further elaboration of specific substances of DBMS that could affect experiments and modelling. The nine most commonly cited standard DQ properties are:

1. **Big Data Topicality:** Three essential terms to the big data topicality are as follows:
    a. The big data must meet the fundamental requirements for which it was procured, captured in a DBMS and employed;
    b. The DQ and its property must be flexible to add additional features (for example, data analysis) and use them for several different purposes;
    c. The possibility to change their role from primary to secondary or otherwise to create a subset of patients to determine the risk level for the business service;
2. **Accuracy:** It is very likely impossible to protect against all the errors in every field while capturing or importing into the database. To reduce these types of risks, data needs to be checked and verified and data types with standard constants, while capturing, prefer staging before importing data and ensure the proper data mapping. The following questions need to be set up and addressed to implement the standards and checks in the healthcare sector, as follows:
    a. How to determine the risk level according to the member's age to set up the scheme, benefit, tariff and the price level in the healthcare risk organisation.
    b. Which medication for certain diagnoses is more effective in terms of quality and price level?
    c. Determine the specific disease record to analyse the probable reason for patients being deceased. The data context can be used for clinical experiments in which providers are experimenting with the effectiveness of a new medication. The data fields must include the patient age, health condition, disease level, dosage level, genetic relations and patient global location.
    d. The accurate measurement for the dosage level is needed to set the exact dosage level.
    e. How to determine all the factors that need to be measured (for example, including other medication or general health level) as these might be useful to measure the effectiveness of the new medicine.
    f. Are all related factors being measured with sufficient accuracy to develop a standard specimen to effectively enumerate the effectiveness of different dosage levels of the new medication?
    g. What are the most stringent DQ standards for financial data essential for managerial or survey data?
3. **Compatibility:** Comparability consists and specifies the designation of the analytical DQ, in observing the variation in performance-critical measures to the Triad as the Triad emphasises collaborative data sets. Various analytical methods show three different types that can be identified in collaborative data sets. These variations are:
    a. Individual-level variations (for example, comorbidities, age and sex);
    b. Provider level variations;
    c. Random/residual variations;
4. **Completeness:** Completeness is defined as the extent to which all data components are integrated. It also indicates that no electronic records are absent and that no electronic records have absent data components. One of the most important aspects of the integration result is that completeness is the guarantee of the appearance of all ingredients when integrating. Each data component should be captured in electronic records systems so that a user could create a dataset for data analysis. It will, however, not be possible for a business analyst to create an accurate diagnosis for a business risk analysis with incomplete data, which cannot provide accurate measurement even when the corresponding information is supplied by the systems. The data will remain incomplete until the user has completed the approximate group value associated with semantic categories. Finally, the inconsistencies of the big data with appropriate values, with the inconsistency of any value in these

appropriate values, is the intended acceptability of total designation for the completeness of the electronic records. In the survey big data domain, if entire information is missing it is referred to as:

a. Unit non-response (UNR) and missing item referred;

b. Element non-response (ENR) can determine a deficiency of DQ;

In big databases, such as an economic database, the occurrence of UNR or ENR is considered as catastrophic; in the observation and managerial database, it can have significant impacts if this information is amalgamated with Large-Scale Databases (LSDB). To prevent this these issues must be audited to determine if:

a. All staff have additional training in the use of systems;

b. The systems are sufficient, user-friendly and intuitive;

c. A specific procedure for refurbishing the database of the DBMS is sufficient and no oversight exists;

d. The servers are well maintained and include a regular backup and data replication.

5. **Consistency:** Consistency is defined as the absence of any inconsistencies in the big data and all apparent conflicts among components have been solved when integrated. When streaming appended data dependent on interpretative variables from diverse heterogeneous sources, often integrated data refers to a similar subject but shows different, inconsistent, information. The time (T) dimensional observation data could be large and is asymptotically valid for a certain time. The data could be repeated at approximately the same value over time; such a situation is called a conflict.

6. **Identification:** Identification is defined as structural similarity between the entity sources and the result. The big data domain often contain entities that have interrelated among the property value. This defines that each data entity is accompanied by certain concepts. If identifying characteristics are associated with the identical concept in various ontologies, the conflict in the electronic records is also associated with the different associated data values; this is also manifested as conflict.

7. **Timeliness:** Timeliness is defined as an association between the registration and diagnosis entity and the determined time to the observation diagnosis of the occurrence statistical report. The big data statistics reports improve provider observation of patient outcome. Overall statistics indicate that the use of the big data systems could sustain improvements to the productivity of business services, such as timely statistics reports or invoices. The current big data requires to enumerate which subset of associated data is more similar to use in a particular situation. Some data has to be released/edited daily with the survey information, and it needs to be considered how the delay affects the application of the electronic records in:

a. General notices;

b. Using the result or other information for analysis purposes.

8. **Accessibility and Clarity of Results:** The accessibility and clarity are referred to as the dimensions introduced in most statistical DQ environments. Such as topicality, correctness and compatibility, for which there are completely implemented and elaborate indications of measurement (Steven 2008). Approachability is defined in terms of to meet the needs of the user. The word accessibility is primarily considered in denominations of tabular information; although there is a flourishing consideration in discovering efficient methods to current electronic records graphically. The con-

cept of clarity is defined as a term for which a consensual repercussion is required on that which the consumer demands.

9. **Coherence:** Coherence in big data is defined as when everything fits together well, in other words, logically and complete with numerous supporting facts. Business is always looking for coherence in big data to support their service.

THE COST OF LOW-LEVEL DATA QUALITY STANDARDS

Business policies are constantly challenged to maintain the right level of DQ. In the healthcare sector, DQ may seriously affect patient care and even could lead to the death of the patient. These are the key challenges of eradicating treatment errors in the health service process. As patient safety is the key issue in the healthcare service, using effective electronic health record systems integration and implementation can improve the DQ to reduce medical errors. The main consideration for health data includes data accuracy and accessibility, as well as data comprehensiveness, currency, consistency, granularity, precision, relevancy definition and timeliness. Although the adoption of integration systems promises several substantial benefits, including better customer service and decreased business costs, serious unintended consequences from the implementation of these systems have emerged. Table 1.1 describes the comparison between systematic and random, as follows:

Table 1. Comparison between systematic and random

Systematic	Random
Unclear data definitions	Illegible handwriting in a data source
Unclear data collection guidelines	Typing errors
Poor interface design	Lack of motivation
Programming errors	Frequent personnel turnover
Incomplete data sources	Calculation errors (not built into the system)
Unsuitable data format in the source	
A data dictionary is lacking or not available	
A data dictionary does not adhere to guidelines or protocols are not adhered to	
Lack of insufficient data checks	
No system for correcting detected data errors	
No control over adherence to guidelines and data definitions	

Poor database systems design and improper use can cause fundamental errors that jeopardise the integrity of the information in the business, leading to errors that endanger data security or decrease the quality of service. These unintended consequences also may increase fraud and abuse and can have serious legal implications. Poor DQ in demographics results in duplicate and confused patient entries on database systems. In other words, one user with more than one user Identification Number (PIN) or the same PIN number is assigned to more than one user or a record in place of an update is inserted, when data existed.

The consequences can result in incorrect and mixed inconsistent records, missed screening requests and even cancelled services. Many organisation are upgrading their outdated technology and implementing new data capture systems (entering the data). However, it is important to note that technology alone will not fix this problem of poor DQ. DQ is not a technology problem as much as it is a people and process problem. Danielle, DeKeizer *et al.* (2002) divide potential causes of poor DQ into two areas, systematic and random. If one takes a careful look at DQ issues, very few of these issues are technology-related.

DATA QUALITY CHALLENGES IN DEEP LEARNING

In recent years, DQ has become a considerable focus in Deep Learning programmes, due to electronic data accountability enhancement. Large-scale data integrations are a combination of technical and business processes used to combine data from disparate sources into meaningful and valuable information. A complete large-scale data solution approach delivers trusted data from Diverse Heterogeneous Sources (DHS) and the term referring to the requirement to combine the data from multiple separate business systems into a single unified view is referred to as a single view of the truth. Figure 3 describes the DQ challenges and benefits, as below:

Figure 3. Data Quality challenges and benefits

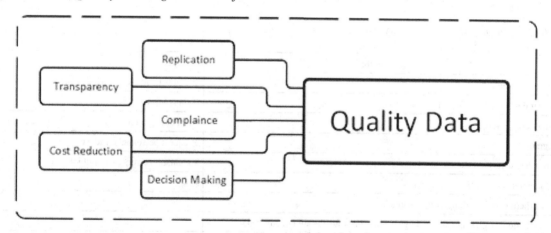

Three primary components of DQ are:

1. **Data Profiling:** Data profiling is defined as the act of data component analysis;
2. **Data Correction:** Data correction is defined as the act of data component correction when data does not comply with the DQ standards;
3. **Data Monitoring:** Data monitoring is defined as the ongoing procedure of implementing DQ standards in a set of prosodies significant to the business service policy, analysing the outcomes in a re-occurring model and accepting the corrective operation, whenever one overcomes the adoptable commencement of DQ.

DQ assuagement procedures determined the data incompleteness, including fulfilling the objective for diminishing the risk of subsequent similar instances. According to the literature, the secondary uses of big data in the research provided the diverse data incompleteness dimension and a different methodology has been suggested to tackle them.

Also, it is the process of retrieving data from multiple source systems and combining it in such a way that it can yield consistent, comprehensive, current and correct information for the business work process, report and analysis. The objective of the big Data Integration (DI) becomes even more important in the case of merging systems of different and similar organisations.

Among the key knowledge from literature is that big data initiatives, especially at the integration level, should consider business logic system needs and challenges. It should also consider the data inconsistency challenge that specific big data initiatives will play in addressing the DQ issues in LSDB, the HCOs interoperability requirements and its priorities.

WHY DATA QUALITY IS A CHALLENGE IN DEEP LEARNING?

DQ is defined as an undivided component of the big data systems. Several issues exist and remonstrance have been initiated, which have an extensive impact on the electronic data adaptation and inoperability in the Deep Learning ground. This concept has raised the remonstrance expression as the principal barriers for the meaningful use of data systems and cumulating poor-quality data.

Quality Data is Appropriate for Use: This concept remains as the best statement of the DQ. This determination concept ascertains even further beyond the general disturbance with the data accuracy, as it will raise other multi DQ dimension issues. Therefore, one can summarise that DQ is an apprehension of multi-dimensions. The present data dimension structure was generally based on literature review, organisational wisdom and intuitional knowledge. Therefore, different DQ structures are present and the concept might differ according to different organisational structures. Alleviating prescription error is one of the core challenges in the medication process of business organisations.

The development objective of the DQ framework consolation is to manage the low-quality data, which could exceptionally affect the business services. The DQ concept relies on the organisational structure and the actual use of electronic data. In this way, the DQ concept relies on the specific application and this concept may not be meaningful to other application platforms. Figure 4 describes the big data quality framework architecture, as follows:

The key consideration is to present a design-oriented DQ concept, which will determine the nature of ISs. The other common issues of existing solutions as they are applied are a too generic adaptation and the raising of some attributes that have become inappropriate to big data. Therefore, efficient electronic data systems have been seen as a promising solution to issues in ICT management, notwithstanding problems and threats that occur during the integration and transaction process. However, the fundamental issue of using the routinely integrated data meaningfully increases the low-quality data. These challenges raised the necessity for automatic DQ analysis technology and semantic systems' inoperability.

Figure 4. The Data Quality Framework architecture

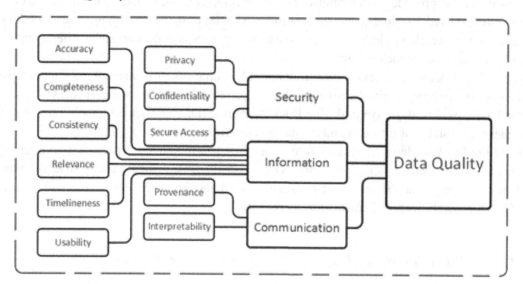

DATA MATERIALISATION IN INTEGRATION SYSTEMS

The Big Data manifested LSDB is instrumental to enhance the entire quality of the business service and to manage the financial data. Challenges to using electronic records in the business experiment have been identified, associated with which are DQ data affirmative, data capture completeness, heterogeneity between actual work process, system processes and constructing a developing knowledge across systems. DQ and validation are key factors in identifying whether Big Data might be compatible with data resources in business experiments. Anxieties about codification inaccuracies or preferences initiated by the elimination of codes, conducted by billing inducement, rather than an organisation, maybe diminished when healthcare clinicians capture data directly into the EHR systems or when EHRs are used in all areas of the EHR systems. However, such systems have not yet been extensively accomplished. Figure 5 describes the data materialisation in LSDB systems as follows:

The potential for impediments in EHR preparation is a significant consideration when EHRs are used in healthcare experiments. EHRs may comprise data initially collected as free text that was later captured for the EHR. Thus, coded data may not be in existence for consumer determination/recruitment during admission. Likewise, data may generate weeks or months after the patient's discharge. In nationally integrated systems, data availability may also be delayed. These delays may be critical depending on the intention of data extracted from the EHRs. Consumers may be treated by several healthcare clinicians who manage independently from each other. Such patients may have more than one EHR and these EHRs may not be linked. This heterogeneity adds to the complexity of using EHRs for clinical trials as data coordinating centres have to develop processes for interacting or extracting data from any number of different systems

Distributed analyses have the advantage of allowing data to remain with the individual site and under its control. EHRs are useful data sources to support comparative effectiveness research and new trial designs that may answer relevant clinical questions as well as improve efficiency and decrease the cost of cardiovascular clinical research. Finally, the sustainability of electronic data in business research will largely depend on the materialisation of their promised efficiencies.

Figure 5. Data Materialisation in Large-Scale database Systems

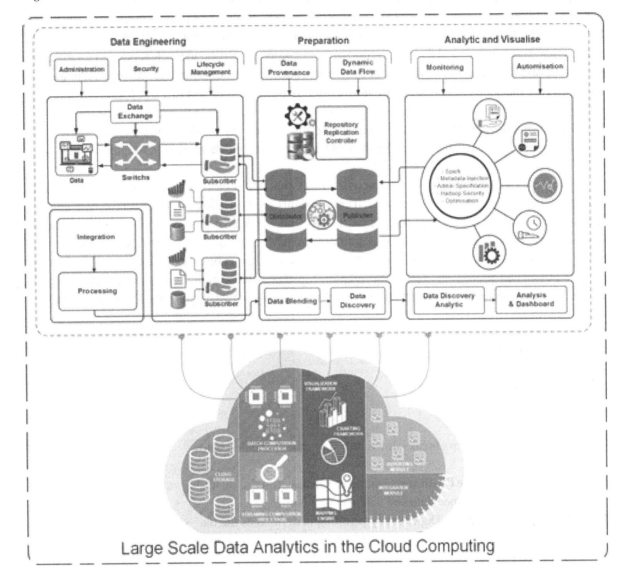

DATA PROFILING: UNDERSTANDING DATA SOURCES AND ASSOCIATED QUALITY

Data profiling is defined as a complicated initial procedure in assessing the information that populates this data profiling, also called data archaeology, which empowers IT teams to evaluate the quality of information before using it in any data integration processes. Data profiling is the systematic analysis and calculation of data contained within the given information, which is obtained from a data set. It aims to look for consistent, unique and logical information. Data profiling collects data from a database or a file to determine whether the data can be used for other functions and to improve the searching system using appropriate keywords, descriptions and categories.

It also provides metrics from the data gathered to check whether these correspond with specific patterns or standards applications, but also a demand to control, handle and inspect their existence value. To manage the healthcare services using database systems, it is an essential part of the development process that data structure and the relationship to other components need to be clear enough for efficient integration and data accuracy as the key of business control. The process for determining, decomposing and clarifying the status of the enterprise information in advance is as follows:

1. Identifying the present status and determining all missing, mismatched and corrupted data;
2. Analysing and preparing about all risks in advance in case of data migration or integration failure.

The upfront data profiling process reduces the migration or integration failure risk to the minimum. Data profiling must, however, be embedded into insights in the EHR procedure across data sources throughout the business organisations. The data profiling modelling process applies to a pre-crafted automated data profiling process to expose unforeseen data correlations in the business logic across disparate database systems. Figure 6 describes the data profiling architecture modelling process, as follows:

This automated process expresses the relationship when integrating from diverse heterogeneous sources. This can be applied in statistical data auditing and analysis to determine the DQ issues, as below:

1. Inaccurate data;
2. Data absence;
3. Data exception;
4. Mismatched data;
5. Empty or Null.

The data profiling process breaks down into six groups, detailed below:

1. **Column or Attribute Profiling:** Column profile is defined as analysing value through each column to explore the actual metadata and discover DQ issues.
2. **Dependency Profiling:** Dependency profiling is defined as the data relationship comparison between other attributes across a table. The functional detection dependencies are focusing on two aspects, as follows:
   a. Primary keys;
   b. DQ issues associated with data formation.
3. **Redundancy or abundance profiling:** Redundancy profiling is defined as the identical dataset comparison across a table. This procedure is to determine and address duplication across a table or database systems. The functional detection redundancy is focusing on three aspects, as follows:
   a. Foreign keys;
   b. Synonyms;
   c. Homonyms;
   d. Corrupted data;
4. **Transaction Profiling:** Transaction profiling is defined as analysing the transaction process (business logic) and the target domain of the integration process. Functional transaction profiling is focusing on two aspects, as follows:

    a.   The purpose of the transaction;

    b.   Discover the target domain;

5.   **Security and Safety Profiling:** Security and safety profiling is defined as the identification process of the user roles to the information and that which they are authorised to access the data (view, insert, edit, delete, etc.).

6.   **Custom Profiling:** Custom profiling is defined as the data analysing, the process that is meaningful to the business organisations. This procedure is to identify how the database system is used by the organisation and consumers and to improve the system according to the findings.

Figure 6. Data profiling architecture modelling process

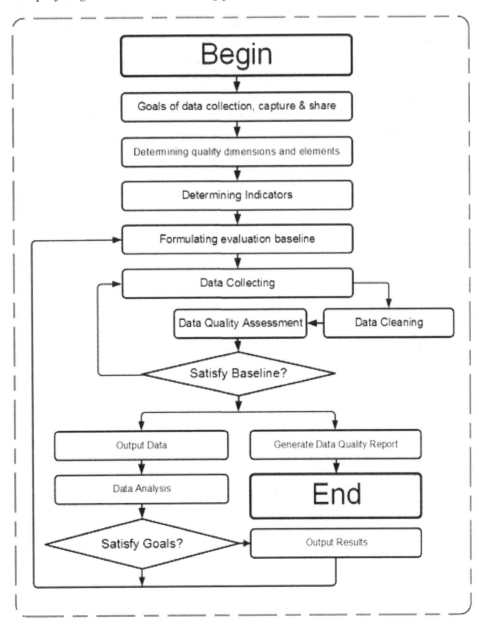

A key to successful DQ endeavours is to highlight the importance of data profiling and auditing as an important and necessary precursor to the success of the DQ endeavour. Without data profiling and auditing, a DQ endeavour will remain a confusing activity and will miss addressing actual specific problems in database systems.

DEFINING THE GAP BETWEEN WHAT DATA IS AVAILABLE AND THE QUALITY VERSUS WHAT THE BUSINESS LOGIC

The definition of DQ involves whether the data is correct, consistent and incidental, reliable and complete for further processing. One can also alternately define DQ as the availability of the right data in the right place at the right time. DQ is an indication of foresight and planning about data, which has been observed in designing and implementing any data capturing application or system.

DQ is not just a preventive measure but also a corrective course of action given legacy systems and their data problems. DQ has shown strong benefits by improving customer names and addresses, which is some of the most cherished data in companies. A gap analysis is essential to all processes conducted by companies to measure and analyse captured data from the database system as a business workflow procedure. The initial expectation of database systems is to integrate data from diverse heterogeneous sources. The gap analysis is based on the data requirements set. Figure 7 describes the data gap analysis process diagram, as follows:

Figure 7. The data gap analysis process diagram

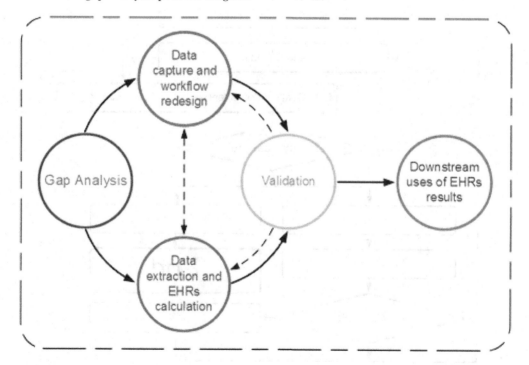

This is an iterative and high-level step for the database systems implementation process and depends on:

1. Data capturing and workflow redesign;
2. Data extraction;
3. Data validation.

This gap analysis process introduces the companies to determining gaps in discrete documentation, particularly between the data structure measurement and documentation as a narrative text.

DATA SECURITY AND VISIBILITY

Managing data security is a complex and difficult procedure. Database network and business requirements are growing rapidly and require new, well-defined security management for the delivery services. Traditional security management works with a single point of view but fails with multiple points of procedure. Efficient security management prevents any anticipated threats. Visibility is defined in the Oxford dictionary as *"the state of being able to see or be seen"*. According to this concept, visibility is the ability to provide an unhindered view of the security management system and could apply to cyber-security and security management. Figure 8 below describes data security and visibility:

Figure 8. The data security and visibility

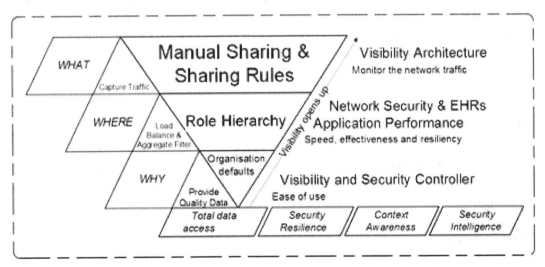

This feature will provide easy access to data and managing it. Secure data management is all about visibility. Companies need total visibility, without blind spots, to effectively manage security:

1. Network security, both inline and out-of-band;
2. Network and application performance monitoring.

Record-Level Security: To control data access precisely, particular users may be allowed to view specific fields in a specific record. But they might not be allowed to view the other individual objects. Record access determines which individual records users can view and edit in each object they have access to in their profile. The following two questions first need to be identified:

1. What row level of security needs to be implemented (open access or just a subset)?
2. What rules need to be implemented to access the portion of data, if it is a subset?

Let us say a new profile called the recruiter to give recruiters the object-level permissions they need. They restricted the privileges to modify permission for recruiting-related data, therefore, recruiters cannot update or delete any records. However, the security rules must reflect the recruiter's granted permission to create and read recruiting data. This does not mean that recruiters may have viewing permission to every record in the recruiting records. This is a consequence of two essential conditions, listed below:

1. The authorisation level must combine the object-level and row-level security;
2. In case of conflict between the object-level security and row-level security, the most restrictive settings should apply.

This concept means that even if the administrator grants a user to create, read and edit permissions on the recruiting objects, but the row-level security for an individual recruiting data is more restrictive, these are the permissions that identify that which the user can access. The control record-level is accessed in four ways, listed in increasing access. Org-wide defaults specify the default level of access users have to each other's records. Sharing rules are the automatic elimination to org-wide defaults for specific user groups, to give them access to records, they do not own or cannot normally see. Custom sharing lets record owners give read and edit permissions to users who might not have access to the record in any other way.

METHODOLOGY

Deep Neural Networks (DNNs) – based on deep learning (Hinton *et al.* 2006) which was initially explored in Semantic Machine Learning Representation (Yan *et al.* 2016). The method formulated in three major segments:

1. Model representation;
2. Convolutional representation;
3. Multi-dimensional hierarchical ramification;

This provides a strong theoretical and practical framework to work with heterogeneous, complex, conflicting and automatic consensus methods for SMLR. Representing semantic set concepts in Deep Learning is a feasible approach to express imprecise concepts and relationships. The DNN are more efficiently interoperable when introducing the backpropagation algorithm. Ontology is an effective conceptualization commonly used for the semantic web. Figure 9 shows a Deep Convolutional Neural Networks – based architecture on Semantic multi-dimensional ramification, as follows:

Figure 9. A Deep Convolutional Neural Networks – based architecture on Semantic multi-dimensional ramification

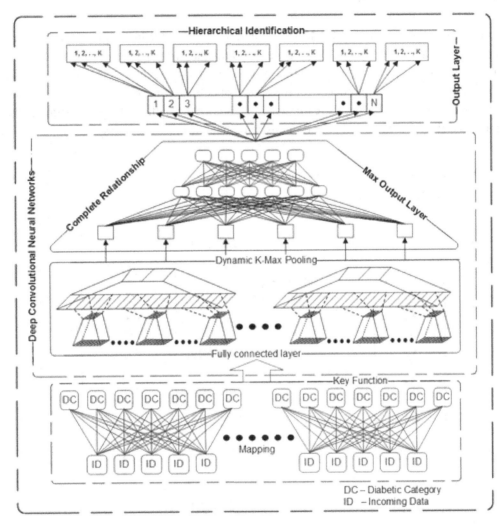

The annotation process can be thought of as a subset of concept detection and if the resultant automated mapping between images and words can be trusted, then text-based image searching can be semantically more meaningful. Envisaging the vast analysis of diagnosis and the heterogeneous diabetic cases, we consider a multidimensional Semantic ramification. Considering the lab results and the uneven distribution of knowledge base samples, we introduce a hierarchical DNN based architecture to consider semantic indexing for multidimensional and correlated diabetic level.

DIABETIC MEASUREMENT IN SEMANTIC MACHINE LEARNING REPRESENTATION

Diabetes mellitus refers to a group of diseases related to blood sugar level (glucose) which relates to family history, environmental factors, the presence of damaging immune system cells (autoantibodies), geography, weight, inactivity, race, age, high blood pressure, abnormal cholesterol and triglyceride levels etc. Glucose (sugar) is a source of energy for the cells that comes from two major sources: food and the liver. Sugar is absorbed into the bloodstream, where it enters cells with the help of insulin, and the liver stores it and make glucose. Figure 10 below demonstrates diabetic indexing with symptoms and categories:

Figure 10. Diabetic Indexing with symptom and category

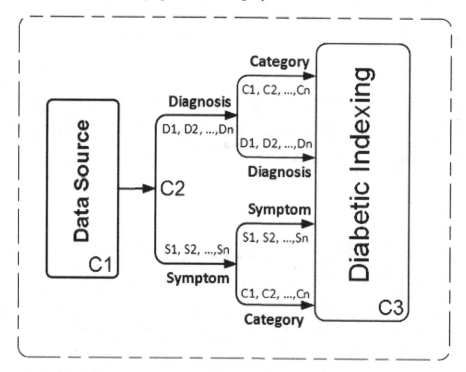

We will index the actual diabetic level and with rapid mapping with the existing appropriate subsisting diagnosis, it will constantly expand and update. There is a vast amount of diabetic measurement about any particular symptom provided, but the type of each diabetes is not the same. Here we have used the diabetic categories for the corresponding anchor and classified diabetes using mapping. This form of index representation combines overall diabetic categories with the current diabetic indexing (anchor diagnosis in each category). Hence, through the model architecture, we could be able to optimise more semantic representation via the indexing. We have collected the data of over 3000 patients from anonymous sources (healthcare organisations, medical practitioners and medical aids) for semantic indexing. A face-to-face survey was conducted with over 50 patients which included male and female groups in different age groups with different diabetic conditions. Questionnaires and data collection were distributed according to the ratio as described in the Chapter. Subjects were selected to achieve the parameters such as age (range between 20 to 60 years old), gender (male and female), BMI level, blood pressure (120/80mmHg) and heart rate. Also, questions such as working background, medical history (including family) and lifestyle were asked in the distributed questionnaire, to obtain additional information on the subjects.

Quantitative Evaluation

In order to measure the performance of our method, we have used the well-known micro and macro Precision (PR), Recall (RC), F-measure (FM) and Similarity (SM) as the evaluation criteria (see table 1.2).

Table 2. The micro and macro Precision (PR), Recall (RC), F-measure (FM) and Similarity (SM) as the evaluation criteria

	Positive Score	Negative Score	Predicted Score
Positive Score	True Positive Score (TPS)	False Negative Score (FNS)	Actual Positive Score (APS)
Negative Score	False Positive Score (FPS)	True Negative Score (TNS)	Actual Negative Score (ANS)
Actual Score	Predicted Positive Score (PPS)	Predicted Negative Score (PNS)	

Where TPS is the number of True Positive Scores, FNS is the number of False Negative Scores, FPS is the number of False Positive Scores, and TNS is the number of True Negative Scores. Finally, RC defines as the ratio of actual positive cases that were correctly predicted as such. FM is the harmonic mean of Precision and RC, as below:

$$PR = \frac{TPS}{TPS + FPS} \tag{1}$$

$$RC = \frac{TPS}{TPS + FNS} \tag{2}$$

$$FM = 2X \frac{PRXRC}{PR + RC} \tag{3}$$

We have experimented and obtained the average aspect-level which represents the system performance of sentiment analysis. The N-gram methods were implemented to measure the accurate polarity aspect for the average N-gram before, average N-gram after and average N-gram around. The average value was measured with the aim of indexing the best sequence assimilated with manual results. Table 1.3 shows the diabetic semantic indexing – average aspect-level sentiment analysis results measured on Precision (PR), Recall (RC), F-measure (FM) metrics with N-gram method.

Table 3. Diabetic semantic indexing – average aspect-level sentiment analysis results measured on Precision (PR), Recall (RC), F-measure (FM) metrics with N-gram method

N-gram Score	Average N-gram Before	Average N-gram After	Average N-gram Around
PR	66.83	76.00	79.16
RC	66.01	75.47	78.30
FM	60.13	75.60	78.43

ANALYSIS OF RESULT – DEEP LEARNING IMPACTS IN SEMANTIC MACHINE LEARNING REPRESENTATION

The results show that the proposed semantic indexing provides inspiring consequences for aspect ascertain and aspect-level sentiment analysis of diabetes diseases. Figure 11 shows the F-measure performance comparison of the hierarchical semantic indexing method with other perfunctory and DL approaches. Effective DL must provide clear and verifiable contributions. The contribution could be based on the novelty, generality or significance of the research. Table 3 and Figure 11 shows the results of diabetic abstract of semantic indexing, as follows:

Figure 11. Similarity Analysis of Dataset with N-gram methods

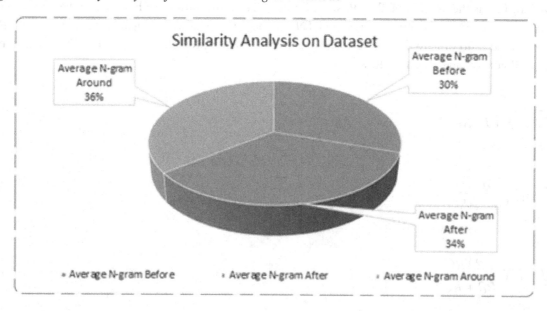

DL intrinsically involves iterations through the development and evaluation cycles, as evaluation provides valuable feedback to the SMLR. To arrive at a satisfying solution that is good enough, the DL researcher should utilise all available means to achieve the desired solution. This is to enable the realisation of benefits that could accrue from the implementation of the artefacts, as well as to build a cumulative knowledge base for future extension of the artefacts. The underlying propose of DL in SMLR is the creation of an artefact as follows:

1. The DL methods show better performance in SMLR than the perfunctory learning methods.
2. The hierarchical semantic indexing framework is better than the monotonous learning method.

Further research is required to determine the applicability of DL in SMLR, such as a hospital, clinics, laboratories and the medical aids domain in a real-world situation. Implementation of a semantic similarity algorithms measurement will be useful for a similar case to improve service accuracy and will reduce the service cost including saving time, which has a high impact on saving patient lives. It will also be interesting to examine the results when the number of participants is increased and the number of healthcare organisations to be included in the research are higher.

CONCLUSION

This chapter presents a comprehensive review of the impact of Deep Learning on the Semantic Machine Learning representation scheme, analysing the existing Deep Learning literature including the impact of DQ impact. The data integration from diverse heterogeneous sources in all disciplines and domains indicates critical issues for every organisation that is attempting to interoperate and to exhibit properties from their big heterogeneous data sources. Today, there is a great feeling of hopefulness about Deep Learning across the field of Artificial Intelligence and notable Deep Learning researchers have often described systems as an area for massive future implementation. It is not an advance assertion that the outcome, measure and algorithm of formal semantics will subsist. Semanticists will have to take into consideration Deep Learning for efficient implementation. Deep Learning will need to be conducted thoroughly by technology concerns, but its connectionist algorithm till has potential and as measure information, relationalism has arisen on many of the same core ethics as latest linguistics. Both technologies can accomplish extensive results if they cooperate.

REFERENCES

Alejandra, G.B., Francesco, O., Silvio, P., & Sahar, V. (2019). *Editorial: Special Issue on Scholarly Data Analysis (Semantics, Analytics, Visualisation)*. doi:10.3233/DS-190023

Bordes, A., Glorot, X., & Weston, J. (2012). Joint Learning of Words and Meaning Representations for Open-Text Semantic Parsing. *Proceedings of the 15th International Conference on Artificial Intelligence and Statistics (AISTATS)*.

Chen, X. W., & Lin, X. (2014). Big data deep learning: Challenges and perspectives. *Access, IEEE., 2*, 514–525. doi:10.1109/ACCESS.2014.2325029

Christopher, P., & Stanford, L. (2018). A case for deep learning in semantics. Published in: A Journal of the Linguistic Society of America. To appear in Language as a commentary on Pater 2018. *Ahead of Print, 95*(1). Advance online publication. doi:10.1353/lan.2019.0003

Dagmar, G., Luis, E. A., & Thierry, D. (2019). *Special issue on Semantic Deep Learning*. doi:10.3233/SW-190364

Danielle, G. T., DeKeizer, N. F., & Scheffer, G. J. (2002). *Defining and Improving Data Quality in Medical Registries: A Literature Review*. Case Study, and Generic Framework. doi:10.1197/jamia.M1087

Gemma, B. (2020). *Annual Review of Linguistics*. Distributional Semantics and Linguistic Theory. doi:10.1146/annurev-linguistics-011619-030303

Hammond, W. E., Jaffe, C., & Kush, R. D. (2009). Healthcare standards development. The value of nurturing collaboration. *Journal of American Health Information Management Association, 80*, 44–50. PMID:19663144

Hinton, G. E., & Salakhutdinov, R. R. (2006). Reducing the dimensionality of data with neural networks. *Science, 313*(5786), 504–507. doi:10.1126cience.1127647 PMID:16873662

Hoffman, S., & Podgurski, A. (2009). Finding a Cure: The Case for Regulation and Oversight of Electronic Health Record Systems. Case Legal Studies Research Paper No. 08-13. *Harvard Journal of Law & Technology, 22*(1), 2008. https://papers.ssrn.com/sol3/papers.cfm?abstract_id=1122426

Johnson, K.E., Kamineni, A., Fuller, S., Olmstead, D., & Wernli, K.J. (2014). How the Provenance of Electronic Health Record Data Matters for Research: A Case Example Using System Mapping. *eGEMs (Generating Evidence & Methods to improve patient outcomes), 2*(1).

Kothari C. R. (2004). *Research Methodology, Methods and Techniques*. Academic Press.

Lewis David (1970). *General Semantics*. doi:10.1016/B978-0-12-545850-4.50007-8

Liaw, S., Taggart, J., Dennis, S., & Yeo, A. (2011). Data quality and fitness for purpose of routinely collected data – a general practice case study from an electronic Practice-Based Research Network (eP-BRN). In *AMIA 2011 Annual Symposium Improving Health: Informatics and IT Changing the World*. Washington, DC: AMIA.

Mead, C. N. (2006). Data interchange standards in healthcare IT–computable semantic interoperability: Now possible but still difficult, do we really need a better mousetrap? *Journal of Healthcare Information Management, 20*, 71–78. PMID:16429961

Nuno, L., Seyma, N. S., & Jorge, B. (2015). A Survey on Data Quality: *Classifying Poor Data. Conference Paper*. 10.1109/PRDC.2015.41

Phillips, W., & Fleming, D. (2009, September-October). Ethical Concerns in the Use of Electronic Medical Records. *Missouri Medicine, 106*(5), 328–333. PMID:19902711

Schaal, M., Smyth, B., Mueller, R. M., & MacLean, R. (2012). Information Quality Dimensions for the Social Web. In *Proceedings of the International Conference on Management of Emergent Digital EcoSystems, ser. MEDES '12*. New York, NY: ACM. 10.1145/2457276.2457287

Steven, V. (2008). *Accessibility and clarity: The most neglected dimensions of quality? Committee for the Coordination of Statistical Activities. Conference on Data Quality for International Organizations,* Rome, Italy.

Veli, N. S., Dipak, K., Pierre, L., Alan, R., Jean, M. R., Karl, A. S., Gyorgy, S., Bedirhan, U., Martti, V., & Pieter, E. Z. (2009). Semantic Interoperability for Better Health and Safer Healthcare. *Deployment and Research Roadmap for Europe.* doi:10.2759/38514

Wu, X., Zhu, X., Wu, G. Q., & Ding, W. (2014). Data mining with big data. *Knowl Data Eng. IEEE Trans., 26*(1), 97–107.

Yan, Y., Xu-Cheng, Y., Bo-Wen, Z., Chun, Y., & Hong-Wei, H. (2016). *Semantic indexing with deep learning: a case study.* doi:10.118641044-016-0007-z

Yue-ting, Z., Fei, W., Chun, C., & Yun-he, P. (2017). *Challenges and opportunities: from big data to knowledge in AI 2.0.* doi:10.1631/FITEE.1601883

Zhang, R., Pakhomov, S., McInnes, B. T., & Melton, G. B. (2011). Evaluating Measures of Redundancy in Clinical Texts. *Proc AMIA,* 1612–1620.

Chapter 3
Semantic and Blockchain Technology

Aswini R.
IFET College of Engineering, India

Padmapriya N.
iD https://orcid.org/0000-0001-5809-3586
IFET College of Engineering, India

ABSTRACT

Blockchain is a distributed ledger with the ability of keeping up the uprightness of exchanges by decentralizing the record among participating clients. The key advancement is that it enables its users to exchange resources over the internet without the requirement for a centralised third party. Also, each 'block' is exceptionally associated with the past blocks by means of digital signature which implies that creation a change to a record without exasperating the previous records in the chain is beyond the realm of imagination, in this way rendering the data tamper-proof. A semantic layer based upon a blockchain framework would join the advantages of adaptable administration disclosure and approval by consensus. This chapter examines the engineering supporting the blockchain and portrays in detail how the information distribution is done, the structure of the block itself, the job of the block header, the block identifier, and the idea of the Genesis block.

INTRODUCTION

Semantic Blockchain is the utilization of Semantic web principles on blockchain based frameworks. The standard advances normal data format and trade conventions on the blockchain, making utilized of the Resource Description Framework (RDF). It permits contrasting a solicitation and numerous resource descriptions by considering semantics of their explanations alluded to a shared ontology. The outcome is a score estimating the semantic distance between the solicitation metadata and comments of accessible chain resources. Ensuing segments discuss the difficulties, favourable circumstances and confinements of blockchain from a security perspective.

DOI: 10.4018/978-1-7998-6697-8.ch003

Blockchain innovation is vigorous like the Internet, yet not at all like the web2 has Internet of today; it stored indistinguishable blocks of data over its network. Consequently, a blockchain cannot be constrained by any single entity nor does it have a solitary purpose of failure. By putting away information over its system, the blockchain wipes out the dangers that accompany information being held halfway. Blockchain systems need incorporated purposes of helplessness that PC programmers can misuse effectively. The present Internet has security issues that are natural to everybody. We as a whole depend on username and secret word accreditations to get to our advantages on the web. Blockchain utilizes encryption innovation to improve security. By enabling information and data to be broadly disseminated, blockchain innovation has made the foundation of the new Internet, web3. In spite of the fact that it was initially contrived for the digital currency Bitcoin, the business and innovation networks are finding numerous utilizations for blockchain. Knowledge of this new innovation will be required by software engineers as well as by all organizations. In the following five to ten years, blockchain will change the plans of action in a wide range of enterprises and maybe change the manner in which individuals work and live.

Technological advances have made a "Semantic Blockchain" feasible. The term semantics as broadly agreed today alludes to this process of making of such digital conventions for getting conviction of meaning. The fundamental(Tim Berners-Lee, 2007)article on the semantic web not just signposted the ascent of activity in this field likewise featured the way that digital systems and the advanced interaction and transaction they empower can and should be supported by digital means for building up conviction of significance. From that point forward another cottage industry has emerged around the formation of digital ontologies and the hypothetical knowledge, strategies, documentations and tools required for their development.

Having taken a gander at the requirement for both conviction of meaning and assurance of arrangement and a portion of the overall solutions for every it is presently worth thinking about how blockchain and semantics can be consolidated in practice (von Wendland, Marcelle,2018) There are two general ways: First it is conceivable to make a blockchain component that permits smart contracts or different protocols to be characterized utilizing a way that mimics a Turing Machine like e.g. a microprocessor; the guidelines here are advising the mechanism precisely HOW to compute an outcome yet give no immediate understanding into what is required. This could be called semantic blockchain with procedural semantics. The subsequent methodology is to make a blockchain system that takes guidelines in the structure details of the necessary outcomes yet without indicating precisely how the outcome is to be computed; The instructions here determine precisely WHAT is required but leave it to the mechanism to locate the exact route for HOW to figure the necessary outcome. This could be called Semantic blockchain with declarative semantics.

While making a smart contract that inserts information sounds direct on paper, actually the mechanics are profoundly unpredictable. A compelling smart contract needs data that interfaces it to setting, permitting the end client and delegates to know who, what, where, when and why the contract will make or lose cash. This robust comprehension of setting is at the core of ventures and risk management; even algorithmic exchanging PCs are working from information that flexibly the specific situation. In any case, we are not at where smart contracts can satisfy their guarantee. The mechanics of smart contracts don't yet have the fundamental backbone of data – the Semantic Web – that permits investors to capture information about an contract in a sensible range of time to settle on a investment choice. This is the following enormous leap forward, and with it come various significant results for capital business sectors.

Semantic Blockchain with Procedural Semantics Early Blockchain endeavors were either focussed on digital money like Bitcoin (Nakamoto, 2009), controlling resource utilize like HashCash(Adam Back,

2002)Byzantine Fault Tolerant state machine replication figuring primitivess to be designed into more extensive solutions. Semantics in those early exertions was either fixed and inferred as in Bitcoin and hash money or expected outside to the mechanism as in Lamports PAXOS and Liskovs PBFT. In the mid 2010's analysts and professionals understood that the computational semantics of stages like Bitcoin could be utilized to develop a wide variety of applications. Hal Hodson's article " Bitcoin moves beyond mere money" (Hodson, 2013) in the New Scientist give an early overview of this action. In any case while Bitcoin permits a specific measure of scripting directly as a component of the design more intricate smart contract expect systems to be united onto Bitcoin. This acknowledgment leads analysts and professionals to investigate manners by which a more extensive scripting language could be embedded into new coin structures. Vitalik Buterin (2014),depicts how Ethereum had been explicitly intended for this reason. [8] gives an expansive review of computational semantics inserted into coins like Bitcoin and Ethereum and their utilization for developing smart contracts. Simultaneously, additionally beginning in the early 2010, specialists and professionals likewise began to search for alternative approaches to execute block chain smart contracts without utilizing coins. Following a line earlier set out by (Cachin, 2017) outstanding amongst other know venture that took this direction is HyperLegder.

The advantages of Knowledge Representation and especially Semantic Web advancements at knowledge revelation level in inescapable heterogeneous framework stacks are notable. This opens the route toward incorporating blockchains with a cosmology based resource/service revelation, utilizing semantics of solicitations and resource depictions to refine recovery methodologies. Semantic-upgraded blockchain frameworks empower revelation foundations for universally useful machine-to-machine trust less commercial centres with negligible or no human intercession over various Decentralized Autonomous Organization (DAOs). This has a few applications with conceivably transformation impact on pertinent parts for smart urban areas and communities.

On the Semantic Web, all data is communicated in statements about resources. Resources are recognized by International or Uniform Resource Identifiers (IRI/URIs). While URIs is extremely useful, they additionally have some innate shortcomings:

- Centralization. While individual URIs can be stamped in a distributed manner, the identifier generation depends on the concentrated DNS framework, which represents a solitary purpose of disappointment or assault.
- Persistence. If there should be an occurrence of deliberate (for example a merger or securing of a legitimate element) or accidental occasions, the persistence of identifiers cannot be ensured.

In spite of the fact that Bitcoin, the primary genuine usage of blockchain, is a decentralized currency and payment framework, the fundamental builds that structure the premise of the framework do not need to be restricted to payment exchanges, records, balances or clients. Rather, blockchain innovation in Bitcoin is simply transaction verified and executed by a scripting language utilizing cryptographic strategies. This implies blockchain is a stage with a scripting language that can explain many use cases other than just cryptographic forms of money.

WHAT IS BLOCKCHAIN INNOVATION?

Blockchain is an appropriated database that keeps up a ceaselessly growing list of records verified from altering and correction. It comprises of data structure blocks that may contain information or program with each blocks holding clusters of individual transactions.

Blockchain comprises of three significant concepts: blocks, nodes and miners.

Blocks

Each chain comprises of numerous blocks and each block has three fundamental components:

- The data in the block.
- A 32-bit whole number called a nonce. The nonce is arbitrarily produced when a block is made, which at that point creates a block header hash.
- The hash is a 256-bit number wedded to the nonce. It must beginning with countless zeroes.

At the point when the first block of a chain is made, a nonce generates the cryptographic hash. The data in the block is viewed as signed and perpetually attached to the nonce and hash except if it is mined.

Miners

Miners make new blocks on the chain through a cycle called mining. In a blockchain each block has its own unique nonce and hash, yet additionally references the hash of the previous block in the chain, so mining a block is not simple, particularly on large chains. Miners utilize unique programming to tackle the staggeringly complex math problem of finding a nonce that creates an acknowledged hash. Since the nonce is just 32 bits and the hash is 256, there are about four billion potential nonce-hash combinations that must be mined before the correct one is found. At the point when that happens miners are said to have discovered the "golden nonce" and their block is added to the chain. Rolling out an improvement to any block earlier in the chain requires re-mining the block with the change, yet the entirety of the blocks that come after. This is the reason it is incredibly hard to control blockchain innovation. Consider it is as "security in math" since finding golden nonces requires a tremendous measure of time and figuring power. At the point when a block is effectively mined, the change is acknowledged by the entirety of the nodes on the system and the miner is compensated monetarily.

Nodes

One of the most significant ideas in blockchain technology is decentralization. No one PC or association can possess the chain. Rather, it is a distributed ledger by means of the nodes associated with the chain. Nodes can be any sort of electronic gadget that keeps up duplicates of the blockchain and keeps the system working. Each node has its own copy of the blockchain and the system should algorithmically affirm any recently mined block for the chain to be refreshed, trusted and confirmed. Since blockchains are straightforward, each activity in the ledger can be easily checked and seen. Every member is given a unique alphanumeric recognizable proof number that shows their transactions. Consolidating public data with a system of checks and balances helps the blockchain keep up integrity and makes trust among clients. Basically, blockchains can be thought of as the scalability of trust through innovation. Each block inside the blockchain is recognized by a hash, produced utilizing the SHA256 cryptographic hash calculation on the header of the block. Each block likewise references a previous block, known as the parent block, through the "previous block hash" field in the block header. As it were, each block contains the hash of its parent inside its own header. The arrangement of hashes connecting each block to its parent makes a chain returning right to the main block at any point made, known as the generic block.

Structure of a Block

A block is a container information structure that totals transactions for incorporation in the public ledger, the blockchain. The block is made of a header, containing metadata, trailed by an extensive rundown of transactions that make up the heft of its size. The block header is 80 bytes, though the normal exchange is in any event 250 bytes and the normal block contains in excess of 500 transactions. A total block, with all transactions, is in this manner 1000 times bigger than the block header.

Regardless of the questionable notoriety of Bitcoin, the blockchain innovation at its centre is naturally positive. It is fundamentally a distributed database, which records transaction happened in a given time range in blocks, chained by methods for cryptographic hashes. The dependability of such a structure originates from the way that each transaction is trusted by accord of most of entities acting in the framework. Blockchain empowers the execution of smart contracts, i.e., software stubs which consequently process the terms of an understanding. As individuals, companies and government depend an ever increasing number of basic information to data frameworks, trust in the computerized world has turned out to be progressively identified with the certainty on given "authorities". The way that such entities could be split or fake stances genuine security and protection issues to the dispersion of dematerialized transactions. This is the motivation behind why blockchain could turn out to be helpful.

The advantages of Knowledge Representation and especially Semantic Web– advancements at resource revelation level in inescapable heterogeneous framework stacks are notable. This opens the path toward coordinating blockchains with a philosophy based resource/administration revelation, utilizing semantics of solicitations and resource portrayals to refine recovery techniques. A semantic-upgraded blockchain essentially amounts to a Service-Oriented Architecture (SOA) for directing enlistment, disclosure, selection and payment activities, executed as appropriated smart contracts approved by consenus.

Steps of Blockchain processing:

1. Add new and undeletable transactions and sort them into blocks.
2. Cryptographically confirm every transaction in the block.
3. Add the new block to the end of the previous immutable blockchain.

Mining

Miners on a Blockchain are nodes that produce blocks by tackling proof of work issues. In the event that a miner delivers a square block that is affirmed by an electronic agreement of nodes then the miner is remunerated with coins. As of October 2017, Bitcoin miners get 12.5 Bitcoins per block. The reward is not the main motivator for miners to continue running their hardware. They likewise get the transaction expenses that Bitcoin clients pay. At present, as there is a gigantic measure of transactions occurring inside the Bitcoin arrange, the transaction expenses have soar. Despite the fact that the charges are deliberate with respect to the sender, miner will consistently organize transfers with higher transaction expenses. Along these lines, except if you are eager to pay a fairly high charge, your transaction may set aside an extremely long effort to be prepared.

Cryptographic keys

A cryptographic key is a series of numbers and letters. Cryptographic keys are made by key generators or keygens. These keygens utilize exceptionally progressed mathematics including prime numbers to make keys.

Protocols

The Blockchain comprises of individual conduct specifications, a huge rules that are programmed into it. Those determinations are called protocols. The usage of explicit protocols basically made Blockchain what it is — a distributed, shared and secured data information base. The Blockchain protocols guarantee that the system runs the manner in which it was planned to by its creators, despite the fact that it is totally independent and is not constrained by anybody. Here are a few instances of protocols actualized in Blockchain:

- Input data for each hash number needs to incorporate the past block's hash number.
- The compensation for effectively mining block abatements considerably after each 210,000 blocks is fixed off.
- In request to keep the measure of time expected to mine one block at around 10 minutes, mining difficulty is recalculated each 2,016 squares.

Proof of Work

The assigning of a transaction in a block is known as a successful conclusion to a proof of work challenge, and is done by extraordinary nodes called miners. Proof of Work is a framework that requires some work from the administration requester, normally significance preparing time by a PC. Delivering a proof of work is an irregular cycle with low likelihood, so regularly a great deal of experimentation is required for a substantial confirmation of work to be produced. With regards to Bitcoins, hash is the thing that fills in as a proof of work.

HOW DOES BLOCKCHAIN WORK?

Blockchain innovation is most likely the best invention since the web itself. It permits value exchange without the requirement for trust or a focal expert. The working guidelines of Blockchain are as per the following:

1. A node begins a transaction by first creating and after that digitally signing it with its private key (made by means of cryptography). A transaction can represent different activities in a blockchain. Most usually this is an information structure that represents exchange of significant worth between

clients on the blockchain network. Transaction data more often than not comprises of some rationale of exchange of value, applicable guidelines, source and goal addresses, and other approval data.

2. A transaction is engendered (overflowed) by utilizing a flooding protocol, called Gossip protocol, to peers that approve the transaction dependent on present criteria. Generally, more than one node is required to check the transaction.

3. Once the transaction is approved, it is incorporated into a block, which is then engendered onto the network. Now, the transaction is viewed as affirmed.

4. The recently made block presently turns out to be a part of the ledger, and the following block connections itself cryptographically back to this block. This connection is a hash pointer. At this stage, the transaction gets its second affirmation and the block gets its first affirmation.

5. Transactions are then reconfirmed each time another block is made. Generally, six affirmations in the bitcoin network are required to consider the transaction last.

Balances - Block Chain

Every single affirmed transaction are incorporated into the block chain. It permits Bitcoin wallets to ascertain their spendable parity so new transaction can be confirmed along these lines guaranteeing they are really claimed by the spender. The integrity and the sequential request of the block chain are upheld with cryptography.

Transactions - Private Keys

A transaction is an exchange of significant worth between Bitcoin wallets that gets incorporated into the block chain. Bitcoin wallets stay quiet bit of information called a private key or seed, which is utilized to sign transaction, giving numerical evidence that they have originated from the proprietor of the wallet. The signature additionally keeps the transaction from being modified by anyone once it has been issued. All transaction is communicated to the network and more often than not starts to be affirmed inside 10-20 minutes, through a procedure called mining. The principle reason for this part of blockchain innovation is to make a safe digital identity reference. Identity depends on ownership of a mix of private and public cryptographic keys. The mix of these keys can be viewed as an adroit type of assent, making an incredibly valuable digital signature. Thus, this digital signature gives solid control of proprietorship.

Figure 1. Digital signature

Processing - Mining

Mining is used to secure and verify bitcoin transactions. It is utilized to affirm pending transactions by incorporating them in the block chain. It upholds a sequential request in the block chain, secures the lack of bias of the system, and enables diverse PCs to concur on the condition of the framework. To be affirmed, transactions must be pressed in a block that fits exceptionally exacting cryptographic principles that will be checked by the system. These principles keep past blocks from being changed in light of the fact that doing as such would discredit all the consequent blocks. Mining likewise makes what might be compared to a focused lottery that keeps any person from effectively adding new blocks sequentially to the block chain. Along these lines, no gathering or people can control what is incorporated into the block chain or supplant portions of the block chain to move back their own spends.

Process of Confirmation

A standout amongst the most imperative parts of blockchain innovation is the manner in which that it affirms and approves transactions. Two people wish to conduct a transaction online, each with a private and a public key, blockchain permits the first person (A) to utilize their private key to attach information in regards to the transaction to the public key of the second person (B). This information together structures some portion of a block, which contains a digital signature just as a timestamp and other pertinent data about the transaction, yet not the identities of the people associated with that transaction. That block is then transmitted over the blockchain system to the majority of the nodes, or other segment portions of the network, which will at that point go about as validators for the transaction.

The majority of this sending of data and approving of blocks requires gigantic measures of computing power. In handy terms, it might appear to be improbable to expect a large number of PCs around the world to all be eager to devote processing power and different assets to this undertaking. One answer for this issue for the blockchain arrange is mining. Mining is identified with a conventional monetary issue called the "awfulness of the commons." Put basically, this idea abridges a circumstance in which people who each demonstration autonomously in their very own personal matters will in general act in manners as opposed to the benefit of all of all clients because of exhausting an asset through their activity at an aggregate dimension. During the blockchain validation process, a person who gives up a little part of his or her computational power so as to give a support of the system in this way acquires a reward. By carrying on of personal responsibility that individual has been boosted to help serve the necessities of the more extensive system.

Chains of Blocks

For blockchain networks, this is a vital advance toward safeguarding that cryptocurrencies cannot be spent in numerous transactions in the meantime, an idea known as double spending. So as to secure against double spending, blockchain systems need to guarantee that cryptocurrencies are both extraordinarily claimed and permeated with esteem. One method for giving this administration is to have the nodes inside the blockchain network go about as segments of the record framework itself, keeping up a history of transaction for each coin in that network by attempting to take care of entangled numerical issues. These nodes serve to affirm or dismiss blocks representing bits of data about transaction. In the event that a larger part of node administrators arrive at a similar answer for an issue, the block is affirmed and it is added to the chain of blocks that exist before it. This new block is timestamped and is probably going to contain data about different parts of past transactions.

This is the place there is space for variety relying on the specific system: some blockchain systems incorporate particular sorts of data in their blocks, while others incorporate diverse arrangements of data.

TYPES OF BLOCKCHAIN IN MARKET AND WHY WE NEED THEM?

The thought emerged that the Bitcoin blockchain could be in certainty utilized for any sort of significant worth transaction or any sort of understanding, for example, P2P protection, P2P vitality exchanging, P2P ride sharing, and so on. Colored Coins and Mastercoin attempted to take care of that issue dependent on the Bitcoin Blockchain Protocol. The Ethereum venture chose to make their own blockchain, with altogether different properties than Bitcoin, decoupling the smart contract layer from the center blockchain protocol, offering a radical better approach to make online markets and programmable transactions known as Smart Contracts. Private establishments like banks understood that they could utilize the center thought of blockchain as a distributed ledger technology (DLT), and make a permissioned blockchain (private or unified), where the validator is an individual from a consortium or separate lawful entities of a similar association. The term blockchain with regards to permissioned private ledger is profoundly questionable and debated. This is the reason the term distributed ledger advances developed as a progressively broad term.

There for the most part three kinds of Blockchains that have risen after Bitcoin acquainted Blockchain with the world.

1. Public Blockchain
2. Private Blockchain
3. Consortium or Federated Blockchain

Public Blockchain

Cutting edge public Blockchain conventions dependent on Proof of Work (PoW) accord calculations are open source and not permissioned. Anybody can take an interest, without consent. (1) Anyone can download the code and begin running an open node on their neighborhood gadget, approving transactions in the system, in this manner taking an interest in the accord procedure – the procedure for figuring out what blocks get added to the chain and what the present state is. (2) Anyone on the world can send transactions through the system and hope to see them incorporated into the blockchain on the off chance that they are legitimate. (3) Anyone can peruse transaction on the public block voyager. Transactions are straightforward, yet mysterious/pseudonumous.

Precedents: Bitcoin, Ethereum, Monero, Dash, Litecoin, Dodgecoin, and so on.
Impacts: (1) Potential to disturb current plans of action through disintermediation.
   (2)   No infrastructure costs: No compelling reason to keep up servers or framework administrators profoundly lessens the expenses of making and running decentralized applications (dApps).

Here nobody is in control and anybody can take an interest in perusing/composing/evaluating the blockchain. Something else is that these kinds of blockchain are open and straightforward subsequently anybody can survey anything at a given purpose of time on an open blockchain.

Private Blockchain

Write authorizations are held incorporated to one association. Read consents might be open or limited to a subjective degree. Precedent applications incorporate database management, evaluating, and so forth which are interior to a solitary organization, thus open lucidness may by and large not be vital by any means. In other cases public audit capacity is desired. Private blockchains are a method for exploiting blockchain innovation by setting up gatherings and members who can check exchanges inside. This puts you at the danger of security ruptures simply like in an incorporated framework, instead of open blockchain verified by diversion theoretic motivating force instruments. Nonetheless, private blockchains have their use case, particularly with regards to versatility and state consistence of information security rules and other administrative issues. They have certain security advantages, and other security weaknesses.

Private blockchain as its name recommends is a private property of an individual or an association. Dissimilar to public blockchain here there is an in control who takes care of vital things, for example, read/write or whom to specifically offer access to peruse or the other way around.

Precedents:, Impacts: (1) Decreases transaction expenses and information redundancies and replaces heritage frameworks, improving archive dealing with and disposing of semi manual consistence systems.

(2) In that sense it tends to be viewed as proportionate to SAP in the 1990's: diminishes costs, however not troublesome!

Consortium or Federated Blockchain

Federated Blockchains work under the authority of a gathering. Rather than public Blockchains, they don't enable any individual with access to the Internet to take part during the time spent checking transactions. Federated Blockchains are quicker and give more transaction protection. Consortium blockchains are for the most part utilized in the financial area. The accord procedure is constrained by a pre-chosen set of nodes; for instance, one may envision a consortium of 15 budgetary establishments, every one of which works a node and of which 10 must sign each block all together for the block to be substantial. The privilege to peruse the blockchain might be public, or confined to the members.

Precedent: R3 (Banks), EWF (Energy), Corda
Impacts: (1) decreases transaction expenses and information redundancies and replaces heritage frameworks, improving report dealing with and disposing of semi manual consistence systems.

(2) In that sense it tends to be viewed as identical to SAP in the 1990's: lessens costs, however not troublesome!

There is a wide cluster of ways to deal with actualizing Blockchain or other Distributed Ledger Technologies. A differing scene of players has risen, including programming specialist organizations that offer programming capacities on higher stack levels than the blockchain conventions themselves. Each methodology has its very own benefits and difficulties.

Table1. Blockchain Implementation Solutions

APPROACH	HOW IT IS DONE	EXAMPLES
IT Services	Build on request	ConsenSys
Blockchain First	Develop using the tools provided by the blockchain	Ethereum, Bitcoin
Development Platforms	Tools for IT Professionals	ERIS, Tendermint, Hyperledger
Vertical Solutions	Industry specific	Axoni, Chain, R3, itBit, Clearmatics
Special APIs & Overlays	DIY building blocks	Blockstack, Factom, Open Assets, Tierion

Here, are a few reasons why Blockchain innovation has turned out to be so famous.

- Versatility: Blockchains is frequently simulated architecture. The chain is still worked by most nodes in case of a gigantic assault against the framework.
- Time decrease: In the financial industry, blockchain can assume a crucial job by permitting the speedier repayment of exchanges as it need not bother with a protracted procedure of check, repayment, and clearance because a single version of tons of the offer record is accessible between all stack holders.
- Reliability: Blockchain affirms and checks the personalities of the invested individuals. This evacuates double records, lessening rates and quickens transactions.
- Unchangeable transactions: By enrolling transactions in sequential request, Blockchain affirms the inalterability, of all activities which implies when any new block has been added to the chain of records; it cannot be evacuated or changed.
- Fraud avoidance: The ideas of shared data and agreement forestall conceivable misfortunes because of extortion or theft. In logistics-based businesses, blockchain as a checking component act to decrease costs.
- Security: Attacking a conventional database is the bringing down of a particular target. With the assistance of Distributed Ledger Technology, each gathering holds a duplicate of the first chain, so the framework stays usable, even the expansive number of different nodes fall.
- Coordinated: Allows gatherings to execute straightforwardly with one another without the requirement for intervening outsiders.
- Decentralized: There are benchmarks runs on how every node trades the blockchain data. This strategy guarantees that all transactions are approved, and every single substantial exchange is included one by one.

TECHNOLOGY FUNDAMENTALS OF BLOCKCHAIN

These are the center blockchain engineering segments:

- Node - client or PC inside the blockchain architecture (every has an independent duplicate of the entire blockchain record)
- Transaction - smallest structure block of a blockchain framework (records, data, and so forth.) that fills in as the reason for blockchain
- Block - an information structure utilized for keeping a lot of transactions which is disseminated to all nodes in the system
- Chain - a succession of blocks in a particular request
- Consensus (consensus convention) - a lot of principles and arrangements to do blockchain activities

SMART CONTRACTS & DAPPS

Algorithms that can self-execute, self-authorize, self-check, and self-compel the execution of an agreement. A smart contract is a mechanized transaction convention that executes the terms of an agreement. The general destinations are to fulfil basic legally binding conditions, (for example, installment terms, liens, secrecy, and even implementation), limit exemptions both pernicious and coincidental, and limit the requirement for confided in middle people. A smart contract is an agreement between at least two gatherings that can be modified electronically and is executed naturally through its basic blockchain because of specific occasions encoded inside the agreement. Distributed ledgers empower the coding of basic gets that will execute when determined conditions are met. Ethereum is an open source blockchain venture that was assembled explicitly to understand this probability. In any case, in its beginning times, Ethereum can possibly use the value of blockchains on a genuinely world-evolving scale. Decentralized applications (dApps) are applications that kept running on a P2P system of PCs as opposed to a solitary PC. dApps, have existed since the coming of P2P systems. They are a sort of programming program intended to exist on the Internet in a manner that is not constrained by any single entity.

1. Decentralized applications do not really need to keep running over a blockchain network. BitTorrent, Popcorn Time, BitMessage, Tor, are for the most part conventional dApps that keep running on a P2P arrange, yet not on a Blockchain (which is a particular sort of P2P network).
2. As restricted to straightforward smart contracts, in the classic sense of Bitcoin, that sends cash from A to B, dApps have a boundless number of members on all sides of the market.

Difference Between dApps and Smart Contracts

dApps are a 'blockchain empowered' site, where the Smart Contract is the thing that enables it to associate with the blockchain. The most effortless approach to comprehend this is to see how conventional sites work.

- The customary web application utilizes HTML, CSS and Javascript to render a page. It will also need to get facts from a database using an API. When you go onto Facebook, the page will call an API to snatch your own information and show them on the page. Customary sites: Front End ® API ® Database
- dApps are like a customary web application. The front end utilizes precisely the same innovation to render the page. The one basic distinction is that rather than an API associating with a Database,

you have a Smart Contract interfacing with a blockchain. dApp empowered site: Front End ® Smart Contract ® Blockchain

Rather than customary, centralized applications, where the backend code is running on incorporated servers, dApps have their backend code running on a decentralized P2P organize. Decentralized applications comprise of the entire bundle, from backend to frontend. The smart contract is just a single piece of the dApp:

1. Frontend and
2. Backend

A smart contract, on the other hand, comprises just of the backend, and frequently just a small piece of the entire dApp. That implies in the event that you need to make a decentralized application on a smart contract framework, you need to join a few smart contracts and depend on outsider frameworks for the front-end.

- Smart contract applications and blockchain

Blockchain is perfect for putting away smart contracts in view of the innovation's security and changelessness. Smart contract information is encrypted on a mutual record, making it difficult to lose the data stored in the blocks. Another preferred standpoint of blockchain innovation being consolidated into smart contracts is adaptability. Engineers can store practically any kind of information inside a blockchain, and they have a wide assortment of transaction choices to browse amid smart contract organization.

CRYPTOCURRENCY MINING

Cryptocurrency mining, or cryptomining, is a procedure in which transactions for different types of cryptocurrency are confirmed and added to the blockchain digital record. Otherwise called cryptocoin mining, altcoin mining, or Bitcoin mining (for the most well-known type of digital money, Bitcoin), currency mining has expanded both as a theme and action as cryptocurrency use itself has developed exponentially over the most recent couple of years. Each time a cryptocurrency transaction is made, a cryptocurrency miner is in charge of guaranteeing the genuineness of data and refreshing the blockchain with the transaction. The mining procedure itself includes contending with different cryptominers to tackle entangled scientific issues with cryptographic hash functions that are related with a block containing the transaction information. The main cryptocurrency miner to figure out the code is compensated by having the capacity to approve the transaction, and as an end-result of the service provided, cryptominers win little measures of digital currency of their own. So as to be focused with different cryptominers, however, a cryptocurrency miner needs a PC with particular equipment.

How to Get Started as a Cryptocurrency Miner

So as to begin mining,, cryptocurrency miners will require committed PC equipment with a particular graphical processing unit (GPU) chip or application-specific integrated circuit (ASIC), adequate cooling implies for the equipment, a dependably on web association, an authentic cryptocurrency mining programming bundle, and participation in both an online cryptocurrency trade just as a web based mining pool.

Hopeful cryptominers ought to likewise realize that as cryptocurrencies have ascended in both fame and esteem, rivalry has expanded considerably too and now incorporates associations and undertakings with more broad assets than most people can rival.

Things to know before mining any cryptocurrency

- A free private database also known as coin wallet. Wallet is a secret key ensured stockpiling for your income and keeps a system wide record of exchanges.
- A free mining programming bundle, similar to this one from AMD
- An enrolment in a web based mining pool, which is a network of diggers who consolidate their PCs to expand productivity and pay security. Mining outside of a pool will in all likelihood mean you won't be the person who explains the scientific assignment.
- Membership at an online currency exchange, where you can trade your mined coins for money or Bitcoin
- An equipment setup found ideally in a cool and cooled space.
- A work area or custom-assembled PC intended for mining.
- An ATI/Nvidia graphics processing unit (GPU) or a particular handling gadget called a mining ASIC chip. The cost will be somewhere in the range of $90 used to $3000 new for each GPU or ASIC chip.
- Personal curiosity. You have to continually peruse research and learn, as mining advances improve in all respects quickly which results in better approaches for streamlining coin mining results. The best coin diggers put in hours consistently concentrating the most ideal approaches to modify and improve their coin mining execution.

Bitcoin mining is deliberately intended to be asset escalated and troublesome with the goal that the quantity of block found every day by miners stays consistent. Individual blocks must contain a proof of work to be viewed as substantial. This confirmation of work is checked by other Bitcoin nodes each time they get a block. Bitcoin utilizes the hashcash verification of work.

The basic role of mining is to permit Bitcoin nodes to come to a protected, alter safe agreement. Mining is likewise the component used to bring Bitcoins into the framework: Miners are paid any transaction charges just as an "appropriation" of recently made coins. This two effectively disseminates new coins in a decentralized way just as propelling individuals to give security to the framework. Bitcoin mining is supposed on the grounds that it looks like the mining of different wares: it requires effort and it gradually makes new cash accessible at a rate that takes after the rate at which items like gold are mined starting from the earliest stage.

A cryptocurrency is one mechanism of trade like customary monetary forms, for example, USD, yet it is intended to trade the advanced data through a procedure made conceivable by specific standards of cryptography. Cryptocurrency is advanced cash and is named a subset of elective monetary forms and virtual monetary standards. Cryptocurrency is a carrier instrument dependent on advanced cryptography. In this sort of cryptocurrency, the holder has of the cash has proprietorship. No other record kept with regards to the personality of the proprietor.

WHY IS SEMANTIC BLOCKCHAIN IMPORTANT?

Semantic Blockchain is an appropriated database that keeps up a ceaselessly developing rundown of institutionalized information records, utilizing for the most part Resource Description Framework (RDF), solidified against altering and correction. Semantic Blockchain is the portrayal of information put away on the blockchain utilizing Linked Data. The characteristic properties of the blockchain as: auditable, discernibility, ensured progression, overly dispersed Security, evidence of uniqueness, responsibility for, and so on should fill in as a lift for Semantic Web. So also, current blockchain stages as Ethereum are missing of Semantic thinking on its segments, for instance on the "smart contracts". Semantic web models are out from numerous years and could be effectively adjusted to these new blockchain based stages. Actually, there is a major space of research to make in the field of "Semantic Blockchains" or "Semantic Distributed Ledgers", and ideally won't remain on the exploration field just, and will take a major hop to the mechanical world. For that it results critical to begin creating applications that blend these 2 universes.

Three that numerous possibles approaches to "semantify" a blockchain are:

1. Map the current substance of the blockchain to RDF. For this are required distinctive instruments and semantic segments.
2. Store RDF Data on the blockchain. This information can contain URI indicating other information store inside the blockchain (non HTTP URIs, for instance: Smart Contracts Addresses).
3. Create another blockchain system (altcoin or from scratch) in view of on Semantic web standards (Handling blockchain metadata with RDF design, empowering SPARQL questions locally, and so forth).

Semantic-improved blockchain frameworks empower disclosure foundations for universally useful machine-to-machine trust less commercial centres with negligible or no human intercession over different Decentralized Autonomous Organization (DAOs). This has a few applications with conceivably change sway on significant segments for smart cities and networks.

- Logistics: Asset tracking and inventory network are among the most prevalent blockchain applications, because of the simple fit with existing industry gauges. The most straightforward methodologies depend on value-based records for resource transfer. Semantic improved blockchains dependent on smart contracts further enable any application rationale to be actualized and embedded in the blockchain, and furthermore bolster discoverable and unquestionable multi-step business forms in multi-party SOAs.
- Industry 4.0: IoT-based assembling profits by blockchain technologies, conceding a decentralized coordinated effort foundation, yet additionally a record for procedure recognizability of generation and quality confirmation. Semantic based blockchain advancement can give more noteworthy organization adaptability and thorough procedure formalization.
- Utility markets: Energy, water and petroleum gas provisioning are progressively depending on sensor systems, low-level advanced control and high-level decision support. Semantic-improved blockchains can firmly support visions like the Smart Grid, as they give both asset arranged revelation forms and a powerful record for contracts and installments, which are required in expansive scale, shared decentralized commercial centres.

- Public sector: Many public administrations to the populace can be made quicker, less expensive and less blunder inclined through procedure and information dematerialization. Blockchain innovation can aid the interfacing of the data frameworks of a few free branches and dimensions of the public organization. Moreover, it assumes the job of unquestionable vault in property exchanges just as confirmation and legal official administrations. Semantic-based querying capacities make data and functionalities progressively available to both residents and decision-makers.
- Financial administrations: Traditional banks and finance foundations, private and public alike, are trying different things with blockchain innovation to decrease working expenses of monetary exchanges the board. Semantic-based methodologies empower a commercial centre of financial administrations, where nuclear structure blocks can be naturally found, contrasted and created all together with give the most reasonable customized arrangements.

BLOCKCHAIN - PAYMENT VERIFICATION

Blockchain wallets are what holds the Bitcoin address and furthermore records all exchanges. To send, get, or store crypto currencies it need an advanced wallet. The Bitcoin address is a code made with a numbers and letters, likewise called an open key. The succession of the open key can be seen by all inside the system. Alongside the public key, there is another key that is kept private (another code). Digital currency clients need to keep their private key sheltered and mystery. Both the keys are connected, without one of the other, it can't make exchanges.

Confirmation (simplified) is the way toward running exchanges through one way numerical conditions called hashes. At the point when another block is made, the majority of its transactions are hashed (now and again, hashed ordinarily), delivering an interesting outcome.

These outcomes are checked by different nodes on the system by re-running the equivalent scientific conditions with similar sources of information and affirming that the yield coordinates precisely. In the event that the yield does not coordinate what that tells the node is that the information sources do not coordinate, either because of a blunder or misrepresentation, and the exchange ought to be overlooked.

This procedure works comparatively for approving single transaction just as approving new blocks. Blockchain innovation is one of the important endowments of innovation in light of its security and confirmation highlight. Blockchain, as you may know, holds all the advanced data in various blocks which are connected to one another by means of a hash codes. Each block holds the hash code of the past connected blog which is created through the qualities put away inside the block. At whatever point somebody endeavours to erase or change the estimations of a specific block, it has code changes which educates the associated obstructs that something is not right. Moreover, at whatever point another transaction is made or a current one is refreshed, most of hubs inside the blockchain frameworks get advised. On the off chance that they acknowledge the changes, the progressions are actualized. Something else, the solicitation is denied.

Figure 2. Payment verification

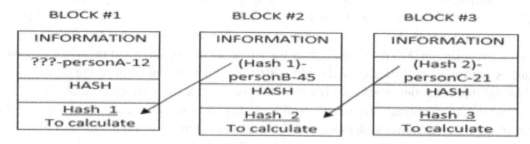

BLOCKCHAIN SECURITY: IS BLOCKCHAIN REALLY SECURE

Anybody can get to the bitcoin organize by means of an anonymous association and submit or get transactions uncovering more than his public key. Notwithstanding in the event that somebody utilizes a similar public key again and again, it's conceivable to associate every one of the transaction to a similar proprietor. The bitcoin organize enables you to create the same number of wallets as you like, each with its very own private and public keys. This enables you to get instalments on various wallets, and there is no chance to get for anybody to realize that you claim every one of these wallets' private keys, except if you send all the got bitcoins to a single wallet.

The absolute number of conceivable bitcoin addresses is

2^{160} or 1461501637330902918203684832716283019655932542976.

This vast number shields the system from conceivable attacks while enabling anybody to claim a wallet.

With this setup, there is as yet a noteworthy security gap that could be misused to review bitcoins in the wake of spending them. Transactions are passed from node to node within the system, so the request in which two transactions achieve every node can be different. An assailant could send a transaction, trust that the partner will dispatch an item, and after that send a reverse transaction back to his very own record. For this situation, a few nodes could get the second transaction before the first and consequently consider the underlying payment transaction invalid, as the transaction information sources would be set apart as effectively spent. How would you know which exchange has been mentioned first? It is not verified to arrange the transaction by timestamp because it could without much of a stretch be counterfeit. In this manner, there is no real way to tell if a transaction occurred before another, and this opens up the potential for extortion.

On the off chance that this occurs, there will be difference among the system nodes with respect to the request of transactions every one of them got. So the blockchain framework has been intended to utilize node consent to arrange transactions and avert the extortion portrayed previously.

The security of individual information, particularly which is put away online is essential and furthermore a human right. For quite a long time, it has been in danger and continually weakened. Blockchain innovation gives an exquisite answer for this issue. Blockchain, as the name demonstrates, is a chain of digital blocks that contain a lot of transactions. Every one of the transaction in a block, structure a Merkel root and a hash is created utilizing it, which is incorporated into the block header. Each block in the blockchain is associated with the past block through the block hash value. This in turns makes the blockchain impervious to any kind of altering, because a programmer would need to change the block containing that transaction just as those connected to it, to maintain a strategic distance from introduction. The blockchain is intended to be unchanging, carefully designed and secure.

Decentralization: Creating a Single Version of the Truth

Generally, anybody needing to store, offer or procedure data has to claim it. This includes making, acquiring or purchasing that data, getting authorization to utilize it (on the off chance that fundamental) and after that guaranteeing everybody knows about any changes. Sound befuddling? It is. Taking care of data along these lines can without much of a stretch become a mind boggling round of phone with several powerless focuses and a high edge for blunder.

Blockchain, then again, disseminates a similar data to each client (or node) on the blockchain organize. When you roll out an improvement, the system approves it and afterward miners (nodes remunerated for refreshing the blockchain) include that transaction into another block, which is then added to the blockchain.

This is decentralization - a solitary adaptation of reality yet no single purpose of disappointment. Change one block, and you did have to change each resulting block before any new blocks could be mined. Something else, nodes would recognize your fake conduct and dispose of your changes. Given there are a huge number of nodes affirming new blocks, it is impossible anybody could beat their combined computing capacity to include an awful one.

Cryptography: The Perfect Disguise

All information on the blockchain is cryptographically hashed; it is prepared to conceal its actual character. Hashing takes any input esteem and applies a scientific calculation (SHA-256 on account of Bitcoin) to create another estimation of a fixed length.

Hashing is like a sort of secret phrase security, a one of a kind ID for delicate information. Each block has a unique hash got from that block's transactions (every transaction ID is additionally hashed) and the hash of the past block. Change the block retroactively, and each former block - the whole history of that blockchain - would likewise need to change. Your private key used to access and move your bitcoins is additionally hashed to turn into a public key, so individuals can send you bitcoins without having the capacity to take them, as well. What makes hashing unique is that it is difficult to figure out. You cannot take an open key, for instance, and conclude the private one. Likewise, one little change in the input esteem makes a completely new hash ID, which implies fraudsters can't pull off rolling out little improvements without invalidating the entire block.

Consensus

Consensus is the brain of the blockchain. It chooses which block to include by contributing nodes against one another a cryptographic race for a Bitcoin prize.

First, nodes approve that the block meets the pre-set guidelines for the Bitcoin blockchain. At that point, miners contend to illuminate a cryptographic riddle dependent on the information contained in that block. At the point when a miner comprehends the riddle, they share their answer with the system. On the off chance that at any rate 51% of the system nodes concur with that arrangement, the block is added to the blockchain.

This specific sort of consensus is called evidence of work. It guarantees each block has experienced an intricate, scientific procedure before turning into an unchanging piece of the blockchain.

The Advantage of Blockchain

- Shared record: It is attaching just appropriated framework shared over the business organize, which makes the framework flexible by wiping out a 'solitary point of failure'.
- Consensus: A transaction is possibly dedicated when all gatherings consent to a system confirmed exchange.
- Provenance: The whole history of a resource is accessible over a blockchain.
- Immutability: Records are permanent and cannot be messed with once dedicated to the mutual record, in this manner making all data reliable.
- Finality: Once a transaction is finished over a blockchain, it can never be returned.
- Smart contracts: Code is worked inside a blockchain that PCs/hubs execute dependent on an activating occasion.

Usecases of Blockchain

- Healthcare
- Education
- Public safety and equity
- Agriculture
- Civil registration
- Defence
- Governance

CONCLUSION

While blockchain's best-known, most utilized and most elevated effect application is Bitcoin, the potential effect of the innovation is a lot more noteworthy and more extensive than virtual monetary standards. Without a doubt, since different applications can 'piggyback' the Bitcoin blockchain, the greatest effects of Bitcoin might be found outside the money area. Exchanges of any sort are generally quicker and less expensive for the client when finished by means of a blockchain, and they likewise advantage from the convention's security. Though exchanges in Europe are frequently quick, shabby and sufficiently secure for most purposes, clients and advocates of blockchain applications regularly observe extra advantages in its straightforwardness and permanence. Undoubtedly, there is a developing pattern towards less trust in money related and administration foundations and more noteworthy social desires for responsibility and obligation. Blockchain innovation could be very integral in a plausibility space for the future world that incorporates both concentrated and decentralized models. Like any new innovation, the blockchain is a thought that at first disturbs, and after some time it could advance the improvement of a bigger biological system that incorporates both the old way and the new innovation. The notoriety of blockchain innovation may likewise mirror a developing social pattern to organize straightforwardness over namelessness.

The most significant impact of blockchain improvement could be found in progressively inconspicuous effects upon expansive social qualities and structures. These effects are related with the qualities that are implanted inside the innovation. All technologies have qualities and legislative issues usually representing the interests of their makers. In this light, the reasons why customary record frameworks position their makers as the central intermediaries are clear: since all exchanges go through them, the makers keep up their situation of intensity and ability to benefit from their clients. In utilizing technologies, individuals reaffirm the qualities and legislative issues that they speak to, so each time these records are utilized to record an exchange, the centrality and vitality of the on-screen character at its middle is reaffirmed. Obviously, a disseminated record without a focal go-between is likewise value laden and political, putting trust in encryption and systems administration innovation and redistributing power from focal specialists to non-progressive and shared structures. In this specific situation, to utilize this sort of blockchain is to partake in a more extensive move that would decrease the trust in and intensity of conventional establishments, for example, banks and governments. The cases investigated in this report uncover a few instances of how blockchain applications encapsulate these qualities. Obviously, for these progressions to be recognizable on a general social dimension would require extremely generous advancement of blockchain to the point where it saturates day by day lives and commonplace schedules

Since mediators are dislodged by the blockchain, such intermediaries cannot be depended upon to manage their task. Accordingly, elective administrative levers must be created to maintain the law and keep up the limit with respect to viable arranging and activity. Four general classes of activity that administration establishments could prepare because of the development of blockchain innovation can be recognized:

- One alternative is to react to 'the issues to which blockchain is an answer' without utilizing blockchain by any means. For instance, if interest for blockchain depends on a longing for more straightforwardness in procedures, at that point residents could be conceded more access to government information and procedures without utilizing blockchain frameworks by any means.
- A second choice is to effectively empower improvement and development of blockchain by the private sector by giving authenticity to their products. For instance, under certain conditions, exchanges on blockchains could be given explicit lawful acknowledgment as records of executed exchanges.
- A third choice is to do the switch of the past one, for example discourage advancement by declining to acknowledge the authenticity of blockchain-based exchanges, for instance by overruling and turning around the conditions in smart contracts.
- A fourth alternative is to embrace a permissioned blockchain in existing frameworks and structures, adequately keeping up the job and intensity of those capable as agent by giving a portion of the essential usefulness of blockchains, yet without offering full decentralization and straightforwardness. This model is now seen in open segment utilization of blockchain innovation, for instance in the UK and Estonia, just as in the private segment.

Varieties and mixes of all four techniques are probably going to be connected to blockchain innovation in various areas and purviews throughout the following decade. For the minute there is little hunger for mediation at a European dimension. In reality, an ongoing European Parliament report on virtual monetary forms recognized the expanded dangers, which will require upgraded administrative limit and satisfactory specialized skill, while requiring a proportionate EU administrative methodology all together not to hamper development at such a beginning time.

To conclude, the way that the blockchain convention gives stages to both great activities and awful activities does not imply that it is an unbiased innovation. In its most flawless structure it advances a redistribution of intensity from central actors across wide networks of companions. While the most optimistic and progressive dreams of blockchain advancement will presumably remain close to dreams, even moderate execution of blockchain may at present advance some level of redistribution and straightforwardness. Blockchain won't improve individuals, yet it may make a portion of the safeguards fundamental in individuals' everyday lives faster, less expensive, progressively secure and increasingly straightforward.

REFERENCES

Back, A. (2002). *Hashcash - a denial of service counter-measure*. https://www.researchgate.net/publication/2482110_Hashcash__A_Denial_of_Service_Counter-Measure

Bartoletti, M., & Pompianu, L. (2017). *An empirical analysis of smart contracts: platforms, applications, and design patterns*. https://arxiv.org/pdf/1703.06322.pdf

Berners-Lee, T., Hendler, J., & Lassila, O. (2001). The Semantic Web. *Scientific American*, (May), 29–37. PMID:11323639

Bryant, M. (2017). *Blockchain may be healthcare's answer to interoperability, data security*. Health Care Dive.

Buterin, D. (n.d.). Smart Contracts: The Blockchain Technology That Will Replace Lawyers. *BlockGeeks*.

Buterin, V. (2014). *A Next Generation Smart Contract & Decentralized Application Platform*. https://www.the-blockchain.com/docs/Ethereum_white_paper-a_next_generation_smart_contract_and_decentralized_application_platform-vitalik-buterin.pdf

Cachin, C. (2017). *Architecture of the Hyperledger Blockchain Fabric*. https://www.zurich.ibm.com/dccl/papers/cachin_dccl.pdf

Carter, J. (2016). *Bitcoin vs distributed ledger vs Ethereum vs blockchain*. http://www.techradar.com/news/internet/bitcoin-vs-distributed-ledger-vs-ethereum-vs-blockchain-1328432

Cole, B. (2016). *Blockchain compliance raises questions of regulatory scope, intent*. Tech Target.

Cuthbertson, A. (2015). *Bitcoin now accepted by 100,000 merchants worldwide*. https://www.ibtimes.co.uk/bitcoin-now-accepted-by-100000-merchants-worldwide-1486613

Dickson, B. (2016). *Blockchain has the potential to revolutionize the supply chain*. Tech Crunch.

Economist Staff. (2015, Oct. 31). Blockchains: The great chain of being sure about things. *The Economist*.

English, M. (2017). *Blockchain and the Semantic Web*. Academic Press.

Getting, B. (2007). *Basic Definitions: Web 1.0, Web. 2.0, Web 3.0*. http://www.practicalecommerce.com/articles/464-Basic-Definitions-Web-1-0-Web-2-0-Web-3-0

Gupta, V. (2017). A Brief History of Blockchain. *Harvard Business Review*.

Hodson, H. (2013). *Bitcoin moves beyond mere money*. https://www.newscientist.com/article/dn24620-bitcoin-moves-beyond-mere-mone

Iansiti, M., & Lakhani, K. R. (2017). The Truth About Blockchain. *Harvard Business Review*.

Nakamoto, S. (2009). *Bitcoin: A Peer-to-Peer Electronic Cash System*, https://bitcoin.org/bitcoin.pdf

Nations, D. (2017). *What Is Web 3.0 and Is It Here Yet?* https://www.lifewire.com/what-is-web-3-0-3486623

O'Reilly, T. (2006). *Web 2.0 Compact Definition: Trying Again*. http://radar.oreilly.com/2006/12/web-20-compact-definition-tryi.html

Prableen, B. (2016). *Bitcoin Vs Ethereum: Driven by Different Purposes*. https://www.investopedia.com/articles/investing/031416/bitcoin-vs-ethereum-driven-different-purposes.asp

Privacy Subcommittee. (2017). *Blockchain Technology and Privacy*. https://www.americanbar.org/content/dam/aba/events/business_law/2017/04/spring/materials/blockchain-tech-201704.authcheckdam.pdf

Ugarte, H. E. (2017). *A more pragmatic Web 3.0: Linked Blockchain Data*. https://semanticblocks.files.wordpress.com/2017/03/linked_blockchain_paper3.pdf

von Wendland, M. (2018). *Semantic Blockchain - A Review of Sematic Blockchain and Distributed Ledger Technology Approaches*. DLT. doi:10.13140/RG.2.2.33005.90088

Williams, M. T. (2014). *Virtual Currencies—Bitcoin Risk. World Bank Conference*, Washington, DC.

Wood, G. (2016). *Polkadot: Vision for a heterogeneous multi-chain framework draft 1*. Available: https://github.com/polkadot-io/polkadotpape/raw/master/PolkaDotPaper

Chapter 4

Structuring Abstraction to Achieve Ontology Modularisation

Zubeida Khan

Council for Scientific and Industrial Research, Pretoria, South Africa

C. Maria Keet

Department of Computer Science, University of Cape Town, South Africa

ABSTRACT

*Large and complex ontologies lead to usage difficulties, thereby hampering the ontology developers'
tasks. Ontology modules have been proposed as a possible solution, which is supported by some algorithms and tools. However, the majority of types of modules, including those based on abstraction, still
rely on manual methods for modularisation. Toward filling this gap in modularisation techniques, the
authors systematised abstractions and selected five types of abstractions relevant for modularisation for
which they created novel algorithms, implemented them, and wrapped them in a GUI, called NOMSA,
to facilitate their use by ontology developers. The algorithms were evaluated quantitatively by assessing the quality of the generated modules. The quality of a module is measured by comparing it to the
benchmark metrics from an existing framework for ontology modularisation. The results show that the
module's quality ranges between average to good, whilst also eliminating manual intervention.*

INTRODUCTION

An ontology is a logic-based model that is used to represent a subject domain in a machine-processable
language for Semantic Web applications. There are various formal definitions presented in the literature
for an ontology. A comprehensive definition for an ontology is as follows: (Guarino, 1998):

*An ontology is a logical theory accounting for the intended meaning of a formal vocabulary, i.e. its
ontological commitment to a particular conceptualization of the world. The intended models of a logical*

DOI: 10.4018/978-1-7998-6697-8.ch004

language using such a vocabulary are constrained by its ontological commitment. An ontology indirectly reflects this commitment (and the underlying conceptualization) by approximating these intended models.

Ontologies are commonly used for some purpose such as enhanced searches across many databases or decision-making support for problems. It consists of entities, organised in a hierarchy, with relations among them and axioms to define such relations. The entities are often constrained and described using the other entities to provide better meaning.

Ontologies that describe large, well-defined domains are consequently large and complex in nature; e.g., the NCBI Taxonomy with its 1,015,206 classes (Federhen, 2012), and likewise SNOMED CT (Donnelly, 2006) and the FMA (Rosse & Mejino, 2003) are well-known to be challenging due to their size. This leads to difficulties for tools and humans alike: tools cannot process them due to computational limitations while humans face cognitive overload for understanding them. Over the last few years, there has been a growth in using modularity to assist with large ontologies (Amato et al., 2015; d'Aquin et al., 2006; Del Vescovo, 2011; Grau et al., 2008; Khan & Keet, 2016b). A module has been defined as follows (Khan & Keet, 2015):

A module M is a subset of a source ontology O, M Ì O, either by abstraction, removal or decomposition, or module M is an ontology existing in a set of modules such that, when combined, make up a larger ontology. Module M is created for some use-case U, and is of a particular type T. T is classified by a set of annotation features P, and is created by using a specific modularization technique MT, and has a set of evaluation metrics EM which is used to assess the quality of module M.

The general idea of modularisation refers to dividing and separating the components of a large system such that it can be recombined into a whole. The purpose of modularity is used to simplify and downsize an ontology for the task at hand, i.e., to modularise a large ontology into smaller ontologies, and it is required in ontology development and use when one needs to hide or delete knowledge that is not required for the use-case (Studer, 2010). Modularisation has been applied to various ontologies to improve usability and assist with complexity; e.g., the myExperiment ontology (Newman et al., 2009), the Semantic Sensor Net ontology (Janowicz & Compton, 2010), several BioPortal ontologies (Del Vescovo et al., 2011), and the FMA ontology (Mikroyannidi et al., 2009).

There are several modularisation methods and tools (Amato et al., 2015; Chen et al., 2019; d'Aquin et al., 2006; Hamdi et al., 2010; Kalyanpur et al., 2006; LeClair et al., 2019). For ontologies that are created in a modular way, however, many of them are created by manual methods (Khan & Keet, 2015). There is tool support for graph partitioning (Kalyanpur et al., 2006), query-based (Natalya Fridman Noy & Musen, 2000) and locality-based (Grau et al., 2008) techniques. We zoom in on the type of modules obtained from abstractions, taken from an existing categorisation of ontology modules (Khan & Keet, 2015). Abstraction is the principle of simplifying complex models by removing some unnecessary details based on some criteria, such as reducing a class hierarchy's depth or removing axioms to fit the ontology in a language of lower expressiveness. The purpose of abstraction, like modularity, is to have a simplified version of an ontology for a specific task or application.

Seeing that automatic techniques for generating these types of modules are lacking (discussed below), we solve this problem by investigating and structuring proposed types of abstractions, which led to the creation of a basic theory from the related works. Based on the theory, several abstractions were selected to fill in the gaps for the lacking tool support and we propose new algorithms for generating abstraction and expressiveness modules. The algorithms have been implemented and are thus the first fully automated abstractions for ontologies. They have been evaluated on adequacy with 128 ontologies. The generated modules have an average to good quality according to typical modularity metrics. The core implementation is also wrapped in a GUI called NOMSA (Novel Ontology Modularisation SoftwAre) for ease of used by the ontology engineer. The objective of the work is two-fold: 1) To create a basic theory of abstraction for ontology modules, and 2) To provide automated tools for generating such modules.

The remainder of the chapter is structured as follows. In the background section, we discuss related works on modularity. This is followed by a section on structuring abstraction towards a theory, which is followed by our new approaches for modularisation. We then present the implementation and experimental evaluation of the algorithms section and a discussion section. Lastly, we provide a conclusion section.

BACKGROUND

There are three broad techniques for creating modules from a larger ontology, including techniques such as graph partitioning, logic-based approaches for locality, and queries. Yet, there is also a heavy reliance on manual methods for module creation: manual methods were used for module creation for 9 out of the 14 module types identified in the framework for ontology modularisation (Khan & Keet, 2015). One well-known approach to create modules, which is also heavily reliant on manual methods, is abstraction, which looks at simplifying an ontology in some way. Several different types of abstraction have been identified and formalised for logical theories and ontologies, notably (Ghidini & Giunchiglia, 2004; Keet, 2005, 2007; Mani, 1998; Pandurang Nayak & Y. Levy, 1995). For instance, one can generalise by exploiting subsumption along the class hierarchy (Ghidini & Giunchiglia, 2004; Keet, 2007; Pandurang Nayak & Y. Levy, 1995), or along a partonomy, among other relations, and 'relevance'-based deletions, however 'relevance' may be specified (Keet, 2007). These types are promising for achieving abstraction, executing it and evaluating whether the resultant module is indeed a good one, but they either require additional user input or have not been implemented.

The notion of abstracting models also has been looked into for managing large conceptual models, such as for Object-Role Modeling (Campbell et al., 1996; Keet, 2005) and Entity-Relationship diagrams (Jaeschke et al., 1994). Their core approach is to use 'relevance' measures by weighting language features. This cannot be reused directly for ontologies, as there are differences in language features and also those rules have not been implemented. To a certain extent related to weighting the language features, is the interplay between an ontology in, say OWL 2 DL and simplifying it into one represented in an OWL Profile (sub-language), or any combination of more/less expressive languages, giving rise to (OWL) 'profile modules' (e.g., (Krötzsch, 2012)) and Protégé v5 has a feature for generating modules in some OWL Profiles[1]. The recently standardised DOL has taken this notion for expressiveness-based networks of modules as its core feature (Mossakowski et al., 2015).

Abstractions for other types of models and languages have been proposed as well (see (de Lara et al., 2013) for an overview), but they have even less features in common with ontologies. De Lara et al.'s (de Lara et al., 2013) four high-level types of abstraction—aggregation, merge, deletion, and view generation—have been proposed also for ontologies and conceptual models, but not the metamodel approach with "structural concepts", for there is less heterogeneity in ontology languages.

Thus what abstraction entails for ontologies varies in the literature, and little has been implemented so as to examine the outcome of such abstraction operations beyond the manual examples given.

Structuring Abstractions Toward a Theory for Abstraction

Informed by the related works, we structure, clarify, and refine those notions of abstraction. Description Logics (DLs) is a formalization that may be used for representing ontologies which is used in the remainder of the Chapter. We assume that the reader is familiar with DLs.

We do not claim that this is an exhaustive list ontologically, but is exhaustive with respect to current proposals. Also, we cast the net for 'abstraction' wide, as in (Fridman et al., 2015): the outcome of an abstraction operation is a simpler artefact (ontology/ logical theory/ conceptual model), or view thereof, that retains certain elements or features of the original one but not all. Cognitively, in the general case, the 'simpler' is expected to be easier to understand because of the lower complexity and should be in some way a smaller artefact than the original. Ontologically, one intentionally removes or ignores certain finer-grained details of the representation of reality, or one's conceptualization thereof, in the abstraction process, i.e., it does not involve denying that certain details exist, but concerns the choice not to deal with that for some reason. We identified the following abstractions with respect to ontologies and related artefacts at the same stratum[2].

1. Abstraction along a hierarchy:
   a. Along a subsumption/class taxonomy: an entity is abstracted into its parent entity (e.g., (Ghidini & Giunchiglia, 2004; Keet, 2007; Pandurang Nayak & Y. Levy, 1995));
   b. Along a partonomy (mereology): an entity is abstracted away into the whole that it is part of (Keet, 2007);
   c. Along a meronymic relation that is not parthood: an entity is abstracted away into the whole that it is part of, such as participation, membership, and constitution (Keet, 2007; Mani, 1998);
   d. Along an arbitrary transitive relation in a domain ontology;
2. Abstraction along axioms with relations:
   a. Along relation chains or composition: this 'shortcuts' a chain/joins; e.g., for $R \mathbin{;} S \mathbin{\hat{o}} T$, to keep T and ignore or delete R and S (where $R \mathbin{^{l}} S \mathbin{^{l}} T$);
   b. Along a class definition, also called folding (Keet, 2007; Mani, 1998), such as removing a class's attributes and relations to other classes;
3. Abstraction based on 'relevance', for which there are various ways in which certain entities are deemed more important than others:
   a. Manual identification of important entities for the subject domain that must remain in the ontology; e.g., in an ontology of pets, the popular ones—cats, dogs—are more important than, say, geckos and snakes (Schulz & Boeker, 2013);
   b. Relative well-connected important entities in the ontology, i.e., those entities participating in a lot of axioms, receive higher weighting cf. the less used ones and orphan entities that are then abstracted away (Natalya F Noy & Musen, 2009);
   c. Syntax-based rules where one language feature is deemed more important for the represented knowledge than another (Campbell et al., 1996; Jaeschke et al., 1994; Keet, 2005); e.g., to provide more weight to existentially quantified relations over universally quantified ones, and therewith the classes involved in it obtain more points as being more important and thus survive the abstraction process;
   d. Hierarchy depth where entities higher up in the hierarchy are deemed more relevant and, e.g., removing everything below a specified depth (de Lara et al., 2013);

4. Abstraction motivated by language expressiveness, i.e., driven by some ontology language's features:

    a. Language feature deletion: simply delete any axiom that uses the offending language features to obtain a module in a less expressive language (Krötzsch, 2012);

    b. Approximation: use a set of rewriting rules to approximate the subject domain semantics of the axiom(s) that is(are) deleted, which typically increases the number of axioms (Botoeva et al., 2010);

    c. Language vocabulary elements: this involves removing certain elements that may be unnecessary for a certain use-case; e.g., data properties.

For this work, we focus on designing algorithms to match those that are lacking for certain module types from an existing ontology modularisation framework and experiment (Khan & Keet, 2015). From the experiment, it was found that for several module types, manual methods were used. We wish to automate the methods for abstraction and expressiveness type modules by selecting the following abstractions to design algorithms for: 2.Generalisation along axioms (b), 3. 'Relevance'-based abstraction (b, d), and 4.Language expressiveness (a, c).

MODULARISATION METHODS INVOLVING ABSTRACTIONS

Within the scope of methods for modularisation, we focus on automating the methods used for generating abstraction modules, based on the types of modules identified in (Khan & Keet, 2015).There are four types of abstraction modules and one type of expressiveness module. To fill this gap, we create algorithms for five types of abstraction, which are listed in Table 1.

We now define and introduce the algorithms for these types. We formally define each of the types of modules together with its corresponding algorithm. The class of an ontology is mentioned in several definitions, and we are referring to the set of axioms describing a class; the same holds for the object property and data property of an ontology.

Table 1.The algorithms that are created for each of the abstractions

Algorithm	Abstraction
AxAbs	2b. Generalisation along axioms with relations: Along a class definition
VocAbs	4c. Language expressiveness: Along vocabulary elements
HLAbs	3d. Relevance -based abstraction: Hierarchy depth
WeiAbs	3b. Relevance -based abstraction: Relative well-connected important entities
FeatExp	4a. Language expressiveness: Language feature deletion

Axiom abstraction (Algorithm 1 (AxAbs)) generates a module without relations between entities; therefore, the technique decreases the horizontal structure of the ontology and makes it a bare taxonomy. Axiom abstraction is formally defined as follows:

Definition 1 (Axiom Abstraction) *Let* $\mathcal{O}$, $\mathcal{O}'$ *be two ontologies.* $\mathcal{S} = \{\alpha_1,...,\alpha_k\}$ *a set of axioms involving at least two classes or a class and a data type, and either at least one object property or data* *property from* $\mathcal{O}$ *(i.e., GCIs). We say that* $\mathcal{O}'$ *is an axiom abstraction module of* $\mathcal{O}$*, if* $\mathcal{O}' \cup \mathcal{S} = \mathcal{O}$ *such that there exists no element of* $\mathcal{S}$ *in* $\mathcal{O}'$ *(i.e.,* $\mathcal{S} \cap \mathcal{O}' = \emptyset$*, hence* $' \subset \mathcal{O}$*.*

For instance, if Professor ⊑ ∃teaches.Course ∈ $\mathcal{S}$ (as it is not a simple subsumption between named classes nor is it a declaration of the Professor class; line 4 of AxAbs), then the axiom will be removed (lines 8-10) resulting in module $\mathcal{O}'$ that will contain just the classes Professor and Course.

Algorithm 1: Axiom abstraction to compute module M (AxAbs).

```
1:Input Ontology O
2:Output Module M
3:for all axiom ∈ O do
4:        if axiom.type==subclass_axiom or axiom.type==declaration_axiom then
5:                cExpression←axiom.getNestedClassExpressions()
6:                cExpressionSet←cExpressionSet+cExpression
// cExpressionSet is a data structure where we store all the class expressions
7:                    for all cExpression ∈ cExpressionSet do
8:                        if cExpression.type ¹class then
9:                            remove axiom
10:                       end if
11:                   end for
12:        else
13:            remove axiom
14:        end if
15:end for
16:M←O
```

Applying <u>vocabulary abstraction</u> to an ontology generates a module where a certain vocabulary element is removed from the ontology.

Definition 2 (Vocabulary abstraction) *Let* $\mathcal{O}, \mathcal{O}'$ *be two ontologies,* $\mathcal{C} = \{\mathcal{C}_1 ... \mathcal{C}_k\}$ *the set of classes in* $\mathcal{O}$*,* $\mathcal{OP} = \{\mathcal{OP}_1 ... \mathcal{OP}_k\}$ *the set of object properties in* $\mathcal{O}$*, and* $\mathcal{DP} = \{\mathcal{DP}_1 ... \mathcal{DP}_k\}$ *the set of data properties in* $\mathcal{O}$*. We say that* $\mathcal{O}'$ *is a vocabulary abstraction module of* $\mathcal{O}$*, if* $\mathcal{O}' \cup \mathcal{C} = \mathcal{O}$ *or* $\mathcal{O}' \cup \mathcal{OP} = \mathcal{O}$ *or* $\mathcal{O}' \cup \mathcal{DP} = \mathcal{O}$ *such that there exists no element of* $\mathcal{C}$*,* $\mathcal{OP}$*, or* $\mathcal{DP}$ *in* $\mathcal{O}'$ *(i.e.,* $\mathcal{C} \cap \mathcal{O}' = \emptyset$*,* $\mathcal{OP} \cap \mathcal{O}' = \emptyset$*,* $\mathcal{DP} \cap \mathcal{O}' = \emptyset$*),* $\mathcal{O}' \subset \mathcal{O}$*.*

Algorithm 2: Vocabulary abstraction to compute module M (VocAbs).

```
1:Input Ontology O, element e, element type t
// e is a named class, object property, or data property and t is the type of
e in O
2:Output Module M
3:        if t==class then
4:                remove e
5:        else if t==object property then
```

```
6:              remove e
7:        else if t==data property then
8:              remove e
9:        else if t==individual then
10:             remove e
11:       end if
12:M¬O
```

For instance, consider a version of the Infectious Disease Ontology (IDO) (Cowell & Smith, 2009) that is linked to the BFO foundational ontology and the developers want to change that to DOLCE for interoperability in a heterogeneous system. Since the domain ontology does not contain any object properties, one could be interested in removing the object properties from the DOLCE-aligned version of the IDO ontology using the vocabulary abstraction algorithm.

High-level abstraction generates a module where entities at a higher level are regarded more important than others (Algorithm 3 (HLAbs)), and is defined as follows, specifying the notion of depth in a taxonomy first:

Definition 3 (Depth) *Let $\mathcal{O}$ be an ontology. A depth in the hierarchy of $\mathcal{O}$ represents the subclass distance between the asserted hierarchy's top-level entity and a given entity; e.g., depth 1 refers only to the top-level classes, depth 2 refers to the top 2 layers of classes (the parent classes and its direct subclasses) and so on.*

Definition 4 (High-level abstraction) *Let $\mathcal{O},\mathcal{O}'$ be two ontologies, n be a depth where n is an integer [3] 1. We say that $\mathcal{O}'$ is a High-level abstraction module of $\mathcal{O}$, if the entities with a depth > n are removed, hence, $\mathcal{O}' \subset \mathcal{O}$.*

Algorithm 3: High-level abstraction to compute module *M* (HLAbs).

```
1:Input Ontology O, levelNumber
2:Output Module M
3:oldSet¬ontology.getAxioms()
4:for all class Î O do
5:        if class.superclasses() is empty then
6:                topLevelClassSet¬topLevelClassSet+class
7:        end if
8:end for
9:counter¬0
10:while counter ¹ levelNumber do
11:        for all topclass Î topLevelClassSet do
12:                newset¬newset+topclass.getAxioms()
13:                        if topclass.subclasses()¹ empty then
14:                                temp¬topclass.subclasses()
15:                        end if
//Repeat lines 3 - 13 for object properties and data properties.
16:        topLevelClassSet.clear()
```

```
17:          topLevelClassSet¬temp
18:          end for
19:end while
20:for all axiom î oldAxioms do
21:          if newAxioms does not contain axiom then
22:                  ontology.remove(axiom)
23:          end if
24:end for
25:M¬O
```

For instance, the GFO-abstract-top module of the GFO ontology in the ROMULUS repository (Khan & Keet, 2016a) is based on the Abstract Top Level layer of GFO which contains mainly two meta-categories: set and item. This module can be generated automatically with HLAbs by setting the depth to 2 (see Figure 1).

Weighted abstraction deals with removing entities from an ontology that are deemed less important than others by assigning weight to the classes, properties, and individuals in an ontology. Our approach for determining this is based on examining entities that other entities are highly dependent on. For instance, in the pizza ontology, the class TomatoTopping is the most widely used, being referenced 61 times by other entities. Weighted abstraction is formally defined in Definition 7, availing of the notions of relative and absolute thresholds, which are introduced first.

Figure 1. Generating a high-level abstraction module with depth = 2 from the GFO ontology

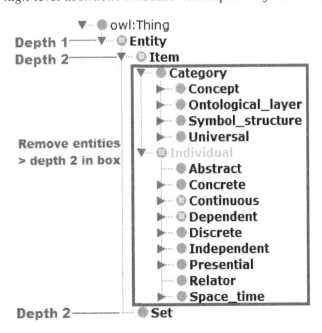

Definition 5 (Relative threshold) *Let $\mathcal{O}$ be an ontology, $\mathcal{E} = \{\mathcal{E}_1...\mathcal{E}_k\}$ be the set of classes, object properties, data properties, and individuals in $\mathcal{O}$. A relative threshold θ is a percentage value to decide*

which elements of $\mathcal{E}$ are to be removed from $\mathcal{O}$. Each element of $\mathcal{E}$ is weighted according to the number of axioms it participates in and ordered according to a position p. If $p(\mathcal{E}_i) < \theta$, $\mathcal{E}_i$ is removed from $\mathcal{O}$.

Definition 6 (Absolute threshold) *Let $\mathcal{O}$ be an ontology, $\mathcal{E} = \{\mathcal{E}_1...\mathcal{E}_k\}$ be the set of classes, object properties, data properties, and individuals in $\mathcal{O}$. An absolute threshold θ is a numerical value to decide which elements of $\mathcal{E}$ are to be removed from $\mathcal{O}$. Each element of $\mathcal{E}$ is weighted according to the number of axioms it participates in and ordered according to a position p, If $p(\mathcal{E}_i) < \theta$, $\mathcal{E}_i$ is removed from $\mathcal{O}$.*

Definition 7 (Weighted abstraction) *Let $\mathcal{O}, \mathcal{O}'$ ¢be two ontologies, $\mathcal{E} = \{\mathcal{E}_1...\mathcal{E}_k\}$ be the set classes, object properties, data properties, and individuals in $\mathcal{O}$. We say that $\mathcal{O}$ ¢ is a weighted abstraction module of $\mathcal{O}$, if elements of $\mathcal{E}$ are removed from $\mathcal{O}$ according to some absolute threshold or relative threshold, hence, $\mathcal{O}, \mathcal{O}'$.*

Algorithm 4 (WeiAbs) generates weighted abstraction modules. For instance, consider modularising the BioTop ontology (Beisswanger et al., 2008) using the weighted abstraction algorithm with $\theta = 4$. For the class Phosphate, it has two referencing axioms: a declaration axiom and the axiom Phosphate ô InorganicMolecularEntity. Since the number of referencing axioms ($p(\mathcal{E}) = 2$) is less than the absolute threshold value (4), the Phosphate class is removed from the ontology.

Algorithm 4: Weighted abstraction to compute module M (WeiAbs).

```
1:Input Ontology O, thresholdPercentage, Weight_array, Class_array
2:Output Module M
3:i¬0
4:for all class Î O do
5:        Weight_array¬Num_of_referencing_axioms
6:        Class_array(i)¬class
7:        i¬i+1
8:end for
9:Sort(Weight_array,Class_array) //Sort Weight_array from low to high, with
Class_array corresponding to Weight_array
10:limit¬thresholdPercentage*|Class_array|
11:for i¬0,limit do
12: remove Class_array(i) from O
13:end for //repeat lines 4-12 for ObjectProperty_array, DataProperty_
array,Individual_array
14:M¬O
```

Feature expressiveness modules deal with removing some axioms of the ontology based on the language features, e.g., cardinality constraints, disjointness, object property features etc. By manipulating complex constructs of the ontology language features, the feature expressiveness algorithm results in a simplified model of the ontology that maybe more suitable for scalability of the ontology-driven information system. We have designed seven rules for this to demonstrate it (discussed below). The algorithm takes these seven rules and removes them from the least important to the most important. At each rule removal, a 'layer' of the ontology is produced where that ontology is represented in a language of lower expressivity than the previous layer. Once the algorithm is complete, seven modules (layers) are produced, each having a lower level of expressivity than the previous. Feature expressiveness is formally defined as follows:

Definition 8 (Feature expressiveness) *Let* $\mathcal{O}, \mathcal{O}'$ *be two ontologies,* $\mathcal{R} = \{\mathcal{R}_1 ... \mathcal{R}_k\}$ *a set of rules describing various OWL language features. We say that* $\mathcal{O}$ ¢ *is a feature expressiveness module of* $\mathcal{O}$ *, if we remove axioms that follow* $\mathcal{R}$ *from* $\mathcal{O}$ *, hence* $\mathcal{O}' \subset \mathcal{O}$ *.*

We decided to assign lower points to those OWL ontology features that serve to restrict and refine entities such as cardinality and property characteristics. We assign higher points to disjointness, equality and inequality, and complex classes since they can be used in conjunction to define new classes. Rule 7 and rule 6 are concerned with OWL features pertaining to class creation, which is why we weight them as the most important; classes are the building blocks in an ontology. Rule 5 is concerned with instance data in an ontology which follows in terms of weighting. Rules 4 to rule 1 are concerned with specialising or refining the existing concepts in the ontology. This weighting is subjective and motivated by the modelling perspective on language features. It is conceivable, and possible if desired, to assign different weights to them; e.g., such that they are motivated by, and aligned with, the various OWL profiles.

In the notation of the rules that follow for the axiom types, *C, D, E* are class descriptions that may be simple (named classes) or complex, *R, S* are object properties, *U, V* are data properties, and *a, b, c* individuals in the vocabulary of the ontology, *n* is a non-negative integer, and all declared knowledge adheres to the OWL 2 DL syntax.

- R1: **Qualified cardinality** in an ontology has an assigned weight of 1 point. *Rules: Remove axioms of the following axiom type, if present: C* ô £ *n R.D, C* ô ^{3} *n R.D, C* ô = *n R.D, C* ô £ *n U.D, C* ô ^{3} *n U.D, C* ô = *n U.D.*

- R2: **Domain and range** weigh 2 points. *Rule: Remove axioms of the following axiom type, if present:* ∃*R.*⊤ > ô *C,* ⊤ ô∀*R.C.*

- R3: **Object Property characteristics** weighs 3 points. *Rule: Remove axioms of the following axiom type, if present (in SROIQ's shorthand notation):* Func(*R*), Func(*R*−), Sym(*R*), Asym(*R*), Trans(*R*), Ref(*R*), Irr(*R*).

- R4: **Disjointness** weighs 4 points. *Rule: Remove axioms of the following axiom type, if present: C* ó *D* ô ⊥*, C* ô ¬*D.*

- R5: **Assertions** weigh 5 points. *Rule: Remove axioms of the following axiom patterns, if present: a: C, R(a,b), U(a,c).*

- R6: **Atomic equivalence and equality** weighs 6 points. *Rule: Remove axioms of the following axiom type, if present: C* ° *D, R* ° *S, U* ° *V, a = b, a* ^{l} *b.*

- R7: **Complex classes** are the most important of the seven rules, which we weigh with 7 points. Rule: *Remove axioms of the following axiom patterns, if present: C* ô *D* ó *E, C* ° *D* ó *E, C* ô *D* ò *E, C* ° *D* ò *E.*

Algorithm 5 (FeatExp) uses these rules to generate feature expressiveness modules. For instance, when modularising the BioTop ontology (Beisswanger et al., 2008), for rule 2, concerning the domain, the axiom ∃processualQuality.⊤ ô Quality is removed from the module, whilst keeping the entities Quality and processualQuality in the module.

Algorithm 5: Feature Expressiveness to compute module *M* (FeatExp).

```
1:Input Ontology O, ruleSet{r₁,..r₇}
2:Output Module moduleSet{M₁,..M₇}
3:i¬1
4:for all axiom Î O do
5:        for all rᵢ Î ruleSet do
6:                if axiom.type is rᵢ then
7:                        remove axiom
8:                end if
9:        end for
10:Mi¬O
11:i¬i+1
12:end for
```

Finally, note that the algorithms are linear for VocAbs and WeiAbs, and quadratic for AxAbs, HLAbs and FeatExp.

ILLUSTRATION OF ALGORITHMS

We now illustrate the algorithms introduced in the previous section with a sample ontology, where we focus on the WeiAbs and FeatExp algorithms. Consider the following axioms in a toy Burger ontology in Figure 2 (entity declaration axioms omitted).

Figure 2. The burger ontology to which the algorithms are applied; see text for details

$BeefPatty \sqsubseteq Patty$	(1)	
$Beefburger \equiv HamBurger$	(2)	
$Beefburger \sqsubseteq Burger$	(3)	
$Cheapburger \sqsubseteq\ \leq 1\ hasFilling.Filling$	(4)	
$Cheapburger \sqsubseteq Burger$	(5)	
$Cheese \sqsubseteq Filling$	(6)	
$Chef \sqsubseteq Person$	(7)	
$Customer \sqsubseteq Person$	(8)	
$HamBurger \equiv Beefburger$	(9)	
$HamBurger \sqsubseteq Burger$	(10)	
$HealthyBurger \sqsubseteq \forall hasFilling.(Lettuce \sqcup Tomato)$	(11)	
$HealthyBurger \sqsubseteq Burger$	(12)	
$Lettuce \sqsubseteq Filling$	(13)	
$Medium \sqsubseteq PattyCook$	(14)	
$PattyCook \equiv Medium \sqcup Rare \sqcup WellDone$	(15)	
$Rare \sqsubseteq PattyCook$	(16)	
$Sauce \sqsubseteq Filling$	(17)	
$Tomato \sqsubseteq Filling$	(18)	
$WellDone \sqsubseteq PattyCook$	(19)	
$WhiteBun \sqsubseteq BurgerBun$	(20)	
$WholeWheatBun \sqsubseteq BurgerBun$	(21)	
$WholeWheatBun \sqsubseteq \neg WhiteBun$	(22)	
$Func(hasBun)$	(23)	
$\exists hasBun.\top \sqsubseteq Burger$	(24)	
$\top \sqsubseteq \forall hasBun.BurgerBun$	(25)	
$\exists hasPatty.\top \sqsubseteq Burger$	(26)	
$\top \sqsubseteq \forall hasPatty.Patty$	(27)	
$\exists hasPattyCook.\top \sqsubseteq Patty$	(28)	
$\top \sqsubseteq \forall hasPattyCook.PattyCook$	(29)	
$MarthasBurger \neq MyBurger$	(30)	
$MarthasBurger : Burger$	(31)	
$MyBurger : Beefburger$	(32)	
$MyBurger : Burger$	(33)	
$MyBurger : Beefburger$	(34)	
$ChefRose : Chef$	(35)	
$cookedBy(MyBurger, ChefRose)$	(36)	

To generate a weighted abstraction module, we apply WeiAbs. Let us assume we wish to create a module whereby we remove 25% of the entities. To achieve this, we set the threshold value to 25%. First, we apply lines 4-8 of WeiAbs, where we weigh each class in the ontology with its number of referencing axioms and we store both the number of referencing axioms and each class in two arrays with corresponding indices. For line 9 of the algorithm, we sort the weight array values from low to high and the class array such that it matches the weight array. In line 10, a limit variable is calculated as the product of the threshold percentage (.25) and the number of classes in the ontology (21) which is rounded off to a value of 5. In lines 11-13, the classes with the 5 lowest values are removed, as displayed in Table 2. The classes in bold font are the 25% of the classes that are deemed less-important than the rest and are to be removed due to having the least number of referencing axioms in the ontology.

Table 2.The classes of the burger ontology with the number of referencing axioms. Those in bold font are the classes to be removed for the resulting module

WhiteBun	2	Medium	3	Patty	4
Customer	2	Lettuce	3	BeefBurger	4
Cheese	2	HealthyBurger	3	BurgerBun	4
Sauce	2	BeefPatty	3	Hamburger	4
Chef	2	Tomato	3	Filling	5
WholeWheatBun	2	WellDone	3	PattyCook	6
Person	3	Rare	3	Burger	7

For the expressiveness feature module, each rule is applied according to the order in FeatExp. For each axiom in the ontology, lines 4-9 of the algorithm are executed, therefore each rule is applied as follows. Applying R1 results in the removal of Axiom 4, R2 removes Axioms 24-29, R3 removes Axiom 23 and R4 removes Axiom 22, and then the assertions in axioms 31-36 are removed (R5), and finally those for equivalence and equality (R6, Axioms 2, 9, and 30) and complex classes (R7), being Axioms 11 and 15.

IMPLEMENTATION AND EVALUATION OF THE ALGORITHMS

To solve the problem of laborious manual modularisation, we have created the tool NOMSA to modularise ontologies, which incorporates the abstraction and expressiveness algorithms presented in Section 4. NOMSA allows the user to upload an ontology (including its imports), and select one of five approaches to modularise it. A module is then generated. NOMSA is a stand-alone Java application and can be downloaded from https://www.dropbox.com/sh/7a1ohvrn705upre/AACcqlFc3Ycd8kcYVTB4OTsFa?dl=0 together with its screencast demonstrating usage and the test files.

We have conducted a performance evaluation against other techniques that create other types of modules and it compared favourably to them, or at least in a similar timeframe. More interesting in the current scope is whether the new modules are any 'good' or 'useful'. For instance, if a certain type of abstraction always generates a module that is about the same size as the original, this is neither a good way of abstracting to generate a module nor useful for the ontology developer; vv., it is. Module quality is difficult to assess, however, and the current evaluation is, to the best of our knowledge, the first attempt to assess it quantitatively.

The selected metrics all have been proposed elsewhere and have been implemented in the TOMM tool that will be used for automated evaluation. Its metrics are summarized here so as to keep the chapter self-contained; see the TOMM documentation (Khan & Keet, 2016b) for longer descriptions and references where they have been proposed first:

- Size is the number of entities in a module |M|, counting classes, object and data properties, and individuals;
- Relative size of the module compared to the original ontology;
- Atomic size is the average size of a group of inter-dependent axioms in a module;
- Appropriateness is measured by mapping the size of an ontology module to some appropriateness function value between 0 and 1 where a module with an optimal size is of value 1;
- Intra-module distance is the distance between all entities in a module by counting the number of relations in the shortest path from one entity to another
- Relative intra-module distance is the difference between distances of entities in a module M to a source ontology O;
- Cohesion refers to the extent to which entities in a module are related to each other;
- Attribute richness is the average number of attributes per class;
- Inheritance richness describes how the knowledge is distributed across the ontology and is defined as the number of subclasses per class in an ontology;
- Correctness states that every axiom that exists in the module also exists in the original ontology; nothing new should be added to the module; and
- Completeness holds if the meaning of every entity is preserved as in the source ontology.

The method for the experiment is as follows:

1. Take a set of ontologies;
2. Run each modularisation tool's algorithm with a subset of 10 randomly selected ontologies from the test files to compare its features to NOMSA;
3. Run the NOMSA tool for each ontology from the test files for all five algorithms;
4. Run the Tool for Ontology Module Metrics (TOMM) (Khan & Keet, 2016b) for NOMSA's modules to acquire metrics; and
5. Conduct an analysis from the metrics for each module.

The materials used for the experiment were as follows: Protégé v4.3 (Musen, 2015), SWOOP (Kalyanpur et al., 2006), OWL Module Extractor (Grau et al., 2008),PROMPT (Natalya Fridman Noy & Musen, 2004), PATO (Stuckenschmidt & Schlicht, 2009), TaxoPart (Hamdi et al., 2010), NOMSA using the default parameters, TOMM (Khan & Keet, 2016b), and 128 ontologies experimentation (Gardiner et al., 2006; Lawrynowicz & Keet, 2016). The default parameters for each algorithm in NOMSA are as follows: element type = object properties in VocAbs, level = 3 in HLAbs, and relative threshold = 50% value in WeiAbs. The set of 128 ontologies were from various domains, and derived from the set of ontologies described elsewhere for experimentation (Gardiner et al., 2006; Lawrynowicz & Keet, 2016). The ontologies in the data set ranged in size from with 0 to 10 520 number of entities. Our tests were carried out on a 3.00 GHz Intel Core 2 Duo PC with 4 GB of memory running Windows 7 Enterprise.

RESULTS

The results of comparing NOMSA's features to the existing modularisation tools are shown in Table 3. For most of the features, NOMSA performs as well as or better than the other tools, with the benefit of full automation of the process. For the level of interaction, NOMSA is automatic; it is possible to run NOMSA without the user providing any initial input parameters. NOMSA includes the greatest number of algorithms in a tool (five) compared to the other tools. Each tool was classified by techniques from the existing framework for modularisation (Khan & Keet, 2015). For techniques, NOMSA used semantic-based abstraction and language simplification techniques; semantic-based abstraction has not been applied in other tools to-date. NOMSA's algorithms take between 2-4 seconds to modularise. The locality-based algorithms have the quickest time (1 second) while partitioning algorithms take longer (6-16 seconds). It was not possible to test PROMPT for time as it was completely user-driven. We do not compare the resultant modules of the other modularisation tools because they all generate different types of modules and their underlying techniques differ.

All 128 ontologies were successfully modularised using all five algorithms in NOMSA and their metrics were generated using the TOMM module metrics tool (Khan & Keet, 2016b). The numerical metrics for the modules are displayed in Table 4 and we discuss the notable metrics here. For the data set in use, all five algorithms result in a reduction of the size of the original ontology, ranging from modules that have a relative size of 0.26 (WeiAbs) to modules that have a size of 0.85 (VocAbs) meaning that WeiAbs and VocAbs results in modules that are 26% and 85% the size of the original ontology, respectively. For the relative intra module distance, the modules of HLAbs and WeiAbs have values greater than 1 (18.66 and 3.96 respectively) meaning that the entities in the module are to that degree closer than in the original ontology; this could aid in human comprehension of an ontology. The rest of the algorithms have values less than 1, meaning that the entities are to that degree further away than in the original ontology. For instance, removing axioms that describe equality between classes simplifies the expressivity of the module for easier tool processing, but increases the distance between classes.

In order to determine whether the modules are of good quality, we can compare the results obtained from the generated modules, to what is expected (we refer to the benchmark dependencies between modularity metrics of the framework for ontology modularity (Khan & Keet, 2016b). Comparing the modules to the dependencies, for WeiAbs and FeatExp modules, all the metric values for the generated modules correspond with what is expected; these modules are of 'good' quality. For AxAbs, VocAbs, and HLAbs, some of the metrics do not correspond to the dependencies. For the 128 modules, AxAbs and HLAbs succeeds to meet 1 out of the 2 expected values for the modules. WeiAbs succeeds to meet 2 out of the 2 expected values for the modules and FeatExp succeeds to meet the 1 expected value for the modules.

Table 3. Comparison of three features of the main modularisation tools against NOMSA and the average running times of the respective algorithms for the test set of ontologies (excluding the time of manual modularisation tasks of the other tools, such as loading the ontology and setting the parameters)

	Level of interaction	Algorithm complexity	Technique	Time (s.)
SWOOP algorithm 1	Semi-automatic	Quadratic	Locality	1
SWOOP algorithm 2	Automatic	Quadratic	Graph partition	6
OWL module extractor	Semi-automatic	Quadratic	Locality	1
PROMPT	User driven	Unknown	Query	-
PATO	Automatic	Unknown	Graph partition	16
Protégé algorithm 1	Semi-automatic	Unknown	Locality	1
Protégé algorithm 2	Automatic	Unknown	Language based	1
Protégé algorithm 3	Semi-automatic	Unknown	Locality	1
Protégé algorithm 4	Semi-automatic	Unknown	Language based	1
TaxoPart	Automatic	Linear	Graph partition	15
NOMSA AxAbs	Automatic	Linear	Semantic based abstraction	3
NOMSA VocABs	Automatic	Linear	Semantic based abstraction	2
NOMSA HLAbs	Automatic	Quadratic	Semantic based abstraction	2
NOMSA WeiAbs	Automatic	Linear	Semantic based abstraction	4
NOMSA FeatExp	Automatic	Quadratic	Language based	3

Table 4. The average values for the metadata for all the generated modules; app. = appropriateness, IMD =intra module distance, coh. = cohesion, AR = attribute richness, IR = inheritance richness, rel. = relative, T(s.)= time in seconds. The metrics that count toward 'good' quality modules are in bold font, the remainder are 'average'

	Size	Atomic Size	App.	IMD	Coh.	AR	IR	Rel. Size	Rel. IMD	T(s.)
AxAbs Modules	238.04	2.34	0.19	866345.6	**0.06**	0.49	4.84	0.71	0.68	3.83
VocAbs Modules	443.38	3.24	0.19	848372.2	**0.06**	0.45	4.78	0.85	0.79	2.47
HLAbs Modules	202.77	3.48	0.24	166797.1	**0.03**	0.47	4.86	0.67	18.66	2.40
WeiAbs Modules	138.58	3.40	0.30	142698.4	**0.07**	0.39	2.72	**0.26**	3.96	3.53
FeatExp Modules	291.89	2.44	0.18	757305.1	**0.06**	0.25	4.80	0.72	0.70	2.83
Original	464.67	3.80	0.15	1866430	0.04	1.04	4.78	-	-	-

We now examine why some of the metrics fail for the algorithms. VocAbs and HLAbs modules are expected to have a large appropriateness value (>0.75) according to the benchmark dependencies. However, based on the calculation of the appropriateness value (Khan & Keet, 2016b), this is only possible where a module has between 167-333 axioms and in some cases a source ontology may have fewer axioms than 167; hence, the source ontology was already not in range and modularising it causes a further decrease in the axioms. For the ontologies of this experiment, for 50 of the 128 source ontologies, the number of axioms were less than 167, which would not result in the optimal appropriateness values. Following these finding, it appears that the appropriateness value needs to be potentially omitted from the dependency diagram for expected metrics. For AxAbs, the correctness measure needs to be true, but it fails meaning that some 'new' axioms were added to the module. Upon examining the TOMM metrics log files, it was found that, by the algorithm removing object properties, other entities have to be changed to be represented in the module. For instance, in the source Pizza ontology, 'France' is represented as using an object property, as follows: MozarellaTopping ô ∃hasCountryOfOrigin.{Italy} and {Italy} ^{1} {France} whereas, in the module using the AxAbs algorithm, 'France' is represented using a named individual, as follows: {France}: Country. TOMM recognizes this axiom as a new axiom in the module.

DISCUSSION

We have inventarised and structured notions of abstraction in the context of ontologies and related artefacts, which encompasses all the known notions of abstraction from the literature. Several categories from the theory were selected to use for automating modularisation ideas that were identified elsewhere (Khan & Keet, 2015) and hitherto could be carried out only manually. Their automation opens the road to examine quantitatively whether such methods are actually effective or not as process of abstraction. Given the results presented in the previous section, it is worthwhile to investigate the success of automating the remaining types of abstraction listed in Section 3.

The algorithms and tool designed for abstraction solve the problems of users' reliance on manual methods for modularity and the lack of abstraction techniques in existing tools. Our experiments show that our algorithms can be used to automatically modularise ontologies thus, it both broadens the scope of the extant set of algorithms for automated modularisation (Grau et al., 2008; Hamdi et al., 2010; Kalyanpur et al., 2006; Musen, 2015; Natalya Fridman Noy & Musen, 2004; Stuckenschmidt & Schlicht, 2009) to enable generation of more types of modules, and it refines and realises theory-based approaches, such as presented in (Ghidini & Giunchiglia, 2004; Keet, 2005, 2007; Mani, 1998; Pandurang Nayak & Y. Levy, 1995) so that it is usable by ontology engineers.

The performance for the algorithms is good; the time taken to modularise the ontologies is fast for all five algorithms (under 5 seconds on average for each ontology). Assessing the quality of the metrics of the modules reveal that for this test set of ontologies, WeiAbs and FeatExp algorithms generate modules of 'good' quality for all its modules according to the expected dependencies. For the remaining three algorithms, they generate some 'good' quality modules, but it is not possible to meet the expected metric values for all the modules; for some of the metrics depend on the source ontology. The resulting modules, are, however, still an improvement compared to the original ontologies; the sizes of the modules have been reduced considerably, and other metrics such as attribute richness, etc., are notably different when compared to the original ontologies, as displayed in Table 2.

The use of existing module metrics uncovered interesting results. The metrics, and the tool that implements them, TOMM, were evaluated on a set of 189 existing ontology modules (Khan & Keet, 2016b). This is slightly different from evaluating the process of generating modules. One may, however, extrapolate from the quality of a module to the process it has created: if the module is not good, then either neither was the process good or neither was the source ontology good, or both. For instance, instead of Schlicht and Stuckenschmidt's appropriateness value having been informed by software modules (Schlicht & Stuckenschmidt, 2006) (and integrated in TOMM as such), this could also be judged or specified upfront by the user or by type of ontology or by more data on the size of current ontologies and modules. Regarding the latter, the quality of the ontology that will be subjected to some abstraction operation: if it has representation issues then the resultant smaller ontology may also have them; OWL's enumerations/one-of—i.e., pretending that an instance is a class (universal/concept/type)—is one such modelling construct that is subject to debate.

CONCLUSION

Fourteen types of abstractions were identified and categorised, which may assist with the understanding of abstraction for achieving ontology modularisation. For five of them, new algorithms were designed to generate abstraction-based modules. They have been implemented in the NOMSA tool to modularise ontologies accordingly, which are the first fully-automated abstractions for ontologies. The quantitative evaluation of the modules' quality with TOMM showed that for the weighted abstractions (WeiAbs) and feature expressiveness (FeatExp) algorithms, the modules match the expected values from the framework for modularity for 'good' quality modules. For the axiom (AxAbs), vocabulary (VocAbs), and high level (HLAbs) abstraction algorithms, some of its modules match the expected values and some fail to match all the values due to the source ontology. All the generated modules, however, are notably different from the source ontologies according to their metrics.

For future work, it is worthwhile to investigate the design and implementation of algorithms and formalisations for the other categories of abstraction structured in Section 3 for ontology modularisation and to examine further the notion of 'good' abstractions and module metrics.

REFERENCES

Amato, F., De Santo, A., Moscato, V., Persia, F., Picariello, A., & Poccia, S. R. (2015). Partitioning of ontologies driven by a structure-based approach. *Proceedings of the 2015 IEEE 9th International Conference on Semantic Computing (IEEE ICSC 2015)*, 320–323. 10.1109/ICOSC.2015.7050827

Beisswanger, E., Schulz, S., Stenzhorn, H., & Hahn, U. (2008). BioTop: An upper domain ontology for the life sciencesA description of its current structure, contents and interfaces to OBO ontologies. *Applied Ontology*, *3*(4), 205–212. doi:10.3233/AO-2008-0057

Botoeva, E., Calvanese, D., & Rodriguez-Muro, M. (2010). *Expressive Approximations in DL-Lite Ontologies BT*. In D. Dicheva & D. Dochev (Eds.), *Artificial Intelligence: Methodology, Systems, and Applications* (pp. 21–31). Springer Berlin Heidelberg.

Campbell, L. J., Halpin, T. A., & Proper, H. A. (1996). Conceptual schemas with abstractions making flat conceptual schemas more comprehensible. *Data & Knowledge Engineering*, *20*(1), 39–85. doi:10.1016/0169-023X(96)00005-5

Chen, J., Alghamdi, G., Schmidt, R. A., Walther, D., & Gao, Y. (2019). Ontology Extraction for Large Ontologies via Modularity and Forgetting. In *Proceedings of the 10th International Conference on Knowledge Capture* (pp. 45–52). 10.1145/3360901.3364424

Cowell, L., & Smith, B. (2009). Infectious Disease Ontology. In Infectious Disease Informatics (pp. 373–395). doi:10.1007/978-1-4419-1327-2_19

d'Aquin, M., Sabou, M., & Motta, E. (2006). *Modularization: a key for the dynamic selection of relevant knowledge components*. Academic Press.

de Lara, J., Guerra, E., & Sánchez Cuadrado, J. (2013). Reusable abstractions for modeling languages. *Information Systems*, *38*(8), 1128–1149. doi:10.1016/j.is.2013.06.001

Del Vescovo, C. (2011). The modular structure of an ontology: Atomic decomposition towards applications. *24th International Workshop on Description Logics*, 466.

Del Vescovo, C., Gessler, D. D. G., Klinov, P., Parsia, B., Sattler, U., Schneider, T., & Winget, A. (2011). In L. Aroyo, C. Welty, H. Alani, J. Taylor, A. Bernstein, L. Kagal, N. Noy, & E. Blomqvist (Eds.), *Decomposition and Modular Structure of BioPortal Ontologies BT - The Semantic Web – ISWC 2011* (pp. 130–145). Springer Berlin Heidelberg. doi:10.1007/978-3-642-25073-6_9

Donnelly, K. (2006). SNOMED-CT: The advanced terminology and coding system for eHealth. *Studies in Health Technology and Informatics*, *121*, 279. PMID:17095826

Federhen, S. (2012). The NCBI Taxonomy database. *Nucleic Acids Research*, *40*(Database issue), D136–D143. doi:10.1093/nar/gkr1178 PMID:22139910

Fridman, L., Stolerman, A., Acharya, S., Brennan, P., Juola, P., Greenstadt, R., & Kam, M. (2015). Multi-modal decision fusion for continuous authentication. *Computers & Electrical Engineering*, *41*, 142–156. doi:10.1016/j.compeleceng.2014.10.018

Gardiner, T., Tsarkov, D., & Horrocks, I. (2006). In I. Cruz, S. Decker, D. Allemang, C. Preist, D. Schwabe, P. Mika, M. Uschold, & L. M. Aroyo (Eds.), *Framework for an Automated Comparison of Description Logic Reasoners BT - The Semantic Web - ISWC 2006* (pp. 654–667). Springer Berlin Heidelberg.

Ghidini, C., & Giunchiglia, F. (2004). *A semantics for abstraction*. Academic Press.

Grau, B. C., Horrocks, I., Kazakov, Y., & Sattler, U. (2008). Modular reuse of ontologies: Theory and practice. *Journal of Artificial Intelligence Research*, *31*, 273–318. doi:10.1613/jair.2375

Guarino, N. (1998). Formal Ontology and Information Systems. In N. Guarino (Ed.), *Proceedings of the 1st International Conference on Formal Ontology in Information Systems (FOIS'98)* (pp. 3–15). IOS Press.

Hamdi, F., Safar, B., Reynaud, C., & Zargayouna, H. (2010). In F. Guillet, G. Ritschard, D. A. Zighed, & H. Briand (Eds.), *Alignment-Based Partitioning of Large-Scale Ontologies BT - Advances in Knowledge Discovery and Management* (pp. 251–269). Springer Berlin Heidelberg. doi:10.1007/978-3-642-00580-0_15

Jaeschke, P., Oberweis, A., & Stucky, W. (1994). In R. A. Elmasri, V. Kouramajian, & B. Thalheim (Eds.), *Extending ER model clustering by relationship clustering BT - Entity-Relationship Approach — ER '93* (pp. 451–462). Springer Berlin Heidelberg.

Janowicz, K., & Compton, M. (2010). *The Stimulus-Sensor-Observation Ontology Design Pattern and its Integration into the Semantic Sensor Network Ontology.* SSN.

Kalyanpur, A., Parsia, B., Sirin, E., Grau, B. C., & Hendler, J. (2006). Swoop: A Web Ontology Editing Browser. *Journal of Web Semantics, 4*(2), 144–153. doi:10.1016/j.websem.2005.10.001

Keet, C. M. (2005). *Using Abstractions to Facilitate Management of Large ORM Models and Ontologies.* In R. Meersman, Z. Tari, & P. Herrero (Eds.), *On the Move to Meaningful Internet Systems 2005: OTM 2005 Workshops* (pp. 603–612). Springer Berlin Heidelberg. doi:10.1007/11575863_80

Keet, C. M. (2007). *Enhancing Comprehension of Ontologies and Conceptual Models Through Abstractions.* In R. Basili & M. T. Pàzienza (Eds.), *AI*IA 2007: Artificial Intelligence and Human-Oriented Computing* (pp. 813–821). Springer Berlin Heidelberg.

Khan, Z. C., & Keet, C. M. (2015). An empirically-based framework for ontology modularisation. *Applied Ontology, 10*(3–4), 171–195. Advance online publication. doi:10.3233/AO-150151

Khan, Z. C., & Keet, C. M. (2016a). ROMULUS: The Repository of Ontologies for MULtiple USes Populated with Mediated Foundational Ontologies. *Journal on Data Semantics, 5*(1), 19–36. Advance online publication. doi:10.100713740-015-0052-1

Khan, Z. C., & Keet, C. M. (2016b). *Dependencies Between Modularity Metrics Towards Improved Modules.* In E. Blomqvist, P. Ciancarini, F. Poggi, & F. Vitali (Eds.), *Knowledge Engineering and Knowledge Management* (pp. 400–415). Springer International Publishing.

Krötzsch, M. (2012). OWL 2 Profiles: An Introduction to Lightweight Ontology Languages. In *Reasoning Web. Semantic Technologies for Advanced Query Answering: 8th International Summer School 2012, Vienna, Austria, September 3-8, 2012. Proceedings* (pp. 112–183). Springer Berlin Heidelberg. 10.1007/978-3-642-33158-9_4

Lawrynowicz, A., & Keet, C. M. (2016). The TDDonto Tool for Test-Driven Development of DL Knowledge bases. *Proceedings of the 29th International Workshop on Description Logics.* http://ceur-ws.org/Vol-1577/paper_15.pdf

LeClair, A., Khédri, R., & Marinache, A. (2019). Toward Measuring Knowledge Loss due to Ontology Modularization. In *Proceedings of the 11th International Joint Conference on Knowledge Discovery, Knowledge Engineering and Knowledge Management, IC3K 2019, Volume 2: KEOD, Vienna, Austria, September 17-19, 2019* (pp. 174–184). 10.5220/0008169301740184

Mani, I. (1998). *A Theory of Granularity and its Application to Problems of Polysemy and Underspecification of Meaning.* Academic Press.

Mikroyannidi, E., Rector, A., & Stevens, R. (2009). Abstracting and generalising the foundational model anatomy (fma) ontology. *Proceedings of the Bio-Ontologies 2009 Conference.*

Mossakowski, T., Codescu, M., Neuhaus, F., & Kutz, O. (2015). *The Distributed Ontology, Modeling and Specification Language – DOL.* In A. Koslow & A. Buchsbaum (Eds.), *The Road to Universal Logic: Festschrift for the 50th Birthday of Jean-Yves Béziau* (Vol. 2, pp. 489–520). Springer International Publishing. doi:10.1007/978-3-319-15368-1_21

Musen, M. A. (2015). The protégé project: A look back and a look forward. *AI Matters, 1*(4), 4–12. doi:10.1145/2757001.2757003 PMID:27239556

Newman, D., Bechhofer, S., & De Roure, D. (2009). *myExperiment: An ontology for e-Research.* Academic Press.

Noy, N. F., & Musen, M. A. (2000). {PROMPT}: Algorithm and Tool for Automated Ontology Merging and Alignment. *Seventeenth National Conference on Artificial Intelligence and Twelfth Conference on on Innovative Applications of Artificial Intelligence (AAAI/IAAI),* 450–455.

Noy, N. F., & Musen, M. A. (2004). Specifying Ontology Views by Traversal. In *The Semantic Web - ISWC 2004: Third International Semantic Web Conference, Hiroshima, Japan,* November 7-11, 2004. *Proceedings* (pp. 713–725). 10.1007/978-3-540-30475-3_49

Noy, N. F., & Musen, M. A. (2009). Traversing Ontologies to Extract Views. In *Modular Ontologies: Concepts, Theories and Techniques for Knowledge Modularization* (pp. 245–260). Springer Berlin Heidelberg. doi:10.1007/978-3-642-01907-4_11

Pandurang Nayak, P., & Levy, Y., A. (1995). A Semantic Theory of Abstractions. *Proceedings of IJCAI-95.*

Rosse, C., & Mejino, J. L. V. Jr. (2003). A reference ontology for biomedical informatics: The Foundational Model of Anatomy. *Journal of Biomedical Informatics, 36*(6), 478–500. doi:10.1016/j.jbi.2003.11.007 PMID:14759820

Schlicht, A., & Stuckenschmidt, H. (2006). Towards Structural Criteria for Ontology Modularization. *Proceedings of the 1st International Workshop on Modular Ontologies, WoMO'06, co-located with the International Semantic Web Conference, ISWC'06.* http://ceur-ws.org/Vol-232/paper7.pdf

Schulz, S., & Boeker, M. (2013). BioTopLite: An Upper Level Ontology for the Life SciencesEvolution, Design and Application. In *Informatik 2013, 43. Jahrestagung der Gesellschaft für Informatik e.V. (GI), Informatik angepasst an Mensch, Organisation und Umwelt, 16.-20. September 2013,* (pp. 1889–1899). https://dl.gi.de/20.500.12116/20620

Stuckenschmidt, H., & Schlicht, A. (2009). *Structure-Based Partitioning of Large Ontologies. BT - Modular Ontologies: Concepts.* Theories and Techniques for Knowledge Modularization., doi:10.1007/978-3-642-01907-4_9

Studer, T. (2010). *Privacy Preserving Modules for Ontologies.* In A. Pnueli, I. Virbitskaite, & A. Voronkov (Eds.), *Perspectives of Systems Informatics* (pp. 380–387). Springer Berlin Heidelberg. doi:10.1007/978-3-642-11486-1_32

ENDNOTES

[1] https://protegewiki.stanford.edu/wiki/P4MoveAxioms#Refactor

[2] That is, we exclude other notions of abstractions in different contexts, e.g., those when needing to deal with going from object in reality to its computerised representation or from individual to its class or set.

Chapter 5
Integrating Semantic Acquaintance for Sentiment Analysis

Neha Gupta

iD https://orcid.org/0000-0003-0905-5457

Manav Rachna International Institute of Research and Studies, Faridabad, India

Rashmi Agrawal

iD https://orcid.org/0000-0003-2095-5069

Manav Rachna International Institute of Research and Studies, Faridabad, India

ABSTRACT

The use of emerging digital information has become significant and exponential, as well as the boom of social media (forms, blogs, and social networks). Sentiment analysis concerns the statistical analysis of the views expressed in written texts. In appropriate evaluations of the emotional context, semantics plays an important role. The analysis is generally done from two viewpoints: how semantics are coded in sentimental instruments, such as lexicon, corporate, and ontological, and how automated systems determine feelings on social data. Two approaches to evaluate sentiments are commonly adopted (i.e., approaches focused on machine learning algorithms and semantic approaches). The precise testing in this area was increased by the already advanced semantic technology. This chapter focuses on semantic guidance-based sentiment analysis approaches. The Twitter/Facebook data will provide a semantically enhanced technique for annotation of sentiment polarity.

INTRODUCTION

Opinions or ideals have become an essential component in making judgment or alternatives for people or businesses. The rapid boom of Web 2.0 over the last decade has improved online organizations and enabled humans to put up their reviews or evaluation on a variety of topics in public domains. This user-generated content (UGC) is an essential statistics supply to help clients make shopping decision,

DOI: 10.4018/978-1-7998-6697-8.ch005

however also provided treasured insights for shops or manufacturers to enhance their marketing strategies and products (Pang & Lee, 2008). Sentiment evaluation deals with the computational treatment of critiques expressed in written texts (Kalra & Agrawal, 2017). In the era of Information explosion, there may be a huge quantity of opinionated statistics generated each day. These generated statistics leads to unstructured records and the analysis of these records to extract useful information is a hard to achieve task. The need to address these unstructured opinionated statistics naturally cause the upward push of sentiment analysis. The addition of already mature semantic technologies to this subject has increased the consequences accuracy. Evaluation of semantic of sentiments is precisely essential method in the internet now a days. Discovering the exact sense and understanding in which a specific sentence was written on the net is very important as there might not be any physical interaction to discover the significance of the sentence. There are a number of techniques to classify the specified sentiment as bad or horrible. This categorization helps us honestly discover the context of a sentence remotely (Gupta & Verma, 2019). The crucial troubles in sentiment evaluation is to express the sentiments in texts and to check whether or not the expressions indicate superb (favorable) or negative (unfavorable) opinions toward the challenge and to evaluate the correctness of the sentences that are classified. The motivation of writing this chapter is to understand the concepts related to sentiment analysis and the importance of semantic in sentiment analysis. The present chapter starts with basic of ontologies and their relation to sentiment analysis. The chapter further discusses semantic ontologies with concept forms and their relationships along with steps to develop a baseline model for simple analysis of sentiment using NLP. At the end of the chapter case study related to the sentiment analysis using R programming on the protests for CAA and NRC in India during December 2019 has been presented. The corpus of the case study has been built by collecting related articles from the Times of India and other leading newspapers of the India. Real time data has been extracted from twitter by applying the most frequent words as hash tags. Finally sentiment analysis techniques have been applied on twitter data to know the opinions of the people of country on the issue of NRC and CAA protest.

ONTOLOGY AND THE SEMANTIC WEB

Today the Internet has become a critical human need. People depend heavily on the Internet for their day-to-day tasks. World Wide Web (WWW) has rapidly become a massive database with some information on all of the interesting things. Most of the web content is primarily designed for human read, computers can only decode layout web pages (Kaur & Agrawal, 2017). Machines generally lack the automated processing of data collected from any website without any knowledge of their semantics.

This has become a concern because users spend a great deal of time comparing multiple websites. Semantic Web provides a solution to this problem. Semantic web is defined as a collection of technologies that enable computers to understand the meaning of metadata based information, i.e., information about the information content. Web Semantic can be applied to integrate information from heterogeneous sources and improve the search process for improved and consistent information (Jalota & Agrawal, 2019). The Semantic technologies allow the ontology to refer to a metadata.

Ontology is a description of a domain knowledge that includes various terminologies of a given domain along with the relationship between existing terms.

Ontology is designed to act as metadata. Ontologies can help to create conceptual search and navigation of semantics for integration of semantically in-order feature. The language structures used to constructs ontologies include: XML, XML Schema, RDF, OWL, and RDF Scheme.

OWL has benefits over other structure languages in that OWL has more facilities to express meaning and semantic than XML and RDF / s. Ontologies built using RDF, OWL etc. are linked in a structured way to express semantic content explicitly and organize semantic boundaries for extracting concrete information (Kalra & Agrawal, 2019).

A semantic ontology can exists as an informal conceptual framework with concept forms and their relationships named and described, if at all, in natural language, Or it may be constructed as a formal semantic domain account, with concept types and systematically defined relationships in a logical language.

However, within the Web environment ontology is not merely a conceptual construct but a concrete, syntactic structure that models a domain's semantics – the conceptual framework – in a machine-understandable language (Gupta & Verma, 2019).

For the purpose of comprehensive and transportable machine understanding, the semantic web relies heavily on the structured ontologies that structure underlying data. Consequently, the performance of the semantic Web is highly dependent on the proliferation of ontology that requires quick and easy ontology engineering and the avoidance of a bottleneck of information gain (Pang & Lee, 2008). Conceptual structures which define the underlying ontology are German to the concept of machine processable data on the semantic Web. By identifying mutual and specific theories of the domain, ontology lets both people and machines interact precisely in order to facilitate semantic exchange. Ontology language editors aid in the development of semantic Web. Thus, the cheap and rapid creation of a domain-specific ontology is crucial to the semantic Web's success.

Limitations of Semantic Ontologies

Ontology helps in delivering solutions for database identification, end-to-end application authentication, authorization, data integrity, confidentiality, coordination and exchange of isolated pieces of information issues (Agrawal & Gupta, 2019). Some of the drawbacks of semantic ontologies are

1. Natural language parsers can function on only single statement at a particular time.
2. It is quite impossible to define the ontology limits of the abstract model of a given domain.
3. Automatic ontology creations, automatic ontology emergence to create new ontologies, and the identification of possible existing relationships between classes to automatically draw the taxonomy hierarchy are needed.
4. Ontology validators are limited and unable to verify all kinds of ontologies, e.g. validation of ontologies on the basis of complex inheritance relations.
5. Domain-specific ontologies are highly dependent on the application domain, and it is not possible to determine the general purpose ontologies from them because of this dependency.
6. The reengineering of semantic enrichment processes for web development consists of relational metadata, which must be built at high speed and low cost based on the abundance of ontologies, which is not currently possible (Agrawal & Gupta, 2019).

Because of these limitations in ontology, it is not currently possible for Semantic Web to achieve the actual objectives of completely structured information over the web in a computer process-able format and making advanced knowledge modeling framework.

NLP AND SENTIMENT ANALYSIS

Sentiment analysis (Pang and Lillian 2008) is a kind of text classiõcation that is used to handle subjective statements. Natural language processing (NLP) is used to gather and study opinion or sentiment words. Determining subjective attitudes in big social data maybe a hotspot in the õeld of data mining and NLP (Hai et al. 2014). Makers are additionally intrigued to realize which highlights of their items are increasingly well known out in the open, so as to settle on proõtable business choices. There is an immense archive of conclusion content accessible at different online sources as sites, gatherings, internet based life, audit sites and so forth. They are developing, with increasingly obstinate content poured in constantly. In the past, manual strategies are used to investigate millions of sentiments & reviews and aggregated them toward a quick and efficient decision making (Liu, 2006). Sentiment analysis strategies carry out the project via automated procedures with minimum or no consumer support. The datasets that are available online may also comprise of objective statements, which no longer make effective contributions in sentiment analysis. These Type of statements are usually segregated at pre-processing stage. Binary Classification can be used to recommend the outcome of sentiment analysis. It may be considered as a multi-class classiõcation problem on a given scale of likeness. Because text is considered as a complex community of words which might be uniquely related to every sentiment therefore graph based definitely evaluation techniques are used for NLP tasks. Opinion mining involves NLP, to retrieve semantics from phrases and words of opinion. NLP will, however, have open problems that may be too challenging to be handled quickly and correctly up to date. Because sentiment analysis frequently uses NLP really well in large scale, it reflects this complicated behavior (Agrawal & Gupta, 2019). NLP's definitions for categorizing textual source material now don't fit with opinion mining, because they are different in nature. Documents with vastly disproportionate identical frequency of words do not always have the same polarity of sentiment. This is because, a fact can be either morally right or wrong in categorizing textual content, and is commonly accepted by all. Because of its subjective existence, a number of opinions may be incorrect about the same thing. Another distinction is that opinion mining is responsive to individual words, in which an unmarried word like NOT can change the meaning of the entire sentence. The transparent challenging conditions are prepositional phrases without the use of NOT words, derogatory and hypothetical sentences, etc. The latter section includes an in-depth overview of NLP problems surrounding the assessment of sentiments. The online resources consists of subjective content material having basic, composite, or complex sentences. Plain sentences have approximately one product's unmarried view, whereas complex sentences have multiple opinions on it (Agrawal & Gupta, 2019). Long sentences have an implied mean and are difficult to test. Standard assessments pertain only to an unmarried person, even though comparative articles have an object or a variety of its aspects examined as opposed to some other object. Comparative viewpoints may be either empirical or contextual. An example of a subjective comparison sentence is "Game X's visual effects are much better than game Y's," while an example of objective comparison expression is

"Game X has twice as many control options as that of Game Y". Opinion mining anticipates an assortment of sentence types, since individuals follow different composing styles so as to communicate in a superior manner.

Normally, conclusion examination for content information can be figured on a few levels, remembering for an individual sentence level, section level, or the whole archive in general. Frequently, notion is registered on the archive overall or a few collections are done subsequent to processing the supposition for singular sentences. There are two major approaches to sentiment analysis (Gupta & Verma, 2019).

- Supervised machine learning or deep learning approaches
- Unsupervised lexicon-based approaches

Usually we need pre-labeled facts for the first strategy, although we do not also have the luxury of a well-labeled training dataset in the second technique. We would therefore want to use unsupervised approaches to predict sentiment through the use of knowledge bases, ontologies, databases, and lexicons with distinctive details, primarily curated and prepared for analysis of sentiment. A lexicon is an encyclopedia, a wordbook or an e-book. Lexicons, in our case, are special dictionaries or vocabularies created to interpret sentiments (Gupta & Agrawal, 2020). Some of these lexicons provide a list of wonderful and terrible polar terms with a few grades aligned with them along with the use of different techniques such as the position of terms, phrases, meaning, sections of expression, phrases, and so on, . Rankings are given to the text documents from which we need to determine the sentiments. After these scores have been aggregated we get the very last sentiment.

TextBlob, along with sentiment analysis, is an excellent open-supply repository for efficient working of NLP tasks. It is additionally a sentiment lexicon (in the form of an XML file) that enables to offer rankings of polarity as well as subjectivity. The polarity rating is a float inside the [-1.0, 1.0] range. The subjectivity is a float in the range [0.0, 1.0] where zero.0 could be very objective and 1.0 may be very subjective.

Following the trends of artificial intelligence, the number of programs built for the processing of natural languages is growing every day with aid of the day. NLP-developed applications would allow for a faster and more effective implementation of infrastructures to remove human strength in many jobs (Niazi & Hussain, 2009). The following are common examples of NLP applications

- Text Classification (Spam Detector etc)
- Sentiment Analysis & Predictions
- Author Recognition systems
- Machine Translation
- Chatbots

Steps to Develop a Baseline Model for Simple Analysis of Sentiment Using NLP

Following steps needs to be followed to develop a baseline model for analysis of sentiment using NLP. The implementation is in python with standard libraries and tools:

1. Identifcation of Dataset
2. Name of the data set: Sentiment Labelled Sentences Data Set

3. Source of data set: UCI Machine Learning Library
4. Basic Information about the data set: 4.This information kit was generated through a user analysis of 3 websites (Amazon, Yelp, Imdb). Such remarks include impressions of restaurants, movies and goods. Two separate emoticons appear in each record in the data set (PORIA & GELBUKH 2013). These are 1: good, 0: bad.
5. Creation of a model of sentiment analysis with the above-mentioned data.
6. Create a Python based Machine Learning model with the sklearn and nltk library.
7. Code writing by library imports. For instance:

   import pandas as pnd

   import numpy as nmp

   import pickle

   import sys

   import os

   import io

8. Now upload and view the data set. For Example:

   input_file = "../data/amazon_cells_labelled.txt"

   amazon = pnd.read_csv(input_file,delimiter='\t',header=None)

   amazon.columns = ['Sentence','Class']

9. Statistical analysis of the data on the basis of following parameters.
   A) Total Count of Each Category
   B) Distribution of All Categories
10. For a very balanced dataset that is having almost equal number of positive and negative classes then pre processing the text by removing special characters, lower string, punctuations, email address, IP address, stop words etc
11. Data pre-cleaning makes the data inside the model ready for use..
12. Build the model by splitting the dataset to test (10%) and training(90%).
13. Test the model with test data and examine the accuracy, precision, recall and f1 results.
14. To test the accuracy of the calculations, create the confusion matrix. Link to plot a confusion matrix can be seen at

   #source: https://www.kaggle.com/grfiv4/plot-a-confusion-matrix

SEMANTIC SEARCH ENGINE

Current keyword-based search engines such as Google can identify internet pages by matching correct tokens or words with tokens or words in internet content inside the consumer's query (Ye & Zang, 2009). There are many disadvantages to this method.

A. Tokens or tokens-like words inside the User Search shall not be taken into account when looking for net sites.

    B. The key-word based search engine gives equal importance to all key phrases whereas consumers challenge them as they think of one category of keywords as important.

C. To get the correct applicable end result, customers might also also want to enter numerous synonyms on his very own to get the desired records which would possibly result into the omission of many treasured net pages.

D. Another trouble is of information overloading. The traditional keyword based absolute search engines like google make it very tedious for user to locate the useful facts from a massive list of search results.

To remedy the above mentioned problems that the customers face, Ontology based semantic steps were developed.

Ontology is primarily based on Semantic Search Engine that which recognizes the meaning of the consumer query and gives the results in a comparative sense.

It is not principally easy to return built-in keyword pages but also the pages which can be used to provide the means available by using the Ontological synonym dataset, created using WordNet, to enter keywords from the user. First the Ontology Synonym Collection uses WordNet and then invokes the provider. In addition, if the similarity is 100%, extra keywords are taken into account to provide the user with the appropriate and accurate results. Approximately the meta facts like URL is provided by the meta-processor.

Following are the Components of a Basic Semantic Search Engine

1. **Development of Ontology:** Ontology with. OWL or. DAML extensions are developed in plain text format.
2. **Crawler for Ontology:** Ontology crawler discovers new ontological content on the web and add it to the library of ontology.
3. Ontology notepad: It is used for the purpose of annotating and publishing web pages to ontologies.
4. Web Crawler: Crawls across the web to find Web pages annotated with ontologies and create knowledge base on Ontology instances.
5. Semantic Searching: understands the context and logical reasoning of the content on the website and offers objective results.
6. **Query Builder:** Query builder is used to construct the user search queries.
7. **Query Pre-processor:** It pre-process the queries and send the queries to the inference engine.
8. **Inference Engine:** Reasoning of the search queries using ontology database and the knowledge base is done by the inference Engine.

SEMANTIC RESOURCES FOR SENTIMENT ANALYSIS

Sentiment and Semantic analysis is an important resource in our network today. It is necessary to find a suitable context and meaning for a selected sentence on the internet because the real meaning of the sentence can not be discovered by physical contact (Tsai & Hsu, 2013). There are large variety of methods and techniques used to identify and classify the argument as good or bad in quality. Such classification virtually helps in defining the context of the sentence (Liu, 2006). The essential questions of sentimental analysis is to identify the expressions of feelings in texts and to check whether the expressions indicate wonderful (favorable) or negative (unfavorable) opinions closer to the subject and how successfully and efficaciously sentences are classified. In the detailed interpretation of the meaning of the expression, Semantics plays a critical role. The role of semantics is studied from two perspectives:

1. The manner in which semantics is represented in sentimental tools like lexica, corpora and ontology.
2. The manner in which automatic systems conduct sentiment evaluations of social media data.

For example, context-dependence and a finer detection of feelings that lead to the assignment of feeling values to elements or to the layout and use of an extensive range of effective labels or to the use of current techniques for finer-grained semantical processing. In the case of semantics, lexical elements should be paired with logical and cognitive problems and other aspects that are concerned about emotions.

Many works in sentiment evaluation try to utilize shallow processing techniques. The not unusual element in a lot of these works is that they merely attempt to pick out sentiment-bearing expressions. No effort has been made to discover which expression simply contributes to the overall sentiment of the text.

Semantic evaluation is critical to recognize the exact meaning conveyed inside the textual content. Some words generally tend to mislead the which means of a given piece of text. For Example:

I like awful boys.

Here the phrase 'like' expresses fine sentiments while the word awful represent negative sentiments.

WSD (Word Sense Disambiguation) is a technique that could been used to get the right sense of the word. Syntactic or structural homes of textual content are used in many NLP applications like gadget translation, speech recognition, named entity recognition, etc.

In general, techniques that are using semantic analysis are high-priced than syntax-based techniques because of the shallow processing involved within the latter. Therefore it is incredibly essential for us to ascertain the precise significance of the expression or else it may result in unfortunate knowledge (in many cases altogether different) on the matter. The key issues in the sentiment assessment are the manner in which sentiments are interpreted in texts and how words indicate a positive or negative (unfavorable) view of the subject. In the present situation, feelings of good or bad polarities for particular topics are extracted from a report instead of the whole document being marked as good or bad in order to include a massive quantity of statistics from one individual paper.Most of their applications aim to classify an entire report into a file subject, which is either specifically or implied. For example, the film form evaluates into wonderful or terrible, implies that all the expressions of sentiment in the evaluation directly represent sentiments towards that film and expressions that contradict it. On the contrary, by studying the relationships between expressions of sentiment and subjects, we can investigate in detail what is and is not required (Niazi & Hussain, 2009). These approaches, therefore, provide a wide variety of incentives for different applications to reach beneficial and unfavorable views on particular topics. It provides strong functions for aggressive research, reputation assessment and the identification of undesirable rumours. For example, huge sums are spent on the evaluation and examination of customer satisfaction. However, the efficacy of such surveys is usually greatly limited (Pang and Lee 2008), considering the amount of money and attempts spent on them, both due to sample length limitations and due to the problems associated with making successful questionnaires. There is thus natural preference for detecting and evaluating inclination, instead of making specific surveys, inside online archives, including blogs, chat rooms and news articles. Human views of these electronic files are easy to understand. Therefore there may have been also significant issues for some organisations, as these documents may have an impact on the general public and terrible rumors in online documents. Let us take an example to interpret the realistic application of sentiment investigation: "Product A is good however expensive." This declaration incorporates a aggregation of statements: "Product A is good" "Product A is expensive" We suppose it's smooth to agree that there is one assertion, Product A is good, it gives a good strong impression, and another statement, product A, is expensive and it has a negative thought. Therefore, we seek to extract any assertion of support additionally to research the benefit of the full context and present it to abandon users who use the findings in line with their program requirements. Sentiment Analysis research therefore involves:

- Sentiment expressions recognition.
- Polarity and expressive power.
- Their relation to the subject.

They are interrelated elements. For example, "XXX beats YY" refers to a positive meaning for XXX and a negative sense for YYY. The word "beats" refers to XXX.

SEMANTIC ORIENTATION AND AGGREGATION

Semantic Orientation

The semantic response to a function f shows whether the view is positive, negative or neutral. Here the figure 1 represents the opinion of the user. Wide variety of literature has been studied for semantic approach to sentiment analysis that classifies the semantic orientation into two kinds of approaches, i.e.

1. corpus based
2. Dictionary or lexicon or knowledge based.

Figure 1. Sentiment Classification Techniques

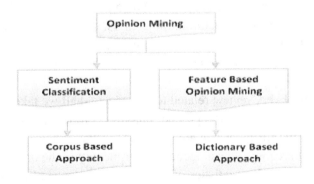

Corpus-based approach suggests data-driven approaches that not only have access to the sentiment labels, but can also be used for the advantage in an ML algorithm. This may simply be a rule-based technique or even a combination of NLP parsing. Corpus also has some specific domain, which will tell the Machine learning algorithm about the variety of the sentiment label for a word depending on its context / domain. Full semantic orientation requires large data sets to satisfy the polarity of the phrases and hence the feeling of the text.

The key drawback with the method is that it is based on the polarity of words contained within the training corpus, and the polarity of word is determined according to the terms in the corpus. Because of the simplification of this approach, this method was well studied in the literature. This method first eliminates sentiment expressions from the unstructured text and then measures the polarity of the words. Most of the sentiment-bearing terms are multi-phrase features in contrast to bag-of-words, e.g., "good movie," "satisfactory cinematography," "satisfactory actors," etc. In literature, the efficiency of a semantic orientation based technology was restricted because of by an insufficient availability of multi-word features.

Dictionary based approach suggests the judging of sentiment based on presence of signaling sentiment words (and perhaps some shorter context, like negations in the front of them) + some kind of counting mechanism to reach at sentiment prediction. In literature, dictionary based method is usually called the most effective (and subsequently of much less accuracy) one. Word based sentiment analysis is a statistical method for evaluating the feeling of a document. In the most successful case, feelings are binary: high or low, but they can be extended to more than one dimension, like anxiety, depression, rage, happiness, etc. This approach is largely based on the predefined list of sentences (or dictionary).

Dictionary-based approach works by identifying the words (for which an opinion has been given), from reviewed textual content then reveals their synonyms and antonyms from dictionary. WordNet or SentiWordNet or any another word network can be used as a dictionary. Corpus based approach helps locate the words of opinion in a particular context orientation, begin with the list of the words of opinion and then locate another word of opinion in a broad corpus. The most useful dictionary to use is Senti-WordNet 3.0. It is publicly accessible lexical tools consisting of "synsets," each with a positive and a negative numerical score of 0 to 1. This score is allocated from the WordNet automatically. This uses a semi-supervised learning process and an iterative algorithm for random walks. The above mentioned method works as follows:

First of all, the system needs to collect the simple and easy to understand sentiment words that have well defined positive or negative orientations. This collection is further extended by the algorithm by searching for its synonyms and antonyms in the WordNet or another online dictionary. The words searched by the algorithm are further added into the seed list to enlarge the collection. Included in the seed list are the following terms. The algorithm continues with the iterations. The cycle stops when new words can no longer be identified. A manual inspection is conducted to clean the list after the cycle had been completed.

Semantic Aggregation: Every review related to a product (shall we take an example of a camera) is mapped with its precise polarities in the product ontology. Product attributes that are at the higher level of the tree overpower the attributes that are at the lower level. When a reviewer talks about certain features of the product that are more advantageous or terrible within the ontology, he is weighting that feature more in comparison to other statistics of all child nodes (ex- light, resolution, coloration and compression). This is because the function of the parent class abstracts data and the characteristics of its child class. The value of the function is captured in the ontological tree by increasing the height of the characteristic node. In case of neutral polarity of the parent function, the polarity of the characteristic node is attributed to the polarities of its younger nodes. Thus data in a particular node is generated by his own data and by the weighted information of all its younger nodes.

In order to assess the record content of the base ode and the polarity of the analysis, the accurate propagation is carried out from the bottom to the top.

Let us create an ontology tree $TR(V1,E1)$ where $V1_i \hat{I} V1$ which is used for setting up a product attribute.

The attribute set of a product $V1i$ consists of the $V1i$ tuple

$$V1_i = \{f1_i, p1_i, h1_i\}$$

Where $f1_i$ is represented as the feature of the product

$P1_i$ represents the polarity score of the product recieved after the review in relation to $f1_i$ and $h1_i$
$H1_i$ represents the height attribute of the product
$E1_{ij} \hat{I} E1$ is s a relationship attribute
$F1_i \hat{I} V1_i$,
$F1_i \hat{I} V1_j$
$V1_i, V1_j \hat{I} V1$.

Let $V1_{ij}$ be the jth child of $V1_i$

The positive sentiment weight (PSW) and negative sentiment weight (NSW) of a vertex $V1_i$ can be calculated using the formula:

$$PSW(V1_i) = h1_i * p1_i$$
$$NSW(V1_i) = h1_i * p1_i$$

The product review polarity is estimated using expected sentiment-weight (ESW) of the ontology tree defined as,

$$ESW(root) = PSW(root) + NSW(root)$$

SEMANTIC APPROACH TO LEXICON ADAPTATION

The sentiment of a term isn't always static, as located in general-cause sentiment lexicons, however rather relies upon at the context wherein the term is used, i.e., it relies upon on its contextual semantics (Liu, 2006). Therefore, the lexicon adaptation technique functions in two predominant step

1. First, given a corpus and a sentiment lexicon, the approach builds a contextual semantic representation for each particular term in the corpus and ultimately uses it to derive the time period's contextual sentiment orientation and strength. The SentiCircle representation version is used to this end. Following the distributional inference, the words co-occurring in specific ways appear to have a common meaning, with certain words within the same corpus, SentiCircle derives the word's contextual semantics from its co-occurrence-styles. Such patterns are then interpreted as

a Geometric Circle & are used to measure the word's conceptual meaning, using simple trigono-metric identities. For each single duration m within the corpus in particular, we are constructing a two Dimensional geometric circle, in which the center of the circle is the time span m and each factor is described as a background ci (i.e., a time period that happens with m inside the identical context).

2. Secondly, rules are applied, mostly in line with the correspondent contextual sentiments, in order to change the previous feelings of the words within the lexicon.

The adaptation process uses a series of antecedent-consistent regulations which determine how their previous feelings in Thelwall-Lexicon are to be up to date in accordance with their SentiMedians' positions (i.e. their contextual feelings). For a term m, it checks, particularly,

1. The prior SOS value of the SentiCircle quadrant in Thelwall-Sexicon and
2. The SentiMedian of m.

The method then chooses the most suitable rule to update the previous feeling and/or opinion of the word.

CASE STUDY: SENTIMENT ANALYSIS ON CAA AND NRC PROTESTS IN INDIA - 2019

To perform the sentiment analysis on the protests held for CAA and NRC in India during December 2019, we created one corpus by collecting related articles from the Times of India and other leading newspapers of the India. The corpus was created for the articles of December 2019 and January 2020 during the peak of the protest.

The aim of this case study is to show the technique of sentiment analysis using R programming. The first objective of this study is to plot a word cloud and identify the most frequent words from the corpus along with the sentiments of these words. These words are used as hash tags to extract the data from the twitter. We extracted real time data from twitter by applying the most frequent words as hash tags. Then we applied sentiment analysis on twitter data to know the opinions of the people of country on the issue of NRC and CAA protest.

Installing Packages and Library

First step for implementing sentiment analysis on R is to install the relevant packages and their corresponding libraries. Some of the important packages which are used in sentiment analysis are-tm, SnowballC, SentimentAnalysis and wordcloud. We read the corpus as text file and loaded the data as corpus.

```
docs <- Corpus(VectorSource(text))
```

First few lines of corpus is shown below-

```
<<SimpleCorpus>>
Metadata:  corpus specific: 1, document level (indexed): 0
Content:  documents: 192
   [1] 20-12-2019 25,000 Citizens Protest CAA At August Kranti
```

```
   [2] Call for "azaadi" or freedom dominated the student-driven pro-
test of over 25,000 Mumbaikars, including 7,000 women, against the Citi-
zenship Amendment Act (CAA) and the proposed National Register of Cit-
izens (NRC) at the historic August Kranti Maidan at Grant Road on
Thursday. The protest was supported by political parties and activists.
```

```
   [3] While organisers said more than one lakh protest-
ers had turned up, police pegged the number at over 25,000.
```

```
   [4] Students from Tata Institute of Social Sciences (TISS), IIT-Bombay and
Mumbai University mobilised their peers and other citizens from across the
city. "The first call was given on my Twitter handle on December 11 and though
I have only a few thousand followers, the tweet was seen by over one lakh in-
dividuals," said Fahad Ahmad, PhD student of TISS who was one of the main or-
ganisers. "I am on 24 WhatsApp groups coordinating with students from across
the city."
```

The sample text is an evidence for the extracted article from Times of India dated 20-12-2019. Before applying the text analysis, the text needs to be transformed. Hence text transformation is an important step while analyzing the text. Here we applied the tm_map() function for text transformation to replace the special characters like- "/", "@" and "|" with space in the text. Subsequent to changeover of special characters with space, text cleaning is done with the same tm_map() function where the content_transformer(tolower) is used to convert all capital letters into lowercase letters and removeNumbers is used to remove the digits from the text.

To remove the common stop words, an inbuilt English stopwords dictionary is used by R which can be accessed as –

```
stopwords("english")
```

The common stopwords are-

```
'but' 'if' 'or' 'because' 'as''we\'re' 'they\'re'  'until' 'while' 'of' 'at'
'by' 'for' 'with' 'about' 'against' 'between' 'into' 'i' 'me' 'my' 'myself'
'we' 'our' 'ours' 'ourselves' 'you' 'your' 'yours' 'yourself' 'yourselves' 'he'
```

'him' 'his' 'through' 'during' 'before' 'after' 'above' 'below' 'to' 'from'
'up' 'down' 'in' 'out' 'on' 'off' 'over' 'more' 'most' 'other' 'some' 'such'
'no' 'nor' 'not' 'only' 'own' 'same' 'so' 'than' 'too' 'very' 'under' 'him-
self' 'she''her' 'hers' 'herself' 'it' 'its' 'itself' 'they' 'them' 'their'
'theirs' 'themselves' 'what' 'which' 'who' 'whom' 'this''that' 'these' 'those'
'am''is' 'are''was' 'were' 'be' 'been' 'being' 'have' 'has' 'you\'ll' 'he\'ll'
'she\'ll' 'we\'ll' 'they\'ll' 'isn\'t' 'aren\'t''wasn\'t' 'weren\'t' 'hasn\'t'
'haven\'t' 'hadn\'t' 'had' 'having' 'do''does' 'did' 'doing' 'would' 'should'
'could' 'ought' 'i\'m' 'you\'re' 'he\'s''she\'s' 'it\'s' 'i\'ve' 'you\'ve'
'we\'ve' 'they\'ve' 'i\'d' 'you\'d' 'he\'d' 'she\'d' 'we\'d' 'they\'d' 'i\'ll'
'again' 'further' 'then' 'once' 'here' 'there' 'when' 'where' 'why' 'how'
'all' 'any' 'both' 'each' 'few'
'doesn\'t' 'don\'t' 'didn\'t' 'won\'t' 'wouldn\'t' 'shan\'t' 'shouldn\'t'
'can\'t' 'cannot' 'couldn\'t' 'mustn\'t'
'let\'s' 'that\'s' 'who\'s' 'what\'s' 'here\'s' 'there\'s' 'when\'s' 'where\'s'
'why\'s' 'how\'s' 'a' 'an' 'the' 'and'

To add more stopwords we need to specify our stopwords as a character vector. In this case we find "said" and "also" as the stopwords and we removed them by applying the following function-

```
docs <- tm_map(docs, removeWords, c("said", "also"))
```

Subsequently punctuation and white spaces are also eliminated. First few lines of the transformed corpus are shown below-

```
<<SimpleCorpus>>
Metadata:  corpus specific: 1, document level (indexed): 0
Content:  documents: 192
  [1]  citizens protest caa august kranti


  [2] call "azaadi" freedom dominated studentdriv-
en protest mumbaikars including women citizenship amendment act
caa proposed national register citizens nrc historic august kranti
maidan grant road thursday protest supported political parties activists

  [3]  organisers one lakh protesters turned police pegged number



  [4] students tata institute social sciences tiss iitbombay mum-
bai university mobilised peers citizens across city " first call giv-
en twitter handle december though thousand followers tweet seen
one lakh individuals" fahad ahmad phd student tiss one main or-
ganisers " whatsapp groups coordinating students across city"
```

```
[5] apart three institutions organis-
ers got support students st xavier's college internation-
al institute population sciences iips wilson college among others


[6] appeals attend rally made protests places " can see people mumbra mira
road govandi bhendi bazaar outraged know allow inequality constitution stop "
activist teesta setalvad
```

To build a term document matrix we applied the following function-

```
D_t_m <- TermDocumentMatrix(docs)
mat <- as.matrix(d_t_m)
var<- sort(rowSums(mat),decreasing=TRUE)
doc <- data.frame(word = names(var),freq=var)
head(doc, 10)
```

This has resulted the output as frequency of each word in descending order. We have shown only first 10 lines of the output by via head().

Table 1. Word frequency table

word	freq	
caa	caa	32
citizenship	citizenship	29
nrc	nrc	28
police	police	27
india	india	26
modi	modi	24
people	people	23
delhi	delhi	23
law	law	20
minister	minister	19

Using this word frequency table we plotted the frequency table of words as shown in figure 2 and generated the word cloud as shown in figure 3 below-

To carry out sentiment analysis of these frequent words we used the SentimentAnalysis package and its library where we used the above generated document term matrix. First few lines of sentiments generated are-

Every document has a word count, a negativity score, a positivity score, and the overall sentiment score.

Figure 2. Word Frequency Plot

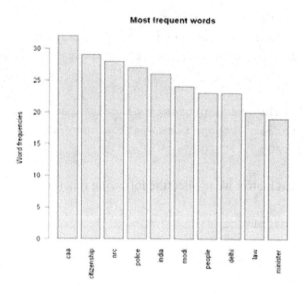

Figure 3. Word cloud

The distribution of overall sentiment can be seen as-

```
summary(sent$SentimentGI)
```

```
Min.   1st Qu.   Median    Mean  3rd Qu.    Max.     NA's
-0.33333  0.00000  0.00000  0.01538  0.05518  0.33333       34
```

After adding the column of words with the sentiment score-

Table 2. Sentiment Analysis of Frequent Words

WordCount	SentimentGI	NegativityGI	PositivityGI
5	-0.20000000	0.20000000	0.00000000
30	0.00000000	0.06666667	0.06666667
8	0.00000000	0.00000000	0.00000000
42	0.04761905	0.00000000	0.04761905
18	0.05555556	0.00000000	0.05555556
24	0.12500000	0.00000000	0.12500000

Table 3. Sentiment score of the words

d[1:6, 1]	WordCount	SentimentGI	NegativityGI	PositivityGI
protest	5	-0.20000000	0.20000000	0.00000000
caa	30	0.06666667	0.10000000	0.16666667
citizenship	8	-0.25000000	0.25000000	0.00000000
india	44	0.06818182	0.00000000	0.06818182
nrc	18	0.11111111	0.00000000	0.11111111
police	26	0.07692308	0.11538462	0.19230769

Performing Sentiment Analysis on Twitter Data based on Hashtags

In 21st century, there has been an exponential rush forward in the online commotion of people across the world. One of the online social platforms is Twitter when people freely express their sentiments. There are several challenges in performing sentiment analysis on the data extracted from the twitter as inhabitants have a dissimilar way of writing and while posting on Twitter, people are least bothered about the correct spelling of words or they may use a lot of slangs which are not proper English words but are used in casual conversations. Hence it has been an interesting research area among researchers from one decade.

By motivating from the above, we have generated the most frequent words from the corpus collected in the above section from various articles in news papers during December 2019 and January 2020 on NRC and CAA and these words have been used as hashtags to extract the relevant data from twitter. Using the twitter API in R we performed data extraction by passing most frequent word as hashtag and extracted top 250 tweets. These tweets were stored as a data frame. First few lines of text of this dataframe can be seen as-

head(tweets.df$text)
1.   'RT @ShayarImran: Participated in KSU protest march and public meeting against #CAA #NRC at Calicutt, Kerala \n@RamyaHaridasMP \n@srinivasiyc…'
2.   '@hfao5 @AnjanPatel7 @SyedAhmedAliER @KTRTRS @trspartyonline @TelanganaCMO @asadowaisi Hyderabadi\'s must protest KCR… https://t.co/T53DB7do14'

3. 'RT @GradjanskiO: Novi protest ce obeleziti puteve Vesicevih rusevina.\n\nUrbicid! Mrznja prema gradjanima!\n\n15.02.2020\n\u23f0 18h\nPlato\n\nDo pobede…'

4. 'RT @SwamiGeetika: #DelhiAssemblyElections2020 \n\nYouth gathered in large numbers to protest after TMC barred distributing Hanuman Chalisa an…'

5. 'RT @anyaparampil: Workers w Venezuelan airline Conviasa tell @ErikaOSanoja their protest of Guaidó\'s arrival in Venezuela is part of "defen…'

6. 'RT @JamesRu55311: We've known for a long time that BBC is already lost, and that they were complicit in their own downfall. Watching them s…'

This data frame is first converted into a vector and then preprocessing is applied before sentiment analysis. The function get_nrc_sentiment() is used to identify the positive and negative words. We then computed the total positive and negative words in the twitter text and the a plot is drawn as shown in figure 4 below. This plot shows the sentiments attached with the corresponding text.

Figure 4. Total Positive And Negative Words In The Twitter Text

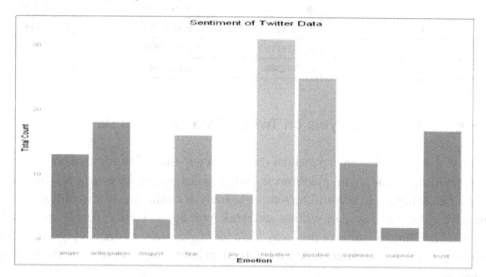

As we can discover here, in the given case more number of negative words are found hence it represents the negative sentiments of the people. Thus we can easily identify and analyse the sentiments of the people based on the key words.

CONCLUSION

The chapter discusses the concepts related to sentiment analysis and the importance of semantic in sentiment analysis. The present chapter has illustrated the basic of ontologies and their relation to sentiment analysis. The chapter has further discussed semantic ontologies with concept forms and their relationships along with steps to develop a baseline model for simple analysis of sentiment using NLP. At the end of the chapter case study related to the sentiment analysis using R programming on the protests for CAA and NRC in India during December 2019 has been presented. The corpus of the case study has been built by collecting related articles from the Times of India and other leading newspapers of the India. Real time data has been extracted from twitter by applying the most frequent words as hash tags. Finally sentiment analysis techniques have been applied on twitter data to know the opinions of the people of country on the issue of NRC and CAA protest. This work can be extended further by applying various sentiment analysis techniques to improve the accuracy of the predicted words. More work is also required to preprocess the data in order to improve the accuracy.

REFERENCES

Agrawal, R., & Gupta, N. (Eds.). (2018). *Extracting Knowledge from Opinion Mining*. IGI Global.

Gupta, N., & Agrawal, R. (2017). Challenges and Security Issues of Distributed Databases. In *NoSQL* (pp. 265–284). Chapman and Hall/CRC.

Gupta, N., & Agrawal, R. (2020). Application and Techniques of Opinion Mining. In *Hybrid Computational Intelligence*. Elsevier.

Gupta, N., & Verma, S. (2019). Tools of Opinion Mining. In *Extracting Knowledge From Opinion Mining* (pp. 179–203). IGI Global.

Hai, Z., Chang, K., Kim, J. J., & Yang, C. C. (2013). Identifying features in opinion mining via intrinsic and extrinsic domain relevance. *IEEE Transactions on Knowledge and Data Engineering*, *26*(3), 623–634. doi:10.1109/TKDE.2013.26

Jalota, C., & Agrawal, R. (2019). Ontology-Based Opinion Mining. In *Extracting Knowledge From Opinion Mining* (pp. 84–103). IGI Global.

Kalra, V., & Aggarwal, R. (2017). Importance of Text Data Preprocessing & Implementation in RapidMiner. In *Proceedings of the First International Conference on Information Technology and Knowledge Management–New Dehli, India* (Vol. 14, pp. 71-75). 10.15439/2017KM46

Kalra, V., & Agrawal, R. (2019). Challenges of Text Analytics in Opinion Mining. In *Extracting Knowledge From Opinion Mining* (pp. 268–282). IGI Global.

Kaur, S., & Agrawal, R. (2018). A Detailed Analysis of Core NLP for Information Extraction. *International Journal of Machine Learning and Networked Collaborative Engineering*, *1*(01), 33–47. doi:10.30991/IJMLNCE.2017v01i01.005

Liu, B. (2006). Mining comparative sentences and relations. In AAAI (Vol. 22). Academic Press.

Medhat, W., Hassan, A., & Korashy, H. (2014). Sentiment analysis algorithms and applications: A survey. *Ain Shams Engineering Journal*, *5*(4), 1093–1113.

Niazi, M., & Hussain, A. (2009). Agent-based tools for modeling and simulation of self-organization in peer-to-peer, ad hoc, and other complex networks. *IEEE Communications Magazine*, *47*(3), 166–173.

Pang, B., & Lee, L. (2008). Opinion mining and sentiment analysis. *Foundations and Trends in Information Retrieval, 2*(1–2), 1–135. doi:10.1561/1500000011

Poria, S., Gelbukh, A., Hussain, A., Howard, N., Das, D., & Bandyopadhyay, S. (2013). Enhanced SenticNet with affective labels for concept-based opinion mining. *IEEE Intelligent Systems, 28*(2), 31–38.

Tsai, A. C. R., Wu, C. E., Tsai, R. T. H., & Hsu, J. Y. J. (2013). Building a concept-level sentiment dictionary based on commonsense knowledge. *IEEE Intelligent Systems, 28*(2), 22–30.

Ye, Q., Zhang, Z., & Law, R. (2009). Sentiment classification of online reviews to travel destinations by supervised machine learning approaches. *Expert Systems with Applications, 36*(3), 6527–6535.

Chapter 6
A Review of the IoT–Based Pervasive Computing Architecture for Microservices in Manufacturing Supply Chain Management

Kamalendu Pal
https://orcid.org/0000-0001-7158-6481
City, University of London, UK

ABSTRACT

Supply chain coordination needs resource and information sharing between business partners. Recent advances in information and communication technology (ICT) enables the evolution of the supply chain industry to meet the new requirements of information sharing architectures due to globalization of supply chain operations. The advent of the internet of things (IoT) technology has since seen a growing interest in architectural design and adaptive frameworks to promote the connection between heterogenous IoT devices and IoT-based information systems. The most widely preferred software architecture in IoT is the semantic web-based service-oriented architecture (SOA), which aims to provide a loosely coupled systems to leverage the use of IoT services at the middle-ware layer to minimise system integration problems. This chapter reviews existing architectural frameworks for integrating IoT devices and identifies the key areas that require further research for industrial information service improvements. Finally, several future research directions in microservice systems are discussed.

INTRODUCTION

Internet of Things (IoT) based computing is one of the promising technologies for the automation of distributed complex information systems. Many researchers and practitioners expressed their views that IoT technology represents the most influential new paradigm for the fourth industrial revolution, which is

DOI: 10.4018/978-1-7998-6697-8.ch006

commonly known as Industry 4.0 (Pal, 2020). It is ushering a new hope in global manufacturing industries by increasing production uptime and reducing operational risks. The IoT based technologies along with service-oriented computing (SOC), data analytics, and cyber-physical systems play an important role in a manufacturing industry supply chain operating environment. In this way, the manufacturing supply chain operation is heavily influenced by the Industry 4.0 information and communication technology (ICT) evolution since it faces the challenge of rapidly growing requirements for agile and efficient reactivity to the rapidly changing global customer demands. Customers are increasingly defining how retail manufacturing businesses design and deploy their supply chain operations. These demanding customers can now do their shopping anywhere and anytime and expect a more fulfilling experience from retailers. However, many retail businesses are dealing with how to find an innovative approach to sourcing, replenishment, and distribution strategies to address the changes. Retail businesses are starting to consider seriously how best to optimize their supply chain operations to face fast-changing customer demand while minimizing operational expenditure.

A retail manufacturing supply chain consists of interconnected activities, and their associated business processes together to provide value-added service to its customers. Customer-engaged retail companies, from automobile dealers to highly attractive summer dressmakers, always need different stakeholders' information for their supply chains. An entire network of manufacturers and distributors, transportation and logistics agencies, warehouses and freight-forwards work together to make sure that the right goods and services are available at the right price, where and when the customers want them. Having supplied value-added services (e.g., products and associated customer services), the supply chain does not terminate. The retail supply chain is comprised of several steps from the front end, through the customer request, supply chain order processing initiation, quality assurance for product and services, relevant training processes for staffs, customer support facilities, to maintenance and replacement facilities.

Figure 1. RFID tagging level at different stages in the apparel manufacturing network

In a typical manufacturing supply chain, raw materials are purchased from suppliers and products are manufactured at one or more manufacturing plants. Then they are transported to intermediated storage (e.g., warehouse, distribution centre) for packing and shipping to retailers or customers (Pal, 2017). The path from supplier to a customer can include several intermediaries such as wholesalers, warehouse, and retailers, depending on the product and markets. In this way, supply chain management relates to business activities such as inbound and outbound transportation, warehousing, and inventory management. Figure 1 presents a simple diagrammatic representation of an apparel manufacturing supply chain, which consists of textile fibre production, fibre dyeing, yarn spinning, knitting and fabrication business process, and finally transported to retail stores (Pal, 2018).

Increased internationalization of retail manufacturing industries is chaining the operational practices of the global retail supply chain, and many retailers have adopted new business models, either by outsourcing or by establishing business-alliances in other countries. Globalization has also led to changes in operational practices, where products are designed and manufactured in one part of the world and sold in another. The retail supply chain has become more global in its geographical scope; the international market is getting more competitive and customer demand oriented. Importantly, this globalized operation also embodies the information systems necessary to monitor these business activities.

As a result, many manufacturing industries are investing in new IoT technology-based solution to harness smooth information sharing ability in supply chain operations. With recent progress in Radio Frequency Identification (RFID) technology, low-cost wireless sensor hardwires, and world wide web technologies, the IoT advance has attracted attention in connecting global manufacturing business activities and sharing operational business information more integrated way (Pal, 2019). In this sense, the IoT refers to a heterogeneous network of physical and virtual objects embedded with electronics, software, sensors, and connectivity to enable objects to achieve greater value and service by exchanging data with other connected objects via the Internet. "Things" in terms of IoT, maybe a field operation robot that assists in a textile production plant, or man-made object that can be assigned an IP address and provided with the ability to transfer data and to interoperate within the existing Internet infrastructure.

These technologies promise to reshape the modus operandi of modern supply chains through enhanced data collection as well as information sharing and analysis between collaborating supply chain business partners. IoT technology supports the capability to connect and integrate both digital and physical business world. The process is quite simple: (i) collect data from real-world objects, (ii) communicate and aggregate those data into information, and (iii) present clear results to systems or users so that deliver actionable insights in an industrial environment. Consequently, the strategic goal of digitization of retail manufacturing industries is evolving to a new automation paradigm, which is essentially flexible and resilient to change. Also, this industrial environment consists of heterogeneous, distributed, intelligent objects – both from the digital and the physical worlds – and operating applications and services for industrial business functions. Since these intelligent IoT-based applications are composed of different types of objects and services, a key aspect for engineering them is their architecture.

Moreover, service-oriented architecture (SOA) offers software parallelism, which can be further classified as an algorithm, programming, data size, and distributed business processes integration. Algorithm parallelism is a process of algorithm implementation for software or an application. The traditional algorithm is based on the concept of sequential processing. Since task execution is linear, the traditional approach will become very counterproductive. To get better parallel performance, the architecture of parallel computing must have enough processors, and adequate global memory access and inter-processor communication of data and control information to enable parallel scalability. When the parallel system is scaled up, the memory and communication systems should also be increased by the architecture of the design. In this way, SOA based software architecture provides a powerful means for supporting the connectivity, interoperability, and integration IoT systems, it forms the backbone of current IoT frameworks. While SOA goals are to mainly improve IoT-based business processes interoperability, its inflexible usage in recent IoT frameworks further resonates the problem of scalability particularly with the huge number of predicted "things". IoT systems tend to expand and with time, a capable SOA framework becomes too immovable to handle system extensibility. Microservice aims to fragment different IoT systems based on the System of Systems (SOS) paradigm to properly serve for system evolution and extensibility. This chapter reviews current IoT integration frameworks and proposes a framework, which can cater a fulfilling solution to the problem of inadequate service integration, scalability, extensibility, and fault tolerance in IoT.

This chapter is organized as follows. Section 2 explains the motivation and challenges in IoT architecture. Section 3 presents some requirements for IoT framework design and review some of the prominent IoT architectures. Section 4 discusses the important issues need to consider in designing an IoT-based architecture to support device connectivity, integration, interoperability, fault tolerance, and scalability. Section 5 concludes the chapter with concluding remarks and lays out future research work.

MOTIVATION AND CHALLENGES

The IoT-based technology infrastructure has motivated many innovative applications of logistics and manufacturing supply chain management in recent years. The ideal IoT vision is that each object has its own Digital Object Identifier (DOI) (Gershenfeld et al., 2004), and it is now achievable to create a global network with objects as the infrastructure through IoT (Kortuem et al., 2010). The goal of IoT is to create a global network infrastructure to facilitate the easy exchange of commodities, services, and information (Liu & Sun, 2011). The application of IoT technology in the industry, such as manufacturing and supply chains, is also known as Industrial IoT (IIoT) (Li et al., 2014). IoT or IIoT has been applied by some enterprises to assist in the collection of real-time information, which has successfully improved and promoted operating efficiency.

In recent years researchers and practitioners are promoting a theme of IoT-based research, which is known as the Internet of People (IoP) (Conti et al., 2017). In IoP, humans play an important role so that design considering aspects as context becomes essential for developing the IoT-based industrial applications. These industrial applications spring up as an evolution of IoT and cyber-physical social systems (CPSSs), which consider the social nature of human beings for the development of this category of systems. In IoP-based system development, its user (i.e., human) is viewed with all possible connectivity through the Internet and self-organizing networks of users as well as physical devices via IoT technology. Besides, IoP design methodology considers devices as the representatives of their owners and they act on behalf of their owners. In this way, users and devices form a complex socio-technical system that lay the foundation of the new generation of IoT-based information system's architecture.

However, there are many challenges and technical issues that are related to the effectiveness of these new generation IoP based software system's architectures. Some of the technical issues are scalability of these architectures, huge data handling capability, the efficiency of real-time data processing ability, and so on. Also, there is no standard architecture for IoT-based software systems which can provide ideal services. Therefore, designing and developing IoT application systems is very challenging. Most of the approaches propose a domain-specific architecture. Consequently, it is worth to use a set of design patterns that could be used to provide end-user applications with self-adaptive and context-aware characteristics, and a reference IoT-based software architecture fulfilling all the IoT system needs in different domains. To do this, a basic IoT system's software architecture needs to be considered first to understand its constituent parts.

Figure 2. Basic IoT system architecture

Figure 2 shows the basic IoT system architecture. This architecture consists of three main components and they are physical sensing layer, IoT middleware layer, and application layer. The physical sensing layer contains embedded devices, which use of sensors to collect real-world industrial operational data. Its gateway component provides the function and protocols for industrial devices to expose their collected data to the IoT network using communication mechanisms (e.g., wireless communication, Ethernet-based communication, GSM, and so on). The middleware layer provides and organizes the interaction between the real-world industrial applications related data and the application layer. The application layer manages the system driven applications, which can be used by the user to send commands to real-world objects over the data communication network via mobile applications.

In this way, interoperability plays a crucial role in exchanging information among heterogeneous architecture and provide relevant services. Current IoT technology-based initiatives focus mainly on applications and devices that address disparate needs of interoperability but offer very limited opportunity for interoperation and connection. It is worth to note that IoT solutions need to support connection and interoperability as a building block to provide mechanisms, processes and security that enable disparate devices and services to be connected. The advantage is that IoT devices and services can communicate with each other and create better efficiencies, enhance ease of use, provide a better capability, greater choice, lead to economies of scale and potentially lower unit cost. Inappropriate interoperability and connection are **exacerbated** by many issues as follows:

- **Standardized Service Description**: There are service standardization issues relating to IoT based applications. It includes naming convention of IoT device services and data description. These issues are important to integrate heterogeneous services. Current trends in IoP related research agenda, particularly in context awareness and data management related issues are investigating the use semantic web technologies (e.g., semantic web services and their standards, Ontology Web Language (OWL)) for IoP based industrial system automation. Researchers are investigating the issues related to diverse naming conventions among disparate social and cultural backgrounds people, and linguistic taxonomy related habits whereby different terms are used to represent similarly or the same entity. The solution of integrating heterogeneous IoT will largely benefit from integrated modelling techniques to provide appropriate knowledge acquisition and representation of the IoT domain.

- **Context-awareness for services:** The inadequate semantics for appropriate service context description is still evident in recent IoT system design. Current IoT systems suffer from insufficient context awareness of services due to inexpertly modelled semantics proliferating various unevenly distributed ontologies and incoherent semantics for services. For proper context-aware data processing in IoT based industrial application domain, a new approach should be utilized to modelling and designing rule engines for services.

- **Device service classification:** Many IoT based information systems utilize cataloguing of device services based on the device categorization. This type of practice attributes service to devices based on the unique identifier of both devices and services. These services are made discoverable if an inquest is made to the service or device identifier. In IoT systems, this practice has long aided device discovery and service discovery but from a machine-to-machine or device-to-device viewpoint in an industrial setting, service discovery is still unconvincing thus, if a device fails and is absent from the system it logs it as an unavailable service even if the same service with a different unique identifier is provisioned for by another device. There must be a new approach to service classification to accommodate such dynamic discovery of services.

- **Information visualisation and analysis:** Recent research initiatives provide limited scope for tailored data collection and visualisation. Tailored data visualisation and analysis from an object's activities and environment can provide invaluable insight into the well-being and the continued adequacy of an industrial operation.

For an IoT based industrial information system's architecture need to be reliable and dependable. It is also essential to have some minimal set of measures that should be satisfied to achieve integration and interoperability in IoT based system. For example, some of the simple measures are – scalability, ease of IoT based system testing, ease of development, appropriate fault tolerance, service coordination, and inter-domain operability. The next section presents an overview of some of the IoT based software system architectures.

REVIEW OF IoT BASED SYSTEM ARCHITECTURES

This section reviews some IoT architectures highlighting the issues that need to be considered by an IoT software architectural proposal. As presented by research works (Al-Qaseemi et al., 2016) (Atzori et al., 2010) that most of the architectural specifications used at the initial stages of IoT research were structured into three layers, each layer is related to one of the three main IoT paradigms (Weyrich & Ebert, 2016).: (i) application (or presentation or semantic) layer, (ii) transportation (or network) layer, and (iii) sensing (or perception or hardware or physical) layer, which is responsible for collecting information. Next, this section presents an overview of four IoT-based software system architectures.

Calvin Framework

The Calvin framework is a hybrid software architecture consists of the IoT-based model and cloud computing-based model to explicate the complexity of distributed computing problems (Person & Angelsmark, 2015). This framework combines ideas from the Actor model and Flow-Based Computing. It divides the IoT-based software application development into four different and sequentially executed well-defined aspects – *describe, connect, deploy,* and *manage.*

- **Describe:** The functional parts of applications, made into reusable components. In a simple sense, Calvin's characteristics is based on actors. These software-based actors consist of actions, communication mechanisms, and triggering events. These triggering events are guided by actions. The actors communicate with their community members using inbuilt communication mechanisms.

Also, in this architecture actors are software components representing hardware devices, business functionality related services, and relevant computation related components. In the "describe" aspect of Calvin's is core functionalities are developed by software components.

- **Connect:** The interactions between components described as graphs. These graphs are implemented in software components using a lightweight intuitive and declarative language, known as *CalvinScript*. This programming language is platform-agnostic, and the initial full-fledged prototype runtime was implemented in python.

- **Deploy:** The instantiation of the application according to the graphs. The initial software architecture was deployed in a distributed runtime environment. Actors functionalities are described and connected which enabling migration between a mesh network of runtimes. The "deploy" aspect improvises a simple deployment pattern bypassing the application script of an intended application for deployment into the runtime environment. Due to the distributed nature of the implementation, deployed actors can manoeuvre across accessible runtimes based on locality, performance requirements, connectivity requirements and resources. The implemented software architecture uses an algorithm to deal with the workload, network congestion-related issues, and manage runtime overload situations.

- **Manage:** The autonomous, dynamic, mapping of components to hardware over the lifetime of the application. It includes aspect involves the management of migrating actors between runtimes, error recovery, scaling, resource usage and updates by the distributed runtime environment.

The Clive framework-based software architecture models a distributed run-time environment and provides multi-tenancy functionality. Also, the Calvin runtime is very lightweight and can be ported to any microcontroller with communication capabilities (a prerequisite for IoT), or run hosted in the cloud, providing a truly heterogeneous application environment. Actors can operate asynchronously and autonomously.

SOCRADES

The SOCRADES, an integration architecture that can serve the requirements of the manufacturing industry (Sa De Souza et al., 2008). This software architecture provides generic components upon which smart manufacturing processes can be modelled. It is a service-oriented based integrated software architecture which provides a generic design facility to aid the manufacturing business process modelling. This architecture uses intelligent objects in manufacturing industries, which represents their behaviour as web services to improve their operational capabilities. Also, this software architecture uses design pattern, and its concept and programming code has been reused from (a European Union research council funded project) SIRENA (Bohn et al., 2006). The SIRENA project proposes and designs an integrated infrastructure for web service-based framework for device supervision and lifecycle management.

SOCRADES software system is composed of four main parts – (i) the Device layer, (ii) middleware layer, (iii) a System Applications and Products (SAP) in the data processing unit (known as xMII Component), and (iv) the enterprise application component, which is a graphical user interface for the end-users.

- The Device Layer comprises the devices on the shop floor. These devices when enabled with the distributed process of web service (DPWS) connect to the SOCRADES middleware for more advanced features. Moreover, since they support web services, they provide the means for a direct connection to Enterprise Applications.

- The middleware of SOCRADES provides connectivity between the device layer and the enterprise application. The central objective of the middleware is to ease the management of devices in the device layer. The most important features of the middleware are – (i) devices access facilitation, (ii) service discovery, (iii) device supervision, (iv) service life cycle management, and (v) security related functionalities. Also, the middleware component provides the communication and cooperation mechanisms with the next layer (e.g., xMII component) and other parts of this architecture.
- The third layer of this architecture is the main centre for data processing. This layer has got main characteristics – for example, non-web service device enabled connectivity, visualization service, graphical modelling, and execution of business logic-based rules, which help to create rich web content for certain business functionalities.
- The fourth and final layer provides the enterprise application user interface. This part of the architecture receives data from the nearby layer using appropriate protocols and use these data for web content creation purpose.

The SOCRADES architecture provides device connectivity and helps to integrate enterprise applications (e.g., enterprise resource planning – ERP system). Its main functionality is based on the service-oriented architecture.

AllJoyn

AllJoyn (Allseen Alliance, 2016) is a collaborative open-source software architecture, which permits hardware devices to communicate with other devices around them. This architecture is flexible, promotes proximal network and cloud connection is optional. The system itself is an open-source project which provides a universal software architecture and core set of system services that enable interoperability among connected products and software applications across manufacturers to create dynamic proximal networks. In other words, the framework provides a proximal network discovery between devices by abstracting out the details of the physical transport and providing a simple-to-use application programming interface (API) for integrating things. Therefore, the complexity of discovering nearby devices is handled by creating sessions (i.e., multiple sessions, point-to-point (P2P), or group sessions) between devices for secure communication between them. Also, this architecture consists of implemented common services and interfaces used by developers to integrate variety of devices, things, or other applications (apps). The architecture depends optimally on cloud services as it runs on a local area network. In this way, devices, and applications (i.e., apps) can communicate within the network using only one gateway agent designed to connect to the Internet. This in turn minimizes security related problems (e.g., devices detailed information leak to the computer network). The AllJoyn architecture consists of two main components: AllJoyn Apps and AllJoyn Routers. These components can both reside on the same or different physical device.

AllJoyn Apps: This component of the architecture provides a way of communication with its local components (i.e., other Apps) using AllJoyn Router. In addition, the AllJoyn App consists of sub-components that are the: AllJoyn App Code, AllJoyn Service Framework and AllJoyn Core Library.

- AllJoyn App Code: This provides algorithmic logical solution for the AllJoyn Apps. It also facilitates access to the AllJoyn Core API by connecting it with the AllJoyn Service framework or the AllJoyn Core Library components to give such access.
- AllJoyn Service Framework: This is the component that implements the common services such as on-boarding a new device for the first time, sending notifications, and controlling a device. These services allow the communication and interoperation between apps and devices.
- AllJoyn Core Library: This component provides access to the API for interaction with the AllJoyn network. It provides support for: session creation, object creation and handling, interface definition of methods, properties and signals and service/device discovery and advertisement.

AllJoyn Routers: This part of the architecture facilitates the communication between different Apps components. The AllJoyn architecture uses three common ways of communication between Apps and Routers.

- Standalone Router: This router operates as a standalone process on a system and it permits the interactions to more than one Apps on the same device as the router. It makes sure that devices can optimize their resources utilization.
- Bundled Router: The router is bundled with an App based on a one-to-one relationship.
- Router on a different device: The router is run on a different device permitting connections from Apps. This is used for embedded devices that are resource constrained. In this way, it will utilize the "Thin" version of the AllJoyn framework with their limited resources.

The AllJoyn architecture follows a common way for the connection, interaction, and integration of things, devices, and apps regardless of their individual operating system, programming language and manufacturers.

FRASAD

The FRASAD framework (Nguyen et al., 2015) is a development focused at allowing developers design their IoT systems utilizing sensor-based networks. This idea is model driven and as such the system code is produced from the designed model via a conversion process. The FRASAD (FRAmework for Sensor Application Development) framework is an extension of research-based framework (Thang et al., 2011) by the inclusion and integration of two layers to the existing sensor node architecture. These two additional layers are the Application Layer (APL) and the Operating System Abstraction Layer (OAL).

The actuality of these two layers is to amplify the level of abstraction and thus concealing the lower levels. To accomplish this, the framework uses a robustly designed Domain Specific Language (DSL) to model the sensor nodes and separate the operating system from the application. The OAL is then contracted to explicate the modelled application based on the particular operating system for development. The OAL is an application generator and its central function is to generate the application code to be deployed in the specified platform. The FRASAD framework inherently follows the Model Driven Architecture (MDA) method by using three levels of abstraction. They are:

- The Computation Independent Model (CIM): used to represent the actual information without detailing the structure of the system or the technology used for its development.

- The Platform Independent Model (PIM): This is the model that provides the application logic and requirements.
- The Platform Specific Model (PSM): The PIM is mapped to the PSM based on the particular operating system of development, using a particularly designed DSL for translating processes. The PSM is operating system specific and may use languages supported by the operating system. FRASAD in a nutshell is a framework which uses a multi-layered MDA with the interaction between layers via some predefined interface. It uses the node-centric model to facilitate the programming of individual sensor nodes using its rule-based programming model.

ISSUES OF IoT SYSTEM ARCHITECTURE DESIGN

This section highlights some of the issues of an IoT-based system architecture which should be considered by a new system proposal. Most of the architectural specifications used at the initial stages of IoT research considered a three-layers (i.e., application, transport, sensing) based design principle (Al-Qasemi et al., 2016) (Atzori et al., 2010) (Weyrich & Ebert, 2016).

Application (or presentation or semantics) layer: This layer uses intelligent computing techniques (e.g., soft-computing based data analysis, smart-algorithmic solutions for service-oriented computing application) to extract valuable information (Atzori et al., 2010). In this way, the data analysis paves an appropriate end-user service. These services offer an interface between users and IoT systems to make judicious decisions (Atzori et al., 2010).

Transport (or network) layer: Transport layer ideally deals with communication network operations (Atzori et al., 2010) in software architecture. This layer is responsible for the transmission of gathered information (Al-Qasemi et al., 2016).

Sensing (or hardware or physical) layer: Harward layer deals with collecting information (Atzorie et al., 2010).

The IoT-based system architecture design phase needs to consider user-centred design philosophy, which helps infrastructure use appropriately (Gubbi et al., 2013). However, most proposals were focused just on the generic aspects of network and, the issues related to sensing (Weyrich & Ebert, 2016) (Gubbi et al., 2013). Those proposals neglect the data presentation issues, which help valuable knowledge creation for the use cases (Weyrich & Ebert, 2016).

A traditional application design approach that combines sensors directly to applications becomes unsuitable (Perera et al., 2014). Regarding flexibility, as highlighted in a research article (Yaqoob et al., 2017), autonomous services needed by IoT users can be supported by constructing an adaptive, context-aware, and reconfigurable service architecture able to handle applications according to its requirements. These issues are essential for IoP applications development where development must focus on the context of the system. Also, a group of researchers (Lagerspetz et al., 2018)supported this view for IoP applications development - "devices also need to obtain information about the social context they are operating in, so they can share resources as their owners would".

To address the problems exhibited by those approaches and the requirements of IoT, such as scalability, flexibility, interoperability, quality of service (QoS), and security among others (Yaqoob et al., 2017), several middleware solutions were introduced as an abstraction layer between the transport and the application layers. However, those middleware solutions focus just on some of the mentioned aspects as stated by (Perera et al., 2014) (Perera et el., 2012). Therefore, an ideal middleware solution or architectural framework that addresses all the aspects required by the IoT is yet to be designed (Perera et al., 2014).

Most of the middleware solutions, such as (Atzori et al., 2010) (Miorandi et al., 2012), proposed for architecting IoT follow a service-oriented architecture (SOA) approach. Despite its advantages for IoT solutions, SOA may become too heavy for being deployed on resource-constrained devices when the system is finally developed as a monolith difficult to be scaled up and evolved. It should be considered that an appropriate SoC degree can ease the traceability between middleware or framework abstractions and components or services.

Furthermore, some of the existing IoT SOA-based middleware solutions rely on several layers that consider support to object abstraction, service management, and service composition (Atzori et al., 2010). However, the definition of specific data models and representations is not properly addressed by such proposals. Consequently, new methods are necessary to adapt SOA concepts to IoT needs (Miorandi et al., 2012).

All the mentioned aspects are paramount for context information management (Al-Qaseemi et al., 2016), as a proposal able to both process the huge amount of data that are continuously generated and decide how to process them to obtain valuable information (Perera et al., 2014) (Issue 5) is necessary, because gathering, modelling, reasoning, and distribution of context plays a critical aspect for IoT. Such context information management is also paramount in IoP, as pointed out in (Miranda et al., 2015). Context-aware computing allows context information linked to sensor data to be stored so that the processing and interpretation can be done more easily and meaningfully. However, many IoT middleware and framework solutions do not provide context-awareness support or the context-aware support they offer do not satisfy other important requirements that IoT demands, such as self-adaptation aspects (Perera et al., 2014).

CONCLUSION

Manufacturers are facing changes on many industry-specific challenges. Advanced manufacturing – in the form of additive manufacturing, advanced materials, smart factories, automated machines, and other technologies – is ushering in a new age of modern production. At the same time, increased connectivity and ever more sophisticated data-gathering and analytics capabilities enabled by the Internet of Things (IoT) have led to a shift towards an information-based economy. With the IoT technology, data, in addition to physical objects, are a source of value – and connectivity makes it possible to build smart supply chains, manufacturing processes, and even end-to-end ecosystems.

As these waves of change continue to shape the competitive landscape, manufacturers must decide how and where to invest in new technologies and identify which ones will drive the most benefits for their organizations. In addition to accurately assessing their current strategic positions, successful manufacturers need a clear articulation of their business objectives, identifying where to play in newly emerging technology ecosystems and what are the technologies, both physical and digital, that they will deploy in pursuit of decisions they make about how to win.

This chapter has reviewed some of the important issues in integrating IoT devices to information processing systems. It has reviewed some of the existing software architecture with much focus on the adapted service-oriented architecture provision. This chapter has also highlight some of the critical issues need to consider in future for IoT-based industrial systems design and development.

The computing paradigm Internet of things and people (IoT-P) facilitates the connection of both virtual and physical generic everyday things or objects, invisibly embedded in our environment, and people using existing and new Internet aspects and network enhancements. IoT-P is related to the growth of the ubiquitous infrastructure in which those objects, some of them on behalf of people, flood the Internet with a high amount of new data that need to be understood. As has been stated, there are lot of issues and challenges that limit the effectiveness and performance of the IoT-P, particularly those related to the IoT reference architectures used that usually focus on sensors and network aspects, neglecting the application domain, information presentation aspects, and other relevant features of IoT-P. In future all these issues will be considered to propose a software architecture, which will help the manufacturing industry automation purpose.

REFERENCES

Al-Qaseemi, S. A., Almulhim, H. A., Almulhim, M. F., & Chaudhry, S. R. (2016). IoT architecture challenges and issues: Lack of standardization. *Proceedings of the 2016 Future Technologies Conference (FTC)*, 731–738.

Allseen Alliance. (2016). *AllJoyn Framework*. Available at https://allseenalliance.org/framework/documentation/learn/architecture

Atzori, L., Iera, A., & Morabito, G. (2010). The Internet of Things: A Survey. *Comput. Network, 54*, 2787–2805.

Bohn, H., Bobek, A., & Golatowski, F. (2006). SIRENA-Service Infrastructure for Real-time Embedded Networked Devices: A service-oriented framework for different domains. *Networking, International Conference on Systems and International Conference on Mobile Communications and Learning Technologies*, 43-43.

Conti, M., & Passarella, A. (2018). The Internet of People: A human and data-centric paradigm for the Next Generation Internet. *Computer Communications, 131*, 51–65.

Conti, M., Passarella, A., & Das, S. (2017). The Internet of People (IoP): A new wave in pervasive mobile computing. *Pervasive and Mobile Computing, 41*, 1–27.

Gershenfeld, N., Krikorian, R., & Cohen, D. (2004). The Internet of things. *Scientific American, 291*(4), 76.

Gubbi, J., Buyya, R., Marusic, S., & Palaniswami, M. (2013). Internet of Things (IoT): A Vision, Architectural Elements, and Future Directions. *Future Generation Computer Systems, 29*, 1645–1660.

Kortuem, G., Kawsar, F., Fitton, D., & Sundramoorthy, V. (2010). Smart objects as building blocks for the Internet of Things. *IEEE Internet Computing, 14*(1), 44–51.

Lagerspetz, E., Flores, H., Mäkitalo, N., Hui, P., Nurmi, P., Tarkoma, S., Passarella, A., Ott, J., Reichl, P., & Conti, M. (2018). Pervasive Communities in the Internet of People. *Proceedings of the 2018 IEEE International Conference on Pervasive Computing and Communications Workshops*, 40–45.

Li, D. X., Wu, H., & Shancang, L. (2014). Internet of Things in Industries: A Survey. *IEEE Transactions on Industrial Informatics*, *10*(4), 2233–2243.

Liu, X., & Sun, Y. (2011). Information flow management of Vendor-Managed Inventory system in automobile parts inbound logistics based on Internet of Things. *Journal of Software*, *6*(7), 1374–1380.

Miorandi, D., Sicari, S., De Pellegrini, F., & Chlamtac, I. (2012). Internet of things: Vision, applications, and research challenges. *Ad Hoc Networks*, *10*, 1497–1516.

Miranda Carpintero, J., Mäkitalo, N., Garcia-Alonso, J., Berrocal, J., Mikkonen, T., Canal, C., & Murillo, J. (2015). From the Internet of Things to the Internet of People. *IEEE Internet Computing*, *19*, 40–47.

Nguyen, X. T., Tran, H. T., Baraki, H., & Geihs, K. (2015). FRASAD: A framework for model-driven IoT application Development. *Internet of Things (WF-IoT), IEEE 2ⁿᵈ World Forum on IoT*, 387-392.

Pal, K. (2017). Supply Chain Coordination Based on Web Services. In H. K. Chan, N. Subramanian, & M. D. Abdulrahman (Eds.), *Supply Chain Management in the Big Data Era* (pp. 137–171). IGI Global Publication.

Pal, K. (2018). A Big Data Framework for Decision Making in Supply Chain. IGI Global.

Pal, K. (2019). Algorithmic Solutions for RFID Tag Anti-Collision Problem in Supply Chain Management. *Procedia Computer Science*, *151*, 929–934.

Pal, K. (2020). Information Sharing for Manufacturing Supply Chain Management Based on Blockchain Technology. In Cross-Industry Use of Blockchain Technology and Opportunities for the Future. IGI Global.

Perera, C., Zaslavsky, A., Christen, P., & Georgakopoulos, D. (2014). Context Aware Computing for The Internet of Things: A Survey. *IEEE Communications Surveys and Tutorials*, *16*, 414–454.

Perera, C., Zaslavsky, A., Christen, P., & Georgakopoulos, D. CA4IOT: Context Awareness for Internet of Things. In *Proceedings of the 2012 IEEE International Conference on Green Computing and Communications*. Besancon, France: IEEE Computer Society.

Person, P., & Angelsmark, O. (2015). Calvin-Merging Cloud and IoT. *Procedia Computer Science*, *52*, 210–217.

Sa De Souza, L. M., Spiess, P., Guinard, D., Kohler, M., Karnouskos, S., & Savio, D. (2008). SOCRADES: A Web Service Based Shop Floor Integration Infrastructure, The Internet of Things. Lecture Notes in Computer Science, 50-67.

Thang, N. X., Zapf, M., & Geihs, K. (2011). Model driven development for data-centric sensor. In Conference on Advances in Mobile Computing and Multimedia. ACM.

Weyrich, M., & Ebert, C. (2016). Reference Architectures for the Internet of Things. *IEEE Software*, *33*, 112–116.

Yaqoob, I., Ahmed, E., Hashem, I. A. T., Ahmed, A. I. A., Gani, A., Imran, M., & Guizani, M. (2017). Internet of Things Architecture: Recent Advances, Taxonomy, Requirements, and Open Challenges. *IEEE Wireless Communications*, *24*, 10–16.

KEY TERMS AND DEFINITIONS

Application Layer: A layer which consists of a set of problem-specific software tools that interact with users, solve problems, process data, and share solutions with other applications.

Communication Layer: A layer which consists of a network of wired/wireless networks, the Internet, and protocols.

Data Service Layer: A layer which consists of private/public cloud and related data management systems.

IoT: The expression "Internet of Things" (IoT), coined back in 1999 by Kevin Ashton, one of co-founder of the Auto-ID Centre at the Massachusetts Institute of Technology, is becoming more and more used in main-stream computing. IoT means "devices or sensors connected world" where things i.e., the smart objects can communicate, monitor surroundings, and take necessary steps to complete certain tasks managed by some external agency or by the connected devices depending on the application context. IoT envisions an eco-system where smart and interconnected objects can sense surrounding changes, communicate with each other, process information and take active roles in decision making.

Microservice: The topic of microservices continues to get significant buzz as businesses build more and more complex solutions. There are many advantages to microservices, and this chapter aggregates them.

Object Layer: A layer which consists of physical objects such as devices, machines, sensors, RFID tags, and readers.

RFID Reader: An RFID transceiver, providing real and possible access to RFID tags information.

RFID Tag: An RFID tag (or transponder), typically consisting of an RF coupling element and a microchip that carries identifying data. Tag functionality may range from simple identification to being able to form ad hoc network.

Service-Oriented Architecture: Service-oriented architecture (SOA) is a style of software design where services are provided to the other components by application components, through a communication protocol over a network. A SOA service is a discrete unit of functionality that can be accessed remotely and acted upon and updated independently, such as retrieving a credit card statement online. SOA is also intended to be independent of vendors, products, and technologies.

Supply Chain Management: Supply chain management encompasses the planning and management of all activities involved in sourcing, procurement, manufacturing, and distribution. Importantly, it also includes coordination and collaboration with channel partners, which can be suppliers, intermediaries, third party service providers, and customers. In essence, supply chain management integrates supply and demand management within and across companies.

Web Ontology Language (OWL): The Web Ontology Language (OWL) is a semantic mark-up language for publishing and sharing ontologies on the Web. OWL is developed as a vocabulary extension of RDF (the Resource Description Framework) and is derived from the DAML + OIL Web Ontology Language.

Section 2
Applications

Chapter 7
Semantic Medical Image Analysis:
An Alternative to Cross-Domain Transfer Learning

Joy Nkechinyere Olawuyi
(iD) https://orcid.org/0000-0003-0385-9788
Adeyemi College of Education, Nigeria

Bernard Ijesunor Akhigbe
(iD) https://orcid.org/0000-0002-0241-4739
Department of Computer Science & Engineering, Obafemi Awolowo University, Nigeria

Babajide Samuel Afolabi
Obafemi Awolowo University, Nigeria

Attoh Okine
University of Delaware, USA

ABSTRACT

The recent advancement in imaging technology, together with the hierarchical feature representation capability of deep learning models, has led to the popularization of deep learning models. Thus, research tends towards the use of deep neural networks as against the hand-crafted machine learning algorithms for solving computational problems involving medical images analysis. This limitation has led to the use of features extracted from non-medical data for training models for medical image analysis, considered optimal for practical implementation in clinical setting because medical images contain semantic contents that are different from that of natural images. Therefore, there is need for an alternative to cross-domain feature-learning. Hence, this chapter discusses the possible ways of harnessing domain-specific features which have semantic contents for development of deep learning models.

DOI: 10.4018/978-1-7998-6697-8.ch007

INTRODUCTION

Semantic Medical Image Analysis (SMIA) might be the "next big thing" in scientific computing (SC) within the context of the healthcare industry basically because its analytics is contingent on semantics in its entirety (i.e. Intention, Meaning, and Context (IMC)). In SMIA resources such as processes, data, tools, document, device, people will be attended to. In the context of Semantic Computing (SC), SMIA is scoped around analytics, integration, description languages for semantics, and interfaces, etc. Additionally, applications that include biomedical systems, SDN, IoT, wearable computing, cloud computing, context awareness, mobile computing, big data, search engines, question answering, multimedia, and services will draw on SC in the 21st century to influence SMIA. The presentation in Table 1 shows what these applications will contribute to (or draw on) SC and aggregate impact on SMIA, which Machine Learning (ML) will benefit from. The sign (Í) show that IMC cannot be applied nor relevant, while (ü) shows it can be applied or relevant.

Table 1. Application and their contribution to SC and aggregate impact on SMIA

Application Type	Contribution To SC	Use SC	Applied to Introduce		
			intention	meaning	context
Biomedical systems	Make data available	Provide semantic wherewithal To support or implement semantic Retrieval	✗	✓	✗
IoT	Make data available from disparate sources	Solve interoperability problem	✗	✓	✓
SDN	Provide room for semantic failover	To cater for collective intelligence	✓	✗	✓
Context Awareness	Provide the context for SC to derive its meaning	To Make context explicit	✓	✓	✓
Wearable Computing	Provide user context's Information	To ensure contexts are interoperable	✓	✓	✓
Cloud Computing	Makes computing Resources available	Helps to achieve portability & interoperability	✓	✓	✓
Big Data	Provide Deep learning Resources & make sense of data	Support meaningful data analytics	✓	✓	✓
Multimedia	Help retrieval of content	To use context to reach varied audience	✗	✗	✓
Question Answering	Provide underlying Framework for SC	Provide deep semantic parsing to get the right response across	✗	✓	✓

*SMIA (Semantic Medical Image Analysis); SC (Semantic Computing)

SMIA rely on Machine Learning Algorithms (MLA) to build implementable models using sample data. These sample data are "training data," which provide the knowledge to train a model or algorithm to have its own information (i.e. experience) to predict outcomes accurately. This happens after training a model without necessarily programming it explicitly to perform the predictive task (Zhang, 2020). Where SC comes in is in the area of understandable insight and applicable intelligence. As such, SC complements MLA to handle the provision of intelligence and insight from data, which the traditional MLachine learning techniques cannot handle.

As is, there has been an explosion in the production of Medical Images (Med-I). This upsurge resulted from the use of Advanced Biomedical Data Collection Devices (ABDCD) that operate digitally with increased throughput (Shung *et al,* 1992; Razzak *et al,* 2018). Though, fueled by the current digital technological revolution, it came with its challenge. For example, in the pre-explosive era of Med-I production the volume of data that exist were easily annotated because they were few with manageable human annotation error. However, in this explosive era it has increasingly become difficult to manage this human error because of the huge volume of Med-I that are still annotated manually. The use of the traditional machine learning technique (i.e. algorithm) has fared well in the tasks of medical image analysis despite the massive volume of data produced by ABDCD that it handles per time. However, despite this successful shift in the paradigm of using computational machine learning models to solve the problem of annotation considering the huge volume of available Med-I data, there is still a disconnect regarding the semantic interpretation of the outcome of such annotation. This lack of interpretive disconnection still make it necessary to augment diagnostic results from High Performing Computational Models (HPCM) with human opinion before decisions are made.

This book chapter makes its contribution by means of presenting a discourse that encapsulates the thematic of ML within the context of SC to facilitate the understanding of medical image analysis through the lens of Deep Learning Techniques (DLT) as an example progressive ML. DLT is a progressive (i.e. advanced) ML technique that is open to exploitation in sundry area of application with benefits that far outweigh that of the traditional ML (tML). As is, its potentials are yet to be fully tapped. One of the major causes of this is the inherent domain-specific challenges that its use is fraught with, which often hinders its application in the development of computational models. The unavailability of professional ground truth or correctly annotated medical data further exacerbate this challenge. It is imperative to now consider the use of DLT since SC can be leveraged in synergy with it to offer the means to crunch the volume of data produced by ABDCD and also provide semantic interpretation of results. With this position, we are optimistic that the challenge of never having sufficient number of qualified personnel to annotate Med-I individually (Lopes and Valiali, 2017) will be a thing of the past.

CONCEPT AND DIFFERENCES OF THE STUDY THEMATIC

This section presents the concept of machine learning from the traditional and progressive perspective within the context of semantic computing. From this concept it is hoped that a better understanding of the synergistic benefits of using the progressive MLA in the healthcare sector with Med-I during the 21st century will be understood in such a way that further research is stimulated regarding the use of DLT within the context of SC.

Traditional Machine Learning

Machine learning is a technology with mathematical and algorithm-based inclinations and a subset of Artificial Intelligence (AI). Based on this mathematical tendency it is applied to build models using sample data. Support vector machines, neural networks, and evolutionary computational entailments, etc form the backbone of MLT. When implementing MLT, a test and training set are often given. This union has implication, which means that there are unlabeled set of example data that are available to machine learners and the labeled set (Zhang, 2020). This computational resourcefulness has made MLT models invaluable to sundry industries. This includes that of the healthcare and other stakeholders in the academia and individuals because it helps to improve targeted outcomes, with reduced cost (Kohli *et al*, 2017) and clinical errors in the healthcare sector. MLT can be relied on to screen large amount of variables to find patterns that accurately predict results (Li and Xu, 2020). Some examples of the traditional MLT are Dimensionality Reduction Technique (DRT), regression, clustering, and classification methods. In the context of this work, "traditional" means the foundational or basic MLT to draw from to get more advanced MLT like transfer learning, ensemble methods, reinforcement learning, and neural networks and deep learning.

The traditional MLTs have issues with their complex network vis-à-vis their setting parameters and training time, as well as leaning time (Chen *et al.,* 2020a). The formal structures (i.e. machines) that MLT has allows it to do learning (i.e. make inference) – a.k.a. model building. This connotes the proposition of expressions that mathematically encapsulate the mechanism through which physical processes lead to observations. Some of the many techniques employed in the use of MLT produce information after processing from data, but do not exactly tally with physical modeling. The information referred to, in this context typically infers whatever assists in the reduction of uncertainty. This explain why a distribution of posterior proportions may characterize "information" or a "learner" since it moderates by way of reducing the uncertainty about a parameter. Parameters in MLT are influencers; hence to increase the sample size of a dataset may give smaller standard errors. However, a focus on "the model" puts uncertainty on the parameters vice versa. MLT settings remain that of high-variability. This orchestrates dealings with the measure of central tendency of uncertainty. So, dealing with the uncertainty of model even carefully usually results in a dominant issue that is tested only by predictive criteria (Clarke *et al.,* 2009; Chen *et al.,* 2020a)

Deep Learning

Learning techniques such as transfer learning, ensemble methods, reinforcement learning, and neural networks and deep learning are more advanced MLT than the traditional MLTs. The traditional MLTs engage in reducing variables at random to obtain set of key variables (i.e. DRT), group observations with related characteristics (i.e. clustering), predict specific values using prior data (regression), and explains a class value that are discrete - that is estimate the prospect of the occurrence of events using data (i.e. classification) (Lisowski, 2020; Li and Xu, 2020). However, advance MLT such as DLT captures patterns that are non-linear in data by means of adding parameters in layers to develop MLT models. They use more layers to foster levels of high abstraction to improve predictions from data inputs. With neural networks DLT finds useful associations amongst a set of outputs and corresponding inputs. The DLT is a subfield of MLT and unlike other MLTs, the intelligence it powers is more huma-like hence it allows the training of agents using data to increase performance (Grossfeld, 2020). DLT's training time, learning speed, and accuracy are the principal features of extended MLT like the DLT (Chen *et al.,* 2020a).

The DLT provide an intelligent model development method that bridges the gap, which exists between the use of insufficient datasets and data-hungry computational models. It particularly offers the opportunity to leapfrog the process of building a new network entirely from the scratch. At this point, self-learning and tuning emerges. These capabilities is what the network of deep learning bring on to complementarily adjust to usually new but similar tasks. The capacity to add new layers and adjust to existing ones make adapting to new tasks possible and learning seamless (Lisowski, 2020; Mazurowski *et al.*, 2019). DLT has been used successfully with non-Med-I data (Li and Xu, 2020). Moreover, there are still more possibilities with its applications. In the healthcare sector MLT is gradually gaining the attention it deserves since its algorithms can examine a large number of variables to discover groupings from which reliable prediction can be made. In Li and Xu, 2020), this procedure of ML was reported to improve prognosis, and its outcome capable of replacing most of the efforts of anatomical pathologists and radiologists to improve diagnosis with high accuracy.

One of the major position highlighted in this work is the understanding that the successful application of MLT to non-medical data and medical data alike (Li and Xu, 2020) has left sufficient Ground Truth (GT). This GT can provide leapfrogging opportunity to harness the DLT to analyze Med-I data. Previously what obtains regarding the analysis of med-I data is to use known features and their semantics from non-medical data to analyze them. This practice is known as cross-domain transfer learning since known features and semantics of non-medical data were applied in this instance to gain insight into the anatomical structure and features of the medical images for their analysis. This "transfer learning" strategy supports the development of high-performance models of medical image analysis using negligible domain-specific data. However, the end-result is not verifiable (Samek *et al*, 2017), hence the need consider an alternative, which this work identifies as the DLT. Based on existing GT as highlighted earlier this work makes its contribution by underscoring the potentials of MLT as a suitable alternative to cross-domain transfer learning for Med-I analysis by a confluence of SC and DLT. Figure 1 shows pictorially the difference between the traditional MLT and the DLT.

Figure 1. A pictorial difference between the traditional MLT and the DLT (Adapted from source: Mazurowski et al., 2019; O'Mahony et al., 2019)

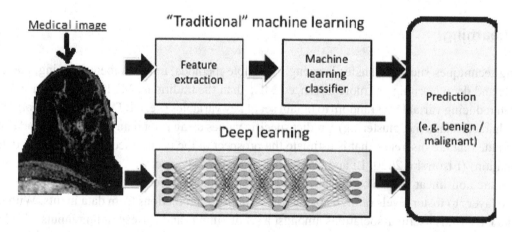

In Mazurowski *et al.* (2019) one of the most achievements of the DLT was reported as being it fared in the classification of ImageNet database that has 14 million natural image annotations (image-net.org) with error rate result that shows its performance to be better when compared to that of humans. Similarly, there are large collections of medical images such as the one from Diagnostic Imaging Dataset Statistical released in 2020 with more than 40 million imaging tests (NHS, 2020). However, the traditional MLTs are inadequate in their capacity to process large volume of data. In Yuan *et al.* (2020), the barrier to

DLT adoption even in the health industry was stressed. The issue of using computational capabilities that are advanced regarding the development of high-tech graphics' and central processing units were highlighted. The integration of big data aspect of Med-I data since DLT is suitable for Med-I and the development of learning algorithms with new trajectories are impediments to be overcomed for DLT to be fully embraced. The medical domain is data-rich enough to keep-off the cross-domain transfer learning.

= Semantic Computing

It is in Semantic Computing (SC) that issues of derivation, integration, description, and the use of semantics (i.e. context, meaning, intention) for all types of data and other resources, device, tool, process, document and people are addressed. The study of SC includes computing technologies such as NLP, AI, software engineering, natural language, data and knowledge engineering, computer systems, signal processing, etc.), and their interactions. These technologies are either engaged to extract or process contents computationally. In this sense the connection that exists between the user of these technologies and the content pushed by them is made through Semantic Analysis (SA). SA is about getting these contents analyzed with the sole purpose of transforming them to machine process-able descriptions (i.e. semantics). This may include semantic integration that incorporates semantics from several sources and content; semantic applications that use the content and its descriptions to handle difficulties; and the semantic Interface that takes users' intentions and interprets them with appropriate expressions any suitable communicative forms or in natural language. If there is a reverse connection, and should it exists users intentions to create content via synthesis and analysis must be recognized and supported (Sheu, 2017). This will foster better user experience particularly when inferentials are to be made.

In the study that involves SC, the design, structure, and handling of digital contents and related technologies to get it done be it natural language processing, AI, and software engineering, etc the end goal is to satisfy the intentions expressed in the needs of users and create better user experience. In the domain of Med-I data analysis the conception of user experience should be about semantics. Being able to make sense out of the data extracted from volumes of Med-I data; interestingly without manual annotation. So, based on the literature semantics is still about annotation in the context of leveraging the features in images for inductive gains (i.e. leveraging observation to reach satisfactory and lifesaving conclusions) (O'Mahony *et al.*, 2019). Therefore as demonstrated in the literature, semantics in the context of Med-I analysis is more than syntax. Syntax entail the manipulation of symbols, but pragmatically the connection of the symbols in a definable way to the users, and the interactions of the symbol with the external world need to be understood. Semantics is about the expressions of states of affairs (i.e. objects) using a language and the certain relations between them. That semantics in general terms is "meaning" particularly of sentences has been identified to be vague (Bołtuc, 2018). In Boltuc (2018), it was debated that should such "meaning" result from the dealings (i.e. interaction) between the real world and users then semantics would definitely be within the context of pragmatics.

Within the context of semantic medical image data analysis as an alternative to the use of cross-domain transfer learning for data analysis the goal is to achieve pragmatism. Effort should be made to avoid the "meaning", which comes from the manipulation of advanced symbols, since it puts the concept of semantics within the context of syntax. To achieve the pragmatic sense of semantic, which is closer to humans, the network approach was recommended as a good start. This is because of the knowledge they form representatively to reconstruct meaning as they relate to concepts.

The Confluence between Semantic Computing and Machine Learning

There a resourceful synergy with the confluence of MLT and SC. In respect of the DLT this synergy is important since it seeks to take annotation out of the hands of Qualified Medical Personnel (QMP). Considering the huge number of Med-I to be annotated the number of QMP is not even adequate for the tasks (Lopes and Valiali, 2017). This makes it necessary to leverage the DLT. Aside from resolving the challenge of annotation automatically, the other advantage of the confluence is the analytic benefit of deploying DLT. This makes the relationship between the DLT and SC symbiotic. The DLT is fittingly employed in the digital domain of image processing to handle difficult problems such as image classification, colourization, segmentation, and detection etc. This is because the technique of DL such as Convolutional Neural Networks (CNN) has been shown to improve the performance of prediction. Moreover, as O'Mahony *et al.* (2019) puts it, both big data and "plentiful" computing resources are needed to make this performance a reality with "super-human accuracy". With the DLT the concept of end-to-end learning is introduced by means of giving the machine a dataset of images that is already annotated. SC can be integrated through the use of semantic annotation-based system to first annotate a given Med-I dataset before feeding it into the computer.

The pursuit of a data driven confluence of techniques with the DLT has been identified. The need for this pursuit was motivated by 1) DLT require lots of data to avoid the development of overfitting model, and 2) to integrate strong connotations regarding semantics data is also the way to go. So, data which is supposed to be a problem in several domains is fortunately not a problem in the health section particularly for semantic medical analysis. Well, for domains where data is a challenge overfitting is resolve by artificially enlarging the dataset using transformations that are label-preserving (O'Mahony *et al.*, 2019). A few approach has been suggested in the literature regarding how to commit in terms of integrating the human level of semantics into machines. In Boltuc (2018) Phenomenal Maps (MP) were suggested as capable of raising machine level of semantic to that of the level of humans. As against the use of phenomenal maps, the syntactic method of communication are not able to raise the semantic level of machines to be comparable to that of humans. Broadly and perceptual as well as activity-based conceptual framework can address this weaknesses. To deliver on MP level of human-like semantics big data analysis (Bandari, 2013) that integrate with external, kinetic, internal are required.

Conceptual or phenomenal maps are suggested as the panacea for weak semantic computing. This is because when applied machines would be help to learn but larger steps can still be taken with more research in the use of MPs. This way semantic computing that is extra strong can be achieved based on MP, and Spinozian maps, etc. These maps are useful in realizing a broader than human phenomenal/perceptual knowledge and ability to process information. A lot of available materials are available for further reading and interested readers are encourage to read them.

STATE-OF-THE-ART OF DEEP LEARNING AND SEMANTIC COMPUTING

This section contains review of the literature in respect of the technique (i.e. method) of DL and SC. The focus is on the state of the art of both techniques in terms of the progress made in the field of computing especially regarding image analysis and by extension Med-I data analysis. This is also expected to highlight the relevance of the integrating techniques in SC and DLT as alternative to the cross-domain approach Med-I data analysis.

Deep Learning Method

The task of analysing data from medical images is daunting, particularly when the volume of image data is on the high side. However the use of machine learning methods is age-long and has contributed making the process better and faster. Before the widespread use of DL methods, the traditional ML algorithms have been used applied. In Carrillo-de-Gea *et al.* (2016) the technique of local binary pattern texture operator was applied to conduct feature for feature segmentation of images. Chest X-Rays (CXR) were successfully classified into normal and pathological features. The application of deep CNN in medical image analysis started with the work of Zhang *et al.* (1994) and Chan *et al.* (1995) with focus on detecting micro-calcification in digital mammography and lung nodules from Computed Tomography (CT) images. Deep learning for chest diagnosis has been documented as studied in Rajpurkar *et al.* (2018). A retrospective comparison of CheXNeXt algorithm to help practicing Radiologist using a CNN model to detect fourteen (14) pathologies from CXR was made. This approach was used on the ChestXray8 dataset. In a similar research work, Tajbakhsh *et al.* (2016) experimented with medical images of different modality to show that pre-trained and trained CNN are capable of satisfactory performance even in the worst case scenario, and when trained from the scratch and fine-tuned the CNNs showed robust attribute to the size of the training datasets. The importance of using large data set for training CNN models from scratch was highlighted in Bar *et al.* (2015), while in Lakhani and Sundaram (2017) using deep CNNs approach the effect of using a very small dataset was reported to hinder the full training of a deep CNN and thus amount to underutilization of its computing network resources.

The other progresses made with the deep CNN include the use of a single trained end-to-end deep CNN to classify skin lesions to identify common cancers (Esteva *et al.*, 2017); the identification of class imbalance in dataset by cascading network models (Kumar and Prabhakar, 2017); the transfer of cross-domain learning on medical images without fine-tuning nor training of dedicated X-ray network from scratch (Baltruschat *et al.*, 2019); the use of deep CNN to detect abnormality and localize them in CXR (Islam *et al.*, 2017); the use of an esemble of deep CNN and Gray-Level co-occurrence matrix to offer the computational resource of a fusion of statistics and multilayer perceptron to extract features (Lai and Deng, 2018); and the use of trained CNN to show that the use of higher image size will produce better validation with minimal training error (Stephen *et al.*, 2019), etc. Other more recent progresses include the use of more novel approach to extend the computational power of DL for image analysis. In Yuan *et al.* (2020) the challenge in using inadequate data, which leads to generalizability concerns and lack of robustness was overcomed through the use of physics-informed learning that uses domain knowledge and process learning as potential remedy. In a similar research an Extreme Method of Learning Algorithm (EMoLA) was proposed by Chen *et al.* (2020a). As a classification method it relied on the polarization decomposition of target technique to assist deep CNN. It made up for the shortcomings of traditional ML network setting, which parameters are complex and training time is discouraging. Previously, Deng *et al.* (2019) and Xu *et al.* (2018) had applied the active learning and DL methods and the method of target decomposition to extract marker samples from polarized images of synthetic aperture radar to find out which feature is effective. Concerns of training time, learning speed, and good accuracy were issues to contend with. However, they became the biggest features and successes of the EMoLA proposed by Chen *et al.* (2020a).

The relevance of DL as an alternative to cross domain learning in semantic Med-I analysis based on the presentations in the foregoing section is in its use for sundry data analysis based on image data. DL can be extended to accommodate other techniques as demonstrated in Yuan *et al.* (2020), Chen *et al.*

(2020a), Deng *et al.* (2019) and Xu *et al.* (2018), etc to achieve better result. This makes the DL technique most useful for Med-I analysis. Before trying a DL - based model on Med-I data there are several image dataset to try the model on. Previously, this was difficult to come by. Therefore, interest in Med-I research with focus on training from scratch is gaining momentum to understanding more about training from the scratch, which already ensures the extraction of domain-specific semantic content of Med-I data. Being a data-hungry technique, the DLT would fare well in this 21 century due to the existence of big data realisation for which there are sufficient grand truth to use data (Bar *et al*, 2015). However, the non-existence of sufficient Ground Truth (GT) to handle the analysis of Med-I still remain a challenge, although it is already receiving attention. GT is usually provided by practicing radiologists who provide the through the annotations of medical images. This present another area of interesting research since the analysis of medical images from a very vantage position require an expensive generation ground truth, which is still almost done of manually (Foncubieta and Muller, 2012). This raises the question of who calls for a proactive look into this challenge since both data availability and GT are important for better Med-I data analysis. This is where this work comes in by highlighting the challenge in the absence of these ingredients - data availability and GT, which is under performance. The submission therefore is that it does not matter how fantastic the DL model is performing in terms of training and learning time, and other metrics.

Semantic Computing for Medical Image Data Analysis

The development of computational models in the era of big data for Med-I analysis has been draggy. This is because of the absence of correctly annotated medical data or professional ground truth. In big data analytics semantics is important. To this end efforts have been made from the onset of image analysis even from within the context of big data conception, which is facilitated with DL to extract high level complex abstraction. This underscores the usefulness of semantic in the analysis of images and Med-I analysis is no exception. In Taouli *et al.* (2018) the different stages at which semantics can be integrated into large-scale processing of images to extract high level complex features at reduced size while preserving characteristics that are important was identified. The place of annotation to achieve high performing computational models in medical image analysis was highlighted in Lopes and Valiali (2017). However, annotation is still supported by non-medical image data, which serves as the basis for "transfer learning". The implication for this is to develop models by using semantic features transferred from non-Med-I databases such as ImageNet that comprises images of natural objects. In Bar *et al.* (2015) this was accomplished using pre-trained weights and this gave good performance using a combination of features that are representative of semantic contents. The semantic contents were introduced by extraction from the CNN and a set of low-level features. These low-level features were incorporated from Med-I (domain features). For knowledge transfer to be accepted from non-medical dataset for the recognition of medical images sufficient semantic details are to be taken seriously.

Other ways of ensuring the presence of the level of semantic details that is okay to support satisfactory SC when in confluence with the use of DL in Med-I analysis are also documented in the literature. Lai and Deng (2018) in their scientific contribution to this studied medical image classification. Their goal was to show that deep features that are extracted using deep model and a fusion of statistic feature and multilayer perceptron can be used to introduce SC to allow semantic features to be adjusted automatically in sufficient proportion to enforce strong semantic. In Shin *et al.* (2016) the application of training a DL model from the scratch to ensure the incorporation of domain-specific semantic content by means of extraction was highlighted. This work supported the claim that Med-I can be trained solely using deep learning models without the need of transferring learned features from a non-medial domain. This consideration is entrenched in the concept of "training from scratch". For SC with DLT semantic contents of Med-I could be extracted both at lower layers of the deep NN and at the higher layers particularly for prediction purposes. However, a standard Med-I dataset for an ML application so as to get expected result should have adequate data volume, annotation and truth (to incorporate semantic), and ensure reusability (Kohli *et al,* 2016). The digital collection of Med-I to allow online annotation is a brilliant idea that can stimulate more research in using annotation to support semantic Med-I analysis.

Aside from the use of annotation to introduce semantic in Med-I data analysis, other approaches have been used. In Taouli *et al.* (2018) a semantic memory that enables the semantic cataloguing of data such that the characteristics of value and quality are identified was proposed. The troubling tasks of semantic segmentation of dataset annotation has been was highlighted O'Mahony *et al.* (2019). This motivates the need to develop automatic semantic segmentation. Recent studies like that of Alalwan *et al.* (2020) in their contribution recognized the importance of Med-I segmentation to support medical decision systems and assist with disease diagnosis. They then proposed a 3D DL model for semantic segmentation with significantly lower trainable and deeper network parameters. The work avoided the use of the traditional CNN and used depth-wise separable convolution which successfully produce effective results and preserved low-level features. Makris *et al.* (2020) in a similar study applied a semantic ontology network for information representation to aid the semantic retrieval of features within the context of named entity disambiguation, which is reproducible for SC and DL in Med-I analysis. In Chen *et al.* (2020b) a means by which useful semantic relation are extracted from patents' documents were proposed. Although, it focus was on contents from non-image documents, the researchers used DLT thus underscoring its potential to work in synergy with other techniques to help bridge the semantic deficient in disease's diagnosis during prognosis in the medical profession. In Kulmanov *et al.* (2020) the significance of ontology was emphasized as capable of provide the computational resource to incorporate semantic through semantic similarity in ML.

The literature is inundated with research work that are motivated by the need to automate the way semantics within the context of SC are incorporated into the computational analysis of images. The use of annotation is more in this regard, thus affirming the fact that it's a technique to look out as researchers consider the effect of the confluence between the use of SC and DLT for Med-I data analysis.

METHODOLOGY

This book chapter is more of presenting a thematic position in respect of the necessary desire to seek an alternative to the use of cross-domain transfer learning in the analysis of Med-I. So far, it is clear that a burgeoning amount of Med-Image data and suitable technique(s) that is synergistic in nature is available for gainful use. This makes it imperative to call the attention of researchers particularly in Med-I analysis and other stakeholders to pay attention to the computational resources that is possible by means of a confluence between DLT and SC in the semantic analysis of Med-I. This section therefore presents a position on possible methodology to draw from to realise the benefits of using the DLT to develop models that can be applied for Med-I analysis.

METHOD

Proposed Methodology

The training of deep learning models from scratch is a huge step towards the elimination of transfer learning, particularly cross-domain transfer learning. Its technicalities allows the extraction of semantic contents and domain specific features for Med-I analysis. The CNN algorithm is proposed as useful in the extraction of salient Med-I features. These features based on other AI usable techniques should be engaged to ensure the analysis of semantic contents to support diagnostic decision making. The Med-I are fed into the earlier layers of the CNN for the purpose of feature extraction. The extracted features are used to determine if there are abnormalities in a test image at the later layers of the network. This proposed approach relieve the challenge of existing methodology that rely on cross-domain transfer learning. With the deep CNN domain-specific transfer learning is proposed.

One of the advantages of transfer learning is having not to learn from the beginning (earlier layers), but later (from higher) layers using the features or patterns from an already existing architecture. This is the gainful expectation in the use of the proposed deep CNN as alternative to cross-domain transfer learning. This proposed methodology supports domain-specific transfer learning, which is consistent with presentation in Mazurowski et al. (2019). The uniqueness of our proposal is that it would allow the earlier layers to extract general characteristics, while the higher (later) layers in synergy will identify complex features. The technique proposed is consistent with what obtains in Mazurowski *et al.* (2019), which was extended in Alalwan *et al.* (2020). Some of the suggested AI-friendly semantic techniques that could be used with the method proposed herein include semantic hashing method, latent semantic analysis, the multi-stain technique that uses bags of word, word hash, and n-gram, etc. Other compatible techniques can be found in the literature (e.g. Taouli *et al.,* 2018).

Documented Methodology

Here we present a few tried and useful methodology of how to carry out DL experiment with the context of Med-I analysis drawing from content (i.e. image) processing and other content (i.e. text) extraction routine for analytic purpose. Inductive learning is particularly encouraged since it is more semantically inclined to deliver strong semantic (Boltuc, 2018) for predictive purpose than the syntactic oriented aspect.

Text-Based DL Semantic Model

The frameworks presented in Chen *et al.* (2020b) fit into this type of model that describes a methodology that guides the development of a DL model, which is helpful in the extraction of semantic features - information from patent documents. The frameworks (see 2a & b) presented in two part - the first framework expressed the characteristic modules for semantic and entity relation recognition as shown in Figure 2a, while the second methodological framework shown in Figure 2b presented the technicalities to verify the characteristics highlighted in Figure 2a. The methodology is novel since the extraction process it typifies were divided into sub-tasks in series of organized pipeline process with the sub-tasks functionally defined as independently as possible to each other. This made it its modularity much better than what exists as described in Chen *et al.* (2020b). On implementation the model demonstrated the ability to relieve the manual rules and human intervention with it domain vocabulary. As shown, once a dataset with sufficient annotation is done along with training for information extraction valuable information and patent attributes were automatically extracted with high accuracy. The motivation to present the model in Figure 2 stems from its novelty and as a recent contribution that show how DL and semantic process automation can be applied to extract patent information from a dataset. Then it was also demonstrated with reproducible result to be better than the traditional methodology that existed before it. However, the caveat of note is to ensure that the corpus to apply in using the methodology has in addition to entity annotations, the semantic relations that ought to exist between entities are well annotated.

Image-Based DL Semantic Model 1

DLT works well with other AI algorithms and its combination with DLT was proposed in Mazurowski *et al.* (2019) and highlighted as having the potential to tremendous influence radiology practice. This scenario to deploy this AI-DLT driven methodology is that in which nearly all or all primary data that is to be utilized in Med-I data analysis is digital. This makes it easy for the SC involving DLT and AI to operate analytically. The work of a radiologist for instance is quite mundane and laborious. It stems from detection of disease from images, diagnosis, and then characterization. The tasks of colocalization presents another round of tasks of interpretation of imaging inspection as a follow-up to previous interventions. This often may require subjective and/or objective assessment. DLT offers the methodological choice to help classify radiological data (see Figure 3). The CNN provision in the DLT offers varying convolutional layers that are connected fully to handle the acquisition variabilities that image classification entail. These variabilities are – variability in patient anatomy and positioning and between examinations, and variability in labeling and modalities to determine anatomic portion for examination. While DLT is particularly significant is that it makes it possible to rely on transfer learning using the shelf features. This significance is reliant on the position already maintained in principle in this work that DLT and SC even in confluence with AI algorithms could be used intelligent to assess the prior imaging of patients, and make valid representation in contrast type and modality as well as determine the location that is of interest to enable smooth prognosis and this will radically reduce the routine tasks of the radiologist. Extended details about the workings of the methodology summarized in Figure 3 are available in Mazurowski *et al.* (2019).

Image-Based DL Semantic Model 2

The methodology applied in Alalwan *et al.* (2020) demonstrates significant improvement from the traditional convolutional methods of the deep CNN. The traditional manual and/or semi-manual segmentation methods that are meant to analyze Med-I to diagnose both tumor and liver cancer are time-consuming and highly subjective and thus prone to error. This motivated the application of the semantic method shown in Figure 4. It uses the philosophy of Med-I segmentation that is realised by an efficient deep learning 3D semantic model of segmentation. The method has a deeper network that is significantly different from the traditional convolution and has considerable lower parameters that are trainable. The depth-wise separable convolution it adopts makes it also different from the traditional DLT. It is advantageous in that its GPU memory requirements are decreased with less cost of computation to achieve high performance. The methods satisfied the cardinal goal of Med-I data analysis, which is to produce effective results while preserving low-level features. In relation to related studies that have used deep CNN this methodology is effective as well as efficient. The details of how to apply this methodology is available for further study in Alalwan *et al.* (2020).

Figure 2. a and b Implementable methodology for semantic Med-I analysis (adapted from Chen et al., 2020b)

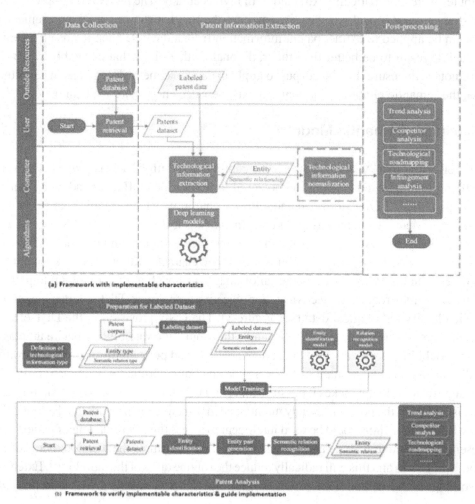

DISCUSSION OF METHODOLOGIES AND FUTURE OF DL WITH SEMANTIC COMPUTING

The literature in respect of Semantic Med-I analysis inundated with techniques that perform at various performance level. The first methodology presented in Figure 2 (a & b) presents the technicalities to use DL to extract semantic attributes that translate easily to information from patent documents. Although this work did not apply Med-I data it highlighted the use of DLT in an experimental for such that the work showed a framework that is capable of reproducibility for further studies. Other researchers can leverage the framework to guide the development of an automated and accurate as well as a capable method of extracting fine-grained information using DLT within the context of SC. While the method by Chen *et al.* (2020b) shown in Figure 2 is from a pragmatic context, the one in Figure 3 is hypothetic. However, the deep learning content and descriptions that yielded result in Figure 2 support the hypothetical approach by Mazurowski *et al.* (2019) presented in Figure 3 that the level of DLT presented though hypothetically can be applied in the real sense. The third methodology by Alalwan *et al.* (2020) in Figure 4 reveal the possibility of hybridizing the deep CNN with usable AI algorithms to handle aspects of the CNN which is in consonant with the hypothetical claim in the method shown in Figure 3 - the method proposed by Mazurowski *et al.* (2019). The advantages exhibited by the method presented in Alalwan *et al.* (2020), which summary is shown in Figure 4 resulted from the use of both DenseNets and UNet links and connections. So, fast training and accurate result is achieved and low-level features maintained. There is also decreased pooling in the pooling layer since standard convolution is adopted with strides. This decreases memory usage and resolution is maintained. Depth-wise convolution that is separable is adopted and this also decreases memory ingestion and computation performance is improved. This work is consistent with the proposition in the literature (Chen *et al.*, 2020b) to uphold the task of semantic segmentation with improved convolution using conformable AI techniques.

Figure 3. An intelligent Deep LT methodological framework for SMIA (adapted from Mazurowski et al., 2019)

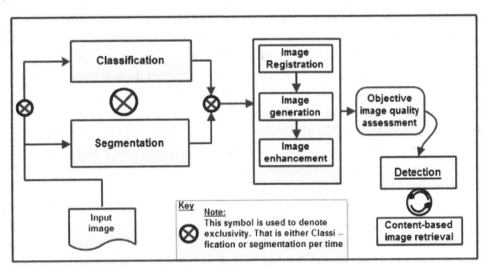

Figure 4. A Proposed methodological 3D Architecture of SMIA for disease (e.g. Tumor & live) Segmentation (adapted from Alalwan et al., 2020)

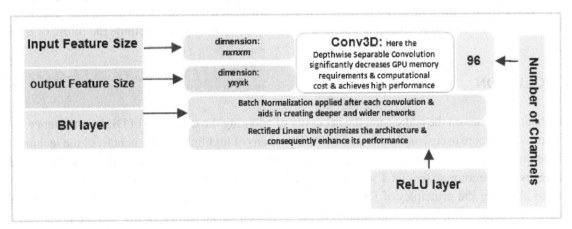

Aside from the existence of reusable methodologies for deep CNN with information on extensibility of the methods, there are useful methodologies too regarding the incorporation of semantics. In Taouli *et al.* (2018) the use of a semantic memory was introduced with a Deep CNN. The approach was proposed to facilitate the characteristic of quality and value through semantic data classification. The semantic memory, which satisfies SC requirements is responsible for coordinating searches that reveals hidden semantics in Med-I. It can also extract features that are complex and of high level quality at reduced size while ensuring the preservation of important characteristics. The work also highlighted the finding that it is possible for such semantic memory to determine images that are associated with other images, which share similar semantic aspects. The research effort in Taouli *et al.* (2018) is particularly significant in this presentation in that SMIA as the "next big thing" particularly in the health section cannot thrive without big data conception. The support the position in this work therefore that the semantic aspect of SMIA can be tied to big data analytics. With this conception semantic can be introduced at strategic position in the DL model.

DLT no doubt will play a key role in SMIA. The future is even now considering the rate at which newer technicalities and use of DLT because of its extensibility are showing up in the literature (Taouli *et al.*, 2018; Mazurowski *et al.*, 2019; Alalwan *et al.*, 2020; Chen *et al.*, 2020a & b). As is there is the possibility that with much research in the use of AI-based techniques for SMIA the mundane tasks of radiologists and other stakeholders who rely on Med-I for diagnosis would be taken over so that they can be committed to other intellectual task that are also important. Even if these stakeholders would need to work hand in hand with the systems that uses DLT the performance of both of them would be better than their individual performance. The aim of any software or innovative and automated technology is not to replace those who have been manually committed to solving the problem technologies are meant to handle. As it were, the technologies are meant to complement them. As befittingly important as the technology highlighted so far sounds for SMIA, there are some challenges to overcome. There are ethical as well as legal challenges to overcome. As Mazurowski *et al.* (2019) puts it, somebody must be responsible for the mistake the computer may make when using the DLT formulated and implemented. As much as this can also be left for research answers, the issue of being able to deploy technology to take over all the tasks of humans is still far from being accomplished. It is also not possible to take over the entire scope of the diagnostic work (i.e. tasks) of stakeholders. It is therefore, not yet uhuru since much work is still needed to change this scope and the green light is visible already showing that it is possible to change this possibility going by by the rapid progress made so far regarding the use of DLT in this context of discourse. Aside from regulatory issues, the question of whether patients will acceptance that humans will be freed from getting involved in their diagnosis and report interpretation is another question to answer. These challenges are crucial in that how they are attended to will determine the future of SMIA

CONCLUSION

This chapter focuses on the addressing the necessity of adopting the technique of DL in confluence with SC to provide a more useful method to do SMIA. By means of highlighting the benefit of the techniques and the presentation of recently used methodologies and discussing the future of DLT and SC and the challenges to overcome so that DLT will be accepted this goal has been addressed. Finally, the concepts so as to highlight the principles of DLT and associated techniques, the progress (i.e. state-of-the-art) made in respect of SMIA, and what obtains in the workflow of stakeholders who handle prognosis on a daily basis. The type of variabilities they face and need to deal with have also been highlighted. It is therefore important to present our submission that DLT in confluence with other AI-based techniques and SC has the capacity to handle the growing amount of data that is turn our regularly. In the full realisation of big data it will also be useful in the capability to assists stakeholder to fully exploit the overarching value SMIA. As part of future work, it will be interesting to consider carry out a gap analysis of DLT and other related technique within the context of SMIA.

REFERENCES

Alalwan, N., Abozeid, A., ElHabshy, A. A., & Alzahrani, A. (2020). Efficient 3D Deep Learning Model for Medical Image Semantic Segmentation. *Alexandria Engineering Journal*. DOI: .2020.10.046 doi:10.1016/j.aej

Baltruschat, I. M., Nickisch, H., Grass, M., Knopp, T., & Saalbach, A. (2019). Comparison of deep learning approaches for multi-label chest X-ray classification. *Scientific Reports*, *9*(1), 1–10. doi:10.103841598-019-42294-8 PMID:31011155

Bandari, R. (2013). *Gestalt Computing and the Study of Content-oriented User Behavior on the Web* (Doctoral dissertation). UCLA.

Bar, Y., Diamant, I., Wolf, L., Lieberman, S., Konen, E., & Greenspan, H. (2015, April). Chest pathology detection using deep learning with non-medical training. In *2015 IEEE 12th international symposium on biomedical imaging (ISBI)* (pp. 294-297). IEEE. 10.1109/ISBI.2015.7163871

Boltuc, P. (2018). Strong semantic computing. *Procedia Computer Science*, *123*, 98–103.

Carrillo-de-Gea, J. M., García-Mateos, G., Fernández-Alemán, J. L., & Hernández-Hernández, J. L. (2016). A computer-aided detection system for digital chest radiographs. *Journal of Healthcare Engineering*, *2016*, 2016. doi:10.1155/2016/8208923 PMID:27372536

Chan, H. P., Wei, D., Helvie, M. A., Sahiner, B., Adler, D. D., Goodsitt, M. M., & Petrick, N. (1995). Computer-aided classification of mammographic masses and normal tissue: Linear discriminant analysis in texture feature space. *Physics in Medicine and Biology*, *40*(5), 857–876. doi:10.1088/0031-9155/40/5/010 PMID:7652012

Chen, G., Wang, L., & Kamruzzaman, M. M. (2020a). Spectral classification of ecological spatial polarization SAR image based on target decomposition algorithm and machine learning. *Neural Computing & Applications*, *32*(10), 5449–5460. doi:10.100700521-019-04624-9

Chen, L., Xu, S., Zhu, L., Zhang, J., Lei, X., & Yang, G. (2020b). A deep learning based method for extracting semantic information from patent documents. *Scientometrics*, *125*(1), 289–312. doi:10.100711192-020-03634-y

Chen, L. C., Zhu, Y., Papandreou, G., Schroff, F., & Adam, H. (2018). Encoder-decoder with atrous separable convolution for semantic image segmentation. In *Proceedings of the European conference on computer vision (ECCV)* (pp. 801-818). 10.1007/978-3-030-01234-2_49

Clarke, B., Fokoue, E., & Zhang, H. H. (2009). *Principles and theory for data mining and machine learning*. Springer Science & Business Media. doi:10.1007/978-0-387-98135-2

Deng, H., Xu, J., Shan, W., and Yuan, C. (2018). Extraction of polarimetric SAR image building area by active deep learning. *Journal of Survey Mapping Science Technology, 35*(3), 278–284.

Esteva, A., Kuprel, B., Novoa, R. A., Ko, J., Swetter, S. M., Blau, H. M., & Thrun, S. (2017). Dermatologist-level classification of skin cancer with deep neural networks. *Nature, 542*(7639), 115–118. doi:10.1038/nature21056 PMID:28117445

Grossfeld, B. (2020). *Deep learning vs machine learning: a simple way to understand the difference*. Retrieved from https://www.zendesk.com/blog/machine-learning-and-deep-learning/

Islam, M. T., Aowal, M. A., Minhaz, A. T., & Ashraf, K. (2017). *Abnormality detection and localization in chest x-rays using deep convolutional neural networks*. arXiv preprint arXiv:1705.09850.

Kohli, M., Prevedello, L. M., Filice, R. W., & Geis, J. R. (2017). Implementing machine learning in radiology practice and research. *AJR. American Journal of Roentgenology, 208*(4), 754–760. doi:10.2214/AJR.16.17224 PMID:28125274

Kohli, M. D., Summers, R. M., & Geis, J. R. (2017). Medical Image Data and Datasets in the Era of Machine Learning. *Journal of Digital Imaging, 30*(4), 392–399. doi:10.100710278-017-9976-3 PMID:28516233

Kulmanov, M., Smaili, F. Z., Gao, X., & Hoehndorf, R. (2020). Semantic similarity and machine learning with ontologies. *Briefings in Bioinformatics*, 1–18. doi:10.1093/bib/bbaa199 PMID:33049044

Kumar, M., & Sheshadri, H. S. (2012). On the classification of imbalanced datasets. *International Journal of Computers and Applications, 44*(8), 1–7. doi:10.5120/6280-8449

Lai, Z., & Deng, H. (2018). Medical Image Classification Based on Deep Features Extracted by Deep Model and Statistic Feature Fusion with Multilayer Perceptron. *Computational Intelligence and Neuroscience, 2018*, 2018. doi:10.1155/2018/2061516 PMID:30298088

Lakhani, P., & Sundaram, B. (2017). Deep learning at chest radiography: Automated classification of pulmonary tuberculosis by using convolutional neural networks. *Radiology, 284*(2), 574–582. doi:10.1148/radiol.2017162326 PMID:28436741

Li, C., & Xu, P. (2020). Application on traffic flow prediction of machine learning in intelligent transportation. *Neural Computing & Applications*, 1–12. doi:10.100700521-018-3699-3 PMID:32292246

Lisowski, E. (2020), *Machine Learning Techniques and Methods*. Retrieved from https://addepto.com/machine-learning-techniques-and-methods/

Lopes, U. K., & Valiati, J. F. (2017). Pre-trained convolutional neural networks as feature extractors for tuberculosis detection. *Computers in Biology and Medicine, 89*, 135–143. doi:10.1016/j.compbiomed.2017.08.001 PMID:28800442

Makris, C., & Simos, M. A. (2020). OTNEL: A Distributed Online Deep Learning Semantic Annotation Methodology. *Big Data and Cognitive Computing, 4*(4), 31. doi:10.3390/bdcc4040031

Mazurowski, M. A., Buda, M., Saha, A., & Bashir, M. R. (2019). Deep learning in radiology: An overview of the concepts and a survey of the state of the art with focus on MRI. *Journal of Magnetic Resonance Imaging, 49*(4), 939–954. doi:10.1002/jmri.26534 PMID:30575178

NHS. (2020). *Diagnostic Imaging Dataset.* Retrieved from https://www.england.nhs.uk/statistics/statistical-work-areas/diagnostic-imaging-dataset/

O'Mahony, N., Campbell, S., Carvalho, A., Harapanahalli, S., Hernandez, G. V., Krpalkova, L., ... Walsh, J. (2019l). Deep learning vs. traditional computer vision. In *Science and Information Conference* (pp. 128-144). Springer.

Rajpurkar, P., Irvin, J., Ball, R. L., Zhu, K., Yang, B., Mehta, H., ... Patel, B. N. (2018). Deep learning for chest radiograph diagnosis: A retrospective comparison of the CheXNeXt algorithm to practicing radiologists. *PLoS Medicine, 15*(11), e1002686. doi:10.1371/journal.pmed.1002686 PMID:30457988

Razzak, M. I., Naz, S., & Zaib, A. (2018). Deep learning for medical image processing: Overview, challenges and the future. In *Classification in BioApps* (pp. 323–350). Springer. doi:10.1007/978-3-319-65981-7_12

Samek, W., Wiegand, T., & Muller, T. (2017). *Explainable Artificial Intelligence: Understanding, Visualizing And Interpreting Deep Learning Models.* arXiv:1708.08296v1 [cs.AI] 28.

Sheu, P. (2017). Semantic computing and cognitive computing/informatics. In *2017 IEEE 16th International Conference on Cognitive Informatics & Cognitive Computing (ICCI* CC)* (pp. 4-4). IEEE.

Shung, K. K., Smith, M. B., & Tsui, B. M. W. (1992). *Principles of Medical Imaging.* Academic Press.

Stephen, O., Sain, M., Maduh, U. J., & Jeong, D. U. (2019). An efficient deep learning approach to pneumonia classification in healthcare. *Journal of Healthcare Engineering, 2019*, 2019. doi:10.1155/2019/4180949 PMID:31049186

Tajbakhsh, N., Shin, J. Y., Gurudu, S. R., Hurst, R. T., Kendall, C. B., Gotway, M. B., & Liang, J. (2016). Convolutional neural networks for medical image analysis: Full training or fine tuning? *IEEE Transactions on Medical Imaging, 35*(5), 1299–1312. doi:10.1109/TMI.2016.2535302 PMID:26978662

Taouli, A., Bensaber, D. A., Keskes, N., Bencherif, K., & Badir, H. (2018). Semantic for Big Data Analysis: A survey. In *Proceedings of the 7th Innovation and New Trends in Information Systems conference, 21-22, December, 2018 in Marrakech Morocco, Algeria* (pp. 163 – 177). Academic Press.

Taouli, A., Bensaber, D. A., Keskes, N., Bencherif, K., & Badir, H. (2018). Semantic for Big Data Analysis: A survey. In *Proceedings of the 7th Innovation and New Trends in Information Systems conference* (pp. 163 – 177). Academic Press.

Xu, J., Yuan, C., Cheng, Y., Zeng, C., & Xu, K. (2018). A classification of polarimetric SAR images based on active deep learning. *Remote Sensing Land Resource, 30*(01), 72–77.

Xu, X., Jiang, X., Ma, C., Du, P., Li, X., Lv, S., ... Lang, G. (2020). A deep learning system to screen novel coronavirus disease 2019 pneumonia. *Engineering., 6*(10), 1122–1129. doi:10.1016/j.eng.2020.04.010 PMID:32837749

Xu, Y., Liu, A., & Huang, L. (2019). Adaptive scale segmentation algorithm for polarimetric SAR image. *Journal of Engineering (Stevenage, England), 2019*(19), 6072–6076. doi:10.1049/joe.2019.0408

Yuan, F. G., Zargar, S. A., Chen, Q., & Wang, S. (2020). Machine learning for structural health monitoring: challenges and opportunities. In *Sensors and Smart Structures Technologies for Civil* (Vol. 11379, p. 1137903). Mechanical, and Aerospace Systems. doi:10.1117/12.2561610

Zhang, W., Doi, K., Giger, M. L., Wu, Y., Nishikawa, R. M., & Schmidt, R. A. (1994). Computerized detection of clustered microcalcifications in digital mammograms using shift-invariant artificial neural network. *Medical Physics, 21*(4), 517–524. doi:10.1118/1.597177 PMID:8058017

Zhang, X.-D. (2020). Machine Learning. In *A Matrix Algebra Approach to Artificial Intelligence* (pp. 223–440). Springer Nature Singapore Pte Ltd., doi:10.1007/978-981-15-2770-8_6

Chapter 8

Creation of Value–Added Services by Retrieving Information From Linked and Open Data Portals

Antonio Sarasa-Cabezuelo

https://orcid.org/0000-0003-3698-7954

Universidad Complutense de Madrid, Spain

ABSTRACT

In recent decades, different initiatives have emerged in public and private institutions with the aim of offering free access to the data generated in their activity to anyone. In particular, there are two types of initiatives: open data portals and linked data portals. Open data portals are characterized in that it offers access to its content in the form of a REST-type web services API that acts as a query language. On the other hand, linked data portals are characterized in that its data is represented using ontologies encoded by RDF triplets of the subject-predicate-object style forming a knowledge graph. This chapter presents a set of value-added service creation cases using the information stored in open data and linked data repositories. The objective is to show the possibilities offered by the exploitation of these repositories in various fields such as education, tourism, or services such as the search for taxis at an airport.

INTRODUCTION

In the last decades, different public and private institutions have emerged that have provided access to enormous amounts of data (Kitchin, 2014) on the activity it is carried out. In general, this information is available free of charge to anyone who wants to consult it or wants to use it to process it. It is true that there are some institutions that sell the data or special permits are required to access it, such as data from hospitals or personal data (Russell, 2013). In particular, there are two prominent initiatives: open data portals and linked data portals. Open data portals are characterized (Hossain et al, 2016) in that access to information is done through a Rest web services (Masse, 2011) API. The API (Michel et al, 2019)

DOI: 10.4018/978-1-7998-6697-8.ch008

acts as a query language so that each service can be configured with a set of parameters that establish what type of data it is able to retrieve, what type of filtering conditions can be done on the data, or the data format in which is retrieved the information. Normally, these portals offer to retrieve the data of the queries done, in the most standard formats such as JSON, XML, CSV and others. Another characteristic of these portals is that normally is available a catalog of the services offered. The catalogs specify each service, the way to invoke it, the parameters that can be configured, and the data formats in which the data can be returned, and even in some cases a test page is offered where these services can be tested. Also in some portals, it is possible to retrieve data directly without the need to invoke web services from any application, so that direct download is allowed in the same data formats mentioned above. One of the advantages of this initiative (Janssen et al, 2016) is the ease of adding an open data portal as the data source of a computer application that exploits the portal data. To do this, calls to web services are embedded within the application code, and the information retrieved in any of the formats can be stored as a document within the directory system or in a database (Larson, 2010). In this way, the information can be processed as if it were local data.

With regard to linked data portals, these are characterized (Hausenblas et al, 2010) by the way in which the information is stored. In this sense, the contents are encoded using domain ontologies that are used to describe the information in the form of RDF triplets of the subject-predicate-object form (Kahan et al, 2002). A property of triplets is that it can be linked together to form a network of related triplets that takes the form of an information graph. Thus, each graph represents the information of a different domain. Furthermore, it is possible to link graphs from different information domains, so that these portals become a great universal knowledge base (Hausenblas et al, 2009). The main advantages of these portals are the ease of creating and maintaining them, since the domain ontologies are created in a particular way in each case and it is the own representation structure of RDF standard that allows the described contents to be related (Heath et al, 2011). Another feature of these portals is the way of retrieving information. To do this, a standard query language called SPARQL (Quilitz et al, 2008) is used. The language syntax is similar to the SQL query language for relational databases. However, it has some differences since it is oriented to retrieve information from a graph, so the data structures or search conditions are adapted to the structure of the graph (Pauwels et al, 2018). The information retrieved through a SPARQL query can be stored in files with the most common data formats such as JSON, XML, CSV, RDF and others. In many portals there is what is called a SPARQL endpoint, which is a place in the portal that offers an interface where to execute SPARQL queries. Retrieval can be done directly from the portal, or it is able to embed retrieval SPARQL queries within the code in a specific programming language, so that just like in open data portals, the information is retrieved and stored local in files or in a database for further processing. In this way, linked data portals can be added to computer applications as a data source (Tsou, 2015).

A common feature in both initiatives is that the form of aggregation of portal data. In both cases, this is done by embedding the SPARQL queries or the web services API, within the application code. In this way, the recovered information is stored locally and can be further processed in any way it is wanted. This form of aggregation is very similar to the so-called mashups (Lee et al, 2012) or processing pipes that exist in programming languages and in other computer systems. Likewise, the aggregation and use that is made of the data has several implications. Firstly, the exploitation of the information on these portals allows the creation of value-added services (Sarasa-Cabezuelo, 2019). Thus, it can be given value to data that in many cases did not have it or increase its value by giving it a different utility than it originally had. For example, there are websites that allow to search for hotels or flights and facilitate the comparison of prices and qualities of different websites. In this case, the value of the information is increased from the customer's perspective because in one place it can be compared the information that under normal conditions it would be need to look for one by one. Other examples of useful combinations are, for example, the combination of data from a meteorological system and data from museums in a city. With these data a service can be created to plan visits to museums in a city taking into account the weather of the day. Another implication of data aggregation is the important dependence of applications on the data it processes (Kallio, 2018). The creation and maintenance of the data is not the property of the application, and is carried out by third parties, so if an important part of the functionality of the application is based on this data, then any problem that occurs in the data source probably affects the operation of the application. For example, in a travel comparison portal, if one of the portals on which the trips are compared stops working, the application that uses this information will not be able to fix it because it depends on the owner of the portal. The third implication is the possibilities of services and functionalities that can be built by combining the information from the open and linked data portals together with the information offered by the sensors available on mobile devices, clothing, household appliances ... Therefore, the number of applications is potentially huge.

The objective of this chapter is to analyze some possible applications of the exploitation of information from open and linked data portals in different fields: education, tourism and customer-oriented services. In order to do this, 3 different applications will be presented that solve specific problems and add value to data that had other different purposes.

The chapter is structured as follows in 4 sections where it will be presented describing specific applications in which information from open data portals or linked data has been used with the aim of facilitating services or solving needs in their respective fields. Section 2 will present an application in the field of education that allows the creation of educational resources using information from the linked data portal Wikidata (Vrandečić, 2012) and the open data portal of the city of Madrid. In section 3, an application in the field of tourism will be presented that allows the planning of tourist visits to museums in the city of Madrid in which information from the open data portal of the city council of Madrid and the Spanish meteorological service is used. Section 4 presents an application in the field of transport, in which a service is created for both clients and drivers of passenger transport services at airport using the information of geolocation, and data from a website specialized in geographic data. Finally, section 5 presents an application in the field of health, in which a service is created to know the prediction that there is an allergy outbreak in a place in Madrid. The chapter ends with a set of conclusions and future work. All the described applications have been developed within the research group to which the author of the chapter belongs.

CASE 1: EDUCATION

This first case focuses on the area of education. A habitual activity of some subjects of the university degree of Art History are visits to museums and monuments. It is an activity programmed by the teacher that consists of the visualization of a set of works by a certain artist. In the plan of the visit, the teacher indicates what stylistic aspects should be observed by the students such as the color used, the geometry of the characters, the subject of the painting... Each artist presents a set of very particular characteristics that may be particular or common to other artists due to the time in which they lived or because they belong to a specific pictorial or artistic movement. In any of the cases, as a result of the activity, the student must answer a set of questions about the visit he has made, and will normally carry out an evaluation of the visit to assess the degree of use and understanding of it. Another requirement when preparing these activities is to generate different visits so that the students do not carry out the same activity. In this sense, the preparation work of this activity for the teacher is usually quite expensive and manual. First, it should look for the works that will be visited in each activity and in which museums these works are displayed. This search is manual because it requires recovering paintings or figures with a set of similar characteristics so that the activities carried out by the students are different but of the same style and difficulty.

There are currently a multitude of linked and open data sources containing information on museums, monuments or artistic works (Sarasa-Cabezuelo et al, 2019). The information from these sources can be exploited to create value-added services (that is, give a different use to the data than it originally had). With this idea, the implementation of a tool to facilitate the work of creating visit activities through the exploitation of information from open data repositories and linked data was proposed. In this sense, an application prototype was implemented in the context of the monuments and museums of the city of Madrid, using Wikidata and the open data portal of the Madrid city council as data sources. The architecture of the application is as follows (Figure 1):

Figure 1. Architecture of the application

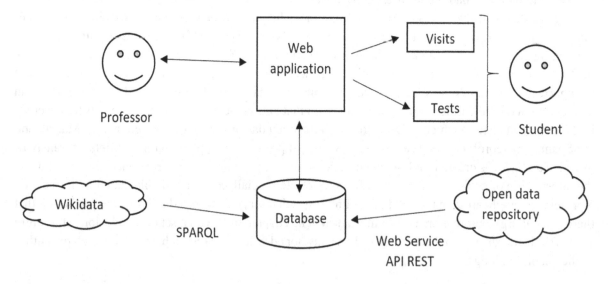

The application retrieves all the available meta-information about the monuments and museums of the city of Madrid and stores it in a local database (this is updated from time to time). Wikidata is a linked data portal, so the way to retrieve information is through SPARQL queries that are embedded within the application code. The same occurs in the open data portal of the city of Madrid except that the information is retrieved by invoking a web service of type rest. In both cases, the result of the queries is retrieved in JSON format, and is stored in a MongoDB type database. The semantic information retrieved from each repository is as follows:

- Wikidata. All the information (date of realization, title, style, painting technique ...) available on the paintings that are exposed in the museum is recovered, as well as the information of each painter (date and place of birth, biography ...)
- Open data portal of the Madrid city council. The administrative information of each museum is retrieved (address, opening hours, cost of tickets...)

Using this data, the value-added service is built by exploiting the stored information through the implemented functions. In the application, there are two interfaces: one oriented towards the teacher and the other oriented towards the student. The teacher has an editor to create visits (Figure 2.a) using a search tool that allows to retrieve paintings or monuments based on artists, artistic styles and other elements. Likewise, from the editor the instructions on how to do the visit are filled in: aspects that must be observed in the work, order of travel of the works in the museum, museum hours, transportation to get to the museum. It is also possible to add the questions that the students must answer once they have done the visit. Finally, the teacher also has an editor available to create an evaluation test associated with each visit. Once, it has been created a visit and it is associated an evaluation test, then it can be published (Figure 2.b). Visits and published tests are visible from the application's student interface.

Figure 2. a. Creation of activities, b. List of activities

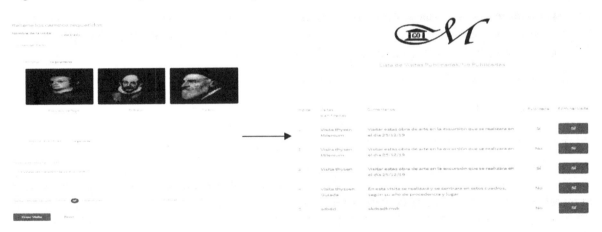

In this way, when a user enters the application as a student, they will find all the visits (and associated assessment tests) that the teacher has published. Then, the student can download the visit in pdf format or view it from the mobile or tablet and carry it out. When the visit has ended, the student answers the questions about the visit in the application and takes the evaluation test associated with the visit. The editor allows to create two types of questions in the evaluation: open questions or questions with various options in which only one of the answers is true. Both the questions about the visit and the evaluation test are registered in the application, and the teacher from their interface can evaluate them and assign a grade. Once they are graded, the student will be able to see the result and the teacher's comments from their interface.

The advantage of this system is that from a set of data generated and maintained by third parties, a system is built that gives a different use to the data than the original one. In addition, the application offers a solution to simplify the teacher's work. The main disadvantage is precisely the dependency of the application on the data since its maintenance depends on third parties, so that if access to the information is interrupted or that data ceases to exist, the application will not work.

On the other hand, there are several lines of future work:

1. Expand the type of questions that can be added to the evaluation of a visit. For example, questions of relation of concepts or questions of cards
2. Transformation of visits and assessment tests into SCORM 2004 learning objects so that they can be viewed in an LMS.
3. Use the geolocation of the mobile phone to recommend that students visit museums that are closer to where they live. This function would obtain the distances from museums to the place where the user is and it would recommend a visit.
4. Exploit the information obtained from the students regarding the visits made and the academic results. In this sense, it could be used, for example, to know if the planned visits have had a good result, or if there has been any concept that they have not understood.
5. Possibility of creating learning paths. A learning path, for example, could be a set of linked visits where paintings by painters belonging to the same artistic movement are used. The system could sequentially recommend visits, so that students who had completed a learning path, obtained a badge.
6. Allow the teacher to create collections of visits and to carry out searches on the information included in each visit such as paintings, museums visited, date the visit was done ... For example, it could be created new visits using information from previous visits.

CASE 2: TOURISM

The following example is contextualized in the field of tourism. When a person visits a city then it arises the problem of what monuments and places to visit. In order to solve this problem, usually tourist use the tourist offices or search in web sites specialized about the city visited. In recent years, with the rise of mobile devices, a huge variety of applications have also emerged with functionalities oriented to help to tourists on the visit to a city (Kaur et al, 2016). Normally, these applications offer services such as the planning of route of visits, information about a particular monument or museum (Dickinson et al, 2014). However, something common in all these applications is that generally the information that it is offered is mostly static and it does not take advantage of other sources of information that could increase its value. With this idea, an Android mobile application has been implemented in order to exploit various sources of information and offer a service oriented to tourists who visit to the city of Madrid. For this, 4 sources of information have been used: the open data portal of the Madrid city council (Open Data Portal Council of Madrid, 2020), the Spanish meteorology service (Open Data Portal Meteorology service, 2020), the open data portal of bus service of the city of Madrid (Open Data Portal of EMT, 2020) and the geolocation information of the mobile phone (Wang et al, 2018). The semantic information retrieved from each repository is as follows:

*   Open data portal of the Madrid City Council. This repository has a catalog of data that is accessible both by direct download and by invoking a web service. In particular, there is a dataset with

information about the museums and monuments of the city of Madrid: opening hours, location, ticket prices, temporary exhibitions... This data set can be retrieved by doing a call to a web service of type REST. In this sense, the application implemented recovers administrative information of each museum (address, opening hours, cost of tickets...)

- Spanish meteorological service. It has an open data portal with information in real time related to weather forecasting: temperatures, rainfall, wind speed, humidity...It is possible to perform queries limited to a specific location, and the result is returned in a json document. In this sense, the application implemented recovers information in real time related about weather forecasting (temperature, wind speed, rainfall...) of zones closers to museums or monuments.
- Open data portal of bus service of the city of Madrid. This portal offers an API of web services such as: buses that offer service in a specific place, bus route for reaching a place both by street name and by geographical coordinates, optimal route between two places... In this sense, the application implemented uses a specific web service that calculate the optimal route from a museum and the geolocation of user. The web service returns the buses and bus stops that user must use in order to reach the museum.

In all cases, the results of requests to the service are retrieved in a json or xml format file that is processed by the application. Figure 3 shows the architecture of the application. As it is shown, the Android application acts as a combination tool for the recovered information. Since the information is retrieved in JSON format, MongoDB has been used as the database so that no complex processing of the information is required. The services offered by the application are implemented as a web services API so it would be simple to use them to create a web application that offers functionality similar to the Android app. On the other hand, every user who uses the application must have an account in the application. User account information is also stored in the database.

Figure 3. Architecture of application

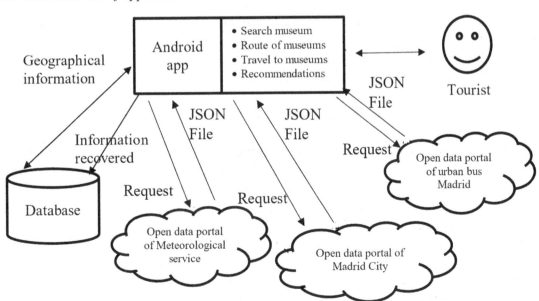

When the user runs the application, the geolocation information of the mobile is retrieved, and it is used to query the three open data sources. On the one hand, all the information about the museums and monuments closest to the user's location are retrieved. For this, the user must have previously configured a search radius. The process consists of taking the geographic coordinates retrieved from the mobile, and calculating the distances to the different monuments and museums (using the information retrieved from the open data portal). Those places that are within the established radius are the candidates to visit. Next, the information to be displayed for each museum is prepared: general information obtained from the open data portal of the Madrid city council, meteorological information obtained from the geographical location of each museum, and images obtained by performing an internet search on each museum. All this information is stored associated, and the user is shown a list with the results. When the user clicks on a selected museum or monument, then all the information retrieved is shown. But it can also perform other operations such as:

1. Find a way to get from where the tourist is to the museum or monument. For this, the geolocation information of the user's mobile and the monument or museum to visit is retrieved, and a query is done to the open data portal of the urban bus service. This query can return the route on foot or using buses to get to the right place.
2. Save the museum or monument to a favorites list.
3. Create a tourist route. First, it is selected a set of museums or monuments. It is recovered the geolocation information of the user's mobile phone and the geographical locations of each museum. Next, it is performed a query in order to find the optimal route to visit the selected museums on foot or by using urban buses.
4. Other information provided by the application is a recommendation about whether or not to visit a museum based on the weather forecast obtained. So if there is rain or it is too cold or hot, the application informs the user of this situation so that it is possible to change museums or tourist routes.

An example of a search is shown in Figure 4. The application using geolocation has retrieved the set of closest places. The user has chosen the "Puerta del Sol". When it is selected, all the information about the monument is displayed. If it is selected information about the location of the monument then a new screen is displayed that shows the distance and the estimated time. In addition, when it is selected the option "Search for a route", then a new screen is shown. This screen describes the route from the geolocation of user to the museum.

The application has several lines of work that could improve it such as:

- The use of real-time information about the number of people who are currently visiting the museum or monument. In some museums there are sensors that provide this information, and in others historical data about the number of visitors of the place at certain times could be used.
- Expand the information offered about each museum or monument, connecting the application with other more specialized sources of information about each place visited or creating its own information base.
- Add functionality of type social network. So, visitors could add and share opinions about the museums or places visited. This information could be used in order to recommend or avoid a visit (for example, it could be recommend to avoid places with too much capacity)

Figure 4. Searching in the app.

The main disadvantage is the dependency of the application on the data since its maintenance depends on third parties, so that if access to the information is interrupted or that data ceases to exist, the application will not work. Another additional application problem is the delays that can occur in the retrieval of information. It is for this reason that the most static information, such as that on general museum data, is not retrieved in real time, and is obtained periodically. However, the transport or weather data is retrieved in real time.

CASE 3: TRANSPORT

Airports have become an essential element of larger cities. In this sense, a common problem for travelers arriving in a city from a plane trip is finding a means of transport that will take them from the airport to their destination in the city. There are several transportation alternatives from an airport such as bus, taxi, subway, or train. In recent years, another alternative has emerged, which are shuttle buses. It is a small private bus that transports several people to different destinations. The main advantages of a shuttle is that it is faster than a means of public transport and is not as expensive as a taxi since the cost is shared among all travelers. The main disadvantage of a shuttle is the delay that occurs in reaching the destinations of the passengers if the stops are very far from each other. This situation becomes critical when the city is very large because in an extreme case two destinations could meet at two ends of the city (Yue et al, 2017).

In order to obtain the optimal route of stops at passenger destinations, the driver normally uses his own experience and decides the order in which they must be carried out (Zafari et al, 2019). Sometimes a geolocation tool such as Google Maps or a similar application can be used. They indicate the best route from one place to another. However, normally these types of tools only work between 2 destinations, but it is not provided a complete route if it is neccesary to do it between a larger set of 2 destinations (Liu et al, 2014). In this sense, the driver should trace the route between each pair of destinations, which does not ensure that the optimal route is found (Yim et al, 2006). Essentially, the problem posed corresponds to the problem of the traveler between cities, in which the problem of visiting n cities without passing through the same city twice and doing it traveling the shortest possible distance arises. However, to this problem it must be considered other additional aspects (Jerby et al, 2006) such as the existence of works, traffic, accidents or other events that may hinder the journey, and which must be taken into account to calculate the optimal route.

To help solve this problem, a mobile application has been created that creates a value-added service using geolocation information from various sources (Zhou et al, 2012). Firstly, the information provided by the passengers themselves about the destination they want to reach is used. On the other hand, the geolocation information of the shuttle driver itself is taken and finally the information and algorithms to obtain optimal routes from a website specialized in geolocation data called MapBox (MapBox, 2020) are used. In this sense, the system takes the destinations declared by the passengers and by the driver, and invokes the MapBox API, which generates the optimal route of stops to be made. The information semantic of route is a sequence ordered of geographical coordinates in the form of latitude and longitude. This sequence is represented graphically. Once the journey has begun, the system indicates to the driver the places through which it must transit. In addition, from time to time, this route is recalculated by making new MapBox calls, thus ensuring that if some extraordinary event has occurred, the route can be changed dynamically. On the other hand, to take into account the problem of extreme distances between two points in the city, the system organizes the routes, establishing service areas to carry out the trips. In this way, each shuttle will only serve a certain set of postal codes. This ensures that the maximum distances between two destinations will never exceed a given distance. The architecture of the application is as follows (Figure 5):

Figure 5. Architecture of the app.

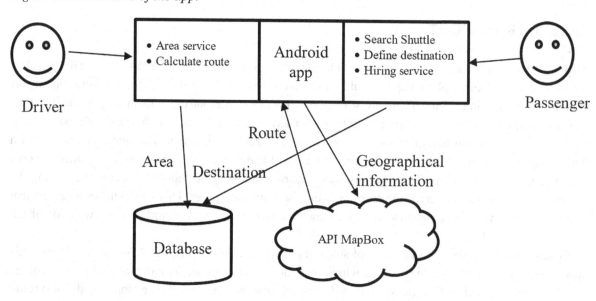

The application has three different interfaces. On the one hand, there is the administrator interface. This user is responsible for defining the different origins of the routes (airports in a city), and for carrying out maintenance work on the application focused on users. On the other hand, there is the driver interface, which establishes in the service area indicating the postal codes of the towns and the maximum number of travelers. Also, it is possible to specify several different routes indicating the times when the routes will be made. And finally there is the traveler interface. This user can carry out a search for the different shuttles that have declared a route to a postal district where the destination to which they want to move is located. Entering the destination shows the different shuttles that reach the destination and the times at which the trip can be done. The traveler will select one of the shuttles. When the journey begins, the driver tells the system to calculate the route according to the data provided, and then shows him the route that the driver will be following. As it progresses along the route, it is recalculated in order to keep it updated in the case of possible events that would make it necessary to change routes. In Figure 6 is shown:

Figure 6. Creating route and using this route.

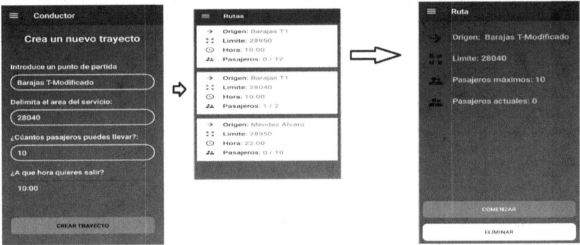

The main advantages of this application is that a value-added service is created from the geolocation information of the destinations of the passengers, the driver and the geographic data offered by the MapBox platform. In this way, it is possible to optimize routes and ensure that passengers will reach their destinations as soon as possible. Likewise, it is a very useful tool for the driver, since it allows him to organize the trip and the stops he must make. On the other hand, the traveler has the advantage of being able to choose between all the possible shuttles that serve the destination area. The main disadvantage is that it is a tool that depends on a third party, in this case the MapBox API. So if there is a problem with this API, the service will stop working.

The application can be improved in several ways:

- Implement an encryption system for users' personal information.
- Establish a price system for each journey and an online payment method.

- Add more functionality to facilitate the estimated time of a journey or to find out which journeys are at a certain time.
- Establish a notification system that keeps users informed of events related to their journeys.
- Improve the delimitation system of the route's stopping area, being able to enter several postal codes or be able to interact directly with the map.

CASE 4: HEALTH

The number of people who have allergies has been increasing over time, among other reasons due to the increase in contamination. In this sense, a common problem that arises in the spring is the appearance of allergy outbreaks to grasses. The possibility of knowing those areas of the cities where pollen accumulations of these plants can occur would be very interesting for people who have this disease.

The likelihood of an allergic outbreak can be predicted with some accuracy by knowing some meteorological data such as humidity, wind speed, temperature, and rainfall to occur. With these values a representative value of the probability that an allergic outbreak to grasses can occur in a specific area can be obtained. Although there are applications in many cities that measure the level of pollen in certain areas, there is no application so specialized that allows predictions to be done in this regard. In order to solve this problem, a pilot application for predicting allergic outbreaks to grasses has been created in the context of the city of Madrid. For this, data is taken from various sources of information in order to generate a prediction: data from the National Meteorological Institute (Open Data Portal Meteorology service, 2020) from which the real-time data of the aforementioned variables are obtained: temperature, humidity, rainfall and air speed; the pollen calendar from the Ministry of Health, the average daily level of pollen grains per cubic meter of air is taken into account, provided by the SEAIC (Spanish Society of Allergology and Clinical Immunology) (SEAIC, 2020) and air quality data taken by the Madrid government (Open Data Portal Madrid government, 2020) from each locality.

Based on the information collected from the different prediction sources, a value will be generated that will represent the level of alert that an outbreak will occur in a given area. In the prediction process, the city is divided into 7 zones taking into account if they has quality sensors. Next, the pollen calendar is used as the basis to make the prediction, since the pollen level is clearly a seasonal data, establishing three different alert levels (Low, Medium and High). In this way, each month is initially classified in one of these levels. Each of these levels has an associated numerical value, which will increase or decrease depending on the other factors included in the algorithm. In this way, the Low level is associated with the value 0, the Middle 1 and the High 2.

Subsequently, the average daily level of pollen grains per cubic meter of air is taken into account, provided by the SEAIC for the previous week. With this data, we calculate the average for the week and we associate a value: if it is less than 200 gr / m3 the value 0 is assigned, if it is between 200 and 1000 gr / m3 the value 1 and for higher quantities the value 2 is assigned. In this way, if the level provided by the pollen calendar is higher than the one assigned taking into account the concentration of pollen in the air, the first one increases by 0.5, while if it is less, the calculated level decreases in the same proportion. In this way we will be obtaining a numerical value that will finally translate into the alert level calculated by the system.

On the other hand, the pollution produced by the particles emitted by the engines of diesel cars, modifies the nature of the pollens, making them more aggressive. Thus, the different pollutants end up being deposited in the soil, affecting the natural development of seeds, roots and plants, altering their physiological characteristics and making pollens more allergic and powerful. In addition, pollution affects the airways, irritating the mucosa of the nose, pharynx and lungs, which aggravates the symptoms of the allergy. This explains why there are more allergies in cities than in the country, although pollen levels are lower. That is why it has been taken into account to define the alert status. For this, the data is taken from the Community of Madrid air quality page about the following pollutants: Nitrogen dioxide, solid particles of 10 thousandths of millimeters of size, solid particles of 2.5 thousandths of millimeters, carbon monoxide, concentration of ozone, sulfur dioxide, and nitrogen monoxide. 0.1 is added to the level previously calculated each time any of the previously described pollutants exceeded limit values established by current legislation on air quality.

Finally, the climate also influences pollen allergies, on rainy days and cloudy and windless days the symptoms decrease, since rain cleans the atmosphere and the absence of wind prevents pollen from moving. On the contrary, warm, dry and windy weather favors a greater distribution of pollen and, consequently, an increase in symptoms. For this, the following data from the National Institute of Meteorology are taken on the predictions for the next three days in each of the different municipalities of the Community of Madrid

- Wind speed (km / h): With a value greater than 30km / h, 0.3 is added to the calculated alert level. Since the wind favours the movement of pollen.
- Probability of precipitation: With a value greater than 30% it is subtracted from the 0.2 level. Rain diminishes the effects, by cleaning the air.
- Minimum relative humidity: With a value greater than 30%, the prediction is decreased by 0.1.
- Maximum relative humidity: With a value greater than 70%, the calculated level is decreased by 0.1, since having higher humidity reduces allergy symptoms such as nasal congestion and itching.
- Minimum temperature: Pollen concentrations are usually higher on hot days. So with a minimum temperature above 20 degrees 0.1 is added to the level.
- Maximum temperature: And with a temperature above 30 degrees 0.1 is also added.

With this calculation, a numerical value is obtained for each municipality and for each of the next three days, this value is rounded and an alert level is assigned. The mapping is shown in Table 1.

Table 1. Mapping calculated value to alert level

Calculated value	Alert level
<1	Low
[1, 2]	Medium
>2	High

In order to display the predictions, a web page (figure 7) has been created that has several sections:

- Home. Information about the page.
- Levels of the day. A map of Madrid divided by municipalities is shown, so if you click on one of them, the pollution levels and atmospheric data of the municipality are shown.
- Predictions. There is a search engine in which if you enter a place in Madrid, the prediction made by the system on the alert level for that place is shown.
- Report us. A form is displayed that allows the user to enter an alert for a municipality in the Community of Madrid, along with a table with the alerts reported to the system during the day (if none have been reported, a message with this information is displayed).
- Notifications. A form is displayed that allows a user to receive an email in their email during the chosen period with the alert level of the selected municipality.

Figure 7. Section "Predictions" of the application.

The architecture of the application is shown in Figure 8.

The main lines of future work are the extension of the application to other areas of Spain and the prediction of allergies to other types of pollens. Likewise, technically the application can be improved in security aspects or have a mobile version. Prediction could also be improved by exploiting other data such as news from newspapers or specialized websites.

The main advantage of this application is that it allows a user to know in real time what the alert level is for an allergic outbreak so that they can avoid the place or prepare if they have to visit it.

Figure 8. Architecture of the application.

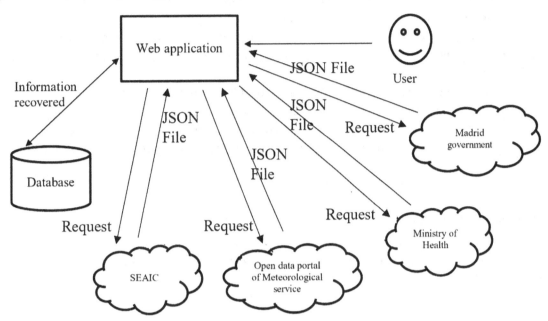

CONCLUSION

There are currently huge amounts of data distributed across the network in the form of open data re-positories and linked data, which are accessible to anyone. These data were created as a result of the activity of an institution for a certain purpose. However, there is the possibility of reusing them and creating applications from them that can give them a different utility than the original one that may be valuable for certain people. In this chapter, 4 concrete examples of data reuse from different sources of open and linked data have been presented to create value-added services that are useful in different areas: education, health, transport or tourism. In all of them, the application architecture is repeated: the data is collected, stored in a persistence system, and the application processes the data to offer a service. In all of them something common is the way to recover the data, either using web services or using SPARQL. The main weakness of these applications is precisely that the data is not the property of the application, and a dependency is created on the owner who maintains it. This weakness is compensated by the utility obtained from the applications. Likewise, the way of building the applications allows to switch to other similar data sources without having to deeply modify the original application.

FUTURE RESEARCH DIRECTIONS

The main lines of future work are:

- Define a process model for applications that are built using open or linked data.
- Create a tool that helps the creation of value-added services.

- In the first application described, you want to allow the creation of SCORM 2004 type learning objects so that the result can be viewed in an LMS.
- In the second application described, it is intended to use other information sensors such as the number of people in a museum and create a recommender of places based on the stored data from other visits.
- In the third application described, it is intended to add functionalities such as payment through the app, or restriction of the service area based on other factors.
- In the fourth described application, it is intended to add to the prediction of allergy outbreaks, other types of pollen that produce allergies as well as extend the scope of action outside Madrid.

ACKNOWLEDGMENT

This research received no specific grant from any funding agency in the public, commercial, or not-for-profit sectors.

REFERENCES

Dickinson, J. E., Ghali, K., Cherrett, T., Speed, C., Davies, N., & Norgate, S. (2014). Tourism and the smartphone app: Capabilities, emerging practice and scope in the travel domain. *Current Issues in Tourism*, *17*(1), 84–101. doi:10.1080/13683500.2012.718323

Hausenblas, M. (2009). Exploiting linked data to build web applications. *IEEE Internet Computing*, *13*(4), 68–73. doi:10.1109/MIC.2009.79

Hausenblas, M., & Karnstedt, M. (2010). Understanding linked open data as a web-scale database. *Proceedings of the second conference on Advances in Databases Knowledge and Data Applications*, 56-61. 10.1109/DBKDA.2010.23

Heath, T., & Bizer, C. (2011). Linked data: Evolving the web into a global data space. *Synthesis Lectures on the Semantic Web: Theory and Technology, 1*(1), 1-136.

Hossain, M. A., Dwivedi, Y. K., & Rana, N. P. (2016). State-of-the-art in open data research: Insights from existing literature and a research agenda. *Journal of Organizational Computing and Electronic Commerce*, *26*(1-2), 14–40. doi:10.1080/10919392.2015.1124007

Janssen, M., Charalabidis, Y., & Zuiderwijk, A. (2012). Benefits, adoption barriers and myths of open data and open government. *Information Systems Management*, *29*(4), 258–268. doi:10.1080/1058053 0.2012.716740

Jerby, S., & Ceder, A. (2006). Optimal routing design for shuttle bus service. *Transportation Research Record: Journal of the Transportation Research Board*, *1971*(1), 14–22. doi:10.1177/0361198106197100102

Kahan, J., Koivunen, M. R., Prud'Hommeaux, E., & Swick, R. R. (2002). Annotea: An open RDF infrastructure for shared Web annotations. *Computer Networks*, *39*(5), 589–608. doi:10.1016/S1389-1286(02)00220-7

Kallio, K. P. (2018). Citizen-subject formation as geosocialization: A methodological approach on 'learning to be citizens'. *Geografiska Annaler. Series B, Human Geography*, *100*(2), 81–96. doi:10.10 80/04353684.2017.1390776

Kaur, K., & Kaur, R. (2016). Internet of things to promote tourism: An insight into smart tourism. *International Journal of Recent Trends in Engineering & Research*, *2*(4), 357–361.

Kitchin, R. (2014). *The data revolution: Big data, open data, data infrastructures and their consequences*. Sage.

Larson, R. R. (2010). Introduction to information retrieval. *Journal of the American Society for Information Science and Technology*, *61*(4), 852–853.

Lee, Y. J., & Kim, J. S. (2012). Automatic web api composition for semantic data mashups. *Proceedings of Fourth International Conference on Computational Intelligence and Communication Networks*, 953-957. 10.1109/CICN.2012.56

Liu, Y., Jia, G., Tao, X., Xu, X., & Dou, W. (2014). A stop planning method over big traffic data for airport shuttle bus. *2014 IEEE Fourth International Conference on Big Data and Cloud Computing*, 63-70. 10.1109/BDCloud.2014.21

MapBox. (2020). https://www.mapbox.com/

Masse, M. (2011). *REST API Design Rulebook: Designing Consistent RESTful Web Service Interfaces*. O'Reilly Media, Inc.

Michel, F., Faron-Zucker, C., Corby, O., & Gandon, F. (2019). Enabling Automatic Discovery and Querying of Web APIs at Web Scale using Linked Data Standards. *Proceedings of the 2019 World Wide Web Conference*, 883-892. 10.1145/3308560.3317073

Open Data Portal Council of Madrid. (2020). https://datos.madrid.es/portal/site/egob/

Open Data Portal Madrid Government. (2020). http://gestiona.madrid.org

Open Data Portal Meteorology Service. (2020). http://www.aemet.es/es/datos_abiertos

Open Data Portal of EMT. (2020). https://opendata.emtmadrid.es/Home

Pauwels, P., McGlinn, K., Törmä, S., & Beetz, J. (2018). Linked Data. Building Information Modeling, 181-197.

Quilitz, B., & Leser, U. (2008). Querying distributed RDF data sources with SPARQL. *Proceedings of European Semantic Web Conference*, 524-538 10.1007/978-3-540-68234-9_39

Russell, M. A. (2013). *Mining the Social Web: Data Mining Facebook, Twitter, LinkedIn, Google+, GitHub, and More*. O'Reilly Media, Inc.

Sarasa-Cabezuelo, A. (2019). Exploitation of Open Data Repositories for the Creation of Value-Added Services. *Proceedings of International Symposium on Distributed Computing and Artificial Intelligence*, 134-141.

Sarasa-Cabezuelo, A., & Fernández-Vindel, J. L. (2019). Merging Open Data Sources to Plan Learning Activities for Online Students. *Proceedings of 23rd International Conference Information Visualisation (IV)*, 306-311. 10.1109/IV.2019.00058

SEAIC (Sociedad Española de Alergología e Inmunología Clínica). (2020). https://www.polenes.com/

Tsou, M. H. (2015). Research challenges and opportunities in mapping social media and Big Data. *Cartography and Geographic Information Science, 42*(1), 70–74. doi:10.1080/15230406.2015.1059251

Vrandečić, D. (2012). Wikidata: A new platform for collaborative data collection. *Proceedings of the 21st International Conference on World Wide Web*, 1063-1064. 10.1145/2187980.2188242

Wang, Y., Zhong, Z., Yang, A., & Jing, N. (2018). Review Rating Prediction on Location-Based Social Networks Using Text, Social Links, and Geolocations. *IEICE Transactions on Information and Systems, 101*(9), 2298–2306. doi:10.1587/transinf.2017EDP7180

Yim, Y. B., & Ceder, A. (2006). Smart feeder/shuttle bus service: Consumer research and design. *Journal of Public Transportation, 9*(1), 5. doi:10.5038/2375-0901.9.1.5

Yue, W. S., Chye, K. K., & Hoy, C. W. (2017). Towards smart mobility in urban spaces: Bus tracking and information application. *AIP Conference Proceedings, 1891*(1), 020145. doi:10.1063/1.5005478

Zafari, F., Gkelias, A., & Leung, K. K. (2019). A survey of indoor localization systems and technologies. *IEEE Communications Surveys and Tutorials, 21*(3), 2568–2599. doi:10.1109/COMST.2019.2911558

Zhou, P., Zheng, Y., & Li, M. (2012). How long to wait? Predicting bus arrival time with mobile phone based participatory sensing. *Proceedings of the 10th international conference on Mobile systems, applications, and services*, 379-392. 10.1145/2307636.2307671

ADDITIONAL READING

Booshehri, M., & Luksch, P. (2016, November). Towards linked open data enabled ontology learning from text. *In Proceedings of the 18th International Conference on Information Integration and Web-based Applications and Services*, pp. 252-256. 10.1145/3011141.3011184

Elzein, N. M., Majid, M. A., Hashem, I. A. T., Yaqoob, I., Alaba, F. A., & Imran, M. (2018). Managing big RDF data in clouds: Challenges, opportunities, and solutions. *Sustainable Cities and Society, 39*, 375–386. doi:10.1016/j.scs.2018.02.019

Hossain, M. A., Dwivedi, Y. K., & Rana, N. P. (2016). State-of-the-art in open data research: Insights from existing literature and a research agenda. *Journal of Organizational Computing and Electronic Commerce, 26*(1-2), 14–40. doi:10.1080/10919392.2015.1124007

Li, T., Levina, E., & Zhu, J. (2019). Prediction models for network-linked data. *The Annals of Applied Statistics*, *13*(1), 132–164. doi:10.1214/18-AOAS1205

Modi, K. J., Garg, S., & Chaudhary, S. (2019). An Integrated Framework for RESTful Web Services Using Linked Open Data. *International Journal of Grid and High Performance Computing*, *11*(2), 24–49. doi:10.4018/IJGHPC.2019040102

Radulovic, F., Mihindukulasooriya, N., García-Castro, R., & Gómez-Pérez, A. (2018). A comprehensive quality model for linked data. *Semantic Web*, *9*(1), 3–24. doi:10.3233/SW-170267

Spahiu, B., Xie, C., Rula, A., Maurino, A., & Cai, H. (2016, May). Profiling similarity links in linked open data. *In 2016 IEEE 32nd International Conference on Data Engineering Workshops (ICDEW)*, pp. 103-108

Sultana, M., Paul, P. P., & Gavrilova, M. L. (2014). Online user interaction traits in web-based social biometrics. In Computer Vision and Image Processing in Intelligent Systems and Multimedia Technologies, pp. 177-190.

KEY TERMS AND DEFINITIONS

Digital Repository: It is a computer application that allows you to store information and offers different services to the user. Essentially it allows searching and retrieving stored information.

Linked Data: It is an initiative that aims to relate data and information to create a large semantic network that can be consulted.

Open Data: It is an initiative that aims to provide the data generated in the institutions so that anyone can use them to exploit them.

RDF: It is a language that allows to represent knowledge using triplets of the subject-predicate-object type.

Web Service: It is a way to implement services on the web, which are associated with web resources.

Wikidata: It is an initiative supported by Wikimedia that maintains a repository of linked data.

SPARQL: It is a query language on documents described in RDF.

Chapter 9
NreASAM:
Towards an Ontology–Based Model for Authentication and Auto–Grading Online Submission of Psychomotor Assessments

A. Kayode Adesemowo
https://orcid.org/0000-0003-1217-1651
Nelson Mandela University, South Africa

Oluwasefunmi 'Tale Arogundade
https://orcid.org/0000-0001-9338-491X
Federal University of Agriculture, Abeokuta, Nigeria

ABSTRACT

Core and integral to the fourth industrial revolution, knowledge economy, and beyond is information and communication technology (ICT); more so, during and post the novel coronavirus pandemic. Yet, there exists a skills gap in ICT networking and networks engineering. Not only do students perceive ICT networking to be difficult to comprehend, lecturers and institutions grapple with the adequacy of ICT networking equipment. Real-life simulators, like the Cisco Packet Tracer, hold the promise of alternate teaching opportunities and evidenced-based environments for (higher-order) assessment. Research in the last decade on ontology for assessments have focused on taxonomy and multiple-choice questions and auto-generation and marking of assessments. This chapter extends the body of knowledge through its ontology-based model for enabling and auto-assessing performance-based and/or pseudo-psychomotor assessment. The auto-grading online submission system assists with authenticity and enables authentic and/or sustainable assessments.

DOI: 10.4018/978-1-7998-6697-8.ch009

INTRODUCTION

Most importantly, what we want to avoid is using old 19th Century teaching methods on new 21st Century technologies to merely dump large volumes of undigested information down large digital diameter pipes to relatively inactive and passive learners. This pump it down a pipe analogy is the "ugly" and uncomfortable reality of online education when done poorly. Unfortunately, too often the default model of online education is just borrowing old delivery methods of teaching and supplanting them onto new online learning spaces and digital technologies with no transformative advantage. – ICDE: International Council for Open and Distance Education

Education is not the learning of facts but the training of the mind to think – Albert Einstein

Beyond a New Era

With the advent of the novel coronavirus disease 2019, known as COVID-19 (WHO, 2020), many higher education institutions (HEI) have either switched to 'online classes' or are in the process of moving to online learning/e-learning (Crawford et al., 2020). Most HEIs are prepping for and/or taking advantage of asynchronous learning (Daniel, 2020). Online learning is not entirely new, it is only being fast-tracked by the COVID-19 pandemic.

This is not just for COVID-19, it is important for the fourth industrial revolution (4IR), digital age, knowledge economy and beyond, as intentional, purposeful, strategic use of *information* is of the essence. The 4IR placed reliance on data, information processing, self-learning, automated processing and transmission. No doubt, 4IR has been viewed as the second information technology (IT) revolution (Lee et al., 2018). In addition to 4IR, the knowledge and creative economy (Craig, n.d.; Goede, 2011), are home to intelligent and smart computing.

During the COVID-19 pandemic, there were lots of remote work and activities. Upon a closer look, one will see that this is in similitude to activities in the 4IR. At the bedrock of the 4IR, knowledge and creative economy and beyond, are (communications and computer) networks, as well as telecommunications. Without these technologies, processes, and capabilities, remote work, activities, and communications will not be enabled, nor will communication and processing of data and information be empowered and enabled effectively and efficiently. Obviously, skills must be developed in these areas, hence, students must be taught.

ICT Networking Skills and Equipment Quagmire

Over and above the general information and communication technology (ICT) skills gap (Mikroyannidis et al., 2018, p. 1),, there are skills gap in the areas of networking and telecommunication, especially ICT networking which is the focus of this paper (Adesemowo, Mhlaba, et al., 2017; Mikroyannidis et al., 2018).

Compounding the scarcity of skills, is the challenge of inadequate physical equipment to go round for students training (Mikroyannidis et al., 2018). In the era of COVID-19, not only are there equipment inadequacy, there are accessibility constraint due to social and physical distancing protocol occasioned by COVID-19 pandemic (Crawford et al., 2020, p. 3). Gaming, virtual reality, augmented reality, animation, simulation, virtual and remote labs are some of the approaches that are being used as stop-gaps (de la Torre et al., 2015, p. 934; Lai & Bower, 2019, p. 32). Remote labs allow for 'controlled' access to physical equipment over the network or Internet (de la Torre et al., 2015, p. 935; Moss & Smith, 2010, p. 331). Virtual and remote labs are integrated with learning management systems (LMS) such as Moodle (de la Torre et al., 2015, p. 935) for collaborative remote sessions.

Increasingly, software-based ICT networking simulators/emulators are put to good use as virtual labs (Makasiranondh et al., 2010; Mikroyannidis et al., 2018; J. Pan & Jain, 2008). These ICT networks simulators have been found to be 'near' replacement for physical equipment or alternatives (Adesemowo & Kende, 2015; Makasiranondh et al., 2010; Moss & Smith, 2010). Although they are suitable for in situ and situated experiment sessions (Mikroyannidis et al., 2018, p. 3), they are not outright replacement though. In the area of situated learning, efforts are being made for web based simulators for teaching ICT network (Mikroyannidis et al., 2018, 2017).

Ontological Approach to Plugging the Gap

An integral part of teaching and learning is assessment. It (assessment) is now an indispensable part of teaching and learning (Lucía Romero et al., 2012), leading to extension into scholarship of teaching, learning and assessment – SoTLA (Adesemowo et al., 2016; Rust, 2011) or scholarship of assessment, learning and teaching – SALT (Janke & Kolar, 2014, p. 3). Romero et al. indicated on-going efforts in the use and integration of ontology for assessment. As would be seen later in this paper, most of the researches are around taxonomy of learning, concept mapping, multiple-choice questions (MCQ) type assessments, and auto-generation of domain-subject assessment.

Training in ICT networking comes with a mix of theoretical knowledge and hands-on practical/experimentation (Mikroyannidis et al., 2018, p. 3). Competencies attainment and cognitive constructive alignment are not just of the essence towards employability but must be critically assessed (Adesemowo, Mhlaba, et al., 2017, p. 2). The informed judgement about students' capabilities, scope of practice and attainments in hands-on skills and real-life assessment are at the root of authentic and most especially sustainable assessment. From a sustainable assessment viewpoint, there is a gap in the use of ontologies in area of simulated and/or psychomotor type of assessment. There is also a gap in simulated/psychomotor assessment integration into (online) e-assessment.

Against this backdrop, the aim (objective) of this chapter is two folds:

1. Exploratory review of ontology for assessment; and
2. Process towards ontology-modelling for psychomotor-related cognitive assessment with a focus on authentication.

Exploratory scoping review (Arksey & O'Malley, 2005; Levac et al., 2010), provides the methodological method for achieving on the first objective. The second uses a mix of ontological modelling and use-case (Arogundade et al., 2014; Shahzad, 2011), and ontology application evaluation (Ekelhart et al., 2009; Steiner & Albert, 2017). For both objectives, the methodological approach is multi-method (Johnson et al., 2007, p. 114; Tako & Kotiadis, 2015, p. 555) informed by plurality across paradigm rather than mixed-methods across qualitative and quantitative approaches (Mingers, 2001, p. 243).

The general perspective of this chapter is process of ontological model for cognitive psychomotor assessment that takes into cognizance authentication and is suitable for digital transformation in the 4IR, knowledge economy and beyond

Paper Structure

This chapter briefly looks at sustainable assessment in the context of (psychomotor and evidence centered design) e-assessment. Attempts at using ontology and the roles of ontology in assessment is reviewed in the following section. Thereafter, the NreASAM (ontological model) is introduced and discussed, which leads to conclusion.

In this chapter, IT and ICT are used interchangeably. Likewise, ICT networking, ICT networks and network engineering. When needed, emphasis is made, or peculiar differences are brought to the fore.

SUSTAINABLE ASSESSMENT AND ICT NETWORKING SIMULATORS

When I started teaching online after many years in a traditional classroom, I discovered that creating coursework for an online setting is not a transcriptional process, in which only the medium by which the content delivery differed, but a translational one in which I needed to use an entirely different set of tools – Phillip A. Ortiz (20 Mar 2020)

As indicated earlier, assessment is an integral part of teaching and learning. More so, ICT is an integral of 4IR, knowledge and creative economy and beyond. Therefore, e-assessment becomes a natural path for assessment (assessing 'IT' with 'IT'); use of and integrating technology (Shute et al., 2016). In this section, we explore sustainable assessment against the notion of informed psychomotor assessment using- and within ICT networking simulator.

Primer on Sustainable Assessment

A question one might ask is what type of assessment would be suitable for 4IR, knowledge and creative economy, and beyond. A simple response would be, one that is indicative of post-study 'realities' and not just content testing. Such is the foundation of sustainable assessment. A key focus of sustainable assessment is producing capable persons who can engage in professional work and contribute to society as an informed citizen and not just as a 'passed' or graduated learner (Boud & Soler, 2016). When institutional learning and teaching strategies are discussed, focus is nearly always on aligning learning outcomes (Adesemowo, Mhlaba, et al., 2017, p. 2). However, do the competencies relate to employability (Ferrel & Gray, 2015) and do the process of assessing enables employability as a long-term factor of learning (Boud & Soler, 2016, p. 401). Sustainable assessment leans towards a concept of learning outcome attainment, post-study competency and employability (Adesemowo, Oyedele, et al., 2017; Boud & Soler, 2016). Sustainable assessment focus is on assessments that equip students with competencies post-study beyond their curriculum contents. Thus, sustainable assessment ensures 'constructive alignment' between teaching system, learning process and assessment tasks; ditto alignment of learning with students' employability.

With the increase use of constructive forms of assessment, there is a greater focus on competency and a view towards employability. A challenge of constructive process of assessing psychomotor skills in ICT networking is the onerous task of higher-order cognitive assessment (Anderson et al., 2001; Heer, 2009). The student with post-study competency and employability attribute must be 'certified' to be the selfsame person that has 'graduated'. Here comes authenticity concern.

Authenticity in this regard relates to 'authentication' That is, in the process of automating assessment of pseudo-psychomotor activities in ICT networking simulators, students should not be allowed to claim another person's work as theirs. Consequentially, this also impacts on validity and reliability of assessment from a pedagogical point of view. Surely, students will always find a way-around, however, the automated assessment system must be robust enough to thwart efforts. Adesemowo, Mhlaba et al.(2017, p. 3) noted that 'authenticity' like the one being considered here, "does not stop students from getting assistance from a third-party to assist them in 'actually doing' the assessment tasks. Where the assessment is proctored, the 'third-party' can be largely addressed".

Nonetheless, when it comes to sustainable assessment, a degree of reliance must be in place. Practically, file-based submission systems, offline or online, suffer the same fate of students' dishonesty. Is the assessment activity done by the system? Is the student submitting their own work for assessment? Is the student getting marks for tasks they actually carried out? The list is inexhaustible.

Packet Tracer Capability for Sustainable Assessment

Considering ICT networking, with the inadequacy of physical equipment and the scalability of hands-on assessment for large classes, network simulators offer alternate platform for psychomotor experimenting and assessing. Two ICT networking simulators that have gained popularity are Graphical Network Simulator 3 (GNS3) and Cisco's Packet Tracer – PT (Adesemowo & Kende, 2015; Mikroyannidis et al., 2018). Adesemowo and Kende, and Mikroyannidis et al, affirmed that GNS3 offers a robust platform in carrying out pseudo-psychomotor activities (in term of scenario-task completeness). However, GNS3 is lacking behind PT as a virtual learning environment (VLE) from a teaching, learning and assessment viewpoint. More so, PT offers out-of-the-box experience for students, has in-built assessment capability and integration. In this paper, the case-study is the Cisco's PT.

Frezzo, Behrens, Mislevy, West, and DiCerbo (2009) affirmed that Packet Tracer is a comprehensive instructional ICT networks simulator for teaching and assessing skills and concepts associated with ICT networking. They further outlined Evidence Centered Design (ECD) capabilities inherent in Packet Tracer. ECD allows for designing assessments in such a way that activities-tasks can be designed at low-level granularity, such that students' activities can be tracked and assessed for varied learning objectives. This is critical in constructivist-connectivism process of assessing psychomotor skills in ICT networking. Readers are referred to Frezzo et al. (2009) for further detail on ECD-based design assessments in PT.

Higher order tasks at Bloom's taxonomy level of 'analyze', 'evaluate' and 'create' levels can be achieved using Packet Tracer. At the intersection of 'analyze', 'evaluate', and 'create' levels, students can be asked to conceptualize, design and configure a secure ICT network to meet the need of an organization. Hence, competencies are assessed

Beyond ECD-based assessments authoring and automatic self-evaluation of activities at Bloom's higher order, PT provides rich application programming interface (API) allowing for low-level interrogation and integration with other systems. Mikroyannidis et al. (2017), innovatively make use of these capabilities and they are extending PT beyond a virtual learning environment (VLE) to an online open education resource (OER) platform with PT Anywhere (Mikroyannidis et al., 2018). Adesemowo, Mhlaba, et al (2017), latched onto this to present an online auto-grading system.

Sustainable Assessment Recap

The Cisco Packet Tracer, apart from its pseudo-psychomotor capability, also offers an evidenced-based environment for assessment. PT can purposefully be engaged as a virtual laboratory and VLE. In addition, PT allows for deep and low-level interaction with its rich API. These pseudo-psychomotor, ECD and API capabilities, provide an enabling and good opportunity for sustainable assessment. The inherent programmability features of PT are perfect basis for including constrainer and (Ontological) knowledge representation system.

Review: Ontology for Assessment

So far, we have looked at the 4IR, knowledge and creative economy, and beyond from the importance of information. Flowing from that, ICT networking came to the fore. It was highlighted that there is a skills gap and there are challenges in training up for the next generation. A feasible workaround to physical equipment is the use of ICT networking simulators like Packet Tracer that is a VLE having ECD-based assessments and rich API that can facilitate sustainable assessment.

This section will now look at assessments and the place of ontology for assessment.

Explorative Review of Ontology for Assessment

Researches in the area of ontology for assessment were identified and highlighted through exploratory scoping review (Arksey & O'Malley, 2005; Levac et al., 2010). Literature search focused on ontology for assessment (the design and/or use of ontology for assessment purposes) and not the assessment of ontologies. Papers focusing on ontology for learning or e-learning or blended learning were given a cursory glance for interest purpose only.

Exploratory search was carried out in Google Scholar because of its reach and completeness (Gusenbauer, 2019). Search using "ontology for assessment" without the quote returned a whopping 628000 entries. Similarly, search with "'ontology" assessment'" returned 710000, whereas narrowed search with "'ontology" "e-assessment'" returned 1100. In a number of instances, returned papers are from the same authors or co-author with iteration of their ontology research project. In three instances, we included earlier and later research studies in instances we felt there are substantial advancement. Flowing from Larsen et al. (2019) reverse search and purposeful inclusion, three others were included. The authors appreciate the reviewers for their inputs as well.

The papers summarized in Table 1 were selected for relevance from the first 120 entries. Two main approaches were observed from the review, and four broad grouping of ontology were identified in the papers reviewed:

The two approaches are:

1. Automated assessment generation
    Most papers in this category explore the generation of MCQ assessment items using different approaches underpinned by ontology.
2. Ontology mapping and concept map
    The second category explore varying approaches of ontology mapping and concept mappings in designing and/or developing assessments.

The four broad grouping of ontology are (Al-Yahya, 2015, p. 69):

- "Domain-Task";
- "Task";
- "Domain"; and
- "Application".

Invariably, when considering ontology for assessments, one must take cognizance of whether the ontology-based assessments will be within one of these four groupings or it will cut across them. Their union, disjoint, and intersection must be considered when considering and designing ontology for assessments.

Table 1. Exploratory review: summary of ontology for assessment

#	Paper	Summary	Coverage	Grouping
1	Romero, L., Gutiérrez, M., & Caliusco, M. L. (2012). Conceptualizing the e-Learning Assessment Domain using an Ontology Network. NB: Update 2015 considered separately	Ontology network, AONet. Conceptualization of e-assessment domain. Support for semi-automatic generation of assessments enriched with rules for considering not only technical aspects of an assessment but also pedagogic.	concept map, ontology-based semi-auto generated assessment	"Application"
2	Orłowski, C., Ziółkowski, A., & Czarnecki, A. (2010). Validation of an Agent and Ontology-Based Information Technology Assessment System.	Ontology-based information technology assessment system. Focus on categorizing and establishing a hierarchy of terms related to IT domains. Performs validation of agents and preserves their functionalities. Can extend agent structure for technical systems to social-technical systems. Possess potential for IT domain assessment.	taxonomy of learning	"Domain"; "Application"
3	Al-Yahya, M. (2014). Ontology-Based Multiple Choice Question Generation.	OntoQue, ontology-based Multiple-Choice Question (MCQ) item generation system. Highlighted shortcomings with ontology-based MCQ item generation systems - educational significance MCQ item; - knowledge level; and - language structure.	ontology auto-generated, MCQ	"Domain-task"; "Application"
4	Litherland, K., Carmichael, P., & Martínez-García, A. (2013). Ontology-based e-Assessment for Accounting Education.	OeLe: ontology-based e-assessment system in the domain of accounting. Uses semantic technologies to offer online assessment. Marks students' free text answers to questions of a conceptual nature. Matches response with a 'concept map' or 'ontology' of domain knowledge expressed by subject specialists.	taxonomy of learning, concept map	"Domain"; "Application"
5	Vinu, E. V., & Kumar, P. S. (2015). Improving Large-Scale Assessment Tests by Ontology Based Approach. *(See also Vinu, E.V., & Kumar, P. S. (2017). Automated generation of assessment tests from domain ontologies. Semantic Web, 8(6), 1023–1047.*	Auto generation of question items for MCQs based on item-response theory (IRT). Knowledge formalized in ontologies to assist Intelligent Tutoring Systems (ITS). Question-Set Selection Heuristics screening techniques: - Property based screening - Concept based screening - Similarity based screening	concept map, MCQ	"Task"; "Application"
6	Romero, L., North, M., Gutiérrez, M., & Caliusco, L. (2015). Pedagogically-Driven Ontology Network for Conceptualizing the e-Learning Assessment Domain.	AONet, ontological network extended to take account of pedagogy. Conceptualizes the e-assessment domain with the aim of supporting the semi-automatic generation of assessment	Ontology-based semi-auto generated assessment, Concept map	"Domain"; "Application"

continues on following page

Table 1. Continued

#	Paper	Summary	Coverage	Grouping
7	Marzano, A., & Notti, A. M. (2015). Eduonto: an ontology for Educational Assessment.	EduOntoWiki: domain specific ontologies on the issues of assessment of learning (assessment) and system (evaluation). Teaching practices are linkable to theoretical constructs of Educational Assessment domain.	Taxonomy of learning, Concept map	"Domain"
8	Alsubait, T., Parsia, B., & Sattler, U. (2012). Automatic generation of analogy questions for student assessment: an Ontology-based approach.	New approach for generating analogies in MCQ format. Shift from delivery model to generation model.	Ontology auto generated assessment, MCQ	"Domain"; "Application"
9	Kumaran, V. S., & Sankar, A. (2013). An Automated Assessment of Students' Learning in e-Learning Using Concept Map and Ontology Mapping.	Concept map based assessment. Derived from students' learning using ontology mapping. Concept maps created by students are converted into ontology, and then mapped with the reference ontology created by the expert.	Ontology-based semi-auto generated assessment, Concept map	"Domain-task"; "Application"
10	Kumaran, V. S., & Sankar, A. (2015). Towards an automated system for short-answer assessment using ontology mapping.	Ontology for assessment ǀ ontology mapping for automated system for assessing short-answers.	Ontology auto assessment, Concept map	"Domain-task"; "Application"
11	Colace, F., & De Santo, M. (2010). Ontology for E-Learning: A Bayesian Approach. IEEE Transactions on Education.	Novel algorithm for ontology building through the use of Bayesian networks. Role of ontologies in context of e-learning and assessment. Introduction of ontologies formalism in e-learning field. Application of algorithm in the assessment process	Taxonomy of learning, Concept map	"Application"
12	Alves da Silva, A., Padilha, F. N., Siqueira, S., Baião, F. A., & Revoredo, K. (2012). Using Concept Maps and Ontology Alignment for Learning Assessment.	Based on educational constructivist theory of Meaningful Learning, concept maps are used from the viewpoint of domain ontologies Learning assessment model supported by the use of concept maps and ontology alignment techniques. 'Near' automation of organization of concepts from student's cognitive structure	Ontology-based semi-auto generated assessment, Taxonomy of learning, Concept map	"Domain-task"; "Application"
13	Al-Yahya, M. (2015). Ontologies in E-Learning: Review of the Literature.	Review of development and use of ontologies in domain of E-Learning systems. - Curriculum Modeling and management; - Describe learning domains (including assessment items); o Ontology mapping (with concept map); o ontology-based assessment system; - Describing learner data (including assessment data); - Describing E-Learning services.	Review.	"Domain-Task", "Task", "Domain", "Application"
14	Kaur, A., & Kumar, M. S. (2018). High Precision Latent Semantic Evaluation for Descriptive Answer Assessment.	Ontology for assessment ǀ Attempt to address keyword matching, sequence matching, quantitative analysis, fuzzy system, rule-based system used by LMS. Use High Precision Latent Semantic Evaluation for students' Descriptive answers; Good assessment between human assessor and computer assessor.	Ontology-concept semi-auto generated assessment, Concept map	"Domain"; "Application"
15	Cubric, M., & Tosic, M. (2011). Towards automatic generation of e-assessment using semantic web technologies.	ontology for assessment ǀ MCQOntology add new ontology elements (annotations), semantic interpretation (mapping between 'domain' and 'target' ontology). Semantic interpretation based on notion of 'question templates' (Bloom's taxonomy, Kolb's learning theory).	Ontology auto generated assessment, MCQ, Concept map	"Domain-task"; "Application";
16	Leshcheva, I., Gorovaya, D., & Leshchev, D. (2010). Ontology-based Assessment Technique.	Ontology as assessment ǀ Descriptive ontology design by students as assessment procedure. Formative and summarizing assessments. Extent and nature of students' knowledge and understanding determined through creating ontology and explaining the processes involved.	Taxonomy of learning, Concept map	"Domain-task";
17	Alsubait, T., Parsia, B., & Sattler, U. (2016). Ontology-Based Multiple Choice Question Generation.	ontology for assessment, ontology-based MCQ item generation system OntoQue holistic view incorporating learning content, learning objectives, lexical knowledge, and scenarios into a single cohesive framework.	Ontology auto generated assessment, MCQ	"Domain"; "Application"

continues on following page

Table 1. Continued

#	Paper	Summary	Coverage	Grouping
	Daramola, O., Afolabi, I., Akinyemi, I., & Oladipupo, O. (2013). Using Ontology-based Information Extraction for Subject-based Auto-grading.	Grading of students' essays and short answers, Automatic essay scoring, informative feedback. Meta-model engine, information extractor, auto-scoring engine, resources repository, domain ontology, WordNet,	Ontology-concept semi-auto assessment,	Domain, Application
	Ajetunmobi, S. A., & Daramola, O. (2017). Ontology-Based Information Extraction for SubjectFocussed Automatic Essay Evaluation.	Subject focused evaluation, knowledge base ontology, UML, information extraction, Semantic similarity matching, web application. Performance evaluation, usability evaluation	Ontology-concept, essay auto assessment,	Domain-task, Application
	Gutierrez, F., Dou, D., Martini, A., Fickas, S., & Zong, H. (2013). Hybrid ontology-based information extraction for automated text grading.	Hybrid Ontology-Based Information Extraction (OBIE), latent semantic analysis, automatic text grading, cell Biology	Ontology-concept semi-auto generated assessment,	Domain, Application
18	Proposed NreASAM	Ontology based framework/mapping for Automated online-submission grading of pseudo-psychomotor assessment. Ontology annotations, semantic interpretation.	Ontology-based auto grading, Taxonomy of learning, Concept map	Domain-task; Application

Source: Authors exploratory review of ontology for assessment

Gap in Ontology for Assessment

In the course of this decade, as evinced from our review, efforts have been put into and as a result, body of literature is forming on ontology for assessments (Ajetunmobi & Daramola, 2017; Al-Yahya, 2014, 2015, Alsubait et al., 2012, 2016; Alves da Silva et al., 2012; Colace & De Santo, 2010; Cubric & Tosic, 2011; Daramola et al., 2013; Gutierrez et al., 2013; Kaur & Kumar, 2018; Kumaran & Sankar, 2013, 2015; Leshcheva et al., 2010; Litherland et al., 2013; Marzano & Notti, 2015; Orłowski et al., 2010; Paneva-Marinova et al., 2012; Lucía Romero et al., 2012; Lucila Romero et al., 2015, 2014; Ellampallil Venugopal Vinu & Kumar, 2015). The development is welcomed and long overdue. However, the focus of most literature is on *taxonomy of learning, concept map, multiple-choice questions type assessments, and ontology-based auto generation and/or marking of assessments*. These are not *enough for sustainable assessment*.

As lofty as these concepts and approaches are, there is yet a gap regarding psychomotor-related cognitive assessment. Romero et al. (2012), highlighted the need to go beyond 'technical' ontology consideration to extend and duly consider educational pedagogies, aligning with Csapó (2012) et al. call for 'technology' advancing assessment in crucial dimensions. As part of extending and approaching from pedagogical viewpoint, this chapter introduces an ontology model that addresses an aspect of sustainable assessment; submission and auto-grading of pseudo-psychomotor assessment of ICT networking, and authentication in assessment generally. Network simulators that are ECD-capable can be integrated into pseudo-psychomotor assessments within the constraints of the underlying ontology. These are made collaborative-aware through further integration with LMS (de la Torre et al., 2015, p. 935).

The four-broad grouping of domain-task, task, domain and application, was taken into consideration in the ontology model introduced in this chapter. The authentication aspect of the ontology model introduced by this chapter cut across domains. At the same time, the instance of a network simulator covers domain-task and application

In the next section, the NreASAM – Non-repudiation e-assessment security architecture model – is introduced, foregrounded by overview of ontology.

NreASAM ONTOLOGY MODEL

Orłowski et al. (2010), described the architecture of an IT assessment model focused on categorizing and establishing a hierarchy of terms relating to IT domains. Their ontology-based model is multi-agent having multiple interfaces and capability for social-technical systems. A similar architecture is evidenced in NreASAM, to be introduced shortly.

Ontology

Before proceeding, it is expedient to discuss the reasons for ontology and not artificial intelligence or recommender system.

Firstly, ontology provides for explicit formal specifications of the terms in a domain and relations among them (Gcaza et al., 2015; Noy & McGuinness, 2001). It also allows for knowledge repository (Al-Yahya, 2015; Lucila Romero et al., 2014) and reasoning (Gcaza et al., 2015; Konys, 2018; J. Z. Pan et al., 2013). Lastly, but not limited, ontology allows for knowledge of use-misuse case (Arogundade et al., 2014).

Although, recommender systems are able to leverage on ontology and/or artificial intelligence in hybridization mode, however they must still overcome cold-start challenge (George & Lal, 2019; Lucía Romero et al., 2012). Hybridization is out of scope for this chapter.

From a formal specification and relationship point of view, ontology finds expression in taxonomy (Al-Yahya, 2015; Noy & McGuinness, 2001) and concept mapping (Alves da Silva et al., 2012; Noy & McGuinness, 2001).

Software development conceptualized, driven and/or underpinned by ontology, allows for scalability, reusability, interoperability and richer description, as well as modularity (Al-Yahya, 2015; J. Z. Pan et al., 2013; Shimizu et al., 2019).

Rationale for NreASAM

From the exploratory review, it comes to fore that developments of ontology for assessments have not been looking at the higher order cognitive level beyond those of reason, analyze and analogy. For ICT networks, a bedrock of 4IR, there is a need for higher order tasks at Bloom's taxonomy level of 'analyse', 'evaluate' and 'create'.

An ontology-based and/or ontology-driven e-assessment, online submission system must allow for 'domain-task' at this (higher) level. More so, such must allow for competencies based, cognitive 'constructive alignment' in line with cognitive constructivist.

However, it is not enough for valid pseudo-psychomotor tasks that supports sustainable assessments to be carried out, accuracy and authentication must also be ensured. This arose because ICT networks simulation-based assessments are nothing, but 'file' based. They are prone to cheating as any other file based submission assessment system (Adesemowo, Mhlaba, et al., 2017; Joy et al., 2005; Koorsse et al., 2016; Webb, 2010). This drawback is the unfortunate dishonest act of a student submitting another student's file or a different file different from the actual assessment activity file. The pedagogical impacts are seen in accuracy, validity and reliability of the assessment.

The need to investigate and design an ontology driven system that assist with authenticity challenges in automated pseudo-psychomotor assessment for ICT networking is of the essence.

Approach Towards Elements of the NreASAM Ontology

Complementary and guiding the approach is the design and development research (DDR) method. Richey and Klein (2014, p. 142) define DDR as "the systematic study of design, development and evaluation processes with the aim of establishing an empirical basis for the creation of instructional and non-instructional products and tools and new or enhanced models that govern their development . It includes the study of the design and development process as a whole, of particular components of the process, or the impact of specific design and development efforts". The following applies in this research project:

Design: leverage on exploratory review to elucidate design elements;
Design: leverage on Arogundade et al. to conceptualize the NreASAM ontology;
Develop: Use Protégé to develop NreASAM ontology;
Develop: iterative software development using programming tools: JAVA, PHP et al;
Process: authentication model, influenced by the NreASAM;
Process: automated grading system;

Arogundade, Jin and Yang (2014), used a use-case approached that adopted part of IEEE 1074-1995 standard (1996) for software development-oriented processes, to develop their ontology. Part of the steps are used in this paper.

- Determine ontology scope and domain and purpose;
  - Informed by exploratory scoping review.
- Elicit important domain terms;
  - Gathered from exploratory review, study of Cisco's Packet Tracers ECD capabilities, study of access control system, and leverage on requirements for online, auto grading system.
- Define classes and class hierarchy;
- Ontology design and coding;
  - Define and design followed iterative ontology development, facilitated by ontology tools: Protégé (Musen & The Protégé Team, 2015), OWLAx (Sarker et al., 2018), OWLGrEd (Bārzdiņš et al., 2010).

The choice of OWLAx and OWLGrEd was informed by Paulheim (2011) "visualization and interaction" components of ontology-enhances user interfaces approaches. Concept, structure and interaction are further based on the "Scope, Structure, Skeleton" elements of Garrett's user experience elements as adapted for ontology by Shahzad (2011).

Elements of the NreASAM ontology

The elements of the NreASAM model will be discussed with a focus on authentication, use-case and annotations.

Authentication

There are four core processes of access control: identification, authentication, authorization and accountability. The degree of need and impact of the four process in each access control system varies.

The NreASAM model provides for identification and authentication. To a lesser extent, authorization takes place. NreASAM works on the concept of non-repudiation model. Students authenticate themselves against the simulator as well as the online system. The students take ownership of their pseudo-psychomotor activity file. The NreASAM becomes a modelled approach of authenticity for use as an effective way of identifying and authenticating student PT files in an automated pseudo-psychomotor assessment system. Further details on authentication are presented in the conceptual NSAM model (Adesemowo, Mhlaba, et al., 2017).

Relevant objects and properties are:

- Login
- PEP_PolicyExtraction;
- requestXACML and respondXACML;
- getXACMLPolicy and putXACMLPolicy;
- PDP and PolicyReposity classes;

The actual (software development) implementation will vary from one learning management system to another. Variations will be informed by the development environment, credential vault/repository et al.

Use-Misuse Case

Beyond authentication, from a use-misuse case viewpoint, object property constrainers are conceptualized, such as:

- Request-and-UploadActivityFile;
- PerformActivities;
- Design-and-UploadActivity;
- Request-and-UpdateMarks;
- Uses;

Annotation

Classes and objects are annotated in the ontology. Although, work is ongoing in this area, the comments are important elements of knowledge representations and domain specific taxonomy.

The annotation for the 'SustainableAssessment' class, shown in Figure 1, is "*It prepares learners for reality of post-study era See Boud and Soler, 2016*", and is of the type 'rdfs:comment'. An annotation like this ensures that academic reference to literature is part and parcel of the ontology.

Figure 1. Sample annotations and class view of Sustainable Assessment

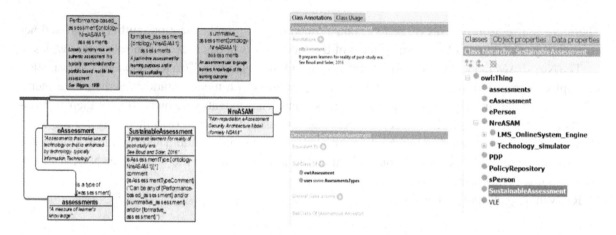

Ontology Mapping and Integration into Software Application

The NreASAM ontology, with the metrics in Table 2, was developed in Protégé, and is part of a bigger ontology-influenced Packet Tracer pseudo-psychomotor auto grading online submission system, as can be seen in Figure 3.

Figure 2. Ontological representation of the NreASAM model with classes and object properties

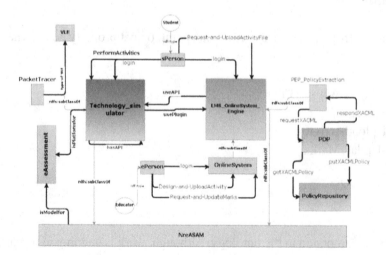

Table 2. NreASAM ontology essential metrics (excluding data properties and disjoints classes)

Elements	metrics
Axiom	136
Logical axiom count	82
Declaration axioms count	38
Class count	15
Object property count	17
Individual count	5
Class axioms: SubClassOf	76
Class axiom: GCI count	33
Individual axioms: ClassAssertion	05
Annotation axioms: AnnotationAssertion	16

Figure 3. NreASAM ontology representation with associations

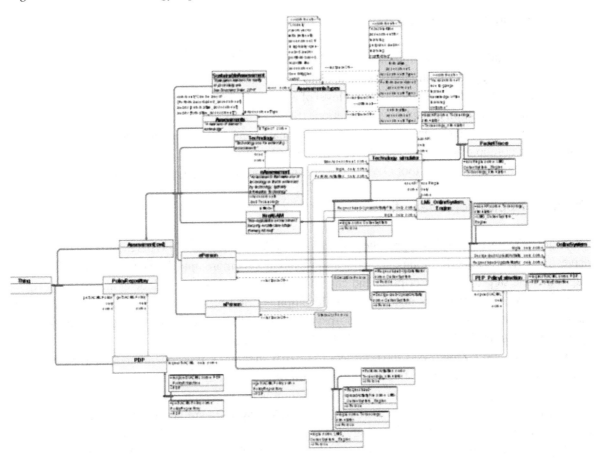

As part of assessment integrity (Adesemowo et al., 2016), the NreASAM define a PEP_PolicyExtraction to interface with "eXtensible Access Control Markup Language" (XACML) based policy decision point (PDP) to reach "Permit" or "Deny" decisions.

The learning management system or online assessment system (LMS) interfaces with the simulator through API calls. The LMS, in this instance Moodle, has inbuilt login authentication. Likewise, the Cisco's Packet Tracer has API calls for login authentication. In this regard, instance of (Cisco Packet Tracer) simulator is included in the online system as a plugin.

Evaluation and NreASAM Driven Auto-Grading Online Submission System

As discussed in the 'introduction' section, the focus of this chapter is not the 'construction' of NreASAM ontology. Rather, the aim is to carry out exploratory review as a process towards ontological-modelling of a system for psychomotor-related cognitive assessments with a focus on authentication (as part of assessments integrity).

Given the aim of the research process, the evaluation need not be formal methods. The more appropriate, in this instance, is the mix of ontological modelling, use-case and ontology application evaluation (Arogundade et al., 2014; Ekelhart et al., 2009; Shahzad, 2011; Steiner & Albert, 2017).

Ontology Consistency Evaluation

As seen from earlier section "approach towards elements of the NreASAM ontology", OWLAx and OWLGrEd ontology-modelling tools were used to conceptualize, model and design NreASAM. They (OWLAx and OWLGrEd) provided the first level of evaluation through their inbuilt 'consistency' check of class/object generation and axioms generation.

Ontology (logical, structure, syntactic coding format) consistency was internally validated within Protégé by a combo of FaCT++ and Pellet reasoners (Arogundade et al., 2014; Tsarkov & Horrocks, 2006), and Manchester online tool OWL Validator: mowl-power.cs.man.ac.uk:8080/validator/.

Ontology Application Evaluation

There are different assessment approaches for ontologies (McDaniel, 2017). Where ontology influences/drives/informs software development, application validation is more apt (Steiner & Albert, 2017) This might include step-by-step description and case study (or use-case) (Arogundade et al., 2014).

The NreASAM model, has influenced the development of a proof-of-concept auto-grading online submission system for Packet Tracer pseudo-psychomotor activity file. It is a web-based system (as a proxy for the targeted LMS system – Moodle) as shown in Figure 4.

As with Orłowski, Ziółkowski and Czarnecki's (2010), in their IT assessment model, NreASAM also modularly interfaces with the rest of the online submission system as shown in Fig. 3. In NreASAM, at the moment, the auto-grading online submission system is influenced by NreASAM, The 'influenced by' speaks to "visualization and interaction" (2011), whereby software are design based on the "concepts, structures and skeletons" of ontology (2011). They guide the approach to conceptualization and ontological modelling in model driven software development (Shahzad, 2011, p. 1081). using ontologies as a base structure for GUI development.

To varying degree, the following aspects of Verma's (2017, fig. 1) 'Abstract Model of Ontology Evaluation' were considered and satisfied:

3.   (limited) User/Expert based Evaluation;
4.   Criteria Based Evaluation;
5.   Context or application level;
6.   Application or Task based

Figure 4. Webpage interface for the auto-grading online submission system

Summary of NreASAM Ontology Model

In the next phase, the auto-grading online submission system will not only be conceptualized by NreASAM, but will directly interact and directly modelled on NreASAM ontology through system API calls between the NreASAM ontology, NreASAM submission system and LMS (Moodle). This will be in-line with the AURUM ontology-based security risk assessment system (Ekelhart et al., 2009), and HMCO bio-ontology system. In AURUM, the prototypical graphical user interface (GUI) was built on top of the ontological model. Likewise, HMCO is a semantic web GUI application using the NetBeans Java IDE, and making use of Protégé ontology Java APIs (Olawande & Segun, 2009).

CONCLUSION AND FUTURE RESEARCH DIRECTIONS

The chapter through exploratory scoping literature review of ontology for assessments has looked into a gap of assessing at higher cognitive level per blooms taxonomy. Most efforts toward ontology for assessments have focused on taxonomy of learning, auto-generation of assessments item, notably multiple-choice questions, and auto-marking of multiple-choice questions and essays.

This chapter contributes to the existing body of work on ontology for assessment in the aspect of authenticity of assessments. The main contribution of this chapter is the exploratory review of ontology for assessment and the presentation of the NreASAM ontology 'model' that will assist with authenticity of online submission system, (especially performance-based and/or pseudo-psychomotor assessments suitable for authentic and/or sustainable assessments). In this instance, the automatic grading of Packet Tracer activity (assessment) files.

Future work on NreASAM will in the immediate be annotations (populating the rdfs:comment properties for classes). By this (rdfs annotation), NreASAM can extend "Domain" and "Application" ontology classification (Al-Yahya, 2015), thereby finding usage in knowledge representation and automatic generation of assessments based on item response theory (E.V. Vinu & Kumar, 2017).

In tandem, the proof of concept online submission webpage will be iteratively developed with NreASAM becoming the primary and main foundational building block. The Packet Tracer auto-grading online submission system will integrate directly with NreASAM through API system calls and ontology-constraint modelling, It will no longer be merely conceptualized using the NreASAM as ontological mapping (Shahzad, 2011, p. 1080).

Further future work, from software engineering and technology enhanced learning viewpoints, will in the long run be centered on greater abstraction, modular and scalable design of the online submission and auto-grading system to suit and adapt to varying LMS.

This chapter has presented and discussed the NreASAM as an ontology model that informs the design of an auto-grading online submission system for ICT networking pseudo-psychomotor assessments. It highlights aspects of advanced concepts, methods, and applications in semantic computing from ontology point of view. Readers should be able to leverage on the approach in this chapter to apply and advance ontology, recommender systems and semantic computing in general to solutions that require constrainer and knowledge reasoning. As many HEIs are rapidly deploying and moving towards technology enhanced learning, especially by starting with online learning, assessments challenges are of concerns. We have presented a concept and development that HEIs can leverage on in the quest during and post COVID-19, as well as in the 4IR, knowledge economy and beyond.

ACKNOWLEDGMENT

This research work was conducted using the Protégé resource (graciously made available by Stanford Center for Biomedical Informatics Research – BMIR), which is supported by grant GM10331601 from the National Institute of General Medical Sciences of the United States National Institutes of Health.

REFERENCES

Adesemowo, A. K., Johannes, H., Goldstone, S., & Terblanche, K. (2016). The experience of introducing secure e-assessment in a South African university first-year foundational ICT networking course. *Africa Education Review*, *13*(1), 67–86. doi:10.1080/18146627.2016.1186922

Adesemowo, A. K., & Kende, N. (2015). Students' Learning Experience of ICT Networking via Simulated Platform at a South African University. In C. A. Shoniregun (Ed.), *IICE-2015 Proceedings* (pp. 65–75). www.iicedu.org/IICE-2015 October/IICE_Home.html

Adesemowo, A. K., Mhlaba, S., Yekela, O., & Ndame, L. (2017). An auto grading online submission system: Case of packet tracer. In A. Mesquita & P. Peres (Eds.), *Proceedings of the 16th European Conference on e-Learning ECEL 2017* (pp. 1–8). Academic Conferences and Publishing International Limited. https://www.academic-bookshop.com/ourshop/prod_6222116-ECEL-2017-PDF-Proceedings-of-the-16th-European-Conference-on-eLearning.html

Adesemowo, A. K., Oyedele, Y., & Oyedele, O. (2017). Text-based sustainable assessment: A case of first-year information and communication technology networking students. *Studies in Educational Evaluation*, *55*, 1–8. doi:10.1016/j.stueduc.2017.04.005

Ajetunmobi, S. A., & Daramola, O. (2017, October). Ontology-Based Information Extraction for SubjectFocussed Automatic Essay Evaluation. *2017 International Conference on Computing Networking and Informatics (ICCNI)*. 10.1109/ICCNI.2017.8123781

Al-Yahya, M. (2014). Ontology-Based Multiple Choice Question Generation. *TheScientificWorldJournal*, *2014*, 1–9. doi:10.1155/2014/274949 PMID:24982937

Al-Yahya, M. (2015). Ontologies in E-Learning: Review of the Literature. *International Journal of Software Engineering and Its Applications*, *9*(2), 67–84.

Alsubait, T., Parsia, B., & Sattler, U. (2012). Automatic generation of analogy questions for student assessment: an Ontology-based approach. *Research in Learning Technology*, *20*(sup1), 19198. doi:10.3402/rlt.v20i0.19198

Alsubait, T., Parsia, B., & Sattler, U. (2016). Ontology-Based Multiple Choice Question Generation. *KI - Künstliche Intelligenz*, *30*(2), 183–188. doi:10.100713218-015-0405-9

Alves da Silva, A., Padilha, F. N., Siqueira, S., Baião, F. A., & Revoredo, K. (2012). Using Concept Maps and Ontology Alignment for Learning Assessment. *IEEE Technology and Engineering Education*, *7*(3), 33–40. https://www.semanticscholar.org/paper/Using-Concept-Maps-and-Ontology-Alignment-for-(-)-Silva-Padilha/0b130e5c2200a15f2c93f210d73a060547a42415

Anderson, L. W., Krathwohl, D. R., & Bloom, B. S. (2001). *A taxonomy for learning, teaching, and assessing: a revision of Bloom's taxonomy of educational objectives*. Longman. http://books.google.com/books?id=bcQlAQAAIAAJ&pgis=1

Arksey, H., & O'Malley, L. (2005). Scoping studies: Towards a methodological framework. *International Journal of Social Research Methodology*, *8*(1), 19–32. doi:10.1080/1364557032000119616

Arogundade, O. T., Jin, Z., & Yang, X. (2014). Towards ontological approach to eliciting risk-based security requirements. *International Journal of Information and Computer Security*, 6(2), 143. doi:10.1504/IJICS.2014.065168

Bārzdiņš, J., Bārzdiņš, G., Čerāns, K., Liepiņš, R., & Sproģis, A. (2010). UML Style Graphical Notation and Editor for OWL 2. In P. Forbrig & H. Günther (Eds.), Perspectives in Business Informatics Research. BIR 2010. Lecture Notes in Business Information Processing (Vol. 64, pp. 102–114). Springer. doi:10.1007/978-3-642-16101-8_9

Boud, D., & Soler, R. (2016). Sustainable assessment revisited. *Assessment & Evaluation in Higher Education*, 41(3), 400–413. doi:10.1080/02602938.2015.1018133

Colace, F., & De Santo, M. (2010). Ontology for E-Learning: A Bayesian Approach. *IEEE Transactions on Education*, 53(2), 223–233. doi:10.1109/TE.2009.2012537

Craig, B. D. (n.d.). *Moving beyond the knowledge economy*. End2End Integration. Retrieved March 23, 2014, from http://www.e2ei.com/site/article.php?id=15

Crawford, J., Butler-Henderson, K., Rudolph, J., Malkawi, B., Glowatz, M., Burton, R., Magni, P. A., & Lam, S. (2020). COVID-19: 20 countries' higher education intra-period digital pedagogy responses. *Journal of Applied Learning & Teaching*, 3(1). Advance online publication. doi:10.37074/jalt.2020.3.1.7

Csapó, B., Ainley, J., Bennett, R. E., Latour, T., & Law, N. (2012). Technological Issues for Computer-Based Assessment. In P. Griffin, B. McGaw, & E. Care (Eds.), *Assessment and Teaching of 21st Century Skills* (pp. 143–230). Springer Netherlands. doi:10.1007/978-94-007-2324-5_4

Cubric, M., & Tosic, M. (2011). Towards automatic generation of e-assessment using semantic web technologies. *International Journal of E-Assessment*, 1(1). https://ijea.org.uk/ijea/index.php/journal/article/view/16

Daniel, S. J. (2020). Education and the COVID-19 pandemic. *Prospects*, 1–6. doi:10.100711125-020-09464-3 PMID:32313309

Daramola, O., Afolabi, I., Akinyemi, I., & Oladipupo, O. (2013). Using Ontology-based Information Extraction for Subject-based Auto-grading. *Proceedings of the International Conference on Knowledge Engineering and Ontology Development: KEOD, (IC3K 2013)*, 1, 373–378. 10.5220/0004625903730378

de la Torre, L., Guinaldo, M., Heradio, R., & Dormido, S. (2015). The Ball and Beam System: A Case Study of Virtual and Remote Lab Enhancement With Moodle. *IEEE Transactions on Industrial Informatics*, 11(4), 934–945. doi:10.1109/TII.2015.2443721

Ekelhart, A., Fenz, S., & Neubauer, T. (2009). AURUM: A Framework for Information Security Risk Management. *Proceedings of the 42nd Hawaii International Conference on System Sciences - HICSS*, 1–10. 10.1109/HICSS.2009.595

Ferrel, G., & Gray, L. (2015, August 31). *Enhancing student employability through technology-supported assessment and feedback*. JISC Guide. https://www.jisc.ac.uk/guides/enhancing-student-employability-through-technology-supported-assessment-and-feedback

Frezzo, D. C., Behrens, J. T., & Mislevy, R. J. (2009). Design Patterns for Learning and Assessment: Facilitating the Introduction of a Complex Simulation-Based Learning Environment into a Community of Instructors. *Journal of Science Education and Technology, 19*(2), 105–114. doi:10.100710956-009-9192-0

Frezzo, D. C., Behrens, J. T., Mislevy, R. J., West, P., & DiCerbo, K. E. (2009). Psychometric and Evidentiary Approaches to Simulation Assessment in Packet Tracer Software. *2009 Fifth International Conference on Networking and Services*, 555–560. 10.1109/ICNS.2009.89

Gcaza, N., von Solms, R., & Jansen Van Vuuren, J. (2015). An Ontology for a National Cyber-Security Culture Environment. In S. M. Furnell & N. L. Clarke (Eds.), *Human Aspects of Information Security & Assurance (HAISA 2015)* (pp. 1–10). Issue Haisa. https://books.google.co.za/books?id=NQJqCwAAQB AJ&pg=PA1&lpg=PA1&dq=An+Ontology+for+a+National+Cyber-Security+Culture+Environment

George, G., & Lal, A. M. (2019). Review of ontology-based recommender systems in e-learning. *Computers & Education, 142*, 103642. doi:10.1016/j.compedu.2019.103642

Goede, M. (2011). The wise society: Beyond the knowledge economy. *Foresight, 13*(1), 36–45. doi:10.1108/14636681111109688

Gusenbauer, M. (2019). Google Scholar to overshadow them all? Comparing the sizes of 12 academic search engines and bibliographic databases. *Scientometrics, 118*(1), 177–214. doi:10.100711192-018-2958-5

Gutierrez, F., Dou, D., Martini, A., Fickas, S., & Zong, H. (2013). Hybrid Ontology-based Information Extraction for Automated Text Grading. *Proceedings - 12th International Conference on Machine Learning and Applications, ICMLA 2013, 1*, 359–364. 10.1109/ICMLA.2013.73

Heer, R. (2009, March). *A Model of Learning Objectives.* https://www.celt.iastate.edu/teaching-resources/effective-practice/revised-blooms-taxonomy/

Janke, K., & Kolar, C. (2014). Recognizing and Disseminating Innovations in Scholarly Teaching and Learning to Support Curricular Change. *Innovations in Pharmacy, 5*(3), 161. doi:10.24926/iip.v5i3.343

Johnson, R. B., Onwuegbuzie, A. J., & Turner, L. A. (2007). Toward a Definition of Mixed Methods Research. *Journal of Mixed Methods Research, 1*(2), 112–133. doi:10.1177/1558689806298224

Joy, M., Griffiths, N., & Boyatt, R. (2005). The boss online submission and assessment system. *Journal of Educational Resources in Computing, 5*(3), 1–27. doi:10.1145/1163405.1163407

Kaur, A., & Kumar, M. S. (2018). High Precision Latent Semantic Evaluation for Descriptive Answer Assessment. *Journal of Computational Science, 14*(10), 1293–1302. doi:10.3844/jcssp.2018.1293.1302

Konys, A. (2018). An Ontology-Based Knowledge Modelling for a Sustainability Assessment Domain. *Sustainability, 10*(2), 300. doi:10.3390u10020300

Koorsse, M., Taljaard, M., & Calitz, A. P. (2016). A Comparison of E-Assessment Assignment Submission Processes in Introductory Computing Courses. In I. C. T. Education (Ed.), *SACLA 2016. Communications in Computer and Information Science* (Vol. 642, pp. 35–42). Springer. doi:10.1007/978-3-319-47680-3_3

Kumaran, V. S., & Sankar, A. (2013). An Automated Assessment of Students' Learning in e-Learning Using Concept Map and Ontology Mapping. In J. Wang & R. Lau (Eds.), Lecture Notes in Computer Science: Vol. 8167. *Advances in Web-Based Learning – ICWL 2013* (pp. 274–283). Springer. doi:10.1007/978-3-642-41175-5_28

Kumaran, V. S., & Sankar, A. (2015). Towards an automated system for short-answer assessment using ontology mapping. *International Arab Journal of E-Technology, 4*(1), 17–24. https://dblp.org/db/journals/iajet/iajet4.html

Lai, J. W. M., & Bower, M. (2019). How is the use of technology in education evaluated? A systematic review. *Computers & Education, 133*, 27–42. doi:10.1016/j.compedu.2019.01.010

Larsen, K. R., Hovorka, D. S., Dennis, A. R., & West, J. D. (2019). Understanding the Elephant: The Discourse Approach to Boundary Identification and Corpus Construction for Theory Review Articles. *Journal of the Association for Information Systems, 20*(7), 887–927. doi:10.17705/1jais.00556

Lee, M., Yun, J., Pyka, A., Won, D., Kodama, F., Schiuma, G., Park, H., Jeon, J., Park, K., Jung, K., Yan, M.-R., Lee, S., & Zhao, X. (2018). How to Respond to the Fourth Industrial Revolution, or the Second Information Technology Revolution? Dynamic New Combinations between Technology, Market, and Society through Open Innovation. *Journal of Open Innovation, 4*(3), 21. doi:10.3390/joitmc4030021

Leshcheva, I., Gorovaya, D., & Leshchev, D. (2010). Ontology-based Assessment Technique. In T. Tiropanis, H. Davis, & P. Carmichael (Eds.), *The 2nd International Workshop on Semantic Web Applications in Higher Education (SemHE'10)* (pp. 1–3). https://eprints.soton.ac.uk/271753/

Levac, D., Colquhoun, H., & O'Brien, K. K. (2010). Scoping studies: Advancing the methodology. *Implementation Science; IS, 5*(1), 69. doi:10.1186/1748-5908-5-69 PMID:20854677

Litherland, K., Carmichael, P., & Martínez-García, A. (2013). Ontology-based e-Assessment for Accounting Education. *Accounting Education, 22*(5), 498–501. doi:10.1080/09639284.2013.824198

Makasiranondh, W., Maj, S. P., & Veal, D. (2010). Pedagogical evaluation of simulation tools usage in Network Technology Education. *World Transactions on Engineering and Technology Education (WTE&TE), 8*(3), 321–326. http://www.wiete.com.au/journals/WTE%26TE/Pages/Vol.8,No.3%282010%29/13-12-Makasiranondh.pdf

Marzano, A., & Notti, A. M. (2015). Eduonto: An ontology for Educational Assessment. *Journal of E-Learning and Knowledge Society, 11*(1), 69–82. doi:10.20368/1971-8829/978

McDaniel, H. M. (2017). An Automated System for the Assessment and Ranking of Domain Ontologies [Georgia State University]. *Computer Science Dissertations.* https://scholarworks.gsu.edu/cs_diss/133

Mikroyannidis, A., Gómez-Goiri, A., Smith, A., & Domingue, J. (2017). Online Experimentation and Interactive Learning Resources for Teaching Network Engineering. *The IEEE Global Engineering Education Conference (EDUCON) 2017*, 181–188. 10.1109/EDUCON.2017.7942845

Mikroyannidis, A., Gómez-Goiri, A., Smith, A., & Domingue, J. (2018). PT Anywhere: A mobile environment for practical learning of network engineering. *Interactive Learning Environments*, 1–15. doi:10.1080/10494820.2018.1541911

Mingers, J. (2001). Combining IS Research Methods: Towards a Pluralist Methodology. *Information Systems Research, 12*(3), 240–259. doi:10.1287/isre.12.3.240.9709

Moss, N., & Smith, A. (2010). Large Scale Delivery of Cisco Networking Academy Program by Blended Distance Learning. *2010 Sixth International Conference on Networking and Services*, 329–334. 10.1109/ICNS.2010.52

Musen, M. A.The Protégé Team. (2015). The protégé project: A look back and a look forward. *AI Matters, 1*(4), 4–12. doi:10.1145/2757001.2757003 PMID:27239556

Noy, N. F., & McGuinness, D. L. (2001). *Ontology Development 101: A Guide to Creating Your First Ontology* (Stanford Knowledge Systems Laboratory Technical Report KSL-01-05 and Stanford Medical Informatics Technical Report SMI-2001-0880). http://www.ksl.stanford.edu/people/dlm/papers/ontology-tutorial-noy-mcguinness-abstract.html

Olawande, D., & Segun, F. (2009). Developing Ontology Support for Human Malaria Control Initiatives. *Nature Precedings*, 1–1. doi:10.1038/npre.2009.3591.1

Orłowski, C., Ziółkowski, A., & Czarnecki, A. (2010). Validation of an Agent and Ontology-Based Information Technology Assessment System. *Cybernetics and Systems, 41*(1), 62–74. doi:10.1080/01969720903408805

Pan, J., & Jain, R. (2008). *A survey of network simulation tools: Current status and future developments*. https://scholar.google.co.za/scholar?oi=bibs&cluster=6577555124204483644&btnI=1&hl=en

Pan, J. Z., Staab, S., Aßmann, U., Ebert, J., & Zhao, Y. (Eds.). (2013). *Ontology-Driven Software Development*. Springer Berlin Heidelberg., doi:10.1007/978-3-642-31226-7

Paneva-Marinova, D., Pavlova-Draganova, L., Draganov, L., & Georgiev, V. (2012). Ontological presentation of analysis method for technology-enhanced learning. *Proceedings of the 13th International Conference on Computer Systems and Technologies - CompSysTech '12*, 384. 10.1145/2383276.2383332

Paulheim, H. (2011). Ontologies in User Interface Development. In *Ontology-based Application Integration* (pp. 61–75). Springer. doi:10.1007/978-1-4614-1430-8_4

Richey, R. C., & Klein, J. D. (2014). Design and development research. In J. M. Spector, M. D. Merrill, J. Elen, & M. J. Bishop (Eds.), *Handbook of Research on Educational Communications and Technology* (4th ed., pp. 141–150). Springer. doi:10.1007/978-1-4614-3185-5_12

Romero, L., Gutierrez, M., & Caliusco, L. (2014). Towards Semantically Enriched E-learning Assessment: Ontology-Based Description of Learning Objects. *2014 IEEE 14th International Conference on Advanced Learning Technologies*, 336–338. 10.1109/ICALT.2014.236

Romero, L., Gutiérrez, M., & Caliusco, M. L. (2012). Conceptualizing the e-Learning Assessment Domain using an Ontology Network. *International Journal of Interactive Multimedia and Artificial Intelligence, 1*(6), 20–28. doi:10.9781/ijimai.2012.163

Romero, L., North, M., Gutiérrez, M., & Caliusco, L. (2015). Pedagogically-Driven Ontology Network for Conceptualizing the e-Learning Assessment Domain. *Journal of Educational Technology & Society, 18*(4), 312–330. doi:10.2307/jeductechsoci.18.4.312

Rust, C. (2011). The Unscholarly Use of Numbers in Our Assessment Practices: What Will Make Us Change? *International Journal for the Scholarship of Teaching and Learning, 5*(1), 1–6. doi:10.20429/ijsotl.2011.050104

Sarker, M. K., Krisnadhi, A. A., & Hitzler, P. (2018). OWLAx: A Protege Plugin to Support Ontology Axiomatization through Diagramming. *Proceedings of the ISWC, 2016,* 1690. https://arxiv.org/abs/1808.10105

Shahzad, S. K. (2011). Ontology-based User Interface Development: User Experience Elements Pattern. *Journal of Universal Computer Science, 17*(7), 1078–1088. doi:10.3217/jucs-017-07-1078

Shimizu, C., Eberhart, A., Karima, N., Hirt, Q., Krisnadhi, A., & Hitzler, P. (2019). A Method for Automatically Generating Schema Diagrams for OWL Ontologies. In B. Villazón-Terrazas & Y. Hidalgo-Delgado (Eds.), *Knowledge Graphs and Semantic Web. KGSWC 2019* (Vol. 1029, pp. 149–161). Springer. doi:10.1007/978-3-030-21395-4_11

Shute, V. J., Leighton, J. P., Jang, E. E., & Chu, M.-W. (2016). Advances in the Science of Assessment. *Educational Assessment, 21*(1), 34–59. doi:10.1080/10627197.2015.1127752

Steiner, C. M., Albert, D., & Wang, S. (2017). Validating domain ontologies: A methodology exemplified for concept maps. *Cogent Education, 4*(1), 1263006. Advance online publication. doi:10.1080/2331186X.2016.1263006

Tako, A. A., & Kotiadis, K. (2015). PartiSim: A multi-methodology framework to support facilitated simulation modelling in healthcare. *European Journal of Operational Research, 244*(2), 555–564. doi:10.1016/j.ejor.2015.01.046

Tsarkov, D., & Horrocks, I. (2006). FaCT++ Description Logic Reasoner: System Description. In U. Furbach & N. Shankar (Eds.), Lecture Notes in Computer Science: Vol. 4130. *Automated Reasoning. IJCAR 2006* (pp. 292–297). Springer. doi:10.1007/11814771_26

Verma, A. (2017, January 18). An abstract framework for ontology evaluation. *Proceedings of the 2016 International Conference on Data Science and Engineering, ICDSE 2016.* 10.1109/ICDSE.2016.7823945

Vinu, E. V., & Kumar, P. S. (2015). Improving Large-Scale Assessment Tests by Ontology Based Approach. *Proceedings of the Twenty-Eighth International Florida Artificial Intelligence Research Society Conference,* 457–462. https://www.aaai.org/ocs/index.php/FLAIRS/FLAIRS15/paper/view/10359

Vinu, E. V., & Kumar, P. S. (2017). Automated generation of assessment tests from domain ontologies. *Semantic Web, 8*(6), 1023–1047. doi:10.3233/SW-170252

Webb, D. C. (2010). Troubleshooting assessment: An authentic problem solving activity for IT education. *Procedia: Social and Behavioral Sciences, 9,* 903–907. doi:10.1016/j.sbspro.2010.12.256

WHO. (2020). *Coronavirus disease 2019 (COVID-19) situation report.* World Health Organisation. https://www.who.int/emergencies/diseases/novel-coronavirus-2019/situation-reports

KEY TERMS AND DEFINITIONS

Bloom's Taxonomy: Bloom's taxonomy is a set of three hierarchical models used to classify educational learning objectives into levels of complexity and specificity. It consists of six major categories: Knowledge, Comprehension, Application, Analysis, Synthesis, and Evaluation.

COVID-19/nCov-19: Coronavirus disease, or novel coronavirus.

NreASAM: Non-repudiation e-assessment security architecture model.

Ontology: A set of concepts and categories or classification representation in a subject area or domain that shows their properties and the relations between them. In this chapter, ontology is not the philosophical study of being.

Sustainable Assessment: Assessment 'that meets the needs of the present and [also] prepares students to meet their own future learning needs' (Boud 2000, p. 151). It is a way of rethinking outcomes, curriculum, and pedagogy away from a focus on disciplinary knowledge to what students can do in the world.

Chapter 10
UcEF for Semantic IR:
An Integrated Context-Based Web Analytics Method

Bernard Ijesunor Akhigbe

https://orcid.org/0000-0002-0241-4739

Department of Computer Science & Engineering, Obafemi Awolowo University, Nigeria

ABSTRACT

At present, keyword-based techniques allow information retrieval (IR) but are unable to capture the conceptualizations in users' information needs and contents. The response to this has been semantic search computing with commendable success. Surprisingly, it is still difficult to evaluate Semantic IR (SIR) and understand the user contexts. The absence of a standardized cognitive user-centred evaluative paradigm (CUcEP) further exacerbates these challenges. This chapter provides the state-of-the-art on IR and SIR evaluation and a systematic review of contexts. Appropriate user-centred theories and the proposed evaluative framework with its integrated-context, web analytic conception, and related data analytic technique are presented. A descriptive approach is adopted, with the conclusion that multiple contexts are essential in SIR evaluation since "searching by meaning" is a multi-dimensional cognitive conception, hence the need to consider the impact of context dynamicity. Finally, the foregrounded semantic items will be applied to standardize the CUcEP in future.

INTRODUCTION

Information Retrieval (IR) systems demonstrate the IR paradigm that allows users to search and retrieve relevant documents that contain the information they need. The Web Search Engine (WeSE) is the most visible example of IR systems since the majority of Internet users rely on it to search the Web (Akhigbe, 2015). Search on the Web is typically modelled as tasks-centric experiences considering the dynamic context of the Web. This fluxing context informs how IR systems operate, and how they are investigated and used (Akhigbe, 2015). This tasks-centric - usage - experiences are bound to change as the inclusive Internet (i.e. Internet of Things - IoT) - that is touted as able to offer limitless possibilities regarding con-

DOI: 10.4018/978-1-7998-6697-8.ch010

nectivity (Malik and Malik, 2020) - enters the stage. More dynamic system collaborations, and cooperation in the form of integration and interoperability (Akhigbe *et al.,* 2016), and diverse IoT applications with varied contexts of deployment with a frequency of continuous change and Disparate Information Sources (DIS) will be prevalent. Enormous amounts of data in dissimilar and badly expressed format will be delivered by the DIS, which will be difficult to understand and exploited by devices and systems. More concerns such as standardization, discovery, and poor IoT information resource descriptions are also expected as causes of retrieval difficulty (Rhayem *et al.,* 2020).

The solution to the foregoing is the Semantic Web IoT (SW-IoT) technologies, which are fast emerging. However, the Semantic Web (SW) is still wanting of a common information structure and standard to make the extraction of meaningful information possible. The keyword-based structure of the SW makes it semantically incapable to resolve issues of context (Malik and Malik, 2020). Its lexicon and semantic structure, therefore, need reworking to shore up its potential to deal with Context and Meaning (C&M) to avoid document misinterpretation. More complex and evolving incompatible (internal) semantics than what exists currently on the Web from varied sources of information will also be avoided. This highlights the need for a cognitive-based approach to the semantic description of terms to aid the retrieval of ambiguous terms based on "relevance". Unfortunately, "relevance" is still considered based on the frequency of query terms expressed in statistical measures (Lashkari *et al.,* 2018). This requires a technical response that approaches semantic retrieval differently from the traditional IR topic and key-words based. The exercise of evaluation has contributed greatly to this regarding retrieval speed, particularly from the non-cognitive context. This is because, in the IR domain evaluation is important for system tuning and improvement (Ferro and Silvello, 2018). However, both the non-cognitive and Cognitive Context of IR Evaluation (CCoIRE) needs rethinking in terms of methodology considering the emerging dynamics to be introduced by the concepts of the SW and the IoT about search and retrieval. The focus of this chapter is on the CCoIRE, which could be exploited to complement the technical response to enhance the potentials of Semantic Information Retrieval (SIR) on the SW. For example, one of the widely used approaches to evaluate SIR is the Information Content Approach (ICA) (Jiang, 2020). However, despite its use, a clear solution is still elusive since the approach is topically inclined. This highlights the need for a "Contextual IR Approach" (CoIRA) within the CCoIRE that promotes the association of Users Information Need (UIN) with semantic concepts to represent real users (Butavicius *et al.,* 2019).

Based on the literature, the strategies offered by the ICA does not completely capture and exploit the conceptualizations that are inherent in UIN, which is contrary to what the CoIRA from the context of CCoIRE will offer. The ICA cannot account for the missing connections that are inherent in the UIN since it is system-centric in its evaluative approach to SIR evaluation. Therefore, the ICA cannot be used to judge the Quality of Semantic IR (QoSIR) and understand important features - in the context users - that account for the right "C&M" of 'Web Contents" vis-à-vis how they are extracted in terms of accuracy of semantic relevance (Mahmood *et al.,* 2020). From the CoIRA perspective the concept of "Relevance" can be studied and understood. Unlike the ICA, the CCoIRE allows the knowledge of "Context" to be used for this examination (Tamine and Daoud, 2018). Therefore, with the CCoIRE methodology, SIR effectiveness can be improved. The CCoIRE approach is still an emerging user-oriented evaluative methodology that is highlighted in the field of IR. Though, research publications within the CCoIRE exist as shown by the section dedicated to evaluation and tool in the ACM conference on human information interaction and retrieval; much is not known about it to promote its adoption for the semantic evaluation of IR. Some researchers with IR system-centric evaluation orientation may not be familiar with the use of CCoIRE philosophy to model "user experience" based on core user-centred theories. Similarly, other researchers who have worked with this user experience based evaluative methodology may not be unacquainted with IR. This chapter seeks to fill this gap by presenting a novel, User-centred Evaluative Framework (UcEF) that is obtained from a synergy of cognitive and measurement theories to replace the usual system-centric evaluative methodology with user-centricity.

The contribution made in this chapter is within the contextual approach to IR evaluation using the descriptivist perspective for its presentation. Since the design of retrieval algorithms (i.e. IR system engine) reached its plateau, the user-centred research (e.g. CCoIRE) has been highlighted as a consensus research path that must be pursued in the IR research community to deliver a much-improved search performance (Liu *et al.*, 2020). This validates this contribution and justifies the contextual user-centred evaluation as suitable for SIR. The UcEF will use its potentials from context dynamicity to guide stakeholders on the inclusion of users' usage experiences as key elements from users' context during an evaluation exercise. It will also guide on the means to formulate Key Performance Indexes (KPIs) using the Web Analytics Method (WAM) to avoid going off the limit. This synergistic application of context dynamicity and the WAM will offer a broad perspective and structure to evaluate the SIR and strengthen the UcEF to aid the definition of evaluation goal and KPIs. The rest of this chapter is arranged as follows. The literature review on the state-of-the-art in IR and SIR evaluation is found in Section 2.0, while discourses on the concept of contexts, etc is in the section 3.0 on methodology. The UcEF framework is in the result section in Section 4.0, while the chapter's conclusion is in Section 5.0.

LITERATURE REVIEW ON STATE-OF-THE-ART OF IR/SIR EVALUATION

The Traditional IR

The system-centred approach to IR evaluation has been standardized in IR literature. This approach focuses on the tweaking of IR engine (or algorithm). The lookup model (see Figure 1) (Bates, 1998) is an earlier model that has served as a standard to examine IR in information-seeking research specifically through the Text Retrieval Conferences (TREC) (Voorhees and Harman, 2005). Nevertheless, this model cannot be used to adequately exemplify multiple query iterations, ill-defined/exploratory needs, and detailed result examination. The assumption underlying the model is that retrieval is only about query formulation. Thus, factors such as information use, task and user context and the context of users' usage experiences are ignored.

Other documented attempts exist in literature to develop better retrieval models in comparison to the lookup model. The interaction model in Figure 2A is one of such classic model, while the model in Figure 2B is the augmented version, which supports user interaction that initiated the concept of Interactive Information Retrieval (IIR). IIR's emphasizes User-system Engagement (UsEng) during search that was followed by the Human-computer Information Retrieval (HcIR). HcIR emphasizes searchers' role during UsEng and the influence of their search experiences, which features can be cognitively modelled to support semantic capabilities (Lopes, 2009).

Figure 1. Lookup model of IR

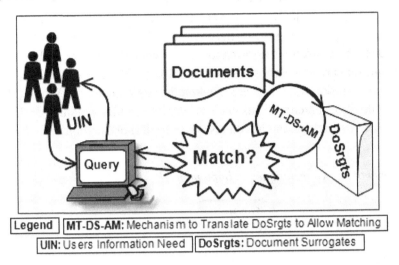

Figure 2. a and b, The Classic and augmented Model of IR
(Adapted from Broder, 2002)

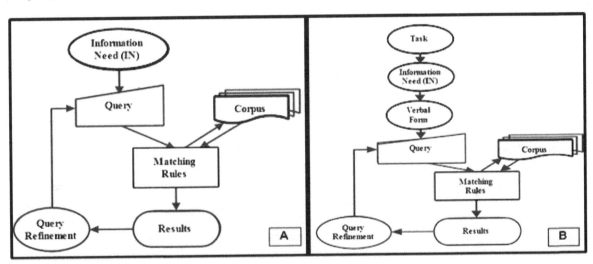

Learnings from these models have revealed that users' information-seeking experiences, the knowledge of task domain or subject-matter expertise, and physical setting can impact effective search (White, 2016). There has been several techniques, with which IR engine has been implemented over the years, which are shown using the taxonomy in Figure 3. One or a combination of these techniques constitute the engine that controls and carry out all the matching in the matching rules module and the exchanges that occur between the matching rules module and the corpus in the model in Figure 2A&B. For brevity, the technicalities of these techniques can be found in (e.g. Baeza-Yates and Ribeiro-Neto, 1999; Broder, 2002; Mitra and Craswell, 2018) and other related texts.

The quest for better retrieval of information has been vigorously pursued over the years. Better search could be delineated cognizant of the IIoT context and the fact that at the centre of IR process is the user (Tamine and Daoud, 2018). This foregrounds the cognitive view of IR. It implies that retrieval should be premised not only on tasks with known information objectives as is with the lookup model, but trail and other cognitive details that are necessary to nurture the IIoT (O'Brien *et al.*, 2020). As shown in Figure 2B UIN is inspired from tasks. But, tasks are dynamic just as humans. As White (2016) puts it, tasks occur from learning through contemplations vis-à-vis the information obtained during search processes (White, 2016). So, better search is search with tasks and trail(s) orientation since both are

Figure 3. A taxonomy of known techniques to implement IR

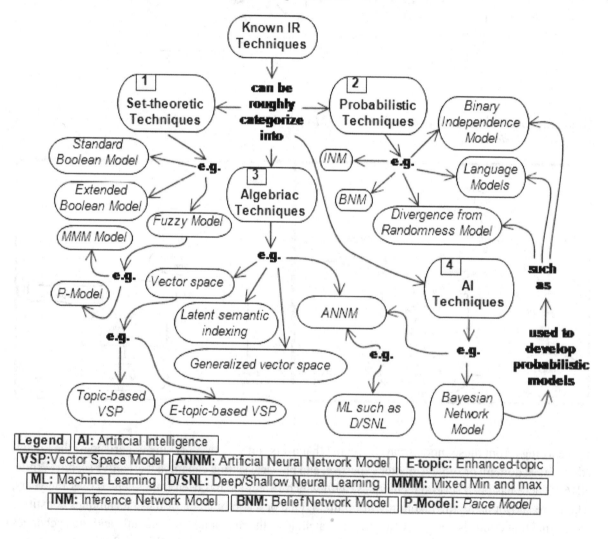

important in determining user satisfaction during system use (O'Brien *et al.*, 2020). Tasks are the atomic representation of UIN. A focus on it implies giving users control and opportunity to do search customization while the system play the role of a guide. The goal is to attain customized and tailored search experiences (and much more) for searchers. This is where Semantic Search Computing (SSC) comes in, though with multifaceted challenges. From the system perspective of SSC the theoretical as well as technological progress is on course. However, both the system and user-centric evaluative facet is still lagging behind. The cognitive view of both the classic IR and SSC (or SIR) is methodically contextual and requires user-centric methodology to study and understand it to advance user modeling with the semantic understanding of queries and documents. Machine learning will benefit from this understanding to realise better search through SSC. That said, the dearth of literature on methodology and theory within the context of user-centricity to use existing large-scale behavioural data even in the context of Big data to understand this cognitive view further exacerbate this challenge.

The SIR for the SW

Over time, the reviews of semantic search have highlighted different approach to SIR evaluation, but basically around the same thematic of investigating the quality of topic relevance. Topic relevance has been the de factor standard for determining the degree to which users queries match the relevant document like what is done in the traditional IR domain. The progression has been basically within the context of using the automatic and human expert judgement approach (Xu *et al.*, 2020) to evaluate the topic relevance of SIR. The approach reported in Newman *et al.* (2010) applied the Bayesian technique that was validated through human judgement to enforce automatic evaluation. Mimno *et al.* (2011) contributed an evaluation metric that automatically identify topics, which does not rely on reference collections or human annotators based on a statistical metric, with significant improvement on topic quality. In an earlier related work by Baazaoui *et al.* (2008) an evaluation protocol that is user driven was proposed to assess the precision measure, which is ordinarily not automatically calculated. Similar recent attempts at proposing evaluative models to evaluate SIR are available in the literature. But, for brevity the research efforts of Xu *et al.* (2020) and Esteva *et al.* (2020) are presented. In Xu *et al.* (2020) an evaluative model was developed to evaluate the topic quality of topical words that are unmatched with any concepts in a mapping ontology that are generated based on document semantics. This method based its evaluation technicalities on semantic patterns and matching concepts. The model was also able to measure a document's relevance in relation to users' information interest. For Esteva *et al.* (2020) topic relevance was examined based on query-document pairs that were annotated into either relevant, partially relevant, or irrelevant. This work's aim was to determine the semantic search performance of a co-search on a combined dataset of the TREC-COVID evaluation dataset and CORD-19 corpus. The findings from the literature available on the evaluation of the SIR is that every attempt to include users' interest as affirmed in Baazaoui *et al.* (2008) and Xu *et al.* (2020) showed clear improvements. On the contrary, the non-inclusion of context affected semantic search performance. In the context of the SW a clear improvement on semantic search is challenged as a context-dependent space. This implies that these models as ingrained in their evaluative frameworks are less user-centred and context deficient. As Tamine and Daoud (2018) highlighted topic relevance is better studied within the limit of context. This chapter, therefore presents a UcEF which is based on the technicalities of context.

METHODOLOGY

This section contains a description of features that strengthens the proposed UcEF for SIR.

The Concept of Contexts

The goal of SIR within the context of SSC is to use queries' "underlying meaning" to achieve information retrieval that satisfies UIN. Contextualizing this is significant. It raises the question of; what ways exist to explore to attach semantics to IR? The use of ontology and other semantic annotation techniques among others has indeed transform keyword (i.e. grammar matching) into meaning matching (i.e., semantic matching) (Chen *et al.*, 2020). But, to what extent has this offered the "reasoning" that is needed within the context of "semantic". User-centred evaluation can help in answering these questions as an approach and exercise. Evidence in the literature (e.g. Iqbal *et al.*, 2005) has shown that lots of large-scale software developments often fail due to insufficient user requirements analysis. This "failure" does not mean systems do not perform their engine responsibility. The question simply is; do the systems in question fulfil their FReq goal? This also needs to be investigated for SIR and as such judge its quality. As a matter of best practice, the FReq aspect of SIR requirements would need to be done in conjunction with the non-FReq. This is because a true representation of stakeholders' perspective is important in that it plays a crucial role both in the formative and summative life of a system. Aside from the complimentary relationship of FReq and NonFReq; their perspective means a lot in the selection of criteria to choose substitute designs to guide implementation (Chung *et al.*, 2000). The multiplicity of stakeholders (see Figure 4) makes this a complex task. The use of the term is ambiguous and thus needs proper delineation to put it in the right context.

Figure 4. Type of stakeholders

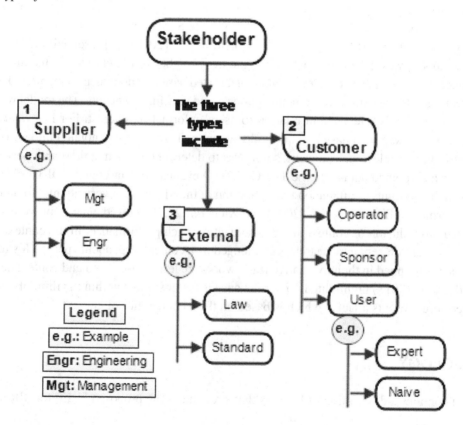

The stakeholder of focus is the user. Its role is important: they use the system or the service the system (in this case SIR) provide. Context can go a lot deeper than this. At one time or the other, the categories of stakeholders in the taxonomy (see Figure 4) to consider may also be important in the context of investigating SIR. The goal of an investigation should determine the stakeholder's context to employ. Context if gotten correctly do assists in understanding systems' requirements. Context does this by separating the outside world from the requirements and capabilities of the system as well as specifies the boundary of the system. In context modelling, a use case is used to represent everything inside the system boundary when identified to express the actual behaviour of the system. What the use case does is to help ascertain the requirement that exists in a specific context from which important features can be learned (Iqbal *et al.,* 2005; Goker and Myrhaug, 2008).

Context is important in the evaluation of systems because it helps to choose metrics and evaluation approaches - methodology from time to time. However, the influence of formative or summative evaluation and what method(s) to use existing quantitative and qualitative methods must be settled. For instance, while formative evaluation studies' intent is to inform on how to improve a system (in terms of its current quality and what it should be in future), the summative evaluation studies seek to provide evidence on whether a system - product is living up to what it was designed to do. Results from both studies are easily translatable to new FReq or non-FReq as the case may be (Khajouei and Farahani, 2020). Usually, quantitative methods provide the wherewithal to carry out a summative evaluation. They also offer the method to identify patterns that are large enough to judge system performance and provide trends that are plausible and sufficient to present criteria to obtain performance ratings to show if a system meets with what is expected of it (Goker and Myrhaug, 2008). The rationale for considering the Quantitative and Qualitative Methods (Q&QM) of evaluation stems from the need to ensure the plausibility of evaluative results.

Users' Context is just one of the many contexts identified in the literature (see Figure 5). It represents aspects of users' situation that influences their information foraging. The users' contexts capture the aspects of user's point of view that are useful and should be drawn from to evaluate search systems (Goker and Myrhaug, 2008; Tamine and Daoud, 2018). The task context (see Figure 5) is part of the user context. Though, conceptualised as system-centric, with SSC in view user-centric conception is needful.

The mental context in the classic IR model highlights the influence of the attitude-behaviour relationship of users of systems. However, the cognitive context of the user context that is missing in existing taxonomy (Goker and Myrhaug, 2008; Tamine and Daoud, 2018), which has now been included (see Figure 5) emphasizes how users acquire knowledge and reach decisions to solve problems. With semantic search, the question of context being a representational and/or interactional problem becomes imperative. First, its delineation suggests that implicit attributes of users' environment in which information activities occur exist. Secondly, the perspective that context arises from performed activities - the interactional aspect, from which the user cannot be separated implies that performed activity have predictable effects on processes. This is significant in that SSC processes can be modelled from this. Aside from this huge leap in the use of context, the study of information seeking behaviour can be leveraged to find the context attributes that matters for SSC applications. Other contexts to consider are the system, query and users' context. The system context is about retrieval systems fulfilling their FReq, while the user-context is about satisfying their IN. Whereas these contexts also exist in the SIR space, their conception (see Figure 5) is important cognizant of the fact that context in IR could either be static and/or dynamic. In the static context, the personal characteristics of users are modelled, whereas in the dynamic context optimising the reuse of users' judgments is paramount. Though empirical associations exist between the characteristics in both contexts, there is a dearth of evaluative frameworks to study and use these variables.

Figure 5. Taxonomy of user context

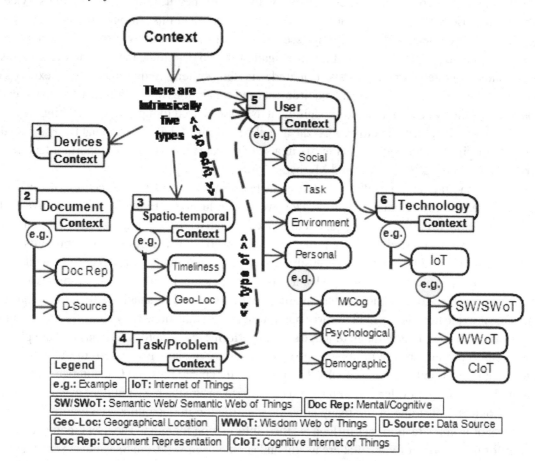

The Multi-Dynamicity of Contexts

The Semantic Web (Sem-Web) presents yet another context, which cannot also be ignored in IR evaluation. Its advent has introduced a multi-dynamicity to the evaluation of search. It is evident in literature that existing semantic techniques, algorithms and standards are bereft of the influence and input from users' usage contexts and experiences that are often misconstrued as interface issues (Croisier, 2012). Sem-Web is fast evolving into the Semantic Web of Things (SWoT) and as a service arm of the IoT (An *et al.,* 2020), it contributes to this multi-dynamicity. IoT's contradiction that includes the manifest diversities of things and the insufficient knowledge of users (An *et al.*, 2020) add to this twist. Relevant feedbacks are classic IR model oriented, but they deviate from the original context of UIN. The semantic approach will help users recalibrate and present concepts and allow them reformat their UIN to semantically reorder documents for retrieval purpose. This semantic philosophy also introduces its own dynamicity that is different from what already obtains in IR evaluation. Before the current demand and influence of the Semantic Web on IR; IR's perspective of user interactivity was driven by the relevance-feedback-based-technique(s), which is also contextual, except it is system based. However, with the Semantic Web, the IR perspective of user interactivity is more contextualized and driven semantically from multi-user contexts. Since better semantic contextualization of IR is expected to emerge and cater for the dearth of complete semantic peculiarities, the obvious question to ask is; from what context should IR be evaluated against the backdrop of the current demand of the Semantic Web or SWoT?

Existing frameworks with user-centred evaluative orientation are framed to evaluate IR in the context of finding texts during user-system interactivity based on the contextual influence of the relevance-feedback-based-technique (Akhigbe *et al.,* 2016). However, the user-centred evaluative framework that is proposed will do things differently as a guide (or protocol) in the evaluation of IR within the context of searching for information content and not just text drawing from users' usage experiences (Ruixiang *et al.,* 2019).

Users' Usage Experiences

Contexts are domain-dependent. They can dovetail into each other based on feature similarity and/or commonality. They could be tricky and also overlap within domains. This is why within the context of evaluation it could be difficult to determine where to stop with one context and begin with the other if not properly understood. With Users' Usage Experience (UUE) context comes an interesting dimension to understand what influence retrieval (Hu *et al.,* 2017). It provides a boundary of operation that serves as a contextual framework that encourages plausible results of evaluation. This is because within the framework both system and users' context can be understood. This is significant in that a system's technological progress is clear in terms of service delivery and fulfilment of FReq. In the context of the user; several interesting features such as interactivity, usability and others are factors to study. It is within this same context that users' requirements - what real users want a system to do are conceived and established (Sutcliffe, 2002). A system's FReq is the users' requirement and within the usage context; the wherewithal to apply the influence(s) of the nonFReq to check and control a system's FReq is learned from users' viewpoint. A large context is involved if UUE is to be totally exploited for advancing systems like SIR within the search space. The UUE postulates that when users use tools, they do not just use them for the sake of using them. They do so within a large context that is mostly user-centric. However, there remains a disconnection between the system and user contexts. A key feature in the user and system context is tasks and can be studied to fix this disconnection.

The theoretical framework underpinning UUE consists of users and (their) task characteristics. Users' personal information infrastructure also contribute to this influence. The constituents of this infrastructure include users' cognitive abilities, task domain knowledge and searching skills (Sarkar *et al.,* 2019). Tasks features provide the leverage to describe IN, and with topics, they make a useful representation of search goals. As such, they are vital elements for modelling users' IN (Kelly, 2009). So, with tasks features subject areas can be accessed cognizant of the understanding of the contexts surrounding IN (Hoenkamp, 2015). Based on this understanding, users' requirements through IN could serve as a means to add extra information to help retrieval systems make sense of queries (Savolainen, 2012). Sense-Making theories like that of Dervin's can guide this conceptualization (Sarkar *et al.,* 2019). Search episodes are viable tools to learn users' sense-making process as per UIN. So, many behavioural data based on Big Data formation that captures users' search episodes can be useful in this regard to derive nonFReq, which can be operationalized to meet the need for Variables and Parameters (Va-&Pa) that machines can learn from to enhance search with SSS. Even hyper-parameters (or knob) could be formulated based on inferences from Va-&Pa to control the balance and technicalities in semantic computing models for retrieval purposes. Interestingly, there exist semantic connotations (or link) that can seamlessly link UIN to its representative query. For example, unconsciously users' information processing ability gets better with the use of search systems. This is the core of UUE that becomes resourceful overtime to advance semantic modelling (Oviatt and Soulier, 2020).

Information Spaces and the Semantic Search Context

There are enormous data on the Internet, and their flow has been identified as one of the challenges that make the retrieval of information ineffective. The varied state of these data (e.g. its structured, semi-structured and unstructured nature) and their veracity in Big Data proportion also exacerbate this challenge (Lozano *et al.*, 2020). There is promise with semantic retrieval using the contextualized approach as a response to this situation. This highlights the essence of conceptions involving user needs vis-à-vis content meanings when significantly harnessed. Another justification for semantic search arises as the collection of data on the Internet continue to grow unprecedentedly at the cost of information overload. In this respect, semantic search would respond through personalization of information, which existing traditional IR cataloguing, classification, among others cannot deal with. This provides the rationale to advance the Semantic Web and the current Web search engine to match this unprecedented amount of data. With IoT in view this information space will be vast, thus requiring that the current level of semantics on the Web be scaled up in varying degrees to support IR (Schoefegger *et al.*, 2013).

The current Information Space (InfoSpcs), though capricious presents a novel way to rethink existing concepts and methods to support the response of semantic scaling. InfoSpcs is a framework oriented concept. It accentuates the set of concepts, relations and system-centred features that exist and is held by IS. It is virtual a system-oriented concept. There also exist the Cognitive Spaces (CogSpcs), which is also a set of concepts and relations that are user-centred features but are held by humans. With these concepts, relations and features InfoSpcs in IS can exhibit exosomatic memories that can inform systems' transformation to become the extension of human memory. There seem to be a one-to-one mapping of InfoSpcs and CogSpcs that will allow this to happen, but requires efforts to map this capability to assist information finding that equates to remembering already known information (Newby, 2002).

User-Centred Oriented Theories

Unconscious Thought Theory

The capacity to process information cannot be overlooked. The information processing theory is grounded in this. For the Unconscious Thought Theory (UTT); it determines how easily users handle and interpret the amounts of information available to them. UTT (a.k.a.) the dual-process theory captures the dissimilar modes of information processing, which captures the conscious awareness of tasks and the cognitive and/ or affective processing of such tasks (Evans, 2008). The affective part of tasks processing takes place outside conscious awareness and does not have anything to do with intuition. However, the unconscious part of UTT applies a goal-dependent technique. Search processes include query formulation and other related cognitive tasks. With affection involved, there are lots of distractions particularly in the face of alternatives to choose from in the bid to satisfy ones IN. The theory hypothesizes that systems could be modelled to become aware of the mind of users. This is subjective and as such susceptible to distraction. This informs that SSS should be able to support users during a search to recover easily in the face of potential distractions. UUT, therefore, draws attention to the mode of thoughts as being circumstance-dependent. The conscious part of the theory suggests a systematic approach to information processing as a way for systems to deal with complex tasks taking advantage of storage capacity, unlike humans. However, the unconscious part is unsystematic and unpredictable. As such, a few research has shown that unconscious thought can handle the combination of information better due to its large processing capacity; though more work is still needed is this respect (Dijksterhuis and Nordgren, 2006; Dijksterhuis *et al.,* 2006; Gao *et al.,* 2012; Abadie and Waroquier, 2019).

The conscious thought part of UTT draws from a top-down principle, unlike the unconscious thought that relies on the bottom-up principle. Implementing both in an evaluative exercise means a probable balance that will make explicit the goal to be reached. This means that users in the circumstance of displaying conscious thought, once a pre-dominant UIN exists in their mind every unsuitable UIN will be ruled out. However, since this process definitely involves some compromises because it is a human "thing"; it will be difficult to realise the exact feedback that is expected thus alarming the fact that this possible inconsistency can negatively affect users' satisfaction. This suggests that every piece of information is better organized and put in a more polarized way. As such, the SIR process can lean on it this way to support users in the right choice of what satisfies their UIN.

Summary of Other Related Theories

A summary of other related user-centric theories is presented as shown in Table 1. There are lots of them in literature. But for brevity Table 1 contains a few that has been useful based on experience in user-centric research. SIR is not only an initiative of soft-technology in orientation with retrieval advantages; it is also user-driven.

Table 1. Summary of a few related user-centred theories

ToT	Implication	Comment	Application	Citation
IFT	Its used to study how technologies and strategies for gathering, seeking, and consuming information can be adapted to the flux of information in the environment	IFT works with the assumption that as much as possible people will try to modify the structure of the environment and the strategies that are needed and if need be to maximize the rate of gaining valuable information	Currently applied to look at affordance in hypertext environment (i.e. within multiple document) and to make sense out of information	Pirolli and Card (1999); Pirolli (2007); Upadhyay (2020); Delgado *et al.* (2020).
CET	Supports the study of how external pressure and/or distractions (in the case of surfing/searching the web with myriads of alternatives) affects internal motivation (the UIN expressed in query) which is the goal that is right to fulfill	This theoretic framework reveals that the external mechanisms of control can interrupt users' sense of autonomy, control and use of IS, and as such are capable of decreasing users' internal motivation	It is applied to understand the dynamics of user cognition during the construction of IR cognitive model	Ryan *et al.* (1983); Shi *et al.* (2017); Ruixiang *et al.* (2019)
ToM	ToM highlights the importance of unavoidably using interpretive models to acquire knowledge about reality.	Provides the grounding to use multi-items to measure cognitive variables	Applied in the sourcing of nonFReq to track the progress of technologies	Kelly (2009); Micheli and Mari (2014)
ToAff	It emphasizes the significance of feelings in the behaviour of humans, and as such weighty responses that are affective could significantly or even primarily influence behavioral intentions	Both theories are about how people's anticipatory visceral feelings influence behavior well above cognitive evaluations impact	To understand and provide insight into the nature and mechanisms of users feelings to make decision	Gao *et al.* (2012); Sha (2017);
CFT	CFT has important implications for the identification of how humans – users switch between mental states, operations or conceptual representations to develop interventions that can facilitate even semantic search during user-system interaction	CFT pursues the goal of systematically supporting people to flexibly use their knowledge, while adapting prior experiences with understandings to fit the needs from new situations that often differ.	Applied to study cognitive flexibility in the context of switching between mental states, operations or conceptual representations	Spiro *et al.* (2003); Lowrey and Kim (2009). Johann *et al.* (2019).

ToT (Type of Theory); Ref. (Reference); IFT (Information Foraging Theory); CET (Cognitive Evaluation Theory); ToM (Theory of Measurement); ToAff (Theory of Affect); CFT (Cognitive Flexibility Theory)

Information Foraging Theory (IFT), on one hand, emphasizes the provision of interactivity with much flexibility to encourage user participation in user-system interaction. For the theory of affect, on the other hand; how meanings are considered based on users' context are highlighted (Burnett and Merchant, 2020). Though, useful to investigate user disposition, mood and emotion; it has been linked to providing insight and learning that fosters innovation and creativity, proactive behaviour, and opportunity evaluation (Nikolaev *et al.,* 2020). Cognitive strategies based on Cognitive Evaluation Theory (CET), are viable elements to study information spaces and learn how to navigate them to build useful texts and corresponding meanings through hypertexts using intertextual linkages (Cho and Afflerbach. 2017; Delgado *et al.,* 2020). Each of these theories (see Table 1) and many other user-centric oriented theories provide the kaleidoscope to simulate different aspects of search as ingrained in the human model. These theoretical models with the right synthesis could be used to model the explicit search scenario to chat the path on how to navigate linked information vis-à-vis the use of affordances in multiple documents to aid semantic retrieval (Naumann, 2015; Salmeron *et al.,* 2018).

Analytic Techniques of User-centred Orientation

IR is a cognitive process (Ruixiang *et al.,* 2019). With Qualitative and Quantitative (Q&Q) methodology, which the WAM introduces into the proposed framework makes it possible to realise cognition from the analytic perspective. Q&Q provides the tool of conceptualization and operationalization. With conceptualization, the cognitive constructs are debriefed of ambiguity and by operationalization, such items are weighted for measurement purpose (Kelly, 2009). This is consistent with the age-long philosophy by Lord Kelvin that; "what you cannot measure you cannot improve". This is also consistent with the goal of UcEva that highlights the need for measurement towards improvement. With the perspective of IR cognitive subjects (or users) with cognitive elements as input multi-dimensionality is introduced. The relationship, which ensures are many, similar and related and modelled mathematically as a matrix of the order of the number of respondents and conceptualized items. This approach is way beyond the conceptions of the use of single items. The mathematical relations behind this is beyond the scope of this chapter. However, the technique of factor analysis presents a data reduction technique to proceed in the data analysis that is required at this point. Some more details about factor analysis are found in section 5.1 as follows.

Factor Analysis

The plausibility and reliability of the Factor Analytic Technique (FAT) can be gauged from the myriads of use it has been put into overtime as found in (e.g. Muley and Tangawade, 2019; Marques *et al.,* 2020), and several other research work. A search for "Factor Analysis" or its variants "Exploratory Factor Analysis", "Confirmatory Factor Analysis", and "Structural Equation Modelling" independently using "Google Scholar" or "ResarchGate" affirms this. FAT is a multivariate statistic tool. The structure of correlation is handled vis-à-vis a set of observables with regards to a significantly reduced number of latent variables (or factors). Principles, namely; the reduction of a large number of variables, factor structure generation from measured variables and latent constructs for theory refinement, and the validation of the structure (Hasan *et al.,* 2020). The classic FA is a computational technique that has its roots in the matrix model, which can be modelled formally as presented in Equation (1);

$$X \in \mathcal{R}^n \tag{1}$$

Where

X = correlation matrix
$\mathcal{R}^n$ = *n-dimensional random vector;*
Σx = *the sum of diagonal matrix – D* and *a* Gramian
$\Sigma x - D$ = Gramian

The Equation in (1) is consistent with the presentation in Hasan *et al.* (2020). The elements of the matrix model in Equation (1) are factors that are correlated and during a typical data analysis exercise using the FAT these factors are decomposed (or reduced) to a factor model. What a factor model expresses is the correlation of say z variables (e.g. $y_1, y_2, \ldots, y_z$), for which there are K observable variables with the assumption that they exist due to a few $q<z$ latent unobservable variables that are known as factors. The link between these factors and observable variables is assumed to be linear. As a result, an observation y_{pn} is further decomposed as

$$y_{pn} = \mu_p + \gamma'_p f_n + e_{pn},$$

where

$\mu p_=$ mean of yp
$\gamma p_=$ q×1 vector, a*nd*
e_{pm}, f_n are uncorrelated

For $p=1 \ldots z$ and $n=1 \ldots K$, y_{pn} is reduced into the sum of two mutually orthogonal components, namely, the shared component - $y_{pn} = \gamma'_p f_n$, and the distinct component $- \omega p_{n=} \mu p +_e pn$ Both derivations are consistent with what obtains in the literature (Hasan *et al.,* 2020). FAT is expansively applied for statistic-based analytic tasks (Williams et al., 2010), and data mining and high dimensional data analytics (Hasan et *al.,* 2020). Some examples of computer-based software that handles FAT computationally are SPSS with AMOS as an add-on, PLS-SEM, Python, R-programming, Stata and others. Based on personal experience AMOS presents the EFA, CFA, SEM and path diagrams better than others.

RESULT

This result section contains the UcEF description for SIR evaluation with the illustration of results that are likely with the UcEF application.

The Framework

In Rico's *et al.* (2019), it was evident that linked data and semantic technologies can have a positive impact on classic search and retrieval scenarios. Thus, like other related work (e.g. Ciampi *et al.*, 2020) the likelihood of introducing semantic computation into existing search systems was highlighted and foreground the possibility of integrating Big Data to strengthen semantic capabilities and enhance interaction models for near real-time analytic searches. Two user-centred methodological frameworks from previous research effort (Akhigbe *et al.*, 2016) were fused synergistically to inform the proposed framework.

The Proposed Framework

The CCP, KbHCI and SCP frames allow the proposed framework to use a broad context in an integrated form that aligns with the concept of semantic search strategy to accommodate the multiple dimensions semantic search requires to be successful. These contexts corroborate what the theory of cognitive flexibility highlighted that semantic is multi-faceted. The User-centred Evaluative Framework (UcEF) (see Figure 6) has three basic components: (i) the contexts, (ii) the WAM and (iii) the Big Data component. The contexts are made up of three sub-components: CCP, KbHCI and SCP. The UcEF is flexible and interactive as indicated by the back and forth arrows. The WAM has 3 phases. Phase 1 receives influence back and forth from the contexts frames. And phase 1's result serves as input into phase 2. The analyze data module of the WAM interacts with the Big Data module and the implement change phase. The back and forth arrow show that change is a continuous affair and subject to how results from data analysis are interpreted. The analyze data module can do without the Big Data component (as in this case), which is waiting for automation, but still futuristic.

The contexts - CCP, KbHCI and SCP are synergistic in a complementary way. KbHCI is about user interface and other HCI concerns. It provides the opportunity to situate the CFT (a.k.a. the constructivist theory) aspect of the framework, while the CCP provides contextualized guidance. This starts with the questions of who, what, why and when to evaluate and specifies a wide range of influencing features - culture and a lot of others. The CCP also highlights the intrinsic context from where the human (information) needs emanates. This means UIN results from the daily interactions that happen with the social, psychological, political and natural environments that are further influenced by societal factors. This is consistent with the practice in Irani (2005) and Taibouni and Chalal (2019). The KbHCI is about user interface issues and other HCI concerns.

The SCP contexts highlight the existence of semantics in how scholars (users in this case) communicate, create, organize, represent and analyze contents. These are worth identifying, and when done they are conceptualized with appropriate operationalization. This is because when users' select what document(s) satisfy their IN, they do so semantically. Both the CCP and the KbHCI presents a conception of activities too that are worth identifying, after which they are conceptualized and operationalized at different points. These activities are intrinsic and a *sine qua non* qualitative (e.g. identification and conceptualization) and quantitative (e.g. operationalization) technicalities to derive decision variables by which the right scale are applied to elicit user-centric data from users. The framework is user-centric: the contexts, the WAM and the Big Data components are meant to pragmatically use HCI considerations to investigate users cognitivist experience during information foraging with a view to learn how users' handle semantics. The WAM provides the guide needed since proposed methods like the UcEF can be off-limits (Fagan, 2014). This way final measures, constructs, factors or non-FReq are made plausible

Figure 6. The UcEF with integrated Context-based WEM

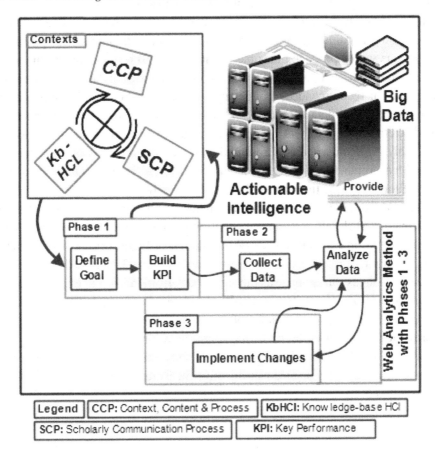

base on statistical modelling. The WAM is a proven technique to determine how effective the virtual space provided by the Web supports users to achieve their Web-based goal (Fagan, 2014). Semantics is a major issue in the virtual space, hence the introduction of the WAM. WAM as a process guide is flexible and integrates easily with sources of knowledge (data), thus making it possible to incorporate the Big Data component. Though the scope of this aspect is beyond this presentation, the integrative module will be needed to use the Big Data architecture as a source of knowledge to enable the provision of automatic data analytic driven context, which can give a semantic update to the SW using users' profile. A pictorial detail of each of the contexts - CCP, KbHCI and SCP are included in the appendix 1 (a, b and c). The following work Fischer (2001) and Stockdale *et al.* (2008) inspired their adoption in the formulation of the proposed UcEF.

Archetypal Methodology

The UcEF is a rigorous evaluative methodology that provides the mechanism to verify and measure system improvements (Webber, 2010). In Phase 1 of the WAM component of the UcEF, goals are defined and refined and then used to build KPIs based on Identified, Conceptualized and Operationalized (ICO) measures. This is done based on input from the contexts component and theory of cognitive flexibility and UTT. Going by what obtains in the literature (e.g. Kuppelwieser and Klaus, 2020), the ICO process would produce Decision Variables (DVs) that are useful and will be used to elicit data as required in Phase 2. The data collected based on fact-finding techniques - like the questionnaire (Nielsen and Hansen, 2014) - are user-oriented data (or ordinal data) that captures the cognitive thoughts of respondents. The factor data analysis technique would produce plausible result with [3] 250 respondents within a sample frame. This is therefore recommended to explore the UcEF paradigm in terms of data analysis technique with the right tool. But, the FAT is recommended, though any other tool can be used depending on research goal to analyse and model cognitive data as required in Phase 2. Based on the UcEF, the choice of technique is strictly at the discretion of researchers and the goal of the evaluation research in question. The result of the statistical analysis should yield a representative model of the factors or nonFReq. This model is also known as the Measurement Model. If the model is well-formulated re-usability and generalizability as an Exploratory FA (EFA) MM that captured users' focus, will be possible.

A higher-order MM from the EFA could be formulated and the reliability tested. This higher model might be a confirmatory MM with a structural equation model to further affirm its validity. The MM is always made up of Actionable Attributes (AA) as shown in Figures 7 and 8. The MM is useful to inform the implementation of relevant changes as required in Phase 3. In case this change is not what is expected appropriate changes can be made as the arrow back from Phase 3 to Phase 2 indicates. This can happen until the right measures or attributes to effect the changes are found. This approach is applicable to ascertain the level of semantic performance of search systems. Formulated AA from the use of the UcEF can be presented as nonFReq by first translating them into users' requirements using personas (Nielsen and Storgaard, 2014). Before the presentation of some sample results (with much brevity) some suggested semantic items that may suffice as subjective measures for SIR evaluation with promise are presented in sub-section 6.4.1.

Semantic Items

From a literature search, the items in Table 2 are suggestive of concepts that can be operationalized to elicit cognitive data for the cognitive user-centred evaluation of semantic search if they are properly conceptualized. Some of the concepts like semantic similarity or relatedness, topic and semantic relativity one way or the other are already being measured using the objective traditional IR metrics from the system-centred perspective. They are still unpopular as subjective measures for user-centred evaluation. However, more studies are recommended to ascertain the effect(s) of the items in future. Definitely, there will be more of these items - measures as research progress to figure out their full subjective potentials.

Example Result

The UcEF presented as shown in Figure 6 based on the postulated archetypal methodology in section 6.2 when applied will result in the sample MM in Figure 7. This MM has *n* number of factors - measures with their items or scales - that are translate-able to nonFreq based on EFA. This MM is a first-order model that has *n*-Factor structure.

A second-order MM could be realised where factors are meant to test if they load successfully on a single factor. For instance, it might be necessary to find out if "semantic" as a variable has a relationship(s) by finding interpretation in another variable(s) as shown in Figure 8 below. Other higher-order MM can be derived. However, their scope is way above this presentation, hence, interested readers are encouraged to consult already recommended text and others as the case may be.

Table 2. Concepts suggestive of subjective measures to evaluate semantic search system

Semantic Item	Conceptualization	Area of Application	Citation					
			Silvello *et al.* (2017)	Jiang (2020)	Kokia and Guilbert (2020)	McNally (2012)	Delacretaz & Marth (2012)	Wenguo & Guangping (2017)
Provenance Event	It means origin – to keep track of full lineage of data since its first creation, allowing users to reconstruct their full history and modifications overtime.	Use to avoid disam-biguation, topic extraction	✓	✗	✗	✗	✗	✗
Concept	AINUTUDTR in SE to CaVoc for a domain	Use to provide user intervention to SAM & formulate RS	✓	✗	✓	✗	✗	✗
Topic	topic detection approaches which is used for detecting relevant topics from documents that are available in online and offline	For semantic-based personalized document retrieval	✓	✗	✓	✗	✗	✓
SemRel	Used for concepts not necessarily similar, but some - how related via many types of relations	Applied using closeness to estimate the semantic relationship between two terms	✗	✓	✓	✗	✗	✗
I/ETI-MuUI	Apply keywords and categories explicitly (manually or/& automatically) & implicitly via algorithm	Use to introduce semantic context	✗	✗	✗	✓	✗	✗
SAanM	semantic value added with content creation so that only suggestions are made to avoid overwhelming users	To support UGC/ Web 2.0 towards semantic retrieval	✗	✗	✗	✗	✓	✗
semantic relativity	Connotes subjectivity in terms of relevant feedback of user interaction; but could be objective in terms of corpus	To reduce ambiguity and have the key -words obtained cover several topics	✗	✗	✗	✗	✗	✓

SE (Semantic Environment); **RS** (Ranking Strategies); **CaVoc** (Create a Vocabulary); **AINUTUDTR** (An Idea, Notion, or a Unit of Thought Used to Define Types of Relationships); **SAM** (Select Appropriate Meaning), **SemRel** (Semantic Relatedness), **I/ETI-MuUI** (Implicit/Explicit Taxonomic Information – Metadata using User Interface); **SAanM** (Semantic Assistant and not Master), **UGC** (User Generated Content)

Figure 7. A sample MM with n factors or actionable attributes

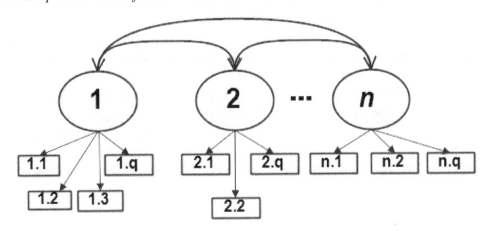

Figure 8. A sample second-order MM with n factors or actionable attributes

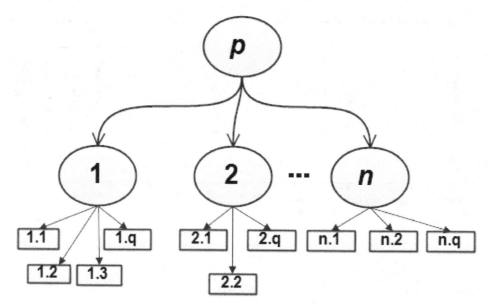

CONCLUSION

Within IR, there is much continuing discussion about the need for further research on the user-centred approach going by the postulations of a key proponent of the UcEva of IR - Saracevic (1995). The postulation is that it is okay to use many approaches in IR evaluation. However, the choice of what approach to use depends on the intent of the evaluation. In this context, both the user and system-centred approaches are needed to nourish each other. This is significant as we get to the cusp of a revolution in which the Intelligent IoT (IIoT) and its components - SWoT, Cognitive Internet of Things and Wisdom Web of Things - will inevitably determine everything and initiate the everything-as-a-service concept (An *et al.,* 2020). While the system-centred evaluative approach will provide the wherewithal to strengthen the technical aspect of SSC, the user-centred aspect will focus on contextual issues and offer the methodology to define strategies based on cognitivism to improve SSS.

Though the focus was on the retrieval of text on the Web, the contribution can also be applied to advance the semantic search of music, video and other data information type. The contributions here is novel in that the presentations were not from (or in) a single chapter. The chapter contains a broad thematic of the state-of-the-art in IR evaluation with a general conception to set the tone for SIR evaluation. To provide a grounding, example theories of user-centred orientation are presented as part of the methodology to contemplate for semantic retrieval evaluation, and the multi-dynamicity of integrated contexts were adopted. Users' context was foregrounded as very relevant in this type of evaluation; first since they are the central element in the IR process (Rinaldi and Russo, 2018). Secondly, because search within the semantic context is about meaning; meaning mainly from the perspective of the users. This makes it imperative to study the user with their usage context from the perspective of how users' form "meanings" and ultimately fulfil the goal of satisfying their UIN. Within this context, this chapter proposed the UcEF.

Since the evaluation of SSS is still at its nascent stage, the perspective of FReq and nonFReq was adopted. This way it is hoped that stakeholders would find the connection between these software engineering principles and keep semantic search advancement on track. Finally, the presentation in this chapter is descriptive rather than prescriptive, which is a weakness, but the expectation is that readers would put their findings from the chapter to practice.

ACKNOWLEDGMENT

I acknowledge the Almighty God first and my family, for their encouragement to put this together during this period of the COVID-19 pandemic. I also acknowledge the editors and reviewers for a good job. Finally, I appreciate Obafemi Awolowo University, Ile-Ife, Nigeria for the opportunity to do the work, which resulted in the report.

REFERENCES

Abadie, M., & Waroquier, L. (2019). Evaluating the benefits of conscious and unconscious thought in complex decision making. *Policy Insights from the Behavioral and Brain Sciences*, *6*(1), 72–78. doi:10.1177/2372732218816998

Akhigbe, B. I. (2015). *Development of a user-centric integrated evaluative model for information retrieval systems* (Unpublished Ph.D. thesis). Postgraduate College, Obafemi Awolowo University, Ile-Ife, Nigeria.

Akhigbe, B. I., Aderibigbe, O. S., Ejidokun, A. O., Afolabi, B. S., & Adagunodo, E. R. (2016a). The web analytics framework: an integrated user-centric evaluative tool. In *Proceedings of International conference on transition from observation to knowledge to intelligence*. University of Lagos.

An, J., Li, G., Ning, B., Jiang, W., & Sun, Y. (2020). Re-sculpturing Semantic Web of Things as a Strategy for Internet of Things' Intrinsic Contradiction. In *Artificial Intelligence in China, LNEE 572* (pp. 67–75). Springer. doi:10.1007/978-981-15-0187-6_66

Baazaoui, H., Aufaure, M.-A., & Soussi, R. (2008). Towards an on- Line Semantic Information Retrieval System based on Fuzzy Ontologies. *Journal of Digital Information Management*, *6*(5), 375–385.

Baeza-Yates, R., & Ribeiro-Neto, B. (1999). *Modern Information Retrieval*. ACM Press/Addison Wesley.

Bates, M. (1989). The design of browsing and berry-picking techniques for the online search interface. *Online Review*, *13*(5), 407–431. doi:10.1108/eb024320

Broder, A. (2002). A taxonomy of web search. *SIGIR Forum*, *36*(2), 3–10.

Burnett, C., & Merchant, G. (2020). Returning to Text: Affect, Meaning Making, and Literacies. *Reading Research Quarterly*, 113–123. doi:10.1002/rrq.303

Butavicius, M. A., Parsons, K. M., McCormac, A., Dennis, S. J., Ceglar, A., Weber, D., Ferguson, L., Treharne, K., Leibbrandt, R., & Powers, D. (2019). Using Semantic Context to Rank the Results of Keyword Search. *Inter. Jour. of HCI*, *35*(9), 725–741. doi:10.1080/10447318.2018.1485263

Chen, X., Li, G., Sun, Y., Chen, H., & Jiang, W. (2020). The Importance of Researching and Developing the Semantic Web of Things. In *Artificial Intelligence in China, LNEE 572* (pp. 637–644). Springer. doi:10.1007/978-981-15-0187-6_76

Cho, B. Y., & Afflerbach, P. (2017). An evolving perspective of constructively responsive reading comprehension strategies in multilayered digital text environments. In S. E. Israel (Ed.), *Handbook of research on reading comprehension* (2nd ed., pp. 109–134). Guilford.

Chung, L., Nixon, B. A., Yu, E., & Mylopoulos, J. (2000). *Non-Functional Requirements in Software Engineering.* Springer. doi:10.1007/978-1-4615-5269-7

Ciampi, M., De Pietro, G., Masciari, E., & Silvestri, S. (2020). Some lessons learned using health data literature for smart information retrieval. In *Proceedings of the 35th Annual ACM Symposium on Applied Computing* (pp. 931-934). 10.1145/3341105.3374128

Croisier, S. (2012). The rise of semantic-aware applications. In W. Maass & T. Kowatsch (Eds.), *Semantic Technologies in Content Management Systems: Trends, Applications and Evaluations* (pp. 23–34). Springer-Verlag. doi:10.1007/978-3-642-24960-0_3

Delacretaz & Marth. (2012). Simplified Semantic Enhancement of JCR-based Content Applications. In Semantic Technologies in Content Management Systems: Trends, Applications and Evaluations. doi:10.1007/978-3-642-24960-0_2

Delgado, P., Lund, E. S., Salmeron, L., & Braten, I. (2020). To click or not to click: Investigating conflict detection and sourcing in a multiple document hypertext environment. *Reading and Writing, 33*(8), 1–24. doi:10.100711145-020-10030-8

Dijksterhuis, A., & Nordgren, L. F. (2006). A theory of unconscious thought. *Perspectives on Psychological Science, 1*(2), 95–109. doi:10.1111/j.1745-6916.2006.00007.x PubMed

Dijksterhuis, A., Bos, M. W., Nordgren, L. F., & Van Baaren, R. B. (2006). On making the right choice: The deliberation-without-attention effect. *Science, 311*(5763), 1005–1007. doi:10.1126/science.1121629 PubMed

Esteva, A., Kale, A., Paulus, R., Hashimoto, K., Yin, W., Radev, D., & Socher, R. (2020). *Co-search: Covid-19 information retrieval with semantic search, question answering, and abstractive summarization.* arXiv preprint arXiv:2006.09595.

Evans, J. S. B. (2008). Dual-processing accounts of reasoning, judgment, and social cog. *Annual Review of Psychology, 59*(1), 255–278. doi:10.1146/annurev.psych.59.103006.093629 PMID:18154502

Fagan, J. C. (2014). The Suitability of Web Analytics Key Performance Indicators in the Academic Library Environment. *Journal of Academic Librarianship, 40*(1), 25–34. doi:10.1016/j.acalib.2013.06.005

Ferro, N., & Silvello, G. (2018). Toward an anatomy of IR system component performances. *Journal of the Association for Information Science and Technology, 69*(2), 187–200. doi:10.1002/asi.23910 PMID:30775406

Fischer, G. (2001). User Modelling in Human-Computer Interaction. *User Modeling and User-Adapted Interaction, 11*(1-2), 65–86. doi:10.1023/A:1011145532042

Gao, J., Zhang, C., Wang, K., & Ba, S. (2012). Understanding Online Purchase Decision Making: The Effects of Unconscious Thought, Information Quality, and Information Quantity. *Decision Support Systems, 53*(4), 772–781. doi:10.1016/j.dss.2012.05.011

Goker, A., & Myrhaug, H. (2008). Evaluation of a mobile information system in context. *Information Processing & Management, 44*(1), 39–65. doi:10.1016/j.ipm.2007.03.011

Hasan, M. M., Wei, S., & Moharrer, A. (2020). *Latent Factor Analysis of Gaussian Distributions under Graphical Constraints.* arXiv preprint arXiv:2001.02712.

Hoenkamp, E. C. (2015). About the 'compromised information need' and optimal interaction as quality measure for search interfaces. In *Proceedings of the 38th international ACM SIGIR conference on research and development in information retrieval* (pp. 835–838). 10.1145/2766462.2767800

Hu, X., Lee, J. H., Bainbridge, D., Choi, K., Organisciak, P., & Downie, J. S. (2017). The MIREX grand challenge: A framework of holistic user-experience evaluation in music information retrieval. *Journal of the Association for Information Science and Technology, 68*(1), 97–112. doi:10.1002/asi.23618

Irani, Z., Sharif, A. M., & Love, P. E. D. (2005). Linking knowledge transformation to information systems evaluation. *European Journal of Information Systems, 14*(3), 213–228. doi:10.1057/palgrave.ejis.3000538

Iqbal, R., Sturm, J., Kulyk, O., Wang, J., & Terken, J. (2005). User-centred design and evaluation of ubiquitous services. In *Proceedings of the 23rd annual international conference on Design of communication: documenting & designing for pervasive information* (pp. 138-145). 10.1145/1085313.1085346

Jiang, Y. (2020). Semantically-enhanced information retrieval using multiple knowledge sources. *Cluster Computing, 23*(4), 1–20. doi:10.100710586-020-03057-7

Johann, V., Konen, T., & Karbach, J. (2019). The unique contribution of working memory, inhibition, cognitive flexibility, and intelligence to reading comprehension and reading speed. *Child Neuropsychology, 26*(3), 324–344. doi:10.1080/09297049.2019.1649381 PMID:31380706

Kelly, D. (2009). Methods for evaluating interactive information retrieval systems with users. *Foundations and Trends in Information Retrieval, 3*(1–2), 1–224. doi:10.1561/1500000012

Khajouei, R., & Farahani, F. (2020). A combination of two methods for evaluating the usability of a hospital information system. *BMC Medical Informatics and Decision Making, 20*(1), 1–10. doi:10.118612911-020-1083-6 PMID:32366248

Kuppelwieser, V. G., & Klaus, P. (2020). Measuring customer experience quality: The EXQ scale revisited. *Journal of Business Research*. Advance online publication. doi:10.1016/j.jbusres.2020.01.042

Lashkari, F., Bagheri, E., & Ghorbani, A. A. (2019). Neural embedding-based indices for semantic search. *Information Processing & Management, 56*(3), 733–755. doi:10.1016/j.ipm.2018.10.015

Liu, J., Liu, C., & Belkin, N. J. (2020). Personalization in text information retrieval: A survey. *Journal of the Association for Information Science and Technology, 71*(3), 349–369. doi:10.1002/asi.24234

Lopes, C. T. (2009). Context features and their use in information retrieval. In *Proceedings of the Third BCS-IRSG Symposium on Future Directions in Information Access* (pp. 36-42). 10.14236/ewic/FDIA2009.7

Lowrey, W., & Kim, K. S. (2009). Online news media and advanced learning: A test of cognitive flexibility theory. *Journal of Broadcasting & Electronic Media, 53*(4), 547–566. doi:10.1080/08838150903323388

Lozano, M. G., Brynielsson, J., Franke, U., Rosell, M., Tjörnhammar, E., Varga, S., & Vlassov, V. (2020). Veracity assessment of online data. *Decision Support Systems, 129*, 113132. doi:10.1016/j.dss.2019.113132

Mahmood, K., Rahmah, M., Ahmed, M. M., & Raza, M. A. (2020). Semantic Information Retrieval Systems Costing in Big Data Environment. In *Int'l Conference on Soft Computing and Data Mining* (pp. 192-201). Springer. 10.1007/978-3-030-36056-6_19

Malik, N., & Malik, S. K. (2020). Using IoT and Semantic Web Technologies for Healthcare and Medical Sector. In V. Jain, R. Wason, J. M. Chatterjee, & D.-N. Le (Eds.), *Ontology-Based Information Retrieval for Healthcare Systems* (pp. 91–116). Wiley & Scrivener Publishing LLC. doi:10.1002/9781119641391.ch5

Marques, R. A. M., Pereira, R. B. D., Peruchi, R. S., Brandão, L. C., Ferreira, J. R., & Davim, J. P. (2020). Multivariate GR&R through factor analysis. *Measurement, 151*, 107107. doi:10.1016/j.measurement.2019.107107

McNally, S. (2012). Empowering the distributed editorial workforce. In W. Maassa & T. Kowatsch (Eds.), *Semantic Technologies in Content Management Systems: Trends, Applications and Evaluations.* Springer-Verlag. doi:10.1007/978-3-642-24960-0_2

Micheli, P., & Mari, L. (2014). The theory and practice of performance measurement. *Mgt Acct Res., 25*(2), 147-156.

Mimno, D., Wallach, H., Talley, E., Leenders, M., & McCallum, A. (2011). Optimizing semantic coherence in topic models. In *Proceedings of the 2011 Conference on Empirical Methods in Natural Language Processing* (pp. 262-272). Academic Press.

Mitra, B., & Craswell, N. (2018). An introduction to neural information retrieval. *Foundations and Trends in Information Retrieval, 13*(1), 1–126. doi:10.1561/1500000061

Muley, A., & Tangawade, A. (2019). Assessment of cosmetic product awareness among female students using data mining technique. *Computational Intelligence in Data Mining,* 289–298. DOI: . doi:10.1007/978-981-13-8676-3_26

Newby, G. B. (2002). The necessity for information space mapping for information retrieval on the semantic web. *Information Research, 7*(4). http://InformationR.net/ir/7-4/paper137.html

Newman, D., Lau, J. H., Grieser, K., & Baldwin, T. (2010). Automatic evaluation of topic coherence. In *Human language technologies: The 2010 annual conference of the North American chapter of the association for computational linguistics* (pp. 100-108). Academic Press.

Nielsen, L., & Storgaard, H. K. (2014). Personas is applicable: a study on the use of personas in Denmark. In *Proceedings of the SIGCHI Conference on Human Factors in Computing Systems* (pp. 1665-1674). 10.1145/2556288.2557080

Nikolaev, B., Shir, N., & Wiklund, J. (2020). Dispositional positive and negative affect and self-employment transitions: The mediating role of job satisfaction. *Entrepreneurship Theory and Practice, 44*(3), 451–474. doi:10.1177/1042258718818357

O'Brien, H. L., Kampen, A., Cole, A. W., & Brennan, K. (2020). The role of domain knowledge in search as learning. In *Proceedings of the 2020 Conference on Human Information Interaction and Retrieval* (pp. 313-317). 10.1145/3343413.3377989

Oviatt, S., & Soulier, L. (2020). *Conversational search for learning technologies. Dagstuhl Report on Conversational Search.* arXiv:2001.02912v1.

Pirolli, P., & Card, S. (1999). Information foraging. *Psychological Review, 106*(4), 643–675. doi:10.1037/0033-295X.106.4.643

Pirolli, P. (2007). *Information foraging theory: Adaptive interaction with information.* Oxford University Press. doi:10.1093/acprof:oso/9780195173321.001.0001

Rhayem, A., Mhiri, M. B. A., & Gargouri, F. (2020). Semantic Web Technologies for the Internet of Things: Systematic Literature Review. *Internet of Things,* 1 - 22.

Rico, M., Vila-Suero, D., Botezan, I., & Gómez-Pérez, A. (2019). Evaluating the impact of semantic technologies on bibliographic systems: A user-centred and comparative approach. *Journal of Web Semantics, 59*, 100500. doi:10.1016/j.websem.2019.03.001

Rieger, O.Y. (2010). Framing digital humanities: The role of new media in humanities scholarship. *First Monday, 15*(10- 4), 1-21. Available at: http://firstmonday.org/ojs/ index.php/fm/article/ view/3198/2628

Rinaldi, A. M., & Russo, C. (2018). User-centered information retrieval using semantic multimedia big data. In *2018 IEEE International Conference on Big Data (Big Data)* (pp. 2304-2313). IEEE. 10.1109/BigData.2018.8622613

Ruixiang, O., Yao, H., Feng, P., & Hui, P. (2019). Research on information retrieval model under scarcity theory and user cognition. *Computers & Electrical Engineering, 76*, 353–363. doi:10.1016/j.compeleceng.2019.04.008

Ryan, R. M., Mims, V., & Koestner, R. (1983). Relation of reward contingency and interpersonal context to intrinsic motivation: A review and test using cognitive evaluation theory. *Journal of Personality and Social Psychology, 45*(4), 736–750. doi:10.1037/0022-3514.45.4.736

Salmeron, L., Kammerer, Y., & Delgado, P. (2018). Non-academic multiple source use on the Internet. In J. L. G. Braasch, I. Braten, & M. T. McCrudden (Eds.), *Handbook of mult-source use* (pp. 285–302). Routledge. doi:10.4324/9781315627496-17

Sarkar, S., Mitsui, M., Liu, J., & Shah, C. (2019). Implicit information need as explicit problems, help, and behavioural signals. *Information Processing & Management*. Advance online publication. doi:10.1016/j.ipm.2019.102069

Savolainen, R. (2012). Conceptualizing information need in context. *Information Research*, *17*(4), paper 534. Available at http://InformationR.net/ir/17-4/paper534.html

Schoefegger, K., Tammet, T., & Granitzer, M. (2013). A survey on socio-semantic information retrieval. *Computer Science Review*, *8*, 25–46. doi:10.1016/j.cosrev.2013.03.001

Selvalakshmi, B., & Subramaniam, M. (2019). Intelligent ontology-based semantic information retrieval using feature selection and classification. *Cluster Computing*, *22*(5), 12871–12881. doi:10.100710586-018-1789-8

Silvello, G., Bordea, G., Ferro, N., Buitelaar, P., & Bogers, T. (2017). Semantic representation and enrichment of information retrieval experimental data. *International Journal on Digital Libraries*, *18*(2), 145–172. doi:10.100700799-016-0172-8

Spiro, R. J., Collins, B. P., Thota, J. J., & Feltovich, P. J. (2003). Cognitive flexibility theory: Hypermedia for complex learning, adaptive knowledge application, and experience acceleration. *Educational Technology*, *43*(5), 5–10.

Sha, W. (2017). Examining the construct validities and influence of affective risk in B2C e-commerce. *Issues in Information Systems*, *18*(4), 46–56.

Shi, W., Connelly, B. L., & Hoskisson, R. E. (2017). External corporate governance and financial fraud: Cognitive evaluation theory insights on agency theory prescriptions. *Strategic Management Journal*, *38*(6), 1268–1286. doi:10.1002mj.2560

Stockdale, R., Standing, C., Love, P. E. D., & Irani, Z. (2008). Revisiting the content, context and process of IS evaluation. In Z. Irani & P. Love (Eds.), *Evaluating Information Systems: Public and Private Sector*. Butterworth-Heinemann & Elsevier. doi:10.1016/B978-0-7506-8587-0.50006-8

Sutcliffe, A. (2002). *User-centred requirements engineering*. Springer. doi:10.1007/978-1-4471-0217-5

Taibouni, N., & Chalal, R. (2019). A toolbox for information system evaluation. In *Proceedings of the 2nd ACM International Conference on Big Data Technologies*, (pp. 283-290). 10.1145/3358528.3358537

Tamine, L., & Daoud, M. (2018). Evaluation in Contextual Information Retrieval: Foundations and Recent Advances within the Challenges of Context Dynamicity and Data Privacy. *ACM Computing Surveys*, *51*(4), 1–36. doi:10.1145/3204940

Upadhyay, P. (2020). Comparing non-visual and visual information foraging on the web. In Extended abstracts of the 2020 CHI conference on human factors in computing systems extended abstracts (pp. 1-8). doi:10.1145/3334480.3383025

Voorhees, E. M., & Harman, D. K. (2005). TREC: Experiment and evaluation in inform. retrieval. MIT Press.

Webber, W. E. (2010). *Measurement in Information Retrieval Evaluation* (Unpublished PhD Thesis). University of Melbourne, Australia.

White, R. W. (2016). *Interactions with search systems*. Cambridge University Press. doi:10.1017/CBO9781139525305

Williams, B., Onsman, A., & Brown, T. (2010). Exploratory factor analysis: A five-step guide for novices. *Journal of Emergency Primary Health Care*, 8(3), 1–13. doi:10.33151/ajp.8.3.93

Xu, Y., Nguyen, H., & Li, Y. (2020). A Semantic Based Approach for Topic Evaluation in Information Filtering. *IEEE Access: Practical Innovations, Open Solutions*, 8, 66977–66988. doi:10.1109/AC-CESS.2020.2985079

APPENDIX

Figure 9.

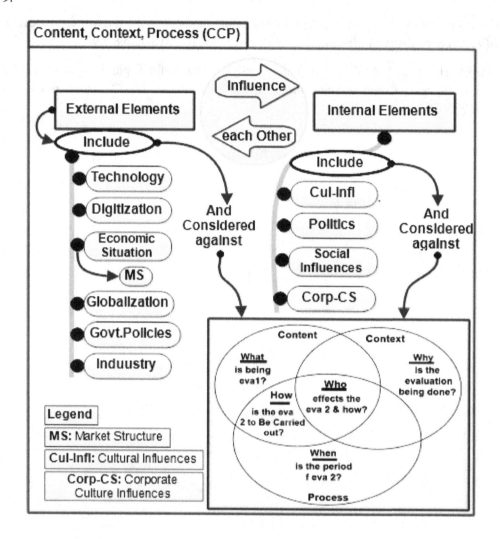

Figure 10.

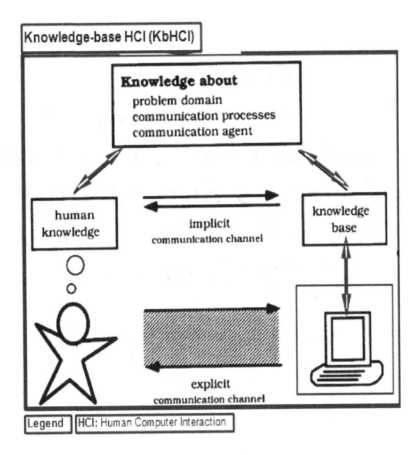

Figure 11.

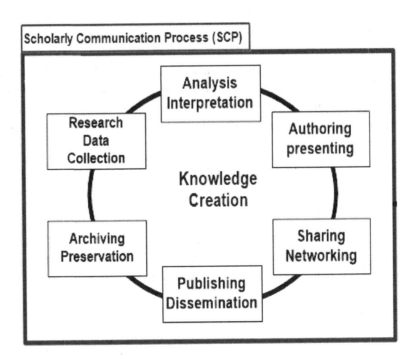

Chapter 11

A Framework to Data Integration for an Internet of Things Supporting Manufacturing Supply Chain Operation

Kamalendu Pal
https://orcid.org/0000-0001-7158-6481
City, University of London, UK

ABSTRACT

With the usage of the technologies like the internet of things (IoT) and Semantic Web service spanning across the spectrum of manufacturing, production, and distribution, typical supply chain management (SCM) systems depend on a multitude of services for operation purpose. The unprecedented growth of valuable data produced by decentralised information systems along the global manufacturing supply chain has led to a persuasive appeal for a semantic approach to integrating distributed data facilities in the field of collaborating logistic services. This technology combines a set of new mechanisms with grounded knowledge representation techniques to address the needs of formal information modelling and reasoning for web-based services. This chapter describes a framework, apparel business decentralised data integration (ABDDI), which exploits knowledge representation techniques and languages (e.g., description logics – DLs) to annotate relevant business activities. Finally, a simple business case is presented to demonstrate the framework's semantic similarity assessment functionality.

INTRODUCTION

All manufacturing business today appreciates the value and consequence of building an effective supply chain as part of enterprise proliferation and profitability (Pal, 2018). There exist different types of the industry-specific supply chain (e.g., automotive, pharmaceutical, apparel, agriculture). In simple, the sup-

DOI: 10.4018/978-1-7998-6697-8.ch011

ply chain is a system with organization, people, technology, activity, information, and resource involved in, to deliver a product or service from suppliers to customers. Supply chain activity transforms natural resources, raw materials, and components into final products, and delivers them to customers. The supply chain network is composed of the enterprises and enterprise departments involved in this process. The most important requirements of supply chain operation are to minimize the inventory, create seamless material and information flow, effective communication must exist among the business-partners, market, sale, purchase, manufacturing plan and control, customer delivery service, after-sales service, and so on. Therefore, a supply chain is a network of facilities and distribution options that performs the functions of material procurement, the transformation of these materials into intermediate and finished products, and delivery of these finished products to customers. This definition, or a modified version of it, has been used by several researchers (e.g. (Lee & Billington, 1993) (Swaminathan, 2001a) (Keskinocak & Tayur, 2001) (Pal, 2017)). Supply Chain Management (SCM) aims at improving the allocation, management, and control of logistical resources. In this way, manufacturing SCM is a set of synchronized activities for integrating suppliers, manufacturers, transporters, and efficient customer service so that the right product or service is delivered at the right quantities, at the right time, to the right places (Pal, 2020) (Pal & Ul-Haque, 2020).

The ultimate objective of SCM is the efficient management of the end-to-end process, which starts with the design of the product or service and ends with the time when it has been sold, consumed, and finally, discarded by the consumer. This complete process includes product design, procurement, planning and forecasting, production, distribution, fulfilment, after-sales support, and end-of-life disposal. Supply chain management issues can be classified into two broad categories: configuration (design-oriented) issues that relate to the basic infrastructure on which the supply chain executes, coordination (execution-oriented) issues that relate to the actual execution of the supply chain.

Configuration-level issues include the following topics:

1. Procurement and Supplier Decisions: Procurement generally involves making buying decisions under conditions of scarcity. At the same time, the requirements criteria for selecting suppliers and the number of suppliers need to be decided. If sound data is available, it is good practice to make use of economic analysis methods such as cost-benefit analysis or cost-utility analysis. Procurement is used to ensure the buyer receives goods, services, or works at the best possible price when aspects such as quality, quantity, time, and location are compared.

2. Production Decisions: This is a multi-criteria decision activity. It includes the decisions regarding production network design (e.g., Where, and how many manufacturing sites should be used for production purpose? How much capacity should be installed at each of these sites? What kind of products and services are going to be supported through the supply chain network?).

3. Distribution Decisions: It is mainly based on infrastructure design decisions (e.g., What kind of distribution channels should a manufacturing company have? How many and where should the distribution centres and retail outlets be situated? What types of transportation services and routes should be used? What types of environmental issues the distribution infrastructure need to be considered?).

4. Information Support Decisions: Managing a manufacturing supply chain involves numerous decisions about the flow of information, product, funds, and coordination. SCM has been instrumental in connecting and smoothing business activities as well as forming various kinds of business rela-

tionships (e.g., Customer Relationship Management, Supplier Relationship Management) among supply chain stakeholders.

Coordination level issues include the following topics:

1. Material Flow Decisions: These decisions include – How much inventory of different product types should be stored to provide the target service levels? Should inventory be carried in finished form or semi-finished form? How often should inventory be replenished? And so many other issues need to be considered.
2. Information Flow Decisions: SCM systems utilize modern Information and Communication Technologies (ICT) to acquire, interpret, retain, and distribute information. The software applications of SCM are ready-made packages, usually targeting a set of tasks, e.g., tracking product-related information during the transportation process. These ready-made package-software applications are mass-customized products that ignore the specific requirements of a certain business sector, and so they are quite problematic. The problem of the appropriate IT solutions for supporting collaboration between supply chain business-partners is not new and it has been approached with several standards and protocols implemented in numerous enterprise information systems.

The application like ERP (Enterprise Resource Planning), CRM (Customer Relationship Management), and WMS (Warehouse Management System) contains valuable data that can be utilized by the decision support systems (DSS). Moreover, the digital transformation of business and society presents enormous growth opportunities offered by technologies such as the Internet of Things (IoT), Big Data, advanced manufacturing, blockchain technologies, and artificial intelligence. This digital transformation is characterized by a fusion of advanced technologies and the integration of physical and digital systems, the predominance of innovative business models and new processes, and the creation of smart products and services.

Figure 1. Diagrammatic representation of the supply chain business process

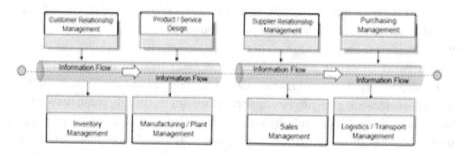

The main goal was to reduce inventory level drastically and to regulate the suppliers' interaction with the production line more effectively. It consisted of two distinct flows through the supply chain organizations: material and information. The scope of the supply chain begins with the source of supply and ends at the point of consumption. It extends much further than simply a concern with the physical movement of materials. Equal emphasis is given to supplier management, purchasing, inventory management, manufacturing management, facilities planning, customer service, information flow, transport, and physical distribution. Some of the important business processes, along the supply chain, are shown in Figure 1.

Also, the important challenges in supporting huge heterogeneous data integration in global supply networks are: (i) increasing number of business alliance partners due to globalization of business processes, (ii) different business practice and infrastructure facilities within participating business-partners, and (iii) differences in data exchange formats and standards among business-partners. Moreover, data capture and transmission mechanisms (e.g., barcoding, radio frequency identification technique, electronic data interchange, wireless networking infrastructure and protocols, global positioning system's capability) produce huge amounts of supply chain transportation data that, if properly controlled and shared, can enhance performance and agility of global supply chain networks. To harness this value-added service of data to global enterprises, a single representation data format is very essential.

As a result, much global manufacturing (e.g., textile and clothing) businesses are investing in new ICT to harness smooth information sharing ability in their supply chain operations (Monteneggro et al., 2007). With the recent progress in Radio Frequency Identification (RFID) technology, low-cost wireless sensor hardwires, and world wide web technologies, the Internet of Things (IoT) advance has attracted attention in connecting global apparel business activities and sharing operational business information. In this context, while IoT technology supports the capability to connect and integrate both digital and physical business entities, enabling the provision of a new type of information system (IS) applications and services. Also, the Semantic Web of Things (SWoT) is ushering a new opportunity in the business community, by integrating the Semantic Web and the IoT technologies. Its objective is to associate semantically rich and easily accessible information to real-world objects, locations, and events, using inexpensive, disposable, and unobtrusive micro-devices, such as RFID tags and wireless sensors. This opportunity provides new types of IS applications and services in many apparel business areas (e.g., manufacturing, inventory management, transportation management). To facilitate this vision, information technologies and software system frameworks must mitigate with typical pervasive computing application related issues: platform heterogeneity; appropriate resource utilization, intelligent intractability of the user, and device volatility, dependence on context, and limitation of device-specific computation power. Hence, the SWoT vision requires pervasive knowledge-based systems with higher degrees of automatic capability in information storage, management, and discovery, also provision of transparent access to information sources for processing.

Most of the IoT technology solutions inherit support from generally stable data communication infra-structures, assistance from centralized brokers for service management and discovery of information. Also, optimization of alternatives information provision has been recently getting prominence, for example, 6LoWPAN (IPv6 over Low Power Wireless Personal Area Networks) (Monteneggro et al., 2007) and the Constrained Application Protocol (CoAP) (Colitti et al., 2011). In parallel attempts, ontologies for device and data annotation were presented, for example - OntoSensor (Russomanno et al., 2005) and the SSN-XG ontology of the World Wide Web Consortium for semantic sensor networks (Lefort et al., 2005). Contemporary research projects, such as UBIWARE (Katasonov et al., 2008), and Sense2Web (Barnaghi et al., 2010), integrate data communication networking and semantic technologies to make software frameworks for semantically enriched IoT application services.

These services are composed of different sources of data originated from real-world objects related to apparel business processes. With many devices in the textile and clothing world, many physical pa-rameters and real-world entities can collaborate in a business service through the data communication networks or the Internet. Thus, there is a need for seamless integration of the physical world with the digital world in IoT. Also, the progress in IoT-enabled device abstraction and integration of different data sources in apparel business is a challenging task. The traditional web service discovery mechanisms are incapable to produce the appropriate result. Because the dynamic heterogeneous nature of IoT generated data requires semantic modelling. Thus, IoT entities need to be formally represented and managed to achieve interoperability.

An important step towards the vision of IoT-based information systems interoperability is the reuse of data collected from widely distributed sensor-enabled devices. Ontology-based semantic modelling helps to capture the capability of entities to represent information and its relationships among other entities to enable efficient information exchange. In this way, semantic modelling in conjunction with service-oriented computing and ontology ushers a scalable means of accessing IoT entities. An ontology simply describes a vocabulary modelling a domain of interest and a specification of the meaning of terms in that vocabulary. Depending on the accuracies of this specification, the notion of ontology encompasses different data or conceptual models (e.g., classifications). In other words, an ontology is a shared conceptualization, and it is used to represent knowledge as a set of concepts related to each other. The structural part of an ontology consists of four key components and they are *classes*, *relations*, *attributes*, and *individuals*. Classes represent the concepts in ontology design, and individuals are the basic, '*ground level*' components or instances of an ontology. Attributes or characteristics represent the features of the classes, and relations describe how the classes and individuals are related to one another.

This chapter presents a semantic knowledge based for IoT related entities in an apparel manufacturing business. Since most of the IoT data, in a textile and clothing industry setting, needs to be made available homogeneously to allow integration from a wide variety of sources. A unified machine-understandable representation of world knowledge is required to put things into common semantic context. The integrated Apparel Business Decentralised Data Integration (ABDDI) framework uses semantic modelling. Particularly, ontologies are used to form a unified knowledge base to support: (a) semantic definition and representation of IoT entities; (b) dynamic service discovery and matching based on user request; and (c) service composition and orchestration in dynamic environments. This chapter considers ontologies as the key component for automatic service-representation, composition, discovery, and orchestration for IoT in dynamic environments. The proposed knowledge base hides the heterogeneity of entities and consequently enables semantic searching and querying capabilities. The presented knowledge base integrates several existing ontologies that were mainly related to sensor resources, web services and extends them for IoT.

The rest of this chapter is organized as follows. Section 2 reviews some of the representative research works on semantic modelling methods for the domain of general IoT-based applications. Section 3 describes the background knowledge about the proposed system. Section 4 presents knowledge representation and reasoning approach. Section 5 explains some of the mathematical concepts using a business case, and it also includes a concept similarity assessment. Section 6 concludes the chapter by discussing relevant research issues and put forward the idea of future research.

RELATED RESEARCH WORKS

In recent decades automatic identification technologies are gaining more and more attraction for industrial applications. These applications are combined with the technologies of RFID, Electronic Product Code (EPC), and sensor-based data communication networks to share application-specific data. Advances in

ICT are bringing into reality the vision of many uniquely identifiable, interconnected objects and things that gather data from diverse physical environments and deliver the information to a variety of innovative applications and services. In this way, the network of objects (e.g., devices, vehicles, machines, containers), embedded with sensors and software has the potential to collect and communicate data over Internet. The inter- and intra-organizational communication and information exchange are perceived to facilitated by IoT capability. This, IoT-based technology adoption can be viewed as an additional capability that may add value to the supply chain industries.

While IoT many applications are used in different supply chain industries (Jandl et el., 2019), industrial IoT (IIoT) focuses especially on industrial usage of IoT devices (Jakl et al., 2018) (Jeschke et al., 2017). Recently, Thomas Moser's research group presented an overview of industrial IoT applications (Jandl et al., 2019) for smart industry (also known as Industry 4.0). With the advent of the IoT, new opportunities and capabilities emerge with relation to the real time monitoring, management and optimization of goods distribution and supply chain. as more and more physical objects in supply chain industries are equipped with barcodes, RFID tags or sensors, transport and logistics companies can perform real-time monitoring of the movement of physical objects from one location to another. The goal is to track a product along the entire supply chain, including material management, production, transportation, and distribution (Karakostas, 2013).

Particularly, the manufacturing companies are changing their IT infrastructure towards the fourth industrial revolution (Lasi et al., 2014). The utilization of artificial intelligence (AI) techniques in cyber-physical systems (CPSs) (Broy et al., 2012) is a typical characteristic of this change (Lee et al., 2014). In this context, flexibility is one of the important criteria for manufacturing companies particularly because of ever shorter market launch times and increasing customer demands for individualization (Cheng et al., 2017; Lasi et al., 2014). To conduct close to reality Industry 4.0 research, researchers are using factory simulation model because companies are often not willing to provide data from and access to their production lines for research purposes.

To get a better understanding of data from various sources, more and more researchers start to concentrate on techniques enabling machines to intelligently understanding IoT data. To use AI applications in practice, contextual operational knowledge must necessarily be available in formal and machine-readable representation (Humm et al., 2020). Semantic web services address the issues of automatic discovering, composing, and executing by providing a declarative, ontological framework for describing them. Using AI methods (e.g., automated planning such as (Marrella, 2018) (Marrella & Mecella, 2018), multi-agent systems for decentralized manufacturing control such as (Ciortea et al., 2018), Case-Based Reasoning (CBR) such as Minor et al., 2014) (Muller, 2018)) to enhance flexibility in cyber-physical production workflows (Bordel Sanchez et al., 2018) (Seiger et al., 2018)) inevitably require such semantic annotations.

Many related research work (Puttonen et al., 2010) (Puttonen et al., 2013) exist that already highlight these issues by using semantic web services (SWS). Moreover, the currently available approaches that use semantic web services in the context of Industry 4.0 focusing only on specific aspects and do not consider the entire context of manufacturing environment. Also, the complex reasoning within the knowledge base makes real-time execution and monitoring of manufacturing processes difficult.

Several research works propose the use of SWSs for smart manufacturing in Industry 4.0 but focusing only on partial aspects and do not consider the entire context of the shop floor. For instance, Puttonen et al. (2013) present an approach to use SWSs for executing manufacturing processes by means of three software agents represented as web services. One of these agents, referred to as Service Monitor, is a specialized web service that carries out semantic web service composition by using planning techniques with respect to a given production goal and the current state of the world that is provided by a domain ontology. Therefore, they use OWL for describing the state of the production system as well as OWL-S and SPARQL expressions for semantically describing the available web services that offer production capabilities.

Since modern Cyber-Physical Production Systems (CPPSs) (Monostori, 2014) consist of many different components and therefore many stakeholders are involved in their development process up to the later use in the manufacturing of products, Lobov et al. (2008) investigated the application of SWSs for orchestration of a flexible control. They propose OWL for modeling a Process Taxonomy, Product Ontology, Equipment Ontology, and Service Ontology and mainly discuss the responsibilities of involved persons for knowledge acquisition and maintenance rather than present their detailed semantic specification.

Many academic and practitioner work-like Henson et al. (Cory et al., 2009) experiment a semantically enhanced sensor service application, known as SemSOS, having the capability to query both high-level knowledge and low-level environmental reading by sensors. Concerning classical sematic-matchmaking approach, different research groups distinguish among full (subsume), potential (intersection-satisðable) and partial (disjoint) match types to represent the relevant knowledge of different types of entities (Colucci et al., 2007) and (Li & Horrocks, 2004) respectively. Similarly, in the ubiquitous infrastructure by queries allow only exact matches with facts derived from a support knowledge base. Non-standard inferences like abduction and contraction are needed to support approximate matches, semantic ranking, and explanations of outcomes (Colucci et al., 2007).

This chapter highlights the requirement for a unified semantic knowledge base for automatic service-representation, discovery, modelling, and composition in dynamic environments. Different research projects try to address these issues with the use of ontologies in prototype system design. For example, semantic commonalities in RFID semantic streams project uses DLs for system modelling purpose (Ruta et al., 2011). This work is of considerable interest, but so far it is somewhat sui generis.

All these schemes are worthy of considerable study, and together they represent the richest characterisation of knowledge-based approach in pervasive service computing so far produced. Moreover, the systems are implemented and can be shown to be capable of generating relevant services using appropriate data streams.

OVERVIEW OF THE FRAMEWORK

The proposed framework uses a model-theoretic semantics modelled in ontologies for IoT generated data modelling purpose. It helps to gather detailed information regarding the characteristics of IoT devices based on their technical requirements. The advantages of this encoding are – (i) interconnecting different classification systems to represent capabilities and properties of constituent parts, (ii) translate characteristics or properties among compound constituent parts, and (iii) aggregate basic properties into complex properties based on the constituents of a superordinate system. Those concepts can be used and adapted for the IoT to enhance the uses of IoT devices in connecting them as a group, create coordination between IoT devices, and improving their interoperability.

One of the main objectives of this framework defines an architecture for IoT, which can be used for other applications also. The design principle in Apparel Business Semantic Data Management (ABDDI) is that any physical/real-world object in global textile and clothing business can have a virtual representation through a Virtual Object (VO). A VO uses a semantic representation of the functionality and conceals the varied identity of the real-world object. Multiple VOs can be combined to form a Composite Virtual Object (CVO) that provides more compact and reliable services. In simple, CVOs are combined to form a service request. Thus, the ABDDI architecture has three layers namely, VO layer, CVO layer and Service layer as shown in Figure 2.

Figure 2. RFID tagging level at different stages in the apparel manufacturing network

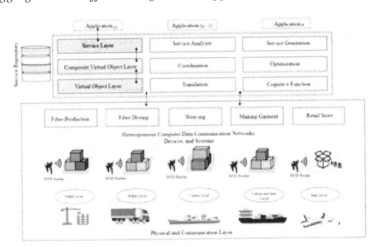

The functionalities of the three layers are presented below:

1. VO layer: Real-world objects are represented in the digital format as VO. End-users can search semantically and retrieve information from any existing VO. Also, actuation can be done through the VO.
2. CVO layer: In this layer VOs are combined to form a service request. This layer generally caters functionality to semantically search and query categories of CVOs for service provision.
3. Service layer: In this layer gets the request from a user and analyse the service requests to determine the categories of CVOs needed for service accomplishment. This layer also performs service composition and orchestration in dynamic cloth and textile business environment.

The ABDDI system also has got other components: *registry*, and *control unit*. Every layer in this framework has a registry holding reference to the available VOs, CVOs, and services. These registries provide methods to semantically search and query existing VOs, CVOs, and services. The control unit regulates access to the VOs, CVOs and services based on the level of the end-user requirements.

KNOWLEDGE REPRESENTATION AND REASONING APPROACH

The main motivation for this chapter stems from Description Logics (DL) [1] based knowledge representation approach in pervasive computing applications along the global apparel supply chain. This DL based knowledge representation systems play a role very much like Database Management Systems

(DBMS). In DL, elementary descriptions are *atomic concepts* and *atomic roles*. Complex descriptions can be built from them inductively with *concept constructors*. In abstract notation, one can use the letters A and B for atomic concepts, the letter R for atomic roles, and the letters C and D for concept descriptions. Possible DL constructors and the related examples are shown in Table 1, and these constructors are used the DLs investigated in this chapter.

Table 1. DLs set of constructors

Constructor Name	Syntax	Explanation
Top concept	⊤	Universal concept. All the objects in the domain.
Bottom concept	⊥	The empty set.
Atomic concept	A	All objects belonging to the set A.
Atomic negation	¬A	All the objects not belonging to the set A.
Conjunction	C⊓D	The objects belonging to both C and D sets.
Disjunction	C⊔D	The objects that are in the extension of either C or D, or both
Value restriction	∀R.C	All the objects participating in the R relation whose rage are all the objects belonging to C set.
Existential restriction	∃R.C	At least one object participating in the relation R.
Concept definition	A ° C	Concepts represent sets of elements and can be viewed as unary predicates.

Resource Representation and Reasoning in Description Logics

The most important and well-known service characterizing reasoning in DL checks for specificity hierarchies, by determining whether a concept description is more specific than other one or, formally, if there is a *subsumption* relation between them.

Definition 1 (Subsumption): *Give two concept descriptions C and D and a TBox τ in a DL L, one can say that D subsumes C with respect to C⊑D if for every model of τ, C⊑I. As a special case, two concepts are equivalent if they subsume each other.*

For example, let us consider the following concept descriptions, referred to different type of garments in an apparel supply chain network: G1 = *SweaterBodyGarment* ⊓ ∀ h*asMain.Color.Red,* and G2 = U*pperBodyGarment* ⊓ ∀ h*asMain.Color.Red.* Then using TBox reasoning – the concept inclusion can be achieved, and the output will be S*weater* ⊑ *UpperBodyGarment.* Hence, given the model, knowledge expressed by G1 is more specific than the one required by G2 with respect to the reasoning mechanism and the definition G2 subsumes G1

Based on subsumption, new reasoning mechanisms can be defined in DLs. The ABDDI system development uses several non-standard reasoning mechanisms (e.g. Least Common Subsumer – LCS).

Definition 2 (Least Common Subsumer): *Let $C_1, ..., C_p$ be p concept descriptions in a DL L. A Least Common Subsumer (LCS) of $C_1, ..., C_p$, denoted by LCS $(C_1, ..., C_p)$ is a concept description E in L. state that the following conditions hold: (i) C_h ⊑ E for h = 1, ..., p; (ii) E is the least L–concept description satisfying (iii) i.e., if E' is an L–concept satisfying C_i ⊑ E' for all i = 1, ..., n, then E ⊑ E'.*

It is worth to show how to model concept collections formalized in ALN (D) according to a compact lossless representation. Such modelling allows finding commonalities in resource annotations formalized in DL.

Definition 3 (Concept Components): *Let C be a concept described in a DL L, with C formalized as* $C^1 ó \ldots C^m$. *The Concept Components of C are defined as follows: if* C^j, *with j = 1,..., m is either a concept name, or a negated concept name, or a concrete feature or a number restriction, then* C^j *is a Concept Component of C; if* $C^j = \forall RE$, *with j = 1 ..., m, then* $\forall R.E^k$ *is a Concept Component of C, for each* E^k *Concept Component of E.*

Definition 4 (Subsumption): *Give two concept descriptions C and D and a TBox* τ *in a DL L, one can say that D subsumes C* $\hat{I}D$ *concerning if for every model of* τ, $C\hat{I}^DI$. *As a special case, two concepts are equivalent if they subsume each other.*

Definition 5 (Least Common Subsumer): *Let C1 ..., Cp be p concept descriptions in a DL L. A Least Common Subsumer (LCS) of C1 ..., Cp denoted by LCS (C1 ..., Cp) is a concept description E in L. state that the following conditions hold: (i) Ch ô E for h = 1, ..., p; (ii) E is the least L–concept description satisfying (iii) i.e., if E' is an L–concept satisfying Ci ô E' for all i = 1, ..., n, then E ô E'.*

Definition 6 (r-Common Subsumer, Informative r-Common Subsumers): *Let* $C_1, \ldots, C_p$ *be p concept descriptions in a DL L, and let be k £ p. A r-Common Subsumer (r-CS) of* $C_1, \ldots, C_p$ *is a concept* $_{D^1}$ *such that D is an LCS of at least r = k/p concepts among* $C_1, \ldots, C_p$. *As a special case, one can define as Informative r-Common Subsumers (IrCS) that specific r-CSs for which r < 1.*

It is worth to show how to model concept collections formalized in ALN (D) according to a compact lossless representation. Such a modelling framework allows finding commonalities in resource annotations formalized in DL.

Definition 7 (Concept Components): *Let C be a concept described in a DL L, with C formalized as* $C^1 ó \ldots C^m$. *The Concept Components of C are defined as follows: if* C^j, *with j = 1,..., m is either a concept name, or a negated concept name, or a concrete feature or a number restriction, then* C^j *is a Concept Component of C; if* $C^j = \forall R.E$, *with j = 1 ..., m, then* $\forall R.E^k$ *is a Concept Component of C, for each* E^k *Concept Component of E.*

Definition 8 (Aggregate Collection Matrix): *Let* $S_1, \ldots, S_n$ *be an aggregate collection, with* $S_i = C_{1i}, .., C_{pi}$ *for i = 1 ... n. Let* $D \hat{I} \{D_1,\ldots,D_m\}$ *be the Concept Components deriving from all the concepts in the aggregate collection. The Aggregate Subsumers Matrix is defined as* $A = (a_{ij})$, *with i = 1 ... n and j = 1 ... m, such that for each i,* $a_{ij} = v$, *with* $0 £ v £ p_i$ *where v is the number of concept descriptions in* S_i *subsumed by the component* D_j.

Definition 9 (Aggregate Model): *Let* $S_1, \ldots, S_n$ *be an aggregate of concept collections; for i = 1 ... n,* S_i *is a concept collection descriptions* C_{ki} *with k = 1 ... p_i. An Aggregate Model for* $S_1, \ldots, S_n$ *and each of this element consists of the pair of items -* $<E, G>$ *with the following characteristics: (i) E represents the subsumers matrix deriving from the collection* $C_1, .., C_p = \hat{E}(C_{ki})$, *with i = 1 ... n and k = 1 ... p_i whose elements* e_{kj} *are calculated by using prognostications to subsumption; and (ii) G is the collection subsumers matrix deriving from the input collection* $S_1, .., S_n$, *whose elements* a_{ij} *are calculated by using information stored in E. In this computation, each row i in G is related to an aggregate collection* S_i *defined as a collection of description* C_{ki} *whose subsumpton relationship with components deriving from* $S_1, .., Sn$ *is stored in E. To this modelling, values* a_{ij} *for each component* D_j *are determined as Concept Component Relative Cardinality* $RC_{D_j}^{S_i}$.

Semantic Similarity Assessment

Before describing the theoretical framework underlying the proposed approach, the employed reasoning services will be shortly recalled in the following subsection to make the chapter self-contained. Furthermore, the proposed algorithmic concept similarity measurement is presented in this section.

In ABSDM, the similarity between two concepts C_i, C_j can be expressed by a number, and its values can fall somewhere between 0 and 1. It may be viewed as a one-directional relation, and its larger values imply a higher similarity between the concepts. The concept similarity is described as follows:

Definition 10 (Concept Similarity): An ontological concept (C) similarity (¶) is considered as a *relation* and it can be defined as ¶: C x C ® [0, 1]. In simple, it is a function from a pair of concepts to a real number between *zero* and *one* expressing the degree of similarity between two concepts such that:

1. $\forall C_1 \in G,\ \partial(C_1, C_1) = 1$
2. $\forall C_1 \in G,\ 0 \leq \partial(C_1, C_1) \leq 1$
3. $\forall C_1, C_2, C_3 \in G,\ \text{IF } Sim_d(C_1, C_2) > Sim_d(C_1, C_3) \text{ THEN } \partial(C_1, C_2) < \partial(C_1, C_3)$

The above properties provide the range of semantic similarity function $¶(C_i, C_j)$. For exactly similar concepts the similarity is $¶(C_1, C_1) = 1$; when two concepts have nothing in common, their similarity is $¶(C_1, C_2) = 0$. In this way, the output of the similarity function should be in the closed interval [0, 1]. Here Sim_d represents the semantic distance and (C_1, C_2, C_3) represent three concepts of graph G. In CSIA, the following semantic similarity (¶) function has been used for computation purpose:

$$\partial(C_1, C_2) = \frac{1}{\deg * Sim_d(C_1, C_2) + 1}$$

Where C_1 and C_2 represent two concepts and 'deg' represents the impact degree of semantic distance on semantic similarity, and it should be between $0 < \deg £ 1$. A weight allocation function is used, as shown below, to compute the semantic similarity between concepts:

$$w(C_m, C_n) = \left[\max(depth(C_m)) + \frac{OrderNumber(C_n)}{TNodes(G) + 1} + 1 \right]^{-1}$$

Where, C_m and C_n represent two nodes directly connected, $\max(depth(C_m))$ represents the maximum depth of the node C_m (the depth of the root node is equal to 0 and 1 for the nodes directly connected to the root node and so on), TNodes(G) and OrderNumber(C_n) represent the total number of nodes in concept graph G and the order number of the node (C_n) between their siblings.

The detail description of these mathematical formalisations is beyond the scope of this chapter.

Semantic Similarity Assessment

In ABDDI, the similarity between two concepts C_i, C_j can be expressed by a number, and its values can fall somewhere between 0 and 1. It may be viewed as a one-directional relation, and its larger values imply a higher similarity between the concepts. The concept similarity is described as follows:

EXAMPLE OF A BUSINESS SCENARIO

A simple apparel manufacturing scenario is used to present a part of ABDDI algorithmic computation.

Algorithm 1. Algorithm for semantic similarity computation

```
input: two concepts (C₁, C₂), root node (Rootₙ), concepts graph (G)
output: semantic similarity value between two concepts
          1:     begin
 2:   if  C₁ and C₂ are same concept then Sim_d  = 0
 3:     else
 4:         if C₁ and C₂ are directly connected then Sim_d  = w (C₁, C₂)
 5:           else
 6:             if idirect path connection exist then
 7:                   S_path01 = ShortestPath (G, C₁, Rootₙ)
 8:                   S_path02 = ShortestPath (G, C₂, Rootₙ)
 9:                   Sim_d = w(S_path01) + w(S_path02) - 2*w(CSPath]
 10:               end if
```

$$11: \qquad \partial\left(C_1, C_2\right) = \frac{1}{\deg * Sim_d + 1}$$

```
           12:           end if
 13:   end if
 14:   return ¶
 15:   end
```

Semantic IoT-based product flow in a retail outlet is considered. Each product is described using semantic-enhanced IoT as an ALN (D) concept expression in OWL language. As the retail apparel product arrive or depart the shop, they are scanned by the gate RFID readers; reading events, including semantic annotation extracted from tags, are fed to a semantic Data Service Management Service (DSMS) which computes Concept Components and subsumption test through a reasoning mechanism.

Let us consider a situation that allows a user to purchase a sweater from an online business. This example considers how a request is matched with service advertised for wool garments selling service. An algorithm (i.e., ALGORITHM 1) tries to perform semantic matching for a relevant sweater. It takes two ontological concepts, the root node (Rootₙ), and the concepts graph (G) as input and computes a semantic similarity between the concepts as output. The part of the concept hierarchy used in this example is shown in Figure 3. Each node of this hierarchy represents a concept. In the experimental comparison, semantic similarity among Wool, Shirt, Sweater, Trouser, Cardigan, Pullover, and Jumper are considered.

Figure 3. The hierarchical concept relationships

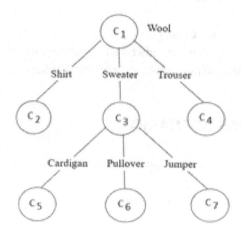

Table 2. The results of various similarity measures

(a) Path similarity						(b) The proposed method				
	C_1	C_2	C_3	C_4	C_5		C_1	C_2	C_3	C_4	C_5
C_1	1.00	0.25	0.50	0.20	0.20	C_1	1.00	0.48	0.65	0.51	0.38
C_2	0.25	1.00	0.50	0.33	0.16	C_2	0.48	1.00	0.65	0.51	0.38
C_3	0.50	0.50	1.00	0.25	0.16	C_3	0.65	0.65	1.00	0.71	0.48
C_4	0.20	0.33	0.25	1.00	0.20	C_4	0.51	0.51	0.71	1.00	0.59
C_5	0.20	0.16	0.16	0.20	1.00	C_5	0.38	0.38	0.48	0.59	1.00

The proposed algorithm (i.e., Algorithm-I) provides semantic similarity between concepts with a high score in comparison to path similarity algorithm. In Table 2, (a) is the result of path similarity [18], and (b) tabulates the results of the proposed Algorithm-I used in ABDDI. In ABDDI similarity measure is flexible and customizable, allowing the consideration of user preferences. This refers to two aspects. Firstly, using the advanced search interface, the user may determine the relative importance of some of the similarity assessment parameter. Second, apart from presenting a single rank for each candidate service, more detailed results may also be provided (e.g., separate values for recall, the degree of match) to facilitate the user in identifying the more suitable service.

CONCLUSION

This chapter presents some of the uses of IoT technologies (e.g., RFID tag-based technology, sensor) in manufacturing industry. In textile and clothing retail industry, RFID technology provides the ability to interact with items (i.e., transport carts, trolleys, keys, and valuable products) without physical contact. Thus, item-level IoT infrastructures not only provide item handling efficiency, but also offer a promising way to capture customers' in-store behavioural data and then gain insight into these data using data mining technology. In this way, these sensing objects and things form the Internet of Things (IoT), which are used to automate different manufacturing business processes (e.g., material management, transportation management, and logistics management). IoT applications rely on real-time context data and allow sending information for driving the behaviours of users in intelligent supply chain environments.

These IoT-based solutions are mostly tailored for vertical applications and systems, utilizing knowledge only from business areas. To realize the full potential of IoT, these specialized silo applications need to be replaced with horizontal collaborative applications, including knowledge acquisition, and sharing capabilities.

One of the main challenges in realizing an IoT system lies in dealing with device and data heterogeneities and fostering the interoperability between devices, information, and services built on top of it. Ontologies and semantic description frameworks play an important role in the IoT as they operate on top of a standardized data interoperability infrastructure and enforce the concept of data uniformity that allows data and data semantics to be described in application-independent ways. In doing so, semantic technologies and ontologies decouple data semantics from application logics, which facilitates information exchange, adaptability, and interoperability among tools and systems.

This chapter describes a unified semantic knowledge base (ABDDI) for IoT related technologies in apparel supply chain management. Semantic modelling is an important component to address issues related to interoperability among different entities to realize the grand vision of IoT. ABDDI's knowledge base comprises of ontologies to model different aspects of apparel business (e.g., IoT resources, location information, contextual information, domain knowledge, policies for the dynamic environment and IoT services). Most of the current work focuses on IoT resources and services, however modelling contextual information in a dynamic environment assists in more accurate knowledge representation for IoT entities.

Real-time data gathering and processing are the main ingredients of modern supply chain operations. To further enhance the potential of this promising application, in future this research will try to propose a unified framework for IoT-based path analytics, which uses both in-store shopping paths and IoT-based purchasing data to mine actionable navigation patterns. In the data pre-processing module, the important problem of how to capture the mainstream shopping path sequences while wiping out redundant and repeated details need to be addressed in detail.

REFERENCES

Baader, F., Calvanese, D., McGuinness, D., Nardi, D., & Patel-Schneider, P. (Eds.). (2002). *The Description Logic Handbook*. Cambridge University Press.

Barnaghi, P., Presser, M., & Moessner, K. (2010). Publishing Linked Sensor Data. *Proceedings of the 3rd International Workshop on Semantic Sensor Networks*.

Bordel Sánchez, B., Alcarria, R., Sánchez de Rivera, D., & Robles, T. (2018). Process execution in CyberPhysical Systems using cloud and Cyber-Physical Internet services. *The Journal of Supercomputing*, *74*(8), 4127–4169. doi:10.100711227-018-2416-4

Broy, M., Cengarle, M. V., & Geisberger, E. (2012). Cyber-Physical Systems: Imminent Challenges. In *Large-Scale Complex IT Syst. Dev., Operat. and Manag. 17th Monterey Workshop*, 7539, 1–28.

Cheng, H., Xue, L., Wang, P., Zeng, P., & Yu, H. (2017). Ontology-based web service integration for flexible manufacturing systems. In *15th Int. Conf. on Ind. Inf.*, (pp. 351–356). IEEE. 10.1109/INDIN.2017.8104797

Ciortea, A., Mayer, S., & Michahelles, F. (2018). Repurposing Manufacturing Lines on the Fly with Multi-agent Systems for the Web of Things. In *Proc. of the 17th Int. Conf. on Autonomous Agents and Multi-Agent Systems*, (pp. 813–822). Int. Found. for Autonomous Agents and Multiagent Systems / ACM.

Colitti, W., Steenhaut, K., Caro, N. De., (2011). *Integrating Wireless Sensor Networks with the Web.* Extending the Internet to Low Power and Lossy Networks (IP+SN).

Colucci, S., Di Noia, T., Pinto, A., Ruta, M., Ragone, A., & Tinelli, E. (2007). A Nonmonotonic Approach to Semantic Matchmaking and Request Refinement in E-Marketplaces. *International Journal of Electronic Commerce*, *12*(2), 127–154. doi:10.2753/JEC1086-4415120205

Cory, A., Henson, J., Pschorr, K., Sheth, A. P., & Thirunarayan, K. (2009). SemSOS: Semantic sensor Observation Service. *Proceedings of the International Symposium on Collaborative Technologies and Systems.*

De Virgilio, R., Di Sciascio, E., Ruta, M., Scioscia, F., & Torlone, R. (2011). Semantic-based rfid data management. In *Unique Radio Innovation for the 21st Century* (pp. 111–141). Springer. doi:10.1007/978-3-642-03462-6_6

Jakl, A., Schoffer, L., Husinsky, M., & Wagner, M. (2018). Agumented Reality for Industry 4.0: Architecture and User Experience. *Proceeding of the 11ᵗʰ Forum Media Technology, CER-WS*, 38-42.

Jandl, C., Nurgazina, J., Schoffer, L., Reichl, C., Wagner, M., & Moser, T. (2019). SensiTrack – A Privacy by Design Concept for Industrial IoT Applications. *Proceeding of the 24th IEEE International Conference on Emerging Technologies and Factory Automation*, 1782-1789. 10.1109/ETFA.2019.8869186

Jeschke, S., Brecher, C., Meisen, T., Ozdemir, D., & Eschert, T. (2017). Industrial Internet of Things and Cyber Manufacturing Systems. In Industrial Internet of Things. Springer.

Karakostas, B. (2013). A DNS architecture for the Internet of things: A case study in transport logistics. *Procedia Computer Science*, *19*, 594–601. doi:10.1016/j.procs.2013.06.079

Katasonov, A., Kaykova, O., Khriyenko, O., Nikitin, S., & Terziyan, V. (2008). Smart Semantic Middleware for the Internet of Things. *Proceedings of the 5th International Conference of Informatics in Control, Automation and Robotics*, 11-15.

Keskinock, P., & Tayur, S. (2001). Quantitive analysis of Internet enabled supply chain. *Interface: a Journal for and About Social Movements*, *31*(2), 70–89. doi:10.1287/inte.31.2.70.10626

Lasi, H., Fettke, P., Kemper, H.-G., Feld, T., & Hoffmann, M. (2014). Industry 4.0. *BISE*, *6*(4), 239–242.

Lastra, J. L. M., & Delamer, I. M. (2006). Semantic Web Services in Factory Automation: Fundamental Insights and Research Roadmap. *IEEE Transactions on Industrial Informatics*, *2*(1), 1–11.

Lee, H. L., & Billington, C. (1992). Managing supply chain inventories: Pitfalls and opportunities. *Sloan Management Review*, *33*(3), 65–77.

Lee, J., Kao, H.-A., & Yang, S. (2014). Service Innovation and Smart Analytics for Industry 4.0 and Big Data Environment. *Procedia CIRP*, *16*, 3–8. doi:10.1016/j.procir.2014.02.001

Lefort, L., Henson, C., Taylor, K., Barnaghi, P., Compton, M., Corcho, O., Garcia-Castro, R., Graybeal, J., Herzog, A., & Janowicz, K. (2005). *Semantic Sensor Network XG Final Report*. W3C Incubator Group Report. http://www.w3.org/2005/Incubator/ssn/XGR-ssn/

Li, L., & Horrocks, I. (2004). A software framework for matchmaking based on semantic web technology. *International Journal of Electronic Commerce*, *8*(4), 39–60. doi:10.1080/10864415.2004.11044307

Lobov, A., Lopez, F. U., Herrera, V. V., Puttonen, J., & Lastra, J. L. M. (2008). Semantic Web Services framework for manufacturing industries. In *Int. Conf. on Rob. and Biomim.*, (pp. 2104–2108). IEEE.

Maass, W., Filler, A. (2006). Towards an infrastructure for semantically annotated physical products. In *INFORMATIK 2006–Informatik für Menschen–Band 2, Beiträge der 36*. Jahrestagung der Gesellschaft für Informatik eV (GI).

Marrella, A. (2018). *Automated Planning for Business Process Management*. Academic Press.

Minor, M., Montani, S., & Recio-García, J. A. (2014). Process-oriented Case-based Reasoning. *Information Systems*, *40*, 103–105. doi:10.1016/j.is.2013.06.004

Monostori, L. (2014). Cyber-physical Production Systems: Roots, Expectations and R&D Challenges. *Procedia CIRP*, *17*, 9–13. doi:10.1016/j.procir.2014.03.115

Montenegro, G., Kushalnagar, N., Hui, J., & Culler, D. (2007). Transmission of IPv6 packets over IEEE 802.15.4 networks. Internet proposed standard RFC, vol. 4944.

Müller, G. (2018). *Workflow Modeling Assistance by Casebased Reasoning*. Springer Fachmedien.

Ocker, F., Kovalenko, I., Barton, K., Tilbury, D., & VogelHeuser, B. (2019). A Framework for Automatic Initialization of Multi-Agent Production Systems Using Semantic Web Technologies. IEEE Robotics and Automation Letters, 4(4), 4330–4337.

Pal, K. (2017). Supply Chain Coordination Based on Web Services. In H. K. Chan, N. Subramanian, & M. D. Abdulrahman (Eds.), *Supply Chain Management in the Big Data Era* (pp. 137–171). IGI Global Publication. doi:10.4018/978-1-5225-0956-1.ch009

Pal, K. (2018). A Big Data Framework for Decision Making in Supply Chain. IGI Global.

Pal, K. (2020). Information Sharing for Manufacturing Supply Chain Management Based on Blockchain Technology. In Cross-Industry Use of Blockchain Technology and Opportunities for the Future. IGI Global. doi:10.4018/978-1-7998-3632-2.ch001

Pal, K., & Ul-Haque, A. (2000). Internet of Things and Blockchain Technology in Apparel Manufacturing Supply Chain Data Management. *Procedia Computer Science*, 450-457.

Puttonen, J., Lobov, A., & Lastra, J. L. M. (2013). Semantics-Based Composition of Factory Automation Processes Encapsulated by Web Services. *IEEE TII*, *9*(4), 2349–2359. doi:10.1109/TII.2012.2220554

Puttonen, J., Lobov, A., Soto, M. A. C., & Lastra, J. L. M. (2010). A Semantic Web Services-based approach for production systems control. *Advanced Engineering Informatics*, *24*(3), 285–299. doi:10.1016/j.aei.2010.05.012

Russomanno, D. J., Kothari, C. R., & Thomas, O. A. (2005). Building a Sensor Ontology: A Practical Approach Leveraging ISO and OGC Models. *2005 International Conference on Artificial Intelligence*, 637-643.

Ruta, M., Colucci, S., Scioscia, F., Di Sciascio, E., & Donini, F. M. (2011). Finding commonalities in RFID semantic streams. *Procedia Computer Science*, *5*, 857–864. doi:10.1016/j.procs.2011.07.118

Seiger, R., Huber, S., & Schlegel, T. (2018). Toward an execution system for self-healing workflows in cyberphysical systems. *Software & Systems Modeling*, *17*(2), 551–572. doi:10.100710270-016-0551-z

Swaminathan, J. M. (2000). *Supply chain management*. In *International Encyclopedia of the Social and Behavioural Sciences*. Elsevier Sciences.

Varelas, G., Voutsakist, E., Raftopoulout, P., Petrakis, E. G. M., & Milios, E. (2005). Semantic Similarity methods in WordNet and their application to information retrieval on the Web. In *Proceedings of the 7th annual ACM international workshop on web information and data management*. Bremen, Germany: ACM. 10.1145/1097047.1097051

KEY TERMS AND DEFINITIONS

Description Logic: Description logics (DL) are a family of formal knowledge representation languages. Many DLs are more expressive than propositional logic, but less expressive than first-order logic.

EPC: Electronic Product Code (EPC), is a low-cost RFID tag designed for consumer products as a replacement for the universal product code (UPC).

Internet of Things: Internet of things (IoT) means networks of things, software, sensors, network connectivity, and embedded 'things' or physical objects. It collects or exchanges data. IoT makes objects sensed or controlled through a network infrastructure, supports integration between physical real world and automated information systems, and brings various effects such as improved productivity or economy in manufacturing industries.

Ontology: Information sharing among supply chain business partners using information systems is an important enabler for supply chain management. There are diverse types of data to be shared across supply chain, namely – *order, inventory, shipment*, and *customer service*. Consequently, information about these issues needs to be shared to achieve efficiency and effectiveness in supply chain management. In this way, information-sharing activities require that human and / or machine agents agree on common and explicit business-related concepts (the shared conceptualization among hardware / software-agents, customers, and service providers) are known as explicit ontologies; and this help to exchange data and derived knowledge out of the data to achieve collaborative goals of business operations.

RFID Reader: An RFID transceiver, providing real and possible access to RFID tags information.

RFID Tag: An RFID tag (or transponder), typically consisting of an RF coupling element and a microchip that carries identifying data. Tag functionality may range from simple identification to being able to form ad hoc network.

Semantic Web Service: A Semantic Web service, like conventional web services, is the server end of a client-server system for machine-to-machine interaction via the Web. Semantic services are a component of the semantic web because they use mark-up which makes data machine-readable in a detailed and sophisticated way (as compared with human-readable HTML which is usually not easily "understood" by computer programs).

Supply Chain Management: Supply chain management encompasses the planning and management of all activities involved in sourcing, procurement, manufacturing, and distribution. Importantly, it also includes coordination and collaboration with channel partners, which can be suppliers, intermediaries, third party service providers, and customers. In essence, supply chain management integrates supply and demand management within and across companies.

Web Ontology Language (OWL): The Web Ontology Language (OWL) is a semantic mark-up language for publishing and sharing ontologies on the Web. OWL is developed as a vocabulary extension of RDF (the Resource Description Framework) and is derived from the DAML + OIL Web Ontology Language.

Chapter 12
Towards Semantic Data Integration in Resource–Limited Settings for Decision Support on Gait–Related Diseases

Olawande Daramola

Cape Peninsula University of Technology, South Africa

Thomas Moser

(iD) https://orcid.org/0000-0002-9220-649X

St. Pölten University of Applied Sciences, Austria

ABSTRACT

Resource-limited settings (RLS) are characterised by lack of access to adequate resources such as ICT infrastructure, qualified medical personnel, healthcare facilities, and affordable healthcare for common people. The potential for the application of AI and clinical decision support systems in RLS are limited due to these challenges. Towards the improvement of the status quo, this chapter presents the conceptual design of a framework for the semantic integration of health data from multiple sources to facilitate decision support for the diagnosis and treatment of gait-related diseases in RLS. The authors describe how the framework can leverage ontologies and knowledge graphs for semantic data integration to achieve this. The plausibility of the proposed framework and the general imperatives for its practical realisation are also presented.

INTRODUCTION

Accurate and prompt treatment decision-making by medical practitioners in dealing with patients is critical to ensuring the health and well-being of patients. It is particularly important when this is done in resource-limited settings (RLS) where several challenges impede good healthcare conditions. Some of the challenges of RLS, which any viable healthcare solution must overcome include the shortage of qualified

DOI: 10.4018/978-1-7998-6697-8.ch012

personnel, lack of good infrastructure, lack of ready access to technology, and high cost of healthcare for common people (Zargaran et al. 2014; Fritz et al., 2015, Daramola & Moser, 2019; Siow et al., 2020). Another challenge is the scarcity of quality data to support Artificial Intelligence (AI) operations. Even when such data exist, they are often in disparate health information systems, which translate to inconsistencies of representations in the schema, semantics, terminologies, data types, and data formats that are used (Dhayne et al., 2018). Also, health data exist in both structured and unstructured forms all of which should be harnessed for effective data-driven decision-making. Thus, the semantic integration of health data sources is necessary for effective data-driven decision support in healthcare. Semantic data integration (SDI) enables heterogeneous health information systems, and health data to be harnessed for meaningful communication and exchange of data while the context of the individual data and systems are preserved (Cheatham & Pesquita, 2017). SDI will ensure that the exchange of data and interpretation of data are consistent irrespective of differences in data labels, data schema, and terminologies that are used by different databases or data (Cheatham & Pesquita, 2017; Vidal et al., 2019; Asfand-E-Yar & Ali, 2020). This will ensure access to all relevant data for accurate data-driven decision-making in healthcare (Shi et al., 2017; Balakrishna et al., 2020).

The advent of new digital technologies such as cloud computing, mobile computing, wearable sensors, Internet of Things (IoT), and linked open data has created new opportunities for semantic integration of heterogeneous data that can facilitate intelligent decision-making. This could aid important clinical processes in the aspects of disease diagnosis, disease treatment, and patient's rehabilitation even if there is a physical distance between the patient and the medical practitioner (Balakrishna et al., 2020). One of the state-of-the-art semantic technologies being used for semantic integration is a knowledge graph. Sundry definitions of a knowledge graph exist and it is difficult to find a consensus definition. However, based on some of the more quoted definitions, we can claim that a knowledge graph describes real-world entities and the relationships that exist between them by using a graphical model of representation. It has a schema that defines classes and entity relations; it captures potential interrelationships between arbitrary entities; and spans several topical domains (Paulheim, 2017). A knowledge graph stores interlinked descriptions of real-world concepts, objects, event, entities, things, situations, and their semantic definitions, which provides a basis to reason on them and derive new knowledge (Ehrlinger & Wöß, 2016; Hogan et al., 2020). It is essentially an ontology plus data instances that are organized based on a graph-based data structure, such that reasoning can be applied on it to generate new knowledge. Well-known organizations like Google, Facebook, Amazon, Microsoft are known to have their AI search operations powered by knowledge graphs (Hogan et al., 2020). The application of AI in healthcare can benefit from semantic data integration through the use of ontologies and knowledge graphs because it will provide a solid basis for data-driven support for clinical healthcare operations. One aspect that is of interest is clinical gait analysis, which is being increasingly used for diagnosis and treatment of neurological and cardiovascular diseases, and chronic diseases in general (Whittle, 2014; di Biase et al., 2020; Dugan et al., 2020).

Gait analysis (GA), which is also known as locomotive analysis entails collecting quantitative data on the pattern of physical movements of a human to understand the etiology of gait defects and the formulation of an appropriate treatment plan (Whittle, 2014; Buongiorno et. al, 2019). GA has been used for disease diagnosis for patients with walking impairment, and the treatment of many neurological disorders and cardiovascular diseases (Tang and Su, 2013; Camps et al., 2018; Buongiorno et al, 2019). Currently, it is possible to obtain real-time information on a patient's gait pattern while the patient is walking both within or outside the hospital environment. Critical gait parameters such as gait speed, cadence, step length, stride length and many more can be measured by using wearable body sensors that are attached to either knee, using sensor-insoles for shoes, or sensors for legs and limbs (Horak et al., 2015; Horsak et al., 2016; Saboor et al., 2020). These gait parameters have been associated with the symptoms of some specific diseases, which make them suitable as a basis for disease diagnoses, disease treatment, gait retraining, and gait rehabilitation of patients that have gait impairment. However, real-time gait analysis is still confronted with several challenges, which include the need to i) improve the precision of diseases diagnosis based on gait factors; ii) adapt real-time gait analysis for application in resource-limited settings; iii) identify specific gait parameters that are more associated with specific types of diseases; and iv) engender gait improvement during gait retraining and gait rehabilitation by using multisensory feedback mechanism (Horak et al., 2015; Zillner & Sonntag, 2012). Hence, there is the need to augment real-time gait analysis predictions with knowledge from other sources to enhance its efficiency (Horak et al., 2015; Zillner & Sonntag, 2012). It is particularly more challenging to attain efficient treatment decision-making for gait-related diseases in resource-limited settings.

This paper presents the conceptual design of a semantic data integration framework for decision support on the diagnosis and treatment of gait-related diseases (SemTreat). The SemTreat framework will harness data from multiple health data sources such as real-time gait analysis data, electronic health records (EHR), textual medical knowledge (TMK), and other open data/knowledge sources to facilitate decision making for the diagnosis and treatment of gait-related diseases in resource-limited settings. Semantic integration enables meaningful communication between heterogeneous systems and platforms. It enables diverse systems to understand one another and engage in meaningful conversation (Noy, 2004; Moser & Biffl, 2012; Shi et al., 2017; Asfand-E-Yar & Ali; 2020). In contrast to existing approaches, the proposed the SemTreat framework will explore the semantic data integration of health data, EHR, epidemiological data, textual medical knowledge, open linked data, and other open data sources to provide decision support for diagnosis and treatment of gait-related diseases in resource-limited settings. With this, the framework will i) provide decision support for medical practitioners and health workers on diagnosis and treatment of patients with gait impairments; ii) help patients to rightly associate symptoms with specific types of diseases, and identify appropriate self-management strategies that could be adopted; iii) aid knowledge retrieval on specific gait-related diseases; iv) support interoperability of clinical care operations among health institutions in RLS; and v) to promote the continuation of care when patients move from their physical location/city of residence to other locations.

Thus, the specific contributions of this paper are as follows:

1. Compared to previous studies, we present the design of a semantic data integration framework that is based on ontologies and knowledge graphs that can be used in resource-limited settings;
2. Provides a conceptual framework for harnessing both structured and unstructured data from multiple sources, which will yield quality data for decision support on gait-related diseases, and generally for healthcare in RLS.
3. Provides insight on the imperatives for the realisation of semantic data integration is RLS.

The rest of this paper is organized as follows. Section 2 presents the background and related work, while Section 3 describes the conceptual design of the SemTreat framework. Section 4 describes the approaches that will be used for the evaluation of the proposed framework. Section 5 discusses the merits and imperatives of the realisation of the proposed framework in resource-limited settings in sub-Saharan Africa. The paper is concluded in Section 6 with a brief note and overview of future work.

BACKGROUND AND RELATED WORK

This section presents background on relevant foundational aspects such as electronic health records (EHR), and gait analysis. It also presents an overview of related work on sensor-based gait analysis and semantic data integration in healthcare.

Electronic Health Records

Electronic health records (EHR) is a repository of personal medical information of individuals. EHR provides a rich source of information on a patient including pathology data, family history, medical history, primary care data, and secondary care data (Lobo et al., 2017; Zhao and Weng, 2011). EHR consists of personal health records of individuals, as such it can facilitate the continuity of care by enabling medical practitioners to access a patient's health record irrespective of their physical location. It can also provide a rich source of data for teaching and research when it is accessed in a way that preserves security and confidentiality of data. According to Botha et al. (2014), the four types of personal health records are i) offline personal records (which are available electronically but not web-based); ii) Web-based organisational health records (which can be accessed online or downloaded for research and computational purposes); iii) Functional personal health records (which are available to support emergency health services irrespective of geographical location); iv) Provider-based personal health records (which contains details of medical history, and administrative information such as appointment schedules); and v) Partial personal health records (which are anonymised patient data that are available online). All these forms of EHR can support digital health technology initiatives in one form or the other either by enabling a better understanding of a patient's condition, informed communication among health workers, support for clinical decision-making, or promoting patient health research. EHR can foster continuity of care in the areas of preventative care, disease diagnosis, treatment decision-making, and patient rehabilitation.

However, there is the need to ensure that interoperability of EHR is not only at the technical, and syntactic levels, but also at the semantic level to ensure that continuity of care is more guaranteed as people move from one location to another across different geographical regions. The existence of different health database standards and systems (data silos) from one country/region to another makes the issue of interoperability of health systems very important (Adebesin et al. 2013; Adenuga et al., 2015).

Recently, the instances of the use of EHR for research purposes have been on the increase. Examples of these include cardiovascular disease (CVD) research using linked bespoke studies and electronic health records (CALIBER) (Morley et al., 2014). The goal of CALIBER is to provide evidence to inform health care and public health policy for CVDs across different stages of translation, by using the linkages to electronic health records to provide new scientific opportunities. CALIBER entails i) linkages of multiple EHR sources such longitudinal primary care data from various sources, and procedure data from hospital episode statistics, and data from the National Office of Statistics; ii) linkages of bespoke investigator-led cohort studies to registry data to provide new means of ascertaining, validating and phenotyping disease; iii) a common data model in which routine EHR data are made research ready, and sharable, by defining and curating with meta-data variables on risk factors, CVDs and non-cardiovascular comorbidities; and iv) ensuring transparency of all data.

HealthID[1], is an initiative of Discovery health, South Africa – a health insurance provider – which enables medical doctors to gain access to patients' electronic records including their medical history, hospital visits, and test results. This enables medical practitioners to have an accurate picture of the health status of patients to ensure the accuracy of care. The Smart Open Services for European Patients (epSOS) project is designed to enable interoperability of health services across Europe for the benefits of citizens as they move across European member countries. Fonseca et al. (2015), described the OpenNCP as a framework that caters for the security, legal and interoperability requirements of the epSOS project. The OpenNCP framework facilitates the secure interconnection of health infrastructures of member countries through an open-source software platform. It offers a comprehensive set of features and services that will enable national and regional e-Health platforms to interoperate and set up cross-border services that are compliant with epSOS, by making minimal changes to the existing e-health infrastructure.

The openEHR initiative is aimed at promoting interoperability between electronic health records systems through the use of open data and standards for the development of health information systems. It uses open standards for the access, management, storage, and retrieval of EHR (Hak et al., 2020). The OpenEHR promotes semantic interoperability by encouraging the use of the same data structure based on predefined archetypes by different types of health systems. Asaria et al. (2016) discuss the challenges and opportunities that are associated with the use of linked EHR in health economics and outcomes research (HEOR) when it is used to estimate healthcare costs. The identified challenges and opportunities were in the areas of how to i) handle and organise data of large sizes and sensitivity; ii) extract clinical endpoints from datasets; and iii) to use routinely collected data for the costing of resource use. Martinez-Costa et al. (2014) describe the semantichealthnet as a semantic resource that is composed of OWL DL framework and some ontology content patterns. Semantichealthnet can support heterogeneous representations of the same clinical information and allows the semantic exploitation the clinical information by using description logics reasoning.

Many of the EHR approaches are focused on the interoperability of EHR (Adebesin et al., 2013; Adenuga et al., 2015; Fonseca et al., 2015; Martinez-Costa et al., 2014), and the use of EHR for informed decision making on patient's treatment (Asaria et al., 2016; Lobo et al., 2017; Morley et al., 2014; Zhao and Weng, 2011). So far, the use of EHR to support gait analysis-based disease diagnosis is not yet commonplace in the literature. EHR can be integrated with real-time gait data as a basis for accurate disease diagnosis, and formulation of a suitable treatment plan for a patient.

Gait Analysis

Gait analysis involves the systematic study of human locomotion through clinical examination by medical experts with the aid of instrumentation that measure specific body movement parameters. Gait analysis has been applied productively in the fields of medical care, sports, security, and human fitness. In healthcare, gait parameters have been used successfully for disease diagnosis, disease prognosis, and patient rehabilitation (Whittle, 2014; Badiye et al., 2020). Gait analysis has proved very useful in the treatment and care of patients with neurological and cardiovascular diseases that are known to cause gait abnormalities such Parkinson's disease, and other chronic diseases like diabetes and tuberculosis (Buongiorno et. al, 2019; Kumari et al., 2018; di Biase et al., 2020; Dugan et al., 2020).

Gait analysis entails the study of human gait either through visual assessment, cameras, and sensors. Gait represents the periodic movement of limbs (hands, feet). It consists of different phases which define the walking pattern within the gait cycle (Whittle, 2014; di Biase et al., 2020; Dugan et al., 2020). The gait cycle consists of the stance phase which corresponds to when the foot is on the ground and the swing phase which is when the foot is in a swing position away from the ground. The sub-phases of the stance phase are initial contact, loading response, mid-stance, terminal stance, and pre-swing; while the sub-phases of the swing phase are the initial swing, mid-swing, and terminal swing (Tao et al., 2012; Chen et al., 2016).

In recent times, the application of wearable sensor-based methods for gait analysis has been on the increase compared to non-wearable sensor-based methods such as vision-based, environment-based, Radio Frequency (RF) methods. The non-wearable methods rely on specialised facilities that are located in dedicated laboratories, which makes them more expensive to implement. However, sensor-based gait analysis is cheaper and can be used to collect data on gait parameters outside the immediate /specialised environments that does not obstruct the daily activities of the patient (Saboor et al., 2020).

RELATED WORK

The review of related work in this section is focussed on sensor-based gait analysis and semantic data integration in healthcare through knowledge graphs.

Sensor-Based Gait Analysis

So far, many instances of sensor-based of gait analysis have been reported in the literature, particularly to aid the treatment of diseases that are associated with gait impairment such as neurological disorders and cardiovascular diseases (Horak et al., 2015; Tang and Su, 2013; Saboor et al., 2020).

Instances of gait data have been reported in the literature. Chereshnev & Kertész-Farkas (2017) presents human gait data on activities such as walking, running, sitting down, walking the stairs collection that was collected from six wearable inertial sensors attached to the body of participants. This is to serve the purpose of activity recognition and foster an understanding of how the different parts of the body move relative to each other. The data is useful for healthcare-related studies such as recognition for gait impairment or gait abnormalities, and gait rehabilitation. It can also be used for virtual reality, simulation, robotics, and gaming software applications. However, the experiment and data collection was not carried out in a resource-limited setting. GaitRec (Horsak et al., 2020) is an annotated large-scale dataset of gait data that was collected through bi-lateral ground reaction force (GRF) walking trials of over 200 patients. The dataset is prepared to be able to support machine learning operations on gait analysis and help researchers to classify gait patterns of patients. The data was collected in a specialised lab with equipment to measure ground reaction forces associated with gait, and not in RLS.

Horsak et al. (2016), reports on the investigation of the effect of sonification on gait parameters. To do this, an evaluation of a pair of instrumented insoles for real-time sonification of gait (SONIGait) was done to assess its immediate effects on spatio-temporal gait parameters. The study involved six male and six female participants that were conveniently selected. The result showed that the sonification of gait led to the generation of auditory feedback to participants that had an impact on their walking cadence. Participants were found to exhibit decreased cadence and differences in gait velocity when walking with sonification. The approach was adjudged to have the potential to support gait rehabilitation and gait retraining for patients with gait impairment. The gait experimentation was done by a force distribution measurement system (FDM) that is situated in a lab environment, which is not suitable for RSL. Camps et al. (2018) used a deep learning approach to detect freezing of gait (FOG) episodes in patients with Parkinson's disease (PD). Data was collected from 21 PD patients who are prone to FOG episodes by placing an inertial measurement unit on their waists. A feed-forward 1D-ConvNet, that was used for analysis achieved about 90% for the geometric mean between sensitivity and specificity in terms of performance, which was an improvement over the state-of-the-art methods. Also, Buongiorno et al. (2019) performed machine learning-based classification and rating of Parkinson's Disease (PD) patients using artificial neural network (ANN) and support vector machine (SVM). The experiment involved the use of a simple and low-cost clinical tool that can extract postural and kinematic features with the Microsoft Kinect v2 sensor to classify and rate PD. Sixteen participants that were classified as PD patients rated, and fourteen healthy paired subjects making a total of thirty subjects participated in the study. The result of the gait analysis revealed that the ANN classifier performed best with 89.4% accuracy in classification, and 95.0% accuracy in rating the severity of PD. In the aspect of finger and foot-tapping analysis, the SVM was found to perform better in the classification of healthy subjects compared to PD patients. The studies did not require semantic data integration or focused on providing decision-support in a resource-limited setting. It was mainly focused on experimentation and analysis of PD.

In Kumari et al. (2018), the Wearable Internet of Things (WIoT) architecture was used to develop a prototype of a wearable human activity device for monitoring and tracking patients with cerebral palsy. The device was used to collect data on both Hemiplegic and Diplegic gait activities. The data was visualized and represented using two different methods (1D,2D) for the 9-axis motion data, and was presented to a deep convolutional neural network (DCNN). It was found that both sets of data are suitable to train a DCNN so that the subtle differences that exist between normal and abnormal gaits can be detected through the convolution of images that takes place in DCNN. The authors opine that considering the cost-effectiveness of the approach, the design could be suitable for use in low- and medium-income countries (LMICs). The objective of the study does not include the need for semantic data integration as a precursor for gait analysis or decision support for treatment of gait-related diseases.

Systematic literature reviews on wearable sensor-based gait analysis have been reported in (Chen et al., 2016; Brognara et al., 2019; Saboor et al., 2020). The most recent systematic review by Saboor et al. (2020) focused on sensor-based gait analysis and machine learning with 33 primary studies eventually selected. However, most of the solutions that were reported in the systematic review were not designed for RLS, hence the ability of the proposed solutions to function in RLS cannot be verified. Another issue is that semantic integration of data is required for the application of AI in RLS which most of the existing approaches to sensor-based gait analysis did not consider. Hence, the need to augment gait prediction with other sources of health data such as EHR and open linked data is paramount, which is what distinguishes our proposed framework for previous research efforts on sensor-based gait analysis.

Knowledge Graph for Semantic Data Integration in Healthcare

Shi et al. (2017), proposed a novel model was used to organize and integrate disparate textual medical knowledge (TMK) and health data from various sources into conceptual graphs. A framework was then used to automatically extract knowledge accurately into knowledge graphs which can support semantic querying and reasoning. Efficient chain referencing was attained by using a contextual pruning algorithm that produced a better inference result with high precision (92%) and recall (96%). Prototypes and services were presented to demonstrate the practicality and effectiveness of the concept. Vidal et al. (2019), presents a knowledge-driven framework that receives biomedical big data sources and integrates them into a knowledge graph. The framework enables knowledge exploration and discovery by using semantic data integration methods to identify entities that have an equivalent meaning in the real-world. The framework receives big data input from different sources such as clinical notes, structured data, scientific publications, and images and generates a knowledge graph from which new knowledge in form of patterns and relationship between entities can be inferred. The framework architecture consists of four components which are knowledge extraction, knowledge graph creation, knowledge management and discovery, and data access control and privacy. This enables the knowledge graph to facilitate the semantic description, integration, and curation of big biomedical data.

Nentidis et al. (2020), describes how a framework that automatically retrieves and integrates disease-specific knowledge was used to realise a current and up-to-date semantic graph, called the iASiS Open Data Graph. The open-source semantic graph was applied to realise three disease-specific knowledge graphs which are for Lung Cancer, Dementia, and Duchenne Muscular Dystrophy. Example queries were used to assess the potential and limitations of the knowledge graphs. Messina et al. (2017), described BioGrakn as a graph-based semantic database that combines the power of knowledge graphs and machine learning to solve problems in the biomedical science domain. It was designed to address the problem of lack of structural organization and interoperability of publicly available biological resources to ensure the semantic integrity of data. It is built on top of GRAKAN.AI which is an integrated database that enables researchers to handle complex data. GRAKAN.AI consists of two parts which are Grakn and Graql. Grakn can be shared and replicated over a network of distributed machines and has an underlying underlining data structure of a labelled and direct hypergraph, while Gradl is a graph query language that uses machine reasoning to retrieve the knowledge that is explicitly stored and implicitly derived from Grakn. Also, Zhang et al. (2020) proposed the Health Knowledge Graph Builder (HKGB) as an end-to-end platform to construct disease-specific and extensible cross-lingual health knowledge graphs from multiple sources. The HKGB offers a technical means to integrate heterogeneous data resources and enhance knowledge-based services. HKGB was used to create a knowledge graph for the cardiovascular domain by working with a local hospital, which was also extended to create a knowledge graph for knee osteoarthritis. The HKGB was designed to leverage the input of expert clinicians in the process of developing the health knowledge graph.

From the review of literature on knowledge graphs for semantic data integration in healthcare, we did not find any study that is focused on the creation disease-specific knowledge graphs with a focus of capturing knowledge on gait analysis to influence the treatment and diagnosis of gait-related diseases. Besides, the previous studies were not addressed to the context of RLS as conceived in our study. This makes our proposed framework unique in terms of focus and perspective compared to other approaches for semantic data integration in healthcare that are based knowledge graph.

METHODOLOGY

This section presents the conceptual design of the framework for the semantic integration of health data sources for diagnosis and treatment of gait-related diseases (SemTreat). We now describe the requirements of the proposed framework, the layers of its architecture, and an overview of the knowledge graph construction process. The section was concluded with a discussion of the potential use cases of the SemTreat framework.

SemTreat Requirements Elicitation

The requirements were gathered to understand both the technical as well as the user requirements for the semantic integration of linked EHR, epidemiological data, open linked data, and real-time gait data. This was done with the help of a requirements analyst, medical experts, and epidemiologists to elicit knowledge from the domain experts and relevant stakeholders. During the requirements elicitation process, the following stakeholders of the SemTreat framework were identified: medical practitioners, patients, and governmental organizations.

The requirements of the SemTreat framework are structured into the following categories (Daramola & Moser, 2019):

- practicability of the SemTreat framework
  - centralized overview of distributed health data of a single patient: should be usable both by the patient as well as by medical practitioners that have been granted such authorised access
- functionality in resource-limited settings
  - limited internet/ mobile data connectivity regarding both signal strength as well as bandwidth;
  - electrical power availability
  - accessibility of technology to patients in terms of cost of devices and internet data
- usability of the SemTreat framework's applications (mobile)
  - smartphone vs. regular mobile phone version
  - usage should also be possible (in a limited way) with low literacy as well as low technical affinity (e.g. elderly persons)
- privacy and data protection
  - personal health data is very sensitive information and needs to be well protected
  - each patient should be able to define for which other parties he/she wants to share the personal health data
  - aggregated but anonymized health data should be available for usage by governmental organizations, e.g. for statistical analysis, data analytics, and strategic planning

Overview of the SemTreat Architecture

The SemTreat architecture is conceptualised to facilitate a framework that enables the integration of health data from various sources and support the process of decision-making in the diagnosis and treatment of gait-related diseases in resource-limited settings.

The architecture consists of four layers (see Figure 1), which are described as follows (Daramola & Moser, 2019):

User services Layer: this layer presents a user with opportunities to access the various services that the SemTreat architecture affords. This includes search and query services, recommendations, health education, and diagnosis.

Business Logic Layer: This layer enables the SemTreat architecture to construct an appropriate response to a user's query promptly. The various algorithms and computational modules that perform machine-learning-based prediction from data, expert systems diagnosis, recommendations on health and wellness requests from users, and semantic analysis are contained in this layer. The components of this layer function based on raw data and semantic web data that are retrieved by using SPARQL endpoints in form of RDF triples from specific knowledge graphs (KG) in the lower level of the SemTreat architecture.

Knowledge Graph Resources Layer: this layer is composed of different knowledge graphs that have been pre-constructed through semantic data integration of various data and knowledge sources for to create disease-specific knowledge graphs such as tuberculosis knowledge graph (TB_KG), HIV

Figure 1. Conceptual View of the SemTreat Architecture (Daramola and Moser, 2019)

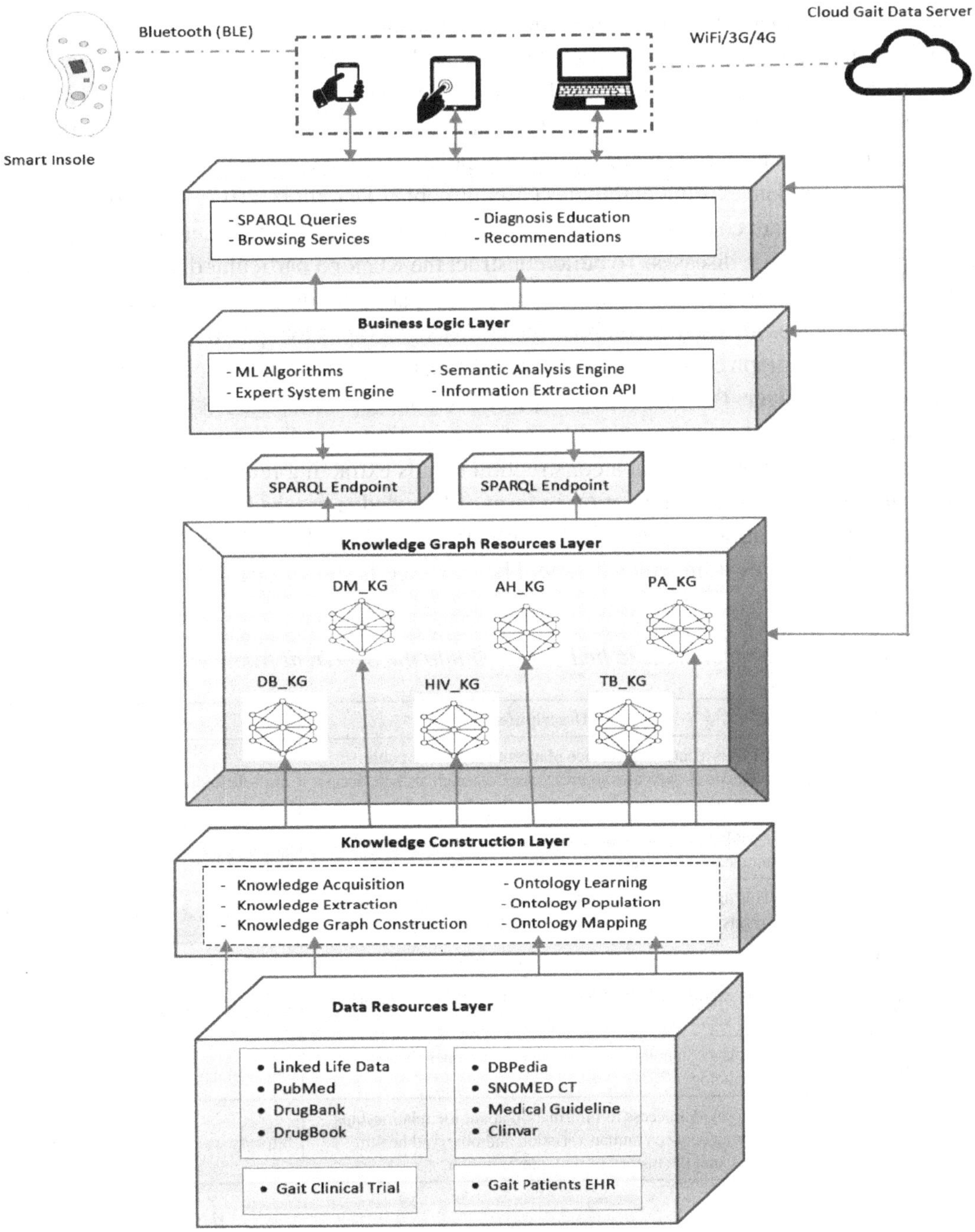

AIDS knowledge graph (HIV_KG), Diabetes knowledge graph (DB_KG), Dementia knowledge graph (DM_KG), Alzheimer's Disease knowledge graph (AH_KG), Parkinson's Disease knowledge graph (PA_KG). This way, each knowledge graph will provide a one-stop access point to all data sources that can support efficient diagnosis and treatment of a specific gait-related disease. For example, the Tuberculosis Knowledge graph (TB_KG) will be a product of semantic integration of various data sources that can aid intelligent search algorithms, machine learning algorithms, and expert system applications that require such available knowledge on tuberculosis to construct the right response to a user query. This also applies to other disease-specific knowledge graphs.

Knowledge Graph Construction Layer: this layer subsumes the various offline activities that will facilitate the construction of relevant knowledge graphs (KG) from multiple health data sources. Key operations that are deployed at this level include ontology learning, ontology population, and information extraction from multiple health data sources. The ontology learning operation will involve the creation of ontologies from textual sources, while ontology population will focus on creating data instances from textual sources to populate existing ontologies (Ajetunmobi & Daramola, 2017; Daramola et al., 2013). The knowledge graphs are constructed by aggregating data from diverse relevant open sources to build a rich data pool for specific diseases. To build/construct the KG for a particular disease, the clinical gait data, and electronic health records of gait patients of that particular disease, epidemiological data, and open linked data sources are used to compose the knowledge graphs for specific diseases. A bottom-up method for knowledge graph construction is applied to create the knowledge graph for a specific disease.

Data Resources Layer: this is a suite of open health data resources, and sources of textual medical knowledge (TMK) that provide a good basis for generating a credible knowledgebase for specific types of diseases. The knowledge graph construction entails extracting relevant knowledge from these sources, ensuring their semantic integration in form of knowledge graphs in a way that can be used by web services and computational modules at run-time for decision making. A description of some of the medical knowledge sources from which data will be extracted is shown in Table 1.

Table 1. Medical Knowledge Sources to be integrated into the SemTreat framework.

S/n	Sources	Description	Web Link
1	Linked Life Data (LLD)	LLD as a data-as-a-service platform enables 25 public biomedical databases to be accessed through a single access point	http://linkedlifedata.com/
2	PubMed	PubMed contains over 29 million open access articles from biomedical literature.	https://www.ncbi.nlm.nih.gov/pubmed/
3	DrugBank	This database contains information on drug data and drug targets. It can be accessed using an API.	https://www.drugbank.ca/
4	DrugBook	This is an e-book that offers rich textual knowledge on drugs	
5	DBPedia	This exposes data in Wikipedia in the form of a database for open access	https://wiki.dbpedia.org/
6	SNOMED CT	This is a comprehensive vocabulary of clinical healthcare terminology.	https://www.snomed.org/
7	Clinvar	this provides access to information about the relationships asserted between human variation and observed health status, and the history of that interpretation.	https://www.ncbi.nlm.nih.gov/clinvar/

The Bottom-Up Knowledge Graph Construction Process

A crucial initial investment that must be made for the realization of the proposed framework is to create knowledge graphs for specific diseases such as Tuberculosis (TB_KG), HIV AIDS (HIV_KG), Diabetes (DB_KG), Dementia (DM_KG), Parkinson's Disease (PA_KG). The knowledge graphs will create a pool of knowledge resources from multiple health data sources that can be leveraged for real-time decision support by software applications that are being used by healthcare professionals and other users. The bottom-up approach to knowledge construction entails extracting knowledge instances from relevant multiple data/knowledge resources, fusing the extracted knowledge and the creation of ontological knowledgebase that is tuned to create a knowledge graph that meets predefined requirements (Zhao et al. 2018). It consists of 5 main phases, which are knowledge acquisition, knowledge extraction, knowledge fusion, knowledge graph storage, and knowledge retrieval and visualization (see Figure 2).

Figure 2. Overview of the Bottom-up Knowledge Graph Construction Process

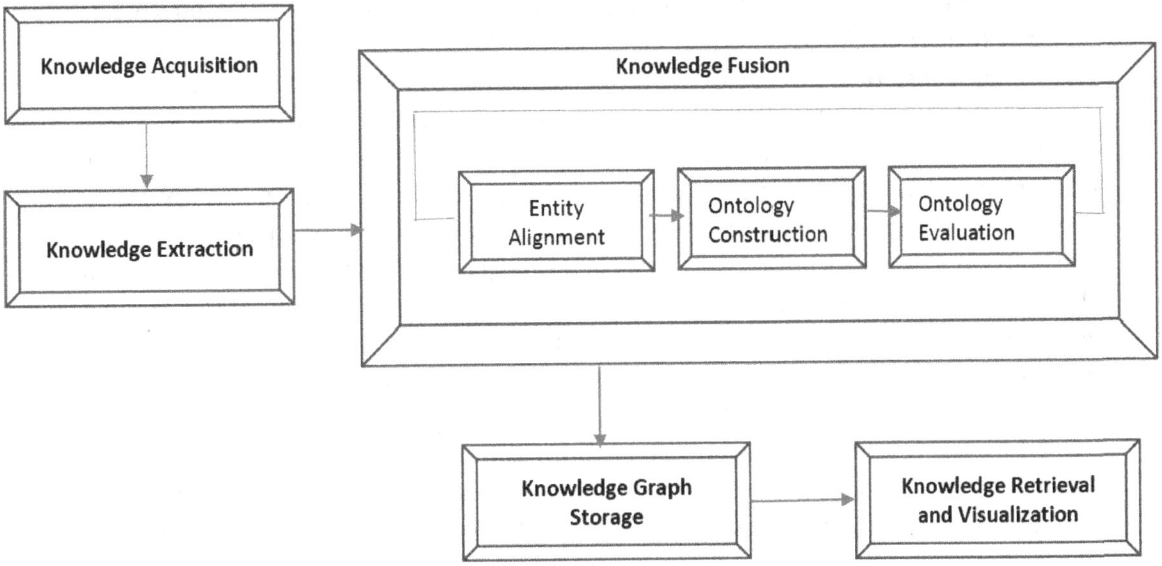

The stages of knowledge graph construction are described as follows:

1. **Knowledge acquisition**: this involves identifying relevant textual medical knowledge resources such as PubMed, DrugBank, DrugBook, SNOMED CT (see Table 1), and organisational health records on gait cases in the form of EHR for specific diseases from which knowledge instances can be extracted. In resource-limited settings, knowledge acquisition will require a more elaborate process to ensure that all data that are relevant for knowledge generation purposes and identified and transformed from their original form to electronic form. These may entail the following:
   a.   Identify all relevant manual data sources;

b.   Convert data from the manual form to electronic form using low-cost technology such as optical character recognition (OCR) scanners to convert paper-based records into an electronic form that can be stored on the computer system;

c.   Captured electronic data have to be inspected and revised by a medical expert to ensure that the data are complete, meaningful, and useful;

d.   The acquired electronic data should be stored as text files, Excel files or in a relational database.

e.   Use of relevant APIs to pull data from identified open textual medical knowledge sources such as SNOMED CT, PubMed, DrugBank, DrugBook

f.   Conversion of EHR, and gait cases data, from their native format to semantic web formats such as OWL, RDF/OWL, RDF/XML format to provide a basis for their semantic readability and interpretation. Several open-source tools can be used to achieve this. These include FRED (Gangemi et al., 2017) - converts natural text to linked data in RDF/OWL format; Protégé DataMaster (Nyulas et al., 2007), Ontobase (Yabloko, 2011) (converts a database to RDF/OWL ontology); Sheet2RDF (http://art.uniroma2.it/sheet2rdf/), Spread2RDF(https://github.com/marcelotto/spread2rdf) -converts spreadsheet to RDF format. Others include: R2RML, D2R, Virtuoso, Morph, r2rml4net, db2triples, ultra-wrap, Quest, Virtuoso, ultra-wrap, Oracle SW (Zhang et al., 2020)

2.   **Knowledge extraction**: this entails extracting knowledge from different types of data (structured, unstructured, semi-structured) that have been acquired in different formats such as XML, JSON, HTML and later transformed to RDF format. The key activities involved are entity extraction, relationship extraction and attribute extraction. Named-entity recognition is a key part of entity extraction where specific noun entities such as names of persons, things, places, events, and other real-world entities are identified with the right meaning associated to them. The semantic relationships that exist between entities are deduced during relationship extraction, while the attributes of entities are derived during attribute extraction. The identification of entities, entity attributes and entity relationships are important to create an accurate conceptual hierarchy within a knowledge graph. The operations of knowledge extraction will be deeply rooted in natural language processing (NLP), and Machine learning algorithms such as Conditional Random fields, Support Vector Machines (SVM), hidden Markov Models (HMM) will be explored for entity extraction, while the use of open knowledge sources such as DBPedia, Wikipedia are essential for relationship extraction, and attributes extraction.

3.   **Knowledge Fusion**: this entails entity alignment that involves entity resolution and entity matching. This is then followed by the construction and evaluation of an ontology. These three procedures are undertaken iteratively until a knowledge graph that matches the set of predefined requirements is attained. The structure of general ontology such as FOAF will be used to construct the ontology.

4.   **Knowledge Graph Storage**: this will entail storing the ontology in the form of a NoSQL database or a graph database. Ne04j which is an open-source knowledge graph will be used to store the knowledge graphs to be created. A graph database allows nodes, edges, and properties of graphs to be stored which is suitable for the structure of a knowledge graph. Graph databases have graph query languages and support some graph mining algorithms.

5.   **Knowledge Retrieval and Visualization**: this entails the implementation of a user-friendly interface where results of the SPARQL query will be displayed in a way that is sensible and insightful to the user. Semantic retrieval will be executed to ensure that meaningful answers to user queries are

provided. Visualization of the knowledge graph results will be done by using tools such as *IsaViz, xyjigsaw, OpenLink Data Explorer.*

Possible Use Cases of the SemTreat Framework

In this section, we present two use cases of the SemTreat framework as relevant to a patient, and a doctor by using exemplary narratives.

Case 1. Mr. X is a 70 years old male with gait impairment due to Tuberculosis (TB) ailment. X wants to receive a recommendation on suitable recreational activities as a form of self-management that can aid his wellness. As a result of wearing a smart insole for 3 months, gait data such as his cadence, gait speed, step length, and stride length was constantly monitored and recorded over the 3 months. Since X is domiciled in a resource-limited setting, gait data were temporarily stored in his mobile device from time to time before being subsequently transferred to the cloud storage via WiFi or mobile (3G/4G) connectivity. When X seeks recommendation to be advised on the type of recreational activities that could help to improve his fitness, the recommendation for Mr X, will be based on the level of severity of TB ailment as inferred from the stored gait patterns that are inherent in his gait data, and the diverse forms of knowledge about TB that are stored in TB KG. This will include using the documentation of TB treatment cases, clinical trials, epidemiological data, and TB knowledge from diverse sources as contained in the TB knowledge graph, and the EHR of Mr. X to construct appropriate recommendation results for him.

Case 2. Dr. Y is an expert in the treatment of Type II Diabetes and needs to respond to a request for advice from Patient B, female, who is a Type II Diabetes Patient that is well-known to Dr. Y but is currently in a remote location. The severity of Patient B's ailment has affected her gait, and because of this, she has been wearing the smart insole device for real-time gait analysis for the past 2 months. Dr. Y wants to use the expert diagnosis service of the SemTreat framework as a decision support tool to respond to Patient B's query. The request from Patient B is that she has witnessed some symptoms lately that appear strange and needs to know what is going on. The request of Patient B, just as any other request of the same nature is uniquely identified by the personal medical record number/medical insurance number of Patient B. Dr. Y needs to access the electronic health record of Patient B to know her medical history. An encrypted message from Dr. Y asking Patient B to give consent/permission to Dr. Y to access her medical records is sent to Patient B. Patient B must give an approval/ consent before access is granted to Dr. Y. Once the permission to access personal EHR is granted by Patient B, her pre-stored gait data also becomes available for the SemTreat algorithms to use to construct medical advice on Patient B's case for the consideration of Dr. Y. By using the combination of relevant extracted knowledge from the Diabetes KG, Gait Data, and EHR of Patient B, Dr. Y will receive machine learning-based decision support on how to respond to the request from Patient B.

EVALUATION CONCEPT

The evaluation concept for the SemTreat framework will be guided by two perspectives. The first perspective of the evaluation will focus on performance and usability. For this, the emphasis will be on the atomic/individual user-based services that the SemTreat framework affords to assess their performance and usability. The services, such as expert diagnosis, health recommender system, and information search shall be experimentally evaluated by using standard performance metrics such as FI, recall, precision, and accuracy by using human experts as the gold standard. Also, the usability of the user-based services shall be assessed both within and outside the clinic environment to determine users' perceptions of the services. The usability evaluation shall be done mainly through qualitative evaluation by user experiment feedbacks, questionnaire surveys, interviews, and case studies. The second perspective of the evaluation is to assess the practicability and effectiveness of the framework in terms of its support for treatment decision-making for selected gait-related diseases from the viewpoints of patients/users, and medical practitioners. The emphasis of this particular evaluation is to determine whether the framework can indeed attain its envisioned goals for resource-limited settings. It is also to determine whether it can be integrated effectively into the operational workflow of medical practitioners for use, and also the daily lifestyle of an average user/patient. To do this, the Goal Question Metric (GQM) paradigm (Basili et al., 1994) will be used to conduct a holistic evaluation of the framework to assess the extent to which it can attain the goals and objectives that are associated with providing support for treatment decision making in resource-limited settings.

MERITS AND IMPERATIVES OF THE PROPOSED FRAMEWORK

In this section, we present the advantages of the proposed SemTreat framework for resource-limited settings, and imperatives for its realisation.

Merits of the SemTreat Framework

Currently, there is a dearth of sufficient medical personnel for healthcare in resource-limited settings in most sub-Saharan African countries (SSA). The doctor-patient ratio in most of the African countries is quite low. So far, the scope of application of AI for healthcare in SSA is small and scarce. A technical solution that is derived from the proposed SemTreat framework could help to enhance healthcare delivery in rural settings across SSA. The creation of knowledge graphs that embody semantic data integration in RLS will amongst others:

1. enable disparate health data silos to be combined to support AI operations to aid patients treatment and management in healthcare in a context preserving way. This means that heterogenous data from different multiple sources can be utilised in a useful way without altering their original structure, content, format, or meaning;
2. ensure that structured and unstructured data are harnessed for clinical decision-support activities in RLS;
3. provide a platform for the evolution of knowledge as data continue to grow dynamically. Relevant algorithms of the knowledge graph construction process can be re-executed from time to time to leverage new data that are available in the diverse sources. This will ensure that new knowledge can be derived continuously in a dynamic way;
4. ensure that contextual medical knowledge in RLS become available in a standard format that can be harnessed to greater uses locally and globally. This is because knowledge graphs are usually built based on specified World Wide Web Consortium (3WC) standards which make them interoperable.

Imperatives for Realisation of SemTreat Framework

Most parts of SSA can be described as resource-limited settings because of several forms of resource limitations that exist. These limitations include lack of ICT infrastructure, lack of quality data, lack of infrastructure for data integration and technical integration of health information systems. These challenges must be surmounted to achieve the goal of utilising AI technologies for improved healthcare in RLS. Therefore, the imperatives for the realisation of the proposed framework in resource-limited settings in SSA include the following:

1. **A Framework for Data Curation**: A systematic approach for the curation of health data does not yet exist in most parts of SSA. Although a vast amount of health data are generated from medical cases, most of the data are not in the form that is usable for computational purposes. Data exist mostly in manual form, and where they are electronic, they are incomplete and inconsistent in terms of content and representation. Data curation entails the identification of relevant data sources, the transformation of the data, integration of data with other sources, and eliminate redundancies. The goal of health data curation is to engender data quality that will enable the application of artificial intelligence (AI) in healthcare (Stonebraker et al., 2013; Satti et al., 2020). Thus a systematic procedure for health data curation in resource-limited settings in SSA is a necessity.

2. **Open Standards for Electronic Health Records**: As more health institutions identify the need for automation of healthcare operations, open standards for electronic health records must be adopted. This will aid interoperability among health institutions.

3. **Adoption of e-Health Standards**: So far, not many African-based institutions have subscribed to the adoption of e-health standards in specific salient areas such as messaging standards, content and content standards, identifier standards, clinical terminology standards, electronic health records standards, and access and security control standards. According to Adebesin et al. (2013), the absence of wide adoption of standards in many African institutions is due to several factors which include a) limited participation in the process of developing the standards; b) lack of understanding of the importance of the use of standards at the national level; c) lack of a guideline for implementation of standards; d) lack of human resource capacity to develop standards; and e) lack of foundational infrastructure for the adoption and utilisation of standards.

4. **Governance Framework for AI Adoption in Healthcare**: So far, there is a lack of policy and ethical framework that guides the use of AI in healthcare in most SSA countries. Salient issues that relate to accountability for AI results, ethical usage, trust, security and privacy of information, and the social impact of AI adoption for healthcare delivery are not yet clearly defined in most SSA countries. This has to be addressed to promote more advanced applications of AI for healthcare in SSA countries.

CONCLUSION AND FUTURE WORK

In this paper, we have presented the description of a conceptual framework (SemTreat) that can enable the semantic integration of multiple health data sources for treatment decision-making for gait-related diseases in resource-limited settings. The framework affords a suite of user-based services that can aid the decision-making process of medical practitioners, and help users/patients in the area of self-management for healthy living and wellness. The SemTreat framework is presented as capable of leveraging aggregated semantic knowledge from diverse sources to deliver intelligent services such as search and browsing, health recommendations, and expert disease diagnosis while providing support for low cost and affordable technologies for real-time gait analysis.

However, the eventual realisation of the SemTreat framework depends on giving attention to some additional non-functional requirements that will ensure the overall success of the framework. This includes the following:

- **Security:** dealing with health information requires that all data must be treated with security by ensuring that that personal data of patients are protected and the data privacy is not compromised.
- **Accessibility**: the framework must provide easy ways for people to assess its resources particularly for people in resource-limited settings where the existence of advanced ICT infrastructure is a rarity.
- **Cost**: there must be an emphasis on the use of low-cost technologies that are affordable for poor people. This includes the use of low-cost sensor technologies and ensuring that the design and product development is suitable for resource-limited settings.
- **Other dependability attributes**: the framework must also possess other dependability attributes apart from security such as reliability, availability, and maintainability to be a viable option for deployment in resource-limited settings.

We also discussed the merits, and the imperatives for the realisation of the framework on a wide scale in resource-limited settings in sub-Saharan African countries with a recommendation to pay specific attention to the adoption of open standards for electronic health records, adoption of general standards for electronic healthcare, and the need for the establishment of a governance framework for the adoption of AI for healthcare.

For future work, we have an immediate objective to implement a prototype of the proposed system in resource-limited settings in South Africa, and then scale the same to other contexts in SSA. We will also evaluate the digital technology framework in terms of usability and effectiveness in resource-limited settings.

ACKNOWLEDGMENT

This work was supported by the Centre for International Cooperation & Mobility (ICM) of the Austrian Agency for International Cooperation in Education and Research (OeAD-GmbH) under Grant No. ZA 10/2019. It is also supported by the National Research Foundation of South Africa under Grant No. STGR 180414320796.

REFERENCES

Adebesin, F., Foster, R., Kotzé, P., & Van Greunen, D. (2013). A Review of Interoperability Standards in E-health and Imperatives for their Adoption in Africa. *South African Computer Journal, 50.*

Adenuga, O. A., Kekwaletswe, R. M., & Coleman, A. (2015). eHealth integration and interoperability issues: Towards a solution through enterprise architecture. *Health Information Science and Systems*, *3*(1), 1. doi:10.118613755-015-0009-7 PMID:26167279

Aldred, L., van der Aalst, W., Dumas, M., & ter Hofstede, A. (2006). Understanding the challenges in getting together: The semantics of decoupling in middleware. *BPM Center Report BPM-06-19, BPM-center. org.*

Asaria, M., Grasic, K., & Walker, S. (2016). Using linked electronic health records to estimate healthcare costs: Key challenges and opportunities. *PharmacoEconomics*, *34*(2), 155–160. doi:10.100740273-015-0358-8 PMID:26645571

Asfand-E-Yar, M., & Ali, R. (2020). Semantic Integration of Heterogeneous Databases of Same Domain Using Ontology. *IEEE Access : Practical Innovations, Open Solutions*, *8*, 77903–77919.

Badiye, A., Kathane, P., & Krishan, K. (2020). Forensic Gait Analysis. In StatPearls. StatPearls Publishing.

Balakrishna, S., Thirumaran, M., & Solanki, V. K. (2020). IoT sensor data integration in healthcare using semantics and machine learning approaches. In *A Handbook of Internet of Things in Biomedical and Cyber-Physical System* (pp. 275–300). Springer.

Basili, V. R., & HD, C. G. R. (1994). The goal question metric approach. In *Encyclopedia of Software Engineering*. Wiley.

Botha, M., Botha, A., & Herselman, M. (2014, December). The Benefits and Challenges of e-Health Applications: A Content Analysis of the South African context. In *Proceedings of The International Conference on Computer Science, Computer Engineering, and Social Media* (pp. 12-14). Academic Press.

Brognara, L., Palumbo, P., Grimm, B., & Palmerini, L. (2019). Assessing gait in Parkinson's disease using wearable motion sensors: A systematic review. *Diseases (Basel, Switzerland)*, *7*(1), 18. doi:10.3390/diseases7010018 PMID:30764502

Buongiorno, D., Bortone, I., Cascarano, G. D., Trotta, G. F., Brunetti, A., & Bevilacqua, V. (2019). A low-cost vision system based on the analysis of motor features for recognition and severity rating of Parkinson's Disease. *BMC Medical Informatics and Decision Making*, *19*(9), 243. doi:10.118612911-019-0987-5 PMID:31830986

Camps, J., Sama, A., Martin, M., Rodriguez-Martin, D., Perez-Lopez, C., Arostegui, J. M. M., ... Prats, A. (2018). Deep learning for freezing of gait detection in Parkinson's disease patients in their homes using a waist-worn inertial measurement unit. *Knowledge-Based Systems*, *139*, 119–131. doi:10.1016/j.knosys.2017.10.017

Cheatham, M., & Pesquita, C. (2017). Semantic data integration. In *Handbook of big data technologies* (pp. 263–305). Springer.

Chen, S., Lach, J., Lo, B., & Yang, G. Z. (2016). Toward pervasive gait analysis with wearable sensors: A systematic review. *IEEE Journal of Biomedical and Health Informatics*, *20*(6), 1521–1537. doi:10.1109/JBHI.2016.2608720 PMID:28113185

Daramola, O., & Moser, T. (2019). Semantic integration of multiple health data for treatment decision-making in low-resource settings. In *Multi-Conference on Computer Science and Information Systems, MCCSIS 2019 - Proceedings of the International Conference on e-Health 2019* (pp. 43–50). IADIS Press. 10.33965/eh2019_201910L006

Dhayne, H., Kilany, R., Haque, R., & Taher, Y. (2018, December). SeDIE: A semantic-driven engine for integration of healthcare data. In *2018 IEEE International Conference on Bioinformatics and Biomedicine (BIBM)* (pp. 617-622). IEEE. 10.1109/BIBM.2018.8621243

Doan, A., & Halevy, A. Y. (2005). Semantic integration research in the database community: A brief survey. *AI Magazine, 26*(1), 83–83.

Effenberg, A., Fehse, U., & Weber, A. (2011). Movement Sonification: Audiovisual benefits on motor learning. In BIO web of conferences (Vol. 1, p. 00022). EDP Sciences.

Fonseca, M., Karkaletsis, K., Cruz, I. A., Berler, A., & Oliveira, I. C. (2015, May). OpenNCP: a novel framework to foster cross-border e-Health services. In MIE (Vol. 210, pp. 617-621). Academic Press.

Fritz, F., Tilahun, B., & Dugas, M. (2015). Success criteria for electronic medical record implementations in low-resource settings: A systematic review. *Journal of the American Medical Informatics Association: JAMIA, 22*(2), 479–488. doi:10.1093/jamia/ocu038 PMID:25769683

Hak, F., Oliveira, D., Abreu, N., Leuschner, P., Abelha, A., & Santos, M. (2020). An OpenEHR Adoption in a Portuguese Healthcare Facility. *Procedia Computer Science, 170*, 1047–1052. doi:10.1016/j.procs.2020.03.075

Hohpe, G. (2006). 06291 workshop report: Conversation patterns. In *Dagstuhl Seminar Proceedings*. Schloss Dagstuhl-Leibniz-Zentrum für Informatik.

Horak, F., King, L., & Mancini, M. (2015). Role of body-worn movement monitor technology for balance and gait rehabilitation. *Physical Therapy, 95*(3), 461–470. doi:10.2522/ptj.20140253 PMID:25504484

Horsak, B., Dlapka, R., Iber, M., Gorgas, A. M., Kiselka, A., Gradl, C., Siragy, T., & Doppler, J. (2016). SONIGait: A wireless instrumented insole device for real-time sonification of gait. *Journal on Multimodal User Interfaces, 10*(3), 195–206. doi:10.100712193-016-0216-9

Kumari, P., Cooney, N. J., Kim, T. S., & Minhas, A. S. (2018, December). Gait analysis in Spastic Hemiplegia and Diplegia cerebral palsy using a wearable activity tracking device-a data quality analysis for deep convolutional neural networks. In *2018 5th Asia-Pacific World Congress on Computer Science and Engineering (APWC on CSE)* (pp. 1-4). IEEE. 10.1109/APWConCSE46201.2018.8950057

Lobo, J. M., Denton, B. T., Wilson, J. R., Shah, N. D., & Smith, S. A. (2017). Using claims data linked with electronic health records to monitor and improve adherence to medication. *IISE Transactions on Healthcare Systems Engineering, 7*(4), 194–214. doi:10.1080/24725579.2017.1346728

Martinez-Costa, C., Legaz-García, M. C., Schulz, S., & Fernández-Breis, J. T. (2014, June). Ontology-based infrastructure for a meaningful EHR representation and use. In *IEEE-EMBS International Conference on Biomedical and Health Informatics (BHI)* (pp. 535-538). IEEE. 10.1109/BHI.2014.6864420

Min, L., Tian, Q., Lu, X., & Duan, H. (2018). Modeling EHR with the openEHR approach: An exploratory study in China. *BMC Medical Informatics and Decision Making*, *18*(1), 75. doi:10.118612911-018-0650-6 PMID:30157838

Morley, K. I., Wallace, J., Denaxas, S. C., Hunter, R. J., Patel, R. S., Perel, P., Shah, A. D., Timmis, A. D., Schilling, R. J., & Hemingway, H. (2014). Defining disease phenotypes using national linked electronic health records: A case study of atrial fibrillation. *PLoS One*, *9*(11), e110900. doi:10.1371/journal.pone.0110900 PMID:25369203

Moser, T., & Biffl, S. (2011). Semantic integration of software and systems engineering environments. *IEEE Transactions on Systems, Man and Cybernetics. Part C, Applications and Reviews*, *42*(1), 38–50. doi:10.1109/TSMCC.2011.2136377

Noehren, B., Scholz, J., & Davis, I. (2011). The effect of real-time gait retraining on hip kinematics, pain and function in subjects with patellofemoral pain syndrome. *British Journal of Sports Medicine*, *45*(9), 691–696. doi:10.1136/bjsm.2009.069112 PMID:20584755

Noy, N. F. (2004). Semantic integration: A survey of ontology-based approaches. *SIGMOD Record*, *33*(4), 65–70. doi:10.1145/1041410.1041421

Redd, C. B., & Bamberg, S. J. M. (2012). A wireless sensory feedback device for real-time gait feedback and training. *IEEE/ASME Transactions on Mechatronics*, *17*(3), 425–433. doi:10.1109/TMECH.2012.2189014

Rodger, M. W., Young, W. R., & Craig, C. M. (2013). Synthesis of walking sounds for alleviating gait disturbances in Parkinson's disease. *IEEE Transactions on Neural Systems and Rehabilitation Engineering*, *22*(3), 543–548. doi:10.1109/TNSRE.2013.2285410 PMID:24235275

Saboor, A., Kask, T., Kuusik, A., Alam, M. M., Le Moullec, Y., Niazi, I. K., Zoha, A., & Ahmad, R. (2020). Latest Research Trends in Gait Analysis Using Wearable Sensors and Machine Learning: A Systematic Review. *IEEE Access: Practical Innovations, Open Solutions*, *8*, 167830–167864. doi:10.1109/ACCESS.2020.3022818

Satti, F. A., Ali, T., Hussain, J., Khan, W. A., Khattak, A. M., & Lee, S. (2020). Ubiquitous Health Profile (UHPr): A big data curation platform for supporting health data interoperability. *Computing*, *102*(11), 2409–2444. doi:10.100700607-020-00837-2

Shi, L., Li, S., Yang, X., Qi, J., Pan, G., & Zhou, B. (2017). Semantic health knowledge graph: Semantic integration of heterogeneous medical knowledge and services. *BioMed Research International*, *2017*, 2017. doi:10.1155/2017/2858423 PMID:28299322

Siow, W. T., Liew, M. F., Shrestha, B. R., Muchtar, F., & See, K. C. (2020). *Managing COVID-19 in resource-limited settings: critical care considerations*. Academic Press.

Stonebraker, M., Bruckner, D., Ilyas, I. F., Beskales, G., Cherniack, M., Zdonik, S. B., . . . Xu, S. (2013, January). Data Curation at Scale: The Data Tamer System. In Cidr (Vol. 2013). Academic Press.

Tang, W., & Su, D. (2013). Locomotion analysis and its applications in neurological disorders detection: State-of-art review. *Network Modeling and Analysis in Health Informatics and Bioinformatics*, *2*(1), 1–12. doi:10.100713721-012-0020-8

Vidal, M. E., Endris, K. M., Jozashoori, S., Karim, F., & Palma, G. (2019). Semantic data integration of big biomedical data for supporting personalised medicine. In Current Trends in Semantic Web Technologies: Theory and Practice (pp. 25-56). Springer.

Whittle, M. W. (2014). *Gait analysis: an introduction*. Butterworth-Heinemann.

Zargaran, E., Schuurman, N., Nicol, A. J., Matzopoulos, R., Cinnamon, J., Taulu, T., Ricker, B., Garbutt Brown, D. R., Navsaria, P., & Hameed, S. M. (2014). The electronic Trauma Health Record: Design and usability of a novel tablet-based tool for trauma care and injury surveillance in low resource settings. *Journal of the American College of Surgeons*, *218*(1), 41–50. doi:10.1016/j.jamcollsurg.2013.10.001 PMID:24355875

Zhao, D., & Weng, C. (2011). Combining PubMed knowledge and EHR data to develop a weighted Bayesian network for pancreatic cancer prediction. *Journal of Biomedical Informatics*, *44*(5), 859–868. doi:10.1016/j.jbi.2011.05.004 PMID:21642013

Zhao, Z., Han, S. K., & So, I. M. (2018). Architecture of knowledge graph construction techniques. *International Journal of Pure and Applied Mathematics*, *118*(19), 1869–1883.

Zhou, Y., Qureshi, R., & Sacan, A. (2012). Data simulation and regulatory network reconstruction from time-series microarray data using stepwise multiple linear regression. *Network Modeling and Analysis in Health Informatics and Bioinformatics*, *1*(1-2), 3–17. doi:10.100713721-012-0008-4

Zillner, S., & Sonntag, D. (2012). Image metadata reasoning for improved clinical decision support. *Network Modeling and Analysis in Health Informatics and Bioinformatics*, *1*(1-2), 37–46. doi:10.100713721-012-0003-9

ENDNOTE

[1]   HealthID: the technology that puts your patients' health records in your hands, available at: https://www.discovery.co.za/medical-aid/health-id

Compilation of References

Abadie, M., & Waroquier, L. (2019). Evaluating the benefits of conscious and unconscious thought in complex decision making. *Policy Insights from the Behavioral and Brain Sciences*, *6*(1), 72–78. doi:10.1177/2372732218816998

Adebesin, F., Foster, R., Kotzé, P., & Van Greunen, D. (2013). A Review of Interoperability Standards in E-health and Imperatives for their Adoption in Africa. *South African Computer Journal, 50*.

Adenuga, O. A., Kekwaletswe, R. M., & Coleman, A. (2015). eHealth integration and interoperability issues: Towards a solution through enterprise architecture. *Health Information Science and Systems*, *3*(1), 1. doi:10.118613755-015-0009-7 PMID:26167279

Adesemowo, A. K., Mhlaba, S., Yekela, O., & Ndame, L. (2017). An auto grading online submission system: Case of packet tracer. In A. Mesquita & P. Peres (Eds.), *Proceedings of the 16th European Conference on e-Learning ECEL 2017* (pp. 1–8). Academic Conferences and Publishing International Limited. https://www.academic-bookshop.com/ourshop/prod_6222116-ECEL-2017-PDF-Proceedings-of-the-16th-European-Conference-on-eLearning.html

Adesemowo, A. K., Johannes, H., Goldstone, S., & Terblanche, K. (2016). The experience of introducing secure e-assessment in a South African university first-year foundational ICT networking course. *Africa Education Review*, *13*(1), 67–86. doi:10.1080/18146627.2016.1186922

Adesemowo, A. K., & Kende, N. (2015). Students' Learning Experience of ICT Networking via Simulated Platform at a South African University. In C. A. Shoniregun (Ed.), *IICE-2015 Proceedings* (pp. 65–75). www.iicedu.org/IICE-2015 October/IICE_Home.html

Adesemowo, A. K., Oyedele, Y., & Oyedele, O. (2017). Text-based sustainable assessment: A case of first-year information and communication technology networking students. *Studies in Educational Evaluation*, *55*, 1–8. doi:10.1016/j.stueduc.2017.04.005

Agrawal, R., & Gupta, N. (Eds.). (2018). *Extracting Knowledge from Opinion Mining*. IGI Global.

Ajetunmobi, S. A., & Daramola, O. (2017, October). Ontology-Based Information Extraction for SubjectFocussed Automatic Essay Evaluation. *2017 International Conference on Computing Networking and Informatics (ICCNI)*. 10.1109/ICCNI.2017.8123781

Akhigbe, B. I. (2015). *Development of a user-centric integrated evaluative model for information retrieval systems* (Unpublished Ph.D. thesis). Postgraduate College, Obafemi Awolowo University, Ile-Ife, Nigeria.

Akhigbe, B. I., Aderibigbe, O. S., Ejidokun, A. O., Afolabi, B. S., & Adagunodo, E. R. (2016a). The web analytics framework: an integrated user-centric evaluative tool. In *Proceedings of International conference on transition from observation to knowledge to intelligence*. University of Lagos.

Alalwan, N., Abozeid, A., ElHabshy, A. A., & Alzahrani, A. (2020). Efficient 3D Deep Learning Model for Medical Image Semantic Segmentation. *Alexandria Engineering Journal.* DOI: .2020.10.046 doi:10.1016/j.aej

Aldred, L., van der Aalst, W., Dumas, M., & ter Hofstede, A. (2006). Understanding the challenges in getting together: The semantics of decoupling in middleware. *BPM Center Report BPM-06-19, BPMcenter. org.*

Alejandra, G.B., Francesco, O., Silvio, P., & Sahar, V. (2019). *Editorial: Special Issue on Scholarly Data Analysis (Semantics, Analytics, Visualisation).* doi:10.3233/DS-190023

Algosaibi, A. A., Albahli, S., & Melton, A. (2015). World Wide Web: A survey of its development and possible future trends. In *The 16th International Conference on Internet Computing and Big Data-ICOMP* (Vol. 15, pp. 79-84). Academic Press.

Allen, M. (2017). Web 2.0: An argument against convergence. In *Media Convergence and Deconvergence* (pp. 177–196). Palgrave Macmillan. doi:10.1007/978-3-319-51289-1_9

Allseen Alliance. (2016). *AllJoyn Framework.* Available at https://allseenalliance.org/framework/documentation/learn/architecture

Al-Qaseemi, S. A., Almulhim, H. A., Almulhim, M. F., & Chaudhry, S. R. (2016). IoT architecture challenges and issues: Lack of standardization. *Proceedings of the 2016 Future Technologies Conference (FTC),* 731–738.

Alsubait, T., Parsia, B., & Sattler, U. (2012). Automatic generation of analogy questions for student assessment: an Ontology-based approach. *Research in Learning Technology, 20*(sup1), 19198. doi:10.3402/rlt.v20i0.19198

Alsubait, T., Parsia, B., & Sattler, U. (2016). Ontology-Based Multiple Choice Question Generation. *KI - Künstliche Intelligenz, 30*(2), 183–188. doi:10.100713218-015-0405-9

Alves da Silva, A., Padilha, F. N., Siqueira, S., Baião, F. A., & Revoredo, K. (2012). Using Concept Maps and Ontology Alignment for Learning Assessment. *IEEE Technology and Engineering Education, 7*(3), 33–40. https://www.semanticscholar.org/paper/Using-Concept-Maps-and-Ontology-Alignment-for-(-)-Silva-Padilha/0b130e5c2200a15f2c93f210d73a060547a42415

Al-Yahya, M. (2014). Ontology-Based Multiple Choice Question Generation. *TheScientificWorldJournal, 2014,* 1–9. doi:10.1155/2014/274949 PMID:24982937

Al-Yahya, M. (2015). Ontologies in E-Learning: Review of the Literature. *International Journal of Software Engineering and Its Applications, 9*(2), 67–84.

Amato, F., De Santo, A., Moscato, V., Persia, F., Picariello, A., & Poccia, S. R. (2015). Partitioning of ontologies driven by a structure-based approach. *Proceedings of the 2015 IEEE 9th International Conference on Semantic Computing (IEEE ICSC 2015),* 320–323. 10.1109/ICOSC.2015.7050827

Anderson, L. W., Krathwohl, D. R., & Bloom, B. S. (2001). *A taxonomy for learning, teaching, and assessing: a revision of Bloom's taxonomy of educational objectives.* Longman. http://books.google.com/books?id=bcQlAQAAIAAJ&pgis=1

An, J., Li, G., Ning, B., Jiang, W., & Sun, Y. (2020). Re-sculpturing Semantic Web of Things as a Strategy for Internet of Things' Intrinsic Contradiction. In *Artificial Intelligence in China, LNEE 572* (pp. 67–75). Springer. doi:10.1007/978-981-15-0187-6_66

Arksey, H., & O'Malley, L. (2005). Scoping studies: Towards a methodological framework. *International Journal of Social Research Methodology, 8*(1), 19–32. doi:10.1080/1364557032000119616

Arogundade, O. T., Jin, Z., & Yang, X. (2014). Towards ontological approach to eliciting risk-based security requirements. *International Journal of Information and Computer Security, 6*(2), 143. doi:10.1504/IJICS.2014.065168

Asaria, M., Grasic, K., & Walker, S. (2016). Using linked electronic health records to estimate healthcare costs: Key challenges and opportunities. *PharmacoEconomics, 34*(2), 155–160. doi:10.100740273-015-0358-8 PMID:26645571

Asfand-E-Yar, M., & Ali, R. (2020). Semantic Integration of Heterogeneous Databases of Same Domain Using Ontology. *IEEE Access : Practical Innovations, Open Solutions, 8*, 77903–77919.

Atzori, L., Iera, A., & Morabito, G. (2010). The Internet of Things: A Survey. *Comput. Network, 54*, 2787–2805.

Baader, F., Calvanese, D., McGuinness, D., Nardi, D., & Patel-Schneider, P. (Eds.). (2002). *The Description Logic Handbook*. Cambridge University Press.

Baazaoui, H., Aufaure, M.-A., & Soussi, R. (2008). Towards an on- Line Semantic Information Retrieval System based on Fuzzy Ontologies. *Journal of Digital Information Management, 6*(5), 375–385.

Back, A. (2002). *Hashcash - a denial of service counter-measure.* https://www.researchgate.net/publication/2482110_Hashcash__A_Denial_of_Service_Counter-Measure

Badiye, A., Kathane, P., & Krishan, K. (2020). Forensic Gait Analysis. In StatPearls. StatPearls Publishing.

Baeza-Yates, R., & Ribeiro-Neto, B. (1999). *Modern Information Retrieval*. ACM Press/Addison Wesley.

Balakrishna, S., Thirumaran, M., & Solanki, V. K. (2020). IoT sensor data integration in healthcare using semantics and machine learning approaches. In *A Handbook of Internet of Things in Biomedical and Cyber-Physical System* (pp. 275–300). Springer.

Baltruschat, I. M., Nickisch, H., Grass, M., Knopp, T., & Saalbach, A. (2019). Comparison of deep learning approaches for multi-label chest X-ray classification. *Scientific Reports, 9*(1), 1–10. doi:10.103841598-019-42294-8 PMID:31011155

Bandari, R. (2013). *Gestalt Computing and the Study of Content-oriented User Behavior on the Web* (Doctoral dissertation). UCLA.

Bar, Y., Diamant, I., Wolf, L., Lieberman, S., Konen, E., & Greenspan, H. (2015, April). Chest pathology detection using deep learning with non-medical training. In *2015 IEEE 12th international symposium on biomedical imaging (ISBI)* (pp. 294-297). IEEE. 10.1109/ISBI.2015.7163871

Barnaghi, P., Presser, M., & Moessner, K. (2010). Publishing Linked Sensor Data. *Proceedings of the 3rd International Workshop on Semantic Sensor Networks.*

Bartoletti, M., & Pompianu, L. (2017). *An empirical analysis of smart contracts: platforms, applications, and design patterns.* https://arxiv.org/pdf/1703.06322.pdf

Bārzdiņš, J., Bārzdiņš, G., Čerāns, K., Liepiņš, R., & Sproģis, A. (2010). UML Style Graphical Notation and Editor for OWL 2. In P. Forbrig & H. Günther (Eds.), Perspectives in Business Informatics Research. BIR 2010. Lecture Notes in Business Information Processing (Vol. 64, pp. 102–114). Springer. doi:10.1007/978-3-642-16101-8_9

Basili, V. R., & HD, C. G. R. (1994). The goal question metric approach. In *Encyclopedia of Software Engineering*. Wiley.

Bates, M. (1989). The design of browsing and berry-picking techniques for the online search interface. *Online Review, 13*(5), 407–431. doi:10.1108/eb024320

Beisswanger, E., Schulz, S., Stenzhorn, H., & Hahn, U. (2008). BioTop: An upper domain ontology for the life sciencesA description of its current structure, contents and interfaces to OBO ontologies. *Applied Ontology*, *3*(4), 205–212. doi:10.3233/AO-2008-0057

Berners-Lee, T., & Fischetti, M. (2001). *Weaving the Web: The original design and ultimate destiny of the World Wide Web by its inventor*. DIANE Publishing Company.

Berners-Lee, T., Hendler, J., & Lassila, O. (2001). The Semantic Web. *Scientific American*, (May), 29–37. PMID:11323639

Berners-Lee, T., Hendler, J., & Lassila, O. (2001). The semantic web. *Scientific American*, *284*(5), 28–37. doi:10.1038 cientificamerican0501-34 PMID:11341160

Bernstein, A., Hendler, J., & Noy, N. (2016). A new look at the semantic web. *Communications of the ACM*, *59*(9), 1–5. doi:10.1145/2890489

Biega, J., Kuzey, E., & Suchanek, F. M. (2013, May). Inside YAGO2s: a transparent information extraction architecture. In *Proceedings of the 22nd International Conference on World Wide Web* (pp. 325-328). 10.1145/2487788.2487935

Biundo, S., & Wendemuth, A. (Eds.). (2017). *Companion technology: a paradigm shift in human-technology interaction*. Springer. doi:10.1007/978-3-319-43665-4

Bizer, C. (2009). The emerging web of linked data. *IEEE Intelligent Systems*, *24*(5), 87–92. doi:10.1109/MIS.2009.102

Bohn, H., Bobek, A., & Golatowski, F. (2006). SIRENA-Service Infrastructure for Real-time Embedded Networked Devices: A service-oriented framework for different domains. *Networking, International Conference on Systems and International Conference on Mobile Communications and Learning Technologies*, 43-43.

Bohring, H., & Auer, S. (2015). Mapping XML to OWL ontologies. In *Marktplatz Internet: Von e-Learning bis e-Payment, 13*. Leipziger Informatik-Tage (LIT 2005).

Bolívar, M. P. R. (2018). *Smart Technologies for Smart Governments*. Springer. doi:10.1007/978-3-319-58577-2

Boltuc, P. (2018). Strong semantic computing. *Procedia Computer Science*, *123*, 98–103.

Bordel Sánchez, B., Alcarria, R., Sánchez de Rivera, D., & Robles, T. (2018). Process execution in CyberPhysical Systems using cloud and Cyber-Physical Internet services. *The Journal of Supercomputing*, *74*(8), 4127–4169. doi:10.100711227-018-2416-4

Bordes, A., Glorot, X., & Weston, J. (2012). Joint Learning of Words and Meaning Representations for Open-Text Semantic Parsing. *Proceedings of the 15th International Conference on Artificial Intelligence and Statistics (AISTATS)*.

Botha, M., Botha, A., & Herselman, M. (2014, December). The Benefits and Challenges of e-Health Applications: A Content Analysis of the South African context. In *Proceedings of The International Conference on Computer Science, Computer Engineering, and Social Media* (pp. 12-14). Academic Press.

Botoeva, E., Calvanese, D., & Rodriguez-Muro, M. (2010). *Expressive Approximations in DL-Lite Ontologies BT*. In D. Dicheva & D. Dochev (Eds.), *Artificial Intelligence: Methodology, Systems, and Applications* (pp. 21–31). Springer Berlin Heidelberg.

Boud, D., & Soler, R. (2016). Sustainable assessment revisited. *Assessment & Evaluation in Higher Education*, *41*(3), 400–413. doi:10.1080/02602938.2015.1018133

Brambilla, M., Ceri, S., Della Valle, E., Volonterio, R., & Acero Salazar, F. X. (2017). Extracting emerging knowledge from social media. In *Proceedings of the 26th International Conference on World Wide Web* (pp. 795-804). International World Wide Web Conferences Steering Committee. 10.1145/3038912.3052697

Broder, A. (2002). A taxonomy of web search. *SIGIR Forum, 36*(2), 3–10.

Brognara, L., Palumbo, P., Grimm, B., & Palmerini, L. (2019). Assessing gait in Parkinson's disease using wearable motion sensors: A systematic review. *Diseases (Basel, Switzerland), 7*(1), 18. doi:10.3390/diseases7010018 PMID:30764502

Broy, M., Cengarle, M. V., & Geisberger, E. (2012). Cyber-Physical Systems: Imminent Challenges. In *Large-Scale Complex IT Syst. Dev., Operat. and Manag. 17th Monterey Workshop*, 7539, 1–28.

Bryant, M. (2017). *Blockchain may be healthcare's answer to interoperability, data security*. Health Care Dive.

Buongiorno, D., Bortone, I., Cascarano, G. D., Trotta, G. F., Brunetti, A., & Bevilacqua, V. (2019). A low-cost vision system based on the analysis of motor features for recognition and severity rating of Parkinson's Disease. *BMC Medical Informatics and Decision Making, 19*(9), 243. doi:10.118612911-019-0987-5 PMID:31830986

Burnett, C., & Merchant, G. (2020). Returning to Text: Affect, Meaning Making, and Literacies. *Reading Research Quarterly*, 113–123. doi:10.1002/rrq.303

Butavicius, M. A., Parsons, K. M., McCormac, A., Dennis, S. J., Ceglar, A., Weber, D., Ferguson, L., Treharne, K., Leibbrandt, R., & Powers, D. (2019). Using Semantic Context to Rank the Results of Keyword Search. *Inter. Jour. of HCI, 35*(9), 725–741. doi:10.1080/10447318.2018.1485263

Buterin, V. (2014). *A Next Generation Smart Contract & Decentralized Application Platform*. https://www.the-blockchain.com/docs/Ethereum_white_paper-a_next_generation_smart_contract_and_decentralized_application_platform-vitalik-buterin.pdf

Buterin, D. (n.d.). Smart Contracts: The Blockchain Technology That Will Replace Lawyers. *BlockGeeks*.

Cachin, C. (2017). *Architecture of the Hyperledger Blockchain Fabric*. https://www.zurich.ibm.com/dccl/papers/cachin_dccl.pdf

Campbell, L. J., Halpin, T. A., & Proper, H. A. (1996). Conceptual schemas with abstractions making flat conceptual schemas more comprehensible. *Data & Knowledge Engineering, 20*(1), 39–85. doi:10.1016/0169-023X(96)00005-5

Camps, J., Sama, A., Martin, M., Rodriguez-Martin, D., Perez-Lopez, C., Arostegui, J. M. M., ... Prats, A. (2018). Deep learning for freezing of gait detection in Parkinson's disease patients in their homes using a waist-worn inertial measurement unit. *Knowledge-Based Systems, 139*, 119–131. doi:10.1016/j.knosys.2017.10.017

Carrillo-de-Gea, J. M., García-Mateos, G., Fernández-Alemán, J. L., & Hernández-Hernández, J. L. (2016). A computer-aided detection system for digital chest radiographs. *Journal of Healthcare Engineering, 2016*, 2016. doi:10.1155/2016/8208923 PMID:27372536

Carroll, J., Herman, I., & Patel-Schneider, P. F. (2015). *OWL 2 web ontology language RDF-based semantics*. W3C Recommendation.

Carter, J. (2016). *Bitcoin vs distributed ledger vs Ethereum vs blockchain*. http://www.techradar.com/news/internet/bitcoin-vs-distributed-ledger-vs-ethereum-vs-blockchain-1328432

Carvalho, R. N., Laskey, K. B., & Costa, P. C. (2017). PR-OWL–a language for defining probabilistic ontologies. *International Journal of Approximate Reasoning, 91*, 56–79. doi:10.1016/j.ijar.2017.08.011

Casanovas, P., Palmirani, M., Peroni, S., van Engers, T., & Vitali, F. (2016). Semantic web for the legal domain: The next step. *Semantic Web, 7*(3), 213–227. doi:10.3233/SW-160224

Chan, H. P., Wei, D., Helvie, M. A., Sahiner, B., Adler, D. D., Goodsitt, M. M., & Petrick, N. (1995). Computer-aided classification of mammographic masses and normal tissue: Linear discriminant analysis in texture feature space. *Physics in Medicine and Biology*, *40*(5), 857–876. doi:10.1088/0031-9155/40/5/010 PMID:7652012

Cheatham, M., & Pesquita, C. (2017). Semantic data integration. In *Handbook of big data technologies* (pp. 263–305). Springer.

Chen, J., Alghamdi, G., Schmidt, R. A., Walther, D., & Gao, Y. (2019). Ontology Extraction for Large Ontologies via Modularity and Forgetting. In *Proceedings of the 10th International Conference on Knowledge Capture* (pp. 45–52). 10.1145/3360901.3364424

Cheng, H., Xue, L., Wang, P., Zeng, P., & Yu, H. (2017). Ontology-based web service integration for flexible manufacturing systems. In *15th Int. Conf. on Ind. Inf.*, (pp. 351–356). IEEE. 10.1109/INDIN.2017.8104797

Chen, G., Wang, L., & Kamruzzaman, M. M. (2020a). Spectral classification of ecological spatial polarization SAR image based on target decomposition algorithm and machine learning. *Neural Computing & Applications*, *32*(10), 5449–5460. doi:10.100700521-019-04624-9

Chen, L. C., Zhu, Y., Papandreou, G., Schroff, F., & Adam, H. (2018). Encoder-decoder with atrous separable convolution for semantic image segmentation. In *Proceedings of the European conference on computer vision (ECCV)* (pp. 801-818). 10.1007/978-3-030-01234-2_49

Chen, L., Xu, S., Zhu, L., Zhang, J., Lei, X., & Yang, G. (2020b). A deep learning based method for extracting semantic information from patent documents. *Scientometrics*, *125*(1), 289–312. doi:10.100711192-020-03634-y

Chen, S., Lach, J., Lo, B., & Yang, G. Z. (2016). Toward pervasive gait analysis with wearable sensors: A systematic review. *IEEE Journal of Biomedical and Health Informatics*, *20*(6), 1521–1537. doi:10.1109/JBHI.2016.2608720 PMID:28113185

Chen, X. W., & Lin, X. (2014). Big data deep learning: Challenges and perspectives. *Access, IEEE.*, *2*, 514–525. doi:10.1109/ACCESS.2014.2325029

Chen, X., Li, G., Sun, Y., Chen, H., & Jiang, W. (2020). The Importance of Researching and Developing the Semantic Web of Things. In *Artificial Intelligence in China, LNEE 572* (pp. 637–644). Springer. doi:10.1007/978-981-15-0187-6_76

Cho, B. Y., & Afflerbach, P. (2017). An evolving perspective of constructively responsive reading comprehension strategies in multilayered digital text environments. In S. E. Israel (Ed.), *Handbook of research on reading comprehension* (2nd ed., pp. 109–134). Guilford.

Choudhury, N. (2014). World wide web and its journey from web 1.0 to web 4.0. *International Journal of Computer Science and Information Technologies*, *5*(6), 8096–8100.

Christopher, P., & Stanford, L. (2018). A case for deep learning in semantics. Published in: A Journal of the Linguistic Society of America. To appear in Language as a commentary on Pater 2018. *Ahead of Print*, *95*(1). Advance online publication. doi:10.1353/lan.2019.0003

Chung, L., Nixon, B. A., Yu, E., & Mylopoulos, J. (2000). *Non-Functional Requirements in Software Engineering*. Springer. doi:10.1007/978-1-4615-5269-7

Ciampi, M., De Pietro, G., Masciari, E., & Silvestri, S. (2020). Some lessons learned using health data literature for smart information retrieval. In *Proceedings of the 35th Annual ACM Symposium on Applied Computing* (pp. 931-934). 10.1145/3341105.3374128

Ciortea, A., Mayer, S., & Michahelles, F. (2018). Repurposing Manufacturing Lines on the Fly with Multi-agent Systems for the Web of Things. In *Proc. of the 17th Int. Conf. on Autonomous Agents and Multi-Agent Systems*, (pp. 813–822). Int. Found. for Autonomous Agents and Multiagent Systems / ACM.

Clarke, B., Fokoue, E., & Zhang, H. H. (2009). *Principles and theory for data mining and machine learning*. Springer Science & Business Media. doi:10.1007/978-0-387-98135-2

Colace, F., & De Santo, M. (2010). Ontology for E-Learning: A Bayesian Approach. *IEEE Transactions on Education*, *53*(2), 223–233. doi:10.1109/TE.2009.2012537

Cole, B. (2016). *Blockchain compliance raises questions of regulatory scope, intent*. Tech Target.

Colitti, W., Steenhaut, K., Caro, N. De., (2011). *Integrating Wireless Sensor Networks with the Web*. Extending the Internet to Low Power and Lossy Networks (IP+SN).

Collins, M. J. (2017). Hypertext Markup Language. In Pro HTML5 with CSS, JavaScript, and Multimedia (pp. 3-14). Apress. doi:10.1007/978-1-4842-2463-2_1

Colucci, S., Di Noia, T., Pinto, A., Ruta, M., Ragone, A., & Tinelli, E. (2007). A Nonmonotonic Approach to Semantic Matchmaking and Request Refinement in E-Marketplaces. *International Journal of Electronic Commerce*, *12*(2), 127–154. doi:10.2753/JEC1086-4415120205

Comer, D. E. (2018). *The Internet book: everything you need to know about computer networking and how the Internet works*. Chapman and Hall/CRC. doi:10.1201/9780429447358

Conti, M., & Passarella, A. (2018). The Internet of People: A human and data-centric paradigm for the Next Generation Internet. *Computer Communications*, *131*, 51–65.

Conti, M., Passarella, A., & Das, S. (2017). The Internet of People (IoP): A new wave in pervasive mobile computing. *Pervasive and Mobile Computing*, *41*, 1–27.

Cory, A., Henson, J., Pschorr, K., Sheth, A. P., & Thirunarayan, K. (2009). SemSOS: Semantic sensor Observation Service. *Proceedings of the International Symposium on Collaborative Technologies and Systems*.

Cowell, L., & Smith, B. (2009). Infectious Disease Ontology. In Infectious Disease Informatics (pp. 373–395). doi:10.1007/978-1-4419-1327-2_19

Craig, B. D. (n.d.). *Moving beyond the knowledge economy*. End2End Integration. Retrieved March 23, 2014, from http://www.e2ei.com/site/article.php?id=15

Crawford, J., Butler-Henderson, K., Rudolph, J., Malkawi, B., Glowatz, M., Burton, R., Magni, P. A., & Lam, S. (2020). COVID-19: 20 countries' higher education intra-period digital pedagogy responses. *Journal of Applied Learning & Teaching*, *3*(1). Advance online publication. doi:10.37074/jalt.2020.3.1.7

Croisier, S. (2012). The rise of semantic-aware applications. In W. Maass & T. Kowatsch (Eds.), *Semantic Technologies in Content Management Systems: Trends, Applications and Evaluations* (pp. 23–34). Springer-Verlag. doi:10.1007/978-3-642-24960-0_3

Csapó, B., Ainley, J., Bennett, R. E., Latour, T., & Law, N. (2012). Technological Issues for Computer-Based Assessment. In P. Griffin, B. McGaw, & E. Care (Eds.), *Assessment and Teaching of 21st Century Skills* (pp. 143–230). Springer Netherlands. doi:10.1007/978-94-007-2324-5_4

Cubric, M., & Tosic, M. (2011). Towards automatic generation of e-assessment using semantic web technologies. *International Journal of E-Assessment*, *1*(1). https://ijea.org.uk/ijea/index.php/journal/article/view/16

Cuthbertson, A. (2015). *Bitcoin now accepted by 100,000 merchants worldwide.* https://www.ibtimes.co.uk/bitcoin-now-accepted-by-100000-merchants-worldwide-1486613

d'Aquin, M., Sabou, M., & Motta, E. (2006). *Modularization: a key for the dynamic selection of relevant knowledge components.* Academic Press.

Dagmar, G., Luis, E. A., & Thierry, D. (2019). *Special issue on Semantic Deep Learning.* doi:10.3233/SW-190364

Danielle, G. T., DeKeizer, N. F., & Scheffer, G. J. (2002). *Defining and Improving Data Quality in Medical Registries: A Literature Review.* Case Study, and Generic Framework. doi:10.1197/jamia.M1087

Daniel, S. J. (2020). Education and the COVID-19 pandemic. *Prospects*, 1–6. doi:10.100711125-020-09464-3 PMID:32313309

Daoust, F. (2018). Report from the World Wide Web Consortium. *SMPTE Motion Imaging Journal*, *127*(8), 72–73. doi:10.5594/JMI.2018.2850378

Daramola, O., & Moser, T. (2019). Semantic integration of multiple health data for treatment decision-making in low-resource settings. In *Multi-Conference on Computer Science and Information Systems, MCCSIS 2019 - Proceedings of the International Conference on e-Health 2019* (pp. 43–50). IADIS Press. 10.33965/eh2019_201910L006

Daramola, O., Afolabi, I., Akinyemi, I., & Oladipupo, O. (2013). Using Ontology-based Information Extraction for Subject-based Auto-grading. *Proceedings of the International Conference on Knowledge Engineering and Ontology Development: KEOD, (IC3K 2013)*, *1*, 373–378. 10.5220/0004625903730378

de la Torre, L., Guinaldo, M., Heradio, R., & Dormido, S. (2015). The Ball and Beam System: A Case Study of Virtual and Remote Lab Enhancement With Moodle. *IEEE Transactions on Industrial Informatics*, *11*(4), 934–945. doi:10.1109/TII.2015.2443721

de Lara, J., Guerra, E., & Sánchez Cuadrado, J. (2013). Reusable abstractions for modeling languages. *Information Systems*, *38*(8), 1128–1149. doi:10.1016/j.is.2013.06.001

De Virgilio, R., Di Sciascio, E., Ruta, M., Scioscia, F., & Torlone, R. (2011). Semantic-based rfid data management. In *Unique Radio Innovation for the 21st Century* (pp. 111–141). Springer. doi:10.1007/978-3-642-03462-6_6

Del Vescovo, C. (2011). The modular structure of an ontology: Atomic decomposition towards applications. *24th International Workshop on Description Logics*, 466.

Del Vescovo, C., Gessler, D. D. G., Klinov, P., Parsia, B., Sattler, U., Schneider, T., & Winget, A. (2011). In L. Aroyo, C. Welty, H. Alani, J. Taylor, A. Bernstein, L. Kagal, N. Noy, & E. Blomqvist (Eds.), *Decomposition and Modular Structure of BioPortal Ontologies BT - The Semantic Web – ISWC 2011* (pp. 130–145). Springer Berlin Heidelberg. doi:10.1007/978-3-642-25073-6_9

Delacretaz & Marth. (2012). Simplified Semantic Enhancement of JCR-based Content Applications. In Semantic Technologies in Content Management Systems: Trends, Applications and Evaluations. doi:10.1007/978-3-642-24960-0_2

Delgado, P., Lund, E. S., Salmeron, L., & Braten, I. (2020). To click or not to click: Investigating conflict detection and sourcing in a multiple document hypertext environment. *Reading and Writing*, *33*(8), 1–24. doi:10.100711145-020-10030-8

Deng, H., Xu, J., Shan, W., and Yuan, C. (2018). Extraction of polarimetric SAR image building area by active deep learning. *Journal of Survey Mapping Science Technology, 35*(3), 278–284.

Dhayne, H., Kilany, R., Haque, R., & Taher, Y. (2018, December). SeDIE: A semantic-driven engine for integration of healthcare data. In *2018 IEEE International Conference on Bioinformatics and Biomedicine (BIBM)* (pp. 617-622). IEEE. 10.1109/BIBM.2018.8621243

Dickinson, J. E., Ghali, K., Cherrett, T., Speed, C., Davies, N., & Norgate, S. (2014). Tourism and the smartphone app: Capabilities, emerging practice and scope in the travel domain. *Current Issues in Tourism*, *17*(1), 84–101. doi:10.1080/13683500.2012.718323

Dickson, B. (2016). *Blockchain has the potential to revolutionize the supply chain*. Tech Crunch.

Dijksterhuis, A., Bos, M. W., Nordgren, L. F., & Van Baaren, R. B. (2006). On making the right choice: The deliberation-without-attention effect. *Science*, *311*(5763), 1005–1007. doi:10.1126/science.1121629 PubMed

Dijksterhuis, A., & Nordgren, L. F. (2006). A theory of unconscious thought. *Perspectives on Psychological Science*, *1*(2), 95–109. doi:10.1111/j.1745-6916.2006.00007.x PubMed

Doan, A., & Halevy, A. Y. (2005). Semantic integration research in the database community: A brief survey. *AI Magazine*, *26*(1), 83–83.

Dominic, M., Francis, S., & Pilomenraj, A. (2014). E-learning in web 3.0. *International Journal of Modern Education and Computer Science*, *6*(2), 8–14. doi:10.5815/ijmecs.2014.02.02

Donnelly, K. (2006). SNOMED-CT: The advanced terminology and coding system for eHealth. *Studies in Health Technology and Informatics*, *121*, 279. PMID:17095826

Economist Staff. (2015, Oct. 31). Blockchains: The great chain of being sure about things. *The Economist*.

Effenberg, A., Fehse, U., & Weber, A. (2011). Movement Sonification: Audiovisual benefits on motor learning. In BIO web of conferences (Vol. 1, p. 00022). EDP Sciences.

Ekelhart, A., Fenz, S., & Neubauer, T. (2009). AURUM: A Framework for Information Security Risk Management. *Proceedings of the 42nd Hawaii International Conference on System Sciences - HICSS*, 1–10. 10.1109/HICSS.2009.595

English, M. (2017). *Blockchain and the Semantic Web*. Academic Press.

Erragcha, N., & Romdhane, R. (2014). New faces of marketing in the era of the web: From marketing 1.0 to marketing 3.0. *Journal of Research in Marketing*, *2*(2), 137–142. doi:10.17722/jorm.v2i2.46

Esteva, A., Kale, A., Paulus, R., Hashimoto, K., Yin, W., Radev, D., & Socher, R. (2020). *Co-search: Covid-19 information retrieval with semantic search, question answering, and abstractive summarization*. arXiv preprint arXiv:2006.09595.

Esteva, A., Kuprel, B., Novoa, R. A., Ko, J., Swetter, S. M., Blau, H. M., & Thrun, S. (2017). Dermatologist-level classification of skin cancer with deep neural networks. *Nature*, *542*(7639), 115–118. doi:10.1038/nature21056 PMID:28117445

Estrela, V. V., Monteiro, A. C. B., França, R. P., Iano, Y., Khelassi, A., & Razmjooy, N. (2018). Health 4.0: Applications, management, technologies and review. *Medical Technologies Journal*, *2*(4), 262–276.

Evans, J. S. B. (2008). Dual-processing accounts of reasoning, judgment, and social cog. *Annual Review of Psychology*, *59*(1), 255–278. doi:10.1146/annurev.psych.59.103006.093629 PMID:18154502

Fagan, J. C. (2014). The Suitability of Web Analytics Key Performance Indicators in the Academic Library Environment. *Journal of Academic Librarianship*, *40*(1), 25–34. doi:10.1016/j.acalib.2013.06.005

Faheem, M., Sattar, H., Bajwa, I. S., & Akbar, W. (2018). Relational Database to Resource Description Framework and Its Schema. In *International Conference on Intelligent Technologies and Applications* (pp. 604-617). Springer.

Federhen, S. (2012). The NCBI Taxonomy database. *Nucleic Acids Research*, *40*(Database issue), D136–D143. doi:10.1093/nar/gkr1178 PMID:22139910

Ferrari, S. (2016). Marketing Strategies in The Age of Web 3.0. In Mobile Computing and Wireless Networks: Concepts, Methodologies, Tools, and Applications (pp. 2132-2149). IGI Global.

Ferrel, G., & Gray, L. (2015, August 31). *Enhancing student employability through technology-supported assessment and feedback*. JISC Guide. https://www.jisc.ac.uk/guides/enhancing-student-employability-through-technology-supported-assessment-and-feedback

Ferro, N., & Silvello, G. (2018). Toward an anatomy of IR system component performances. *Journal of the Association for Information Science and Technology*, *69*(2), 187–200. doi:10.1002/asi.23910 PMID:30775406

Feussner, H., Ostler, D., Kranzfelder, M., Kohn, N., Koller, S., Wilhelm, D., & Schneider, A. (2017). Surgery 4.0. In *Health 4.0: How Virtualization and Big Data are Revolutionizing Healthcare* (pp. 91–107). Springer. doi:10.1007/978-3-319-47617-9_5

Fillmore, C. J., & Baker, C. (2010). A-frames approach to semantic analysis. In The Oxford handbook of linguistic analysis. OUP.

Fischer, G. (2001). User Modelling in Human-Computer Interaction. *User Modeling and User-Adapted Interaction*, *11*(1-2), 65–86. doi:10.1023/A:1011145532042

Fonseca, M., Karkaletsis, K., Cruz, I. A., Berler, A., & Oliveira, I. C. (2015, May). OpenNCP: a novel framework to foster cross-border e-Health services. In MIE (Vol. 210, pp. 617-621). Academic Press.

Freire, R., Díaz, J., & Vera, N. (2019). Redes sociales para el aprendizaje significativo: apropiación tecnológica de la web 3.0. In *Conference Proceedings* (*Vol. 3*, No. 1, pp. 160-172). Academic Press.

Frezzo, D. C., Behrens, J. T., & Mislevy, R. J. (2009). Design Patterns for Learning and Assessment: Facilitating the Introduction of a Complex Simulation-Based Learning Environment into a Community of Instructors. *Journal of Science Education and Technology*, *19*(2), 105–114. doi:10.100710956-009-9192-0

Frezzo, D. C., Behrens, J. T., Mislevy, R. J., West, P., & DiCerbo, K. E. (2009). Psychometric and Evidentiary Approaches to Simulation Assessment in Packet Tracer Software. *2009 Fifth International Conference on Networking and Services*, 555–560. 10.1109/ICNS.2009.89

Fridman, L., Stolerman, A., Acharya, S., Brennan, P., Juola, P., Greenstadt, R., & Kam, M. (2015). Multi-modal decision fusion for continuous authentication. *Computers & Electrical Engineering*, *41*, 142–156. doi:10.1016/j.compeleceng.2014.10.018

Fritz, F., Tilahun, B., & Dugas, M. (2015). Success criteria for electronic medical record implementations in low-resource settings: A systematic review. *Journal of the American Medical Informatics Association: JAMIA*, *22*(2), 479–488. doi:10.1093/jamia/ocu038 PMID:25769683

Fugazza, C., Pepe, M., Oggioni, A., Tagliolato, P., & Carrara, P. (2016). Streamlining geospatial metadata in the Semantic Web. *IOP Conference Series. Earth and Environmental Science*, *34*(1), 012009. doi:10.1088/1755-1315/34/1/012009

Gao, J., Zhang, C., Wang, K., & Ba, S. (2012). Understanding Online Purchase Decision Making: The Effects of Unconscious Thought, Information Quality, and Information Quantity. *Decision Support Systems*, *53*(4), 772–781. doi:10.1016/j.dss.2012.05.011

Gardiner, T., Tsarkov, D., & Horrocks, I. (2006). In I. Cruz, S. Decker, D. Allemang, C. Preist, D. Schwabe, P. Mika, M. Uschold, & L. M. Aroyo (Eds.), *Framework for an Automated Comparison of Description Logic Reasoners BT - The Semantic Web - ISWC 2006* (pp. 654–667). Springer Berlin Heidelberg.

Gcaza, N., von Solms, R., & Jansen Van Vuuren, J. (2015). An Ontology for a National Cyber-Security Culture Environment. In S. M. Furnell & N. L. Clarke (Eds.), *Human Aspects of Information Security & Assurance (HAISA 2015)* (pp. 1–10). Issue Haisa. https://books.google.co.za/books?id=NQJqCwAAQBAJ&pg=PA1&lpg=PA1&dq=An+Ontology+for+a+National+Cyber-Security+Culture+Environment

Gemma, B. (2020). *Annual Review of Linguistics*. Distributional Semantics and Linguistic Theory. doi:10.1146/annurev-linguistics-011619-030303

George, G., & Lal, A. M. (2019). Review of ontology-based recommender systems in e-learning. *Computers & Education, 142*, 103642. doi:10.1016/j.compedu.2019.103642

Gershenfeld, N., Krikorian, R., & Cohen, D. (2004). The Internet of things. *Scientific American, 291*(4), 76.

Getting, B. (2007). *Basic Definitions: Web 1.0, Web. 2.0, Web 3.0*. http://www.practicalecommerce.com/articles/464-Basic-Definitions-Web-1-0-Web-2-0-Web-3-0

Ghidini, C., & Giunchiglia, F. (2004). *A semantics for abstraction*. Academic Press.

Goede, M. (2011). The wise society: Beyond the knowledge economy. *Foresight, 13*(1), 36–45. doi:10.1108/14636681111109688

Goker, A., & Myrhaug, H. (2008). Evaluation of a mobile information system in context. *Information Processing & Management, 44*(1), 39–65. doi:10.1016/j.ipm.2007.03.011

Golbeck, J. (2006). Combining provenance with trust in social networks for semantic web content filtering. In *International Provenance and Annotation Workshop* (pp. 101-108). Springer. 10.1007/11890850_12

Grau, B. C., Horrocks, I., Kazakov, Y., & Sattler, U. (2008). Modular reuse of ontologies: Theory and practice. *Journal of Artificial Intelligence Research, 31*, 273–318. doi:10.1613/jair.2375

Gretzel, U. (2015). 9 Web 2.0 and 3.0. *Tongxin Jishu, 5*, 181. doi:10.1515/9783110271355-011

Griffiths, M. D., Kuss, D. J., Billieux, J., & Pontes, H. M. (2016). The evolution of Internet addiction: A global perspective. *Addictive Behaviors, 53*, 193–195. doi:10.1016/j.addbeh.2015.11.001 PMID:26562678

Grossfeld, B. (2020). *Deep learning vs machine learning: a simple way to understand the difference*. Retrieved from https://www.zendesk.com/blog/machine-learning-and-deep-learning/

Guarino, N. (1998). Formal Ontology and Information Systems. In N. Guarino (Ed.), *Proceedings of the 1st International Conference on Formal Ontology in Information Systems (FOIS'98)* (pp. 3–15). IOS Press.

Gubbi, J., Buyya, R., Marusic, S., & Palaniswami, M. (2013). Internet of Things (IoT): A Vision, Architectural Elements, and Future Directions. *Future Generation Computer Systems, 29*, 1645–1660.

Gupta, N., & Agrawal, R. (2017). Challenges and Security Issues of Distributed Databases. In *NoSQL* (pp. 265–284). Chapman and Hall/CRC.

Gupta, N., & Agrawal, R. (2020). Application and Techniques of Opinion Mining. In *Hybrid Computational Intelligence*. Elsevier.

Gupta, N., & Verma, S. (2019). Tools of Opinion Mining. In *Extracting Knowledge From Opinion Mining* (pp. 179–203). IGI Global.

Gupta, V. (2017). A Brief History of Blockchain. *Harvard Business Review.*

Gusenbauer, M. (2019). Google Scholar to overshadow them all? Comparing the sizes of 12 academic search engines and bibliographic databases. *Scientometrics, 118*(1), 177–214. doi:10.100711192-018-2958-5

Gutierrez, F., Dou, D., Martini, A., Fickas, S., & Zong, H. (2013). Hybrid Ontology-based Information Extraction for Automated Text Grading. *Proceedings - 12th International Conference on Machine Learning and Applications, ICMLA 2013, 1*, 359–364. 10.1109/ICMLA.2013.73

Gyrard, A., Patel, P., Datta, S. K., & Ali, M. I. (2017). Semantic web meets internet of things and web of things. In *Proceedings of the 26th International Conference on World Wide Web Companion* (pp. 917-920). International World Wide Web Conferences Steering Committee. 10.1145/3041021.3051100

Hai, Z., Chang, K., Kim, J. J., & Yang, C. C. (2013). Identifying features in opinion mining via intrinsic and extrinsic domain relevance. *IEEE Transactions on Knowledge and Data Engineering, 26*(3), 623–634. doi:10.1109/TKDE.2013.26

Hak, F., Oliveira, D., Abreu, N., Leuschner, P., Abelha, A., & Santos, M. (2020). An OpenEHR Adoption in a Portuguese Healthcare Facility. *Procedia Computer Science, 170*, 1047–1052. doi:10.1016/j.procs.2020.03.075

Hamdi, F., Safar, B., Reynaud, C., & Zargayouna, H. (2010). In F. Guillet, G. Ritschard, D. A. Zighed, & H. Briand (Eds.), *Alignment-Based Partitioning of Large-Scale Ontologies BT - Advances in Knowledge Discovery and Management* (pp. 251–269). Springer Berlin Heidelberg. doi:10.1007/978-3-642-00580-0_15

Hammond, W. E., Jaffe, C., & Kush, R. D. (2009). Healthcare standards development. The value of nurturing collaboration. *Journal of American Health Information Management Association, 80*, 44–50. PMID:19663144

Hasan, M. M., Wei, S., & Moharrer, A. (2020). *Latent Factor Analysis of Gaussian Distributions under Graphical Constraints.* arXiv preprint arXiv:2001.02712.

Hausenblas, M. (2009). Exploiting linked data to build web applications. *IEEE Internet Computing, 13*(4), 68–73. doi:10.1109/MIC.2009.79

Hausenblas, M., & Karnstedt, M. (2010). Understanding linked open data as a web-scale database. *Proceedings of the second conference on Advances in Databases Knowledge and Data Applications*, 56-61. 10.1109/DBKDA.2010.23

Heath, T., & Bizer, C. (2011). Linked data: Evolving the web into a global data space. *Synthesis Lectures on the Semantic Web: Theory and Technology, 1*(1), 1-136.

Heer, R. (2009, March). *A Model of Learning Objectives.* https://www.celt.iastate.edu/teaching-resources/effective-practice/revised-blooms-taxonomy/

Hendler, J. (2009). Web 3.0 Emerging. *Computer, 42*(1), 111–113. doi:10.1109/MC.2009.30

Hinton, G. E., & Salakhutdinov, R. R. (2006). Reducing the dimensionality of data with neural networks. *Science, 313*(5786), 504–507. doi:10.1126cience.1127647 PMID:16873662

Hiremath, B. K., & Kenchakkanavar, A. Y. (2016). An alteration of the web 1.0, web 2.0 and web 3.0: A comparative study. *Imperial Journal of Interdisciplinary Research, 2*(4), 705–710.

Hodson, H. (2013). *Bitcoin moves beyond mere money.* https://www.newscientist.com/article/dn24620-bitcoin-moves-beyond-mere-mone

Hoenkamp, E. C. (2015). About the 'compromised information need' and optimal interaction as quality measure for search interfaces. In *Proceedings of the 38th international ACM SIGIR conference on research and development in information retrieval* (pp. 835–838). 10.1145/2766462.2767800

Hoffman, S., & Podgurski, A. (2009). Finding a Cure: The Case for Regulation and Oversight of Electronic Health Record Systems. Case Legal Studies Research Paper No. 08-13. *Harvard Journal of Law & Technology, 22*(1), 2008. https://papers.ssrn.com/sol3/papers.cfm?abstract_id=1122426

Hohpe, G. (2006). 06291 workshop report: Conversation patterns. In *Dagstuhl Seminar Proceedings*. Schloss Dagstuhl-Leibniz-Zentrum für Informatik.

Horak, F., King, L., & Mancini, M. (2015). Role of body-worn movement monitor technology for balance and gait rehabilitation. *Physical Therapy, 95*(3), 461–470. doi:10.2522/ptj.20140253 PMID:25504484

Horrocks, I., Giese, M., Kharlamov, E., & Waaler, A. (2016). Using semantic technology to tame the data variety challenge. *IEEE Internet Computing, 20*(6), 62–66. doi:10.1109/MIC.2016.121

Horsak, B., Dlapka, R., Iber, M., Gorgas, A. M., Kiselka, A., Gradl, C., Siragy, T., & Doppler, J. (2016). SONIGait: A wireless instrumented insole device for real-time sonification of gait. *Journal on Multimodal User Interfaces, 10*(3), 195–206. doi:10.100712193-016-0216-9

Hossain, M. A., Dwivedi, Y. K., & Rana, N. P. (2016). State-of-the-art in open data research: Insights from existing literature and a research agenda. *Journal of Organizational Computing and Electronic Commerce, 26*(1-2), 14–40. doi :10.1080/10919392.2015.1124007

Hurwitz, J., Kaufman, M., Bowles, A., Nugent, A., Kobielus, J. G., & Kowolenko, M. D. (2015). *Cognitive computing and big data analytics*. John Wiley & Sons.

Hu, X., Lee, J. H., Bainbridge, D., Choi, K., Organisciak, P., & Downie, J. S. (2017). The MIREX grand challenge: A framework of holistic user-experience evaluation in music information retrieval. *Journal of the Association for Information Science and Technology, 68*(1), 97–112. doi:10.1002/asi.23618

Hwang, K., & Chen, M. (2017). *Big-data analytics for cloud, IoT, and cognitive computing*. John Wiley & Sons.

Iansiti, M., & Lakhani, K. R. (2017). The Truth About Blockchain. *Harvard Business Review*.

Iqbal, R., Sturm, J., Kulyk, O., Wang, J., & Terken, J. (2005). User-centred design and evaluation of ubiquitous services. In *Proceedings of the 23rd annual international conference on Design of communication: documenting & designing for pervasive information* (pp. 138-145). 10.1145/1085313.1085346

Irani, Z., Sharif, A. M., & Love, P. E. D. (2005). Linking knowledge transformation to information systems evaluation. *European Journal of Information Systems, 14*(3), 213–228. doi:10.1057/palgrave.ejis.3000538

Irtaza, A., Jaffar, M. A., & Muhammad, M. S. (2015). Content-based image retrieval in a web 3.0 environment. *Multimedia Tools and Applications, 74*(14), 5055–5072. doi:10.100711042-013-1679-2

Islam, M. T., Aowal, M. A., Minhaz, A. T., & Ashraf, K. (2017). *Abnormality detection and localization in chest x-rays using deep convolutional neural networks*. arXiv preprint arXiv:1705.09850.

Jackson, W. (2016). HTML5 History: The Past and Future of HTML Markup. In HTML5 Quick Markup Reference (pp. 1-4). Apress.

Jaeschke, P., Oberweis, A., & Stucky, W. (1994). In R. A. Elmasri, V. Kouramajian, & B. Thalheim (Eds.), *Extending ER model clustering by relationship clustering BT - Entity-Relationship Approach — ER '93* (pp. 451–462). Springer Berlin Heidelberg.

Jakl, A., Schoffer, L., Husinsky, M., & Wagner, M. (2018). Agumented Reality for Industry 4.0: Architecture and User Experience. *Proceeding of the 11*th *Forum Media Technology, CER-WS*, 38-42.

Jalota, C., & Agrawal, R. (2019). Ontology-Based Opinion Mining. In *Extracting Knowledge From Opinion Mining* (pp. 84–103). IGI Global.

Jandl, C., Nurgazina, J., Schoffer, L., Reichl, C., Wagner, M., & Moser, T. (2019). SensiTrack – A Privacy by Design Concept for Industrial IoT Applications. *Proceeding of the 24th IEEE International Conference on Emerging Technologies and Factory Automation*, 1782-1789. 10.1109/ETFA.2019.8869186

Janke, K., & Kolar, C. (2014). Recognizing and Disseminating Innovations in Scholarly Teaching and Learning to Support Curricular Change. *Innovations in Pharmacy*, *5*(3), 161. doi:10.24926/iip.v5i3.343

Janowicz, K., & Compton, M. (2010). *The Stimulus-Sensor-Observation Ontology Design Pattern and its Integration into the Semantic Sensor Network Ontology*. SSN.

Janssen, M., Charalabidis, Y., & Zuiderwijk, A. (2012). Benefits, adoption barriers and myths of open data and open government. *Information Systems Management*, *29*(4), 258–268. doi:10.1080/10580530.2012.716740

Jerby, S., & Ceder, A. (2006). Optimal routing design for shuttle bus service. *Transportation Research Record: Journal of the Transportation Research Board*, *1971*(1), 14–22. doi:10.1177/0361198106197100102

Jeschke, S., Brecher, C., Meisen, T., Ozdemir, D., & Eschert, T. (2017). Industrial Internet of Things and Cyber Manufacturing Systems. In Industrial Internet of Things. Springer.

Jiang, G., Evans, J., Endle, C. M., Solbrig, H. R., & Chute, C. G. (2016). Using Semantic Web technologies for the generation of domain-specific templates to support clinical study metadata standards. *Journal of Biomedical Semantics*, *7*(1), 10. doi:10.118613326-016-0053-5 PMID:26949508

Jiang, Y. (2020). Semantically-enhanced information retrieval using multiple knowledge sources. *Cluster Computing*, *23*(4), 1–20. doi:10.100710586-020-03057-7

Johann, V., Konen, T., & Karbach, J. (2019). The unique contribution of working memory, inhibition, cognitive flexibility, and intelligence to reading comprehension and reading speed. *Child Neuropsychology*, *26*(3), 324–344. doi:10.1080/09297049.2019.1649381 PMID:31380706

Johnson, K.E., Kamineni, A., Fuller, S., Olmstead, D., & Wernli, K.J. (2014). How the Provenance of Electronic Health Record Data Matters for Research: A Case Example Using System Mapping. *eGEMs (Generating Evidence & Methods to improve patient outcomes)*, *2*(1).

Johnson, R. B., Onwuegbuzie, A. J., & Turner, L. A. (2007). Toward a Definition of Mixed Methods Research. *Journal of Mixed Methods Research*, *1*(2), 112–133. doi:10.1177/1558689806298224

Joy, M., Griffiths, N., & Boyatt, R. (2005). The boss online submission and assessment system. *Journal of Educational Resources in Computing*, *5*(3), 1–27. doi:10.1145/1163405.1163407

Kahan, J., Koivunen, M. R., Prud'Hommeaux, E., & Swick, R. R. (2002). Annotea: An open RDF infrastructure for shared Web annotations. *Computer Networks*, *39*(5), 589–608. doi:10.1016/S1389-1286(02)00220-7

Kallio, K. P. (2018). Citizen-subject formation as geosocialization: A methodological approach on 'learning to be citizens'. *Geografiska Annaler. Series B, Human Geography*, *100*(2), 81–96. doi:10.1080/04353684.2017.1390776

Kalra, V., & Aggarwal, R. (2017). Importance of Text Data Preprocessing & Implementation in RapidMiner. In *Proceedings of the First International Conference on Information Technology and Knowledge Management–New Dehli, India* (Vol. 14, pp. 71-75). 10.15439/2017KM46

Kalra, V., & Agrawal, R. (2019). Challenges of Text Analytics in Opinion Mining. In *Extracting Knowledge From Opinion Mining* (pp. 268–282). IGI Global.

Kalyanpur, A., Parsia, B., Sirin, E., Grau, B. C., & Hendler, J. (2006). Swoop: A Web Ontology Editing Browser. *Journal of Web Semantics*, *4*(2), 144–153. doi:10.1016/j.websem.2005.10.001

Karakostas, B. (2013). A DNS architecture for the Internet of things: A case study in transport logistics. *Procedia Computer Science*, *19*, 594–601. doi:10.1016/j.procs.2013.06.079

Katasonov, A., Kaykova, O., Khriyenko, O., Nikitin, S., & Terziyan, V. (2008). Smart Semantic Middleware for the Internet of Things. *Proceedings of the 5th International Conference of Informatics in Control, Automation and Robotics*, 11-15.

Kaur, A., & Kumar, M. S. (2018). High Precision Latent Semantic Evaluation for Descriptive Answer Assessment. *Journal of Computational Science*, *14*(10), 1293–1302. doi:10.3844/jcssp.2018.1293.1302

Kaur, K., & Kaur, R. (2016). Internet of things to promote tourism: An insight into smart tourism. *International Journal of Recent Trends in Engineering & Research*, *2*(4), 357–361.

Kaur, S., & Agrawal, R. (2018). A Detailed Analysis of Core NLP for Information Extraction. *International Journal of Machine Learning and Networked Collaborative Engineering*, *1*(01), 33–47. doi:10.30991/IJMLNCE.2017v01i01.005

Keet, C. M. (2005). *Using Abstractions to Facilitate Management of Large ORM Models and Ontologies*. In R. Meersman, Z. Tari, & P. Herrero (Eds.), *On the Move to Meaningful Internet Systems 2005: OTM 2005 Workshops* (pp. 603–612). Springer Berlin Heidelberg. doi:10.1007/11575863_80

Keet, C. M. (2007). *Enhancing Comprehension of Ontologies and Conceptual Models Through Abstractions*. In R. Basili & M. T. Pazienza (Eds.), *AI*IA 2007: Artificial Intelligence and Human-Oriented Computing* (pp. 813–821). Springer Berlin Heidelberg.

Kelly, D. (2009). Methods for evaluating interactive information retrieval systems with users. *Foundations and Trends in Information Retrieval*, *3*(1–2), 1–224. doi:10.1561/1500000012

Keskinock, P., & Tayur, S. (2001). Quantitive analysis of Internet enabled supply chain. *Interface: a Journal for and About Social Movements*, *31*(2), 70–89. doi:10.1287/inte.31.2.70.10626

Khajouei, R., & Farahani, F. (2020). A combination of two methods for evaluating the usability of a hospital information system. *BMC Medical Informatics and Decision Making*, *20*(1), 1–10. doi:10.1186/2911-020-1083-6 PMID:32366248

Khaled, A., Ouchani, S., & Chohra, C. (2019). Recommendations-based on semantic analysis of social networks in learning environments. *Computers in Human Behavior*, *101*, 435–449. doi:10.1016/j.chb.2018.08.051

Khan, Z. C., & Keet, C. M. (2015). An empirically-based framework for ontology modularisation. *Applied Ontology*, *10*(3–4), 171–195. Advance online publication. doi:10.3233/AO-150151

Khan, Z. C., & Keet, C. M. (2016a). ROMULUS: The Repository of Ontologies for MULtiple USes Populated with Mediated Foundational Ontologies. *Journal on Data Semantics*, *5*(1), 19–36. Advance online publication. doi:10.1007/13740-015-0052-1

Khan, Z. C., & Keet, C. M. (2016b). *Dependencies Between Modularity Metrics Towards Improved Modules*. In E. Blomqvist, P. Ciancarini, F. Poggi, & F. Vitali (Eds.), *Knowledge Engineering and Knowledge Management* (pp. 400–415). Springer International Publishing.

Kitchin, R. (2014). *The data revolution: Big data, open data, data infrastructures and their consequences*. Sage.

Kohli, M. D., Summers, R. M., & Geis, J. R. (2017). Medical Image Data and Datasets in the Era of Machine Learning. *Journal of Digital Imaging*, 30(4), 392–399. doi:10.100710278-017-9976-3 PMID:28516233

Kohli, M., Prevedello, L. M., Filice, R. W., & Geis, J. R. (2017). Implementing machine learning in radiology practice and research. *AJR. American Journal of Roentgenology*, 208(4), 754–760. doi:10.2214/AJR.16.17224 PMID:28125274

Kollmann, T., Lomberg, C., & Peschl, A. (2016). Web 1.0, Web 2.0, and Web 3.0: The development of e-business. In *Encyclopedia of e-commerce development, implementation, and management* (pp. 1139–1148). IGI Global. doi:10.4018/978-1-4666-9787-4.ch081

Konys, A. (2018). An Ontology-Based Knowledge Modelling for a Sustainability Assessment Domain. *Sustainability*, 10(2), 300. doi:10.3390u10020300

Koorsse, M., Taljaard, M., & Calitz, A. P. (2016). A Comparison of E-Assessment Assignment Submission Processes in Introductory Computing Courses. In I. C. T. Education (Ed.), *SACLA 2016. Communications in Computer and Information Science* (Vol. 642, pp. 35–42). Springer. doi:10.1007/978-3-319-47680-3_3

Kortuem, G., Kawsar, F., Fitton, D., & Sundramoorthy, V. (2010). Smart objects as building blocks for the Internet of Things. *IEEE Internet Computing*, 14(1), 44–51.

Kothari C. R. (2004). *Research Methodology, Methods and Techniques*. Academic Press.

Krause, J. (2016). HTML: Hypertext Markup Language. In Introducing Web Development (pp. 39-63). Apress.

Krötzsch, M. (2012). OWL 2 Profiles: An Introduction to Lightweight Ontology Languages. In *Reasoning Web. Semantic Technologies for Advanced Query Answering: 8th International Summer School 2012, Vienna, Austria, September 3-8, 2012. Proceedings* (pp. 112–183). Springer Berlin Heidelberg. 10.1007/978-3-642-33158-9_4

Kulmanov, M., Smaili, F. Z., Gao, X., & Hoehndorf, R. (2020). Semantic similarity and machine learning with ontologies. *Briefings in Bioinformatics*, 1–18. doi:10.1093/bib/bbaa199 PMID:33049044

Kumaran, V. S., & Sankar, A. (2015). Towards an automated system for short-answer assessment using ontology mapping. *International Arab Journal of E-Technology, 4*(1), 17–24. https://dblp.org/db/journals/iajet/iajet4.html

Kumaran, V. S., & Sankar, A. (2013). An Automated Assessment of Students' Learning in e-Learning Using Concept Map and Ontology Mapping. In J. Wang & R. Lau (Eds.), Lecture Notes in Computer Science: Vol. 8167. *Advances in Web-Based Learning – ICWL 2013* (pp. 274–283). Springer. doi:10.1007/978-3-642-41175-5_28

Kumari, P., Cooney, N. J., Kim, T. S., & Minhas, A. S. (2018, December). Gait analysis in Spastic Hemiplegia and Diplegia cerebral palsy using a wearable activity tracking device-a data quality analysis for deep convolutional neural networks. In *2018 5th Asia-Pacific World Congress on Computer Science and Engineering (APWC on CSE)* (pp. 1-4). IEEE. 10.1109/APWConCSE46201.2018.8950057

Kumar, M., & Sheshadri, H. S. (2012). On the classification of imbalanced datasets. *International Journal of Computers and Applications*, 44(8), 1–7. doi:10.5120/6280-8449

Kuppelwieser, V. G., & Klaus, P. (2020). Measuring customer experience quality: The EXQ scale revisited. *Journal of Business Research*. Advance online publication. doi:10.1016/j.jbusres.2020.01.042

Lagerspetz, E., Flores, H., Mäkitalo, N., Hui, P., Nurmi, P., Tarkoma, S., Passarella, A., Ott, J., Reichl, P., & Conti, M. (2018). Pervasive Communities in the Internet of People. *Proceedings of the 2018 IEEE International Conference on Pervasive Computing and Communications Workshops*, 40–45.

Lai, J. W. M., & Bower, M. (2019). How is the use of technology in education evaluated? A systematic review. *Computers & Education, 133*, 27–42. doi:10.1016/j.compedu.2019.01.010

Lai, Z., & Deng, H. (2018). Medical Image Classification Based on Deep Features Extracted by Deep Model and Statistic Feature Fusion with Multilayer Perceptron. *Computational Intelligence and Neuroscience, 2018*, 2018. doi:10.1155/2018/2061516 PMID:30298088

Lakhani, P., & Sundaram, B. (2017). Deep learning at chest radiography: Automated classification of pulmonary tuberculosis by using convolutional neural networks. *Radiology, 284*(2), 574–582. doi:10.1148/radiol.2017162326 PMID:28436741

Larsen, K. R., Hovorka, D. S., Dennis, A. R., & West, J. D. (2019). Understanding the Elephant: The Discourse Approach to Boundary Identification and Corpus Construction for Theory Review Articles. *Journal of the Association for Information Systems, 20*(7), 887–927. doi:10.17705/1jais.00556

Larson, R. R. (2010). Introduction to information retrieval. *Journal of the American Society for Information Science and Technology, 61*(4), 852–853.

Lashkari, F., Bagheri, E., & Ghorbani, A. A. (2019). Neural embedding-based indices for semantic search. *Information Processing & Management, 56*(3), 733–755. doi:10.1016/j.ipm.2018.10.015

Lasi, H., Fettke, P., Kemper, H.-G., Feld, T., & Hoffmann, M. (2014). Industry 4.0. *BISE, 6*(4), 239–242.

Lastra, J. L. M., & Delamer, I. M. (2006). Semantic Web Services in Factory Automation: Fundamental Insights and Research Roadmap. *IEEE Transactions on Industrial Informatics, 2*(1), 1–11.

Lawrynowicz, A., & Keet, C. M. (2016). The TDDonto Tool for Test-Driven Development of DL Knowledge bases. *Proceedings of the 29th International Workshop on Description Logics.* http://ceur-ws.org/Vol-1577/paper_15.pdf

LeClair, A., Khédri, R., & Marinache, A. (2019). Toward Measuring Knowledge Loss due to Ontology Modularization. In *Proceedings of the 11th International Joint Conference on Knowledge Discovery, Knowledge Engineering and Knowledge Management, IC3K 2019, Volume 2: KEOD, Vienna, Austria, September 17-19, 2019* (pp. 174–184). 10.5220/0008169301740184

Lee, H. L., & Billington, C. (1992). Managing supply chain inventories: Pitfalls and opportunities. *Sloan Management Review, 33*(3), 65–77.

Lee, J., Kao, H.-A., & Yang, S. (2014). Service Innovation and Smart Analytics for Industry 4.0 and Big Data Environment. *Procedia CIRP, 16*, 3–8. doi:10.1016/j.procir.2014.02.001

Lee, M., Yun, J., Pyka, A., Won, D., Kodama, F., Schiuma, G., Park, H., Jeon, J., Park, K., Jung, K., Yan, M.-R., Lee, S., & Zhao, X. (2018). How to Respond to the Fourth Industrial Revolution, or the Second Information Technology Revolution? Dynamic New Combinations between Technology, Market, and Society through Open Innovation. *Journal of Open Innovation, 4*(3), 21. doi:10.3390/joitmc4030021

Lee, Y. J., & Kim, J. S. (2012). Automatic web api composition for semantic data mashups. *Proceedings of Fourth International Conference on Computational Intelligence and Communication Networks*, 953-957. 10.1109/CICN.2012.56

Lefort, L., Henson, C., Taylor, K., Barnaghi, P., Compton, M., Corcho, O., Garcia-Castro, R., Graybeal, J., Herzog, A., & Janowicz, K. (2005). *Semantic Sensor Network XG Final Report.* W3C Incubator Group Report. http://www.w3.org/2005/Incubator/ssn/XGR-ssn/

Leshcheva, I., Gorovaya, D., & Leshchev, D. (2010). Ontology-based Assessment Technique. In T. Tiropanis, H. Davis, & P. Carmichael (Eds.), *The 2nd International Workshop on Semantic Web Applications in Higher Education (SemHE'10)* (pp. 1–3). https://eprints.soton.ac.uk/271753/

Levac, D., Colquhoun, H., & O'Brien, K. K. (2010). Scoping studies: Advancing the methodology. *Implementation Science; IS, 5*(1), 69. doi:10.1186/1748-5908-5-69 PMID:20854677

Lewis David (1970). *General Semantics*. doi:10.1016/B978-0-12-545850-4.50007-8

Liaw, S., Taggart, J., Dennis, S., & Yeo, A. (2011). Data quality and fitness for purpose of routinely collected data – a general practice case study from an electronic Practice-Based Research Network (ePBRN). In *AMIA 2011 Annual Symposium Improving Health: Informatics and IT Changing the World*. Washington, DC: AMIA.

Li, C., & Xu, P. (2020). Application on traffic flow prediction of machine learning in intelligent transportation. *Neural Computing & Applications*, 1–12. doi:10.100700521-018-3699-3 PMID:32292246

Li, D. X., Wu, H., & Shancang, L. (2014). Internet of Things in Industries: A Survey. *IEEE Transactions on Industrial Informatics, 10*(4), 2233–2243.

Li, L., & Horrocks, I. (2004). A software framework for matchmaking based on semantic web technology. *International Journal of Electronic Commerce, 8*(4), 39–60. doi:10.1080/10864415.2004.11044307

Lilleberg, J., Zhu, Y., & Zhang, Y. (2015). Support vector machines and word2vec for text classification with semantic features. In *2015 IEEE 14th International Conference on Cognitive Informatics & Cognitive Computing (ICCI* CC)* (pp. 136-140). IEEE. 10.1109/ICCI-CC.2015.7259377

Lisowski, E. (2020), *Machine Learning Techniques and Methods*. Retrieved from https://addepto.com/machine-learning-techniques-and-methods/

Litherland, K., Carmichael, P., & Martínez-García, A. (2013). Ontology-based e-Assessment for Accounting Education. *Accounting Education, 22*(5), 498–501. doi:10.1080/09639284.2013.824198

Liu, B. (2006). Mining comparative sentences and relations. In AAAI (Vol. 22). Academic Press.

Liu, J., Liu, C., & Belkin, N. J. (2020). Personalization in text information retrieval: A survey. *Journal of the Association for Information Science and Technology, 71*(3), 349–369. doi:10.1002/asi.24234

Liu, X., & Sun, Y. (2011). Information flow management of Vendor-Managed Inventory system in automobile parts inbound logistics based on Internet of Things. *Journal of Software, 6*(7), 1374–1380.

Liu, Y., Jia, G., Tao, X., Xu, X., & Dou, W. (2014). A stop planning method over big traffic data for airport shuttle bus. *2014 IEEE Fourth International Conference on Big Data and Cloud Computing*, 63-70. 10.1109/BDCloud.2014.21

Lobo, J. M., Denton, B. T., Wilson, J. R., Shah, N. D., & Smith, S. A. (2017). Using claims data linked with electronic health records to monitor and improve adherence to medication. *IISE Transactions on Healthcare Systems Engineering, 7*(4), 194–214. doi:10.1080/24725579.2017.1346728

Lobov, A., Lopez, F. U., Herrera, V. V., Puttonen, J., & Lastra, J. L. M. (2008). Semantic Web Services framework for manufacturing industries. In *Int. Conf. on Rob. and Biomim.*, (pp. 2104–2108). IEEE.

Lopes, C. T. (2009). Context features and their use in information retrieval. In *Proceedings of the Third BCS-IRSG Symposium on Future Directions in Information Access* (pp. 36-42). 10.14236/ewic/FDIA2009.7

Lopes, U. K., & Valiati, J. F. (2017). Pre-trained convolutional neural networks as feature extractors for tuberculosis detection. *Computers in Biology and Medicine, 89*, 135–143. doi:10.1016/j.compbiomed.2017.08.001 PMID:28800442

Lowrey, W., & Kim, K. S. (2009). Online news media and advanced learning: A test of cognitive flexibility theory. *Journal of Broadcasting & Electronic Media, 53*(4), 547–566. doi:10.1080/08838150903323388

Lozano, M. G., Brynielsson, J., Franke, U., Rosell, M., Tjörnhammar, E., Varga, S., & Vlassov, V. (2020). Veracity assessment of online data. *Decision Support Systems, 129*, 113132. doi:10.1016/j.dss.2019.113132

Lynch, M. P. (2016). *The Internet of Us: Knowing more and understanding less in the age of big data*. WW Norton & Company.

Maass, W., Filler, A. (2006). Towards an infrastructure for semantically annotated physical products. In *INFORMATIK 2006–Informatik für Menschen–Band 2, Beiträge der 36*. Jahrestagung der Gesellschaft für Informatik eV (GI).

Mahdisoltani, F., Biega, J., & Suchanek, F. M. (2013, January). *Yago3: A knowledge base from multilingual Wikipedias*. Academic Press.

Mahmood, K., Rahmah, M., Ahmed, M. M., & Raza, M. A. (2020). Semantic Information Retrieval Systems Costing in Big Data Environment. In *Int'l Conference on Soft Computing and Data Mining* (pp. 192-201). Springer. 10.1007/978-3-030-36056-6_19

Makasiranondh, W., Maj, S. P., & Veal, D. (2010). Pedagogical evaluation of simulation tools usage in Network Technology Education. *World Transactions on Engineering and Technology Education (WTE&TE), 8*(3), 321–326. http://www.wiete.com.au/journals/WTE%26TE/Pages/Vol.8, No.3%282010%29/13-12-Makasiranondh.pdf

Makris, C., & Simos, M. A. (2020). OTNEL: A Distributed Online Deep Learning Semantic Annotation Methodology. *Big Data and Cognitive Computing, 4*(4), 31. doi:10.3390/bdcc4040031

Malik, N., & Malik, S. K. (2020). Using IoT and Semantic Web Technologies for Healthcare and Medical Sector. In V. Jain, R. Wason, J. M. Chatterjee, & D.-N. Le (Eds.), *Ontology-Based Information Retrieval for Healthcare Systems* (pp. 91–116). Wiley & Scrivener Publishing LLC. doi:10.1002/9781119641391.ch5

Mani, I. (1998). *A Theory of Granularity and its Application to Problems of Polysemy and Underspecification of Meaning*. Academic Press.

MapBox. (2020). https://www.mapbox.com/

Marchand, M., & Raymond, L. (2015). Characterizing the IT Artefact through Plato's Ontology: Performance Measurement Systems in the Web 3.0 Era. In Artificial Intelligence Technologies and the Evolution of Web 3.0 (pp. 325-350). IGI Global.

Marques, R. A. M., Pereira, R. B. D., Peruchi, R. S., Brandão, L. C., Ferreira, J. R., & Davim, J. P. (2020). Multivariate GR&R through factor analysis. *Measurement, 151*, 107107. doi:10.1016/j.measurement.2019.107107

Marrella, A. (2018). *Automated Planning for Business Process Management*. Academic Press.

Martinez-Costa, C., Legaz-García, M. C., Schulz, S., & Fernández-Breis, J. T. (2014, June). Ontology-based infrastructure for a meaningful EHR representation and use. In *IEEE-EMBS International Conference on Biomedical and Health Informatics (BHI)* (pp. 535-538). IEEE. 10.1109/BHI.2014.6864420

Marzano, A., & Notti, A. M. (2015). Eduonto: An ontology for Educational Assessment. *Journal of E-Learning and Knowledge Society, 11*(1), 69–82. doi:10.20368/1971-8829/978

Masse, M. (2011). *REST API Design Rulebook: Designing Consistent RESTful Web Service Interfaces*. O'Reilly Media, Inc.

Ma, Z., & Yan, L. (2016). A review of RDF storage in NoSQL databases. In *Managing Big Data in Cloud Computing Environments* (pp. 210–229). IGI Global. doi:10.4018/978-1-4666-9834-5.ch009

Mazurowski, M. A., Buda, M., Saha, A., & Bashir, M. R. (2019). Deep learning in radiology: An overview of the concepts and a survey of the state of the art with focus on MRI. *Journal of Magnetic Resonance Imaging, 49*(4), 939–954. doi:10.1002/jmri.26534 PMID:30575178

McDaniel, H. M. (2017). An Automated System for the Assessment and Ranking of Domain Ontologies [Georgia State University]. *Computer Science Dissertations.* https://scholarworks.gsu.edu/cs_diss/133

Mead, C. N. (2006). Data interchange standards in healthcare IT–computable semantic interoperability: Now possible but still difficult, do we really need a better mousetrap? *Journal of Healthcare Information Management, 20,* 71–78. PMID:16429961

Medhat, W., Hassan, A., & Korashy, H. (2014). Sentiment analysis algorithms and applications: A survey. *Ain Shams Engineering Journal, 5*(4), 1093–1113.

Metz, C. (2007). Web 3.0. *Pc Magazine, 26*(7/8), 74–79.

Michel, F., Faron-Zucker, C., Corby, O., & Gandon, F. (2019). Enabling Automatic Discovery and Querying of Web APIs at Web Scale using Linked Data Standards. *Proceedings of the 2019 World Wide Web Conference,* 883-892. 10.1145/3308560.3317073

Micheli, P., & Mari, L. (2014). The theory and practice of performance measurement. *Mgt Acct Res., 25*(2), 147-156.

Mikroyannidi, E., Rector, A., & Stevens, R. (2009). Abstracting and generalising the foundational model anatomy (fma) ontology. *Proceedings of the Bio-Ontologies 2009 Conference.*

Mikroyannidis, A., Gómez-Goiri, A., Smith, A., & Domingue, J. (2017). Online Experimentation and Interactive Learning Resources for Teaching Network Engineering. *The IEEE Global Engineering Education Conference (EDUCON) 2017,* 181–188. 10.1109/EDUCON.2017.7942845

Mikroyannidis, A., Gómez-Goiri, A., Smith, A., & Domingue, J. (2018). PT Anywhere: A mobile environment for practical learning of network engineering. *Interactive Learning Environments,* 1–15. doi:10.1080/10494820.2018.1541911

Mimno, D., Wallach, H., Talley, E., Leenders, M., & McCallum, A. (2011). Optimizing semantic coherence in topic models. In *Proceedings of the 2011 Conference on Empirical Methods in Natural Language Processing* (pp. 262-272). Academic Press.

Mingers, J. (2001). Combining IS Research Methods: Towards a Pluralist Methodology. *Information Systems Research, 12*(3), 240–259. doi:10.1287/isre.12.3.240.9709

Min, L., Tian, Q., Lu, X., & Duan, H. (2018). Modeling EHR with the openEHR approach: An exploratory study in China. *BMC Medical Informatics and Decision Making, 18*(1), 75. doi:10.118612911-018-0650-6 PMID:30157838

Minor, M., Montani, S., & Recio-García, J. A. (2014). Process-oriented Case-based Reasoning. *Information Systems, 40,* 103–105. doi:10.1016/j.is.2013.06.004

Miorandi, D., Sicari, S., De Pellegrini, F., & Chlamtac, I. (2012). Internet of things: Vision, applications, and research challenges. *Ad Hoc Networks, 10,* 1497–1516.

Miranda Carpintero, J., Mäkitalo, N., Garcia-Alonso, J., Berrocal, J., Mikkonen, T., Canal, C., & Murillo, J. (2015). From the Internet of Things to the Internet of People. *IEEE Internet Computing, 19,* 40–47.

Mitra, B., & Craswell, N. (2018). An introduction to neural information retrieval. *Foundations and Trends in Information Retrieval, 13*(1), 1–126. doi:10.1561/1500000061

Monostori, L. (2014). Cyber-physical Production Systems: Roots, Expectations and R&D Challenges. *Procedia CIRP*, *17*, 9–13. doi:10.1016/j.procir.2014.03.115

Monteiro, A. C. B., Iano, Y., França, R. P., & Razmjooy, N. (2019). WT-MO Algorithm: Automated Hematological Software Based on the Watershed Transform for Blood Cell Count. In Applications of Image Processing and Soft Computing Systems in Agriculture (pp. 39-79). IGI Global.

Montenegro, G., Kushalnagar, N., Hui, J., & Culler, D. (2007). Transmission of IPv6 packets over IEEE 802.15.4 networks. Internet proposed standard RFC, vol. 4944.

Morley, K. I., Wallace, J., Denaxas, S. C., Hunter, R. J., Patel, R. S., Perel, P., Shah, A. D., Timmis, A. D., Schilling, R. J., & Hemingway, H. (2014). Defining disease phenotypes using national linked electronic health records: A case study of atrial fibrillation. *PLoS One*, *9*(11), e110900. doi:10.1371/journal.pone.0110900 PMID:25369203

Moser, T., & Biffl, S. (2011). Semantic integration of software and systems engineering environments. *IEEE Transactions on Systems, Man and Cybernetics. Part C, Applications and Reviews*, *42*(1), 38–50. doi:10.1109/TSMCC.2011.2136377

Mossakowski, T., Codescu, M., Neuhaus, F., & Kutz, O. (2015). *The Distributed Ontology, Modeling and Specification Language – DOL*. In A. Koslow & A. Buchsbaum (Eds.), *The Road to Universal Logic: Festschrift for the 50th Birthday of Jean-Yves Béziau* (Vol. 2, pp. 489–520). Springer International Publishing. doi:10.1007/978-3-319-15368-1_21

Mossberger, K., Tolbert, C. J., & McNeal, R. S. (2007). *Digital citizenship: The Internet, society, and participation*. MIT Press. doi:10.7551/mitpress/7428.001.0001

Moss, N., & Smith, A. (2010). Large Scale Delivery of Cisco Networking Academy Program by Blended Distance Learning. *2010 Sixth International Conference on Networking and Services*, 329–334. 10.1109/ICNS.2010.52

Muley, A., & Tangawade, A. (2019). Assessment of cosmetic product awareness among female students using data mining technique. *Computational Intelligence in Data Mining*, 289–298. DOI: . doi:10.1007/978-981-13-8676-3_26

Müller, G. (2018). *Workflow Modeling Assistance by Casebased Reasoning*. Springer Fachmedien.

Murugesan, S. (Ed.). (2009). *Handbook of Research on Web 2.0, 3.0, and X. 0: Technologies, Business, and Social Applications: Technologies, Business, and Social Applications*. IGI Global.

Musen, M. A. (2015). The protégé project: A look back and a look forward. *AI Matters*, *1*(4), 4–12. doi:10.1145/2757001.2757003 PMID:27239556

Nakamoto, S. (2009). *Bitcoin: A Peer-to-Peer Electronic Cash System*, https://bitcoin.org/bitcoin.pdf

Nasution, M. K., Noah, S. A. M., & Saad, S. (2016). *Social network extraction: Superficial method and information retrieval*. arXiv preprint arXiv:1601.02904.

Nations, D. (2017). *What Is Web 3.0 and Is It Here Yet?* https://www.lifewire.com/what-is-web-3-0-3486623

Nayak, R., Senellart, P., Suchanek, F. M., & Varde, A. S. (2013). Discovering interesting information with advances in web technology. *SIGKDD Explorations*, *14*(2), 63–81. doi:10.1145/2481244.2481255

Newby, G. B. (2002). The necessity for information space mapping for information retrieval on the semantic web. *Information Research*, *7*(4). http://InformationR.net/ir/7-4/paper137.html

Newman, D., Bechhofer, S., & De Roure, D. (2009). *myExperiment: An ontology for e-Research*. Academic Press.

Newman, D., Lau, J. H., Grieser, K., & Baldwin, T. (2010). Automatic evaluation of topic coherence. In *Human language technologies: The 2010 annual conference of the North American chapter of the association for computational linguistics* (pp. 100-108). Academic Press.

Newman, R., Chang, V., Walters, R. J., & Wills, G. B. (2016). Web 2.0—The past and the future. *International Journal of Information Management*, *36*(4), 591–598. doi:10.1016/j.ijinfomgt.2016.03.010

Nguyen, X. T., Tran, H. T., Baraki, H., & Geihs, K. (2015). FRASAD: A framework for model-driven IoT application Development. *Internet of Things (WF-IoT), IEEE 2nd World Forum on IoT*, 387-392.

NHS. (2020). *Diagnostic Imaging Dataset*. Retrieved from https://www.england.nhs.uk/statistics/ statistical-work-areas/ diagnostic-imaging-dataset/

Niazi, M., & Hussain, A. (2009). Agent-based tools for modeling and simulation of self-organization in peer-to-peer, ad hoc, and other complex networks. *IEEE Communications Magazine*, *47*(3), 166–173.

Nielsen, L., & Storgaard, H. K. (2014). Personas is applicable: a study on the use of personas in Denmark. In *Proceedings of the SIGCHI Conference on Human Factors in Computing Systems* (pp. 1665-1674). 10.1145/2556288.2557080

Nikolaev, B., Shir, N., & Wiklund, J. (2020). Dispositional positive and negative affect and self-employment transitions: The mediating role of job satisfaction. *Entrepreneurship Theory and Practice*, *44*(3), 451–474. doi:10.1177/1042258718818357

Noehren, B., Scholz, J., & Davis, I. (2011). The effect of real-time gait retraining on hip kinematics, pain and function in subjects with patellofemoral pain syndrome. *British Journal of Sports Medicine*, *45*(9), 691–696. doi:10.1136/bjsm.2009.069112 PMID:20584755

Noskova, T., Pavlova, T., & Iakovleva, O. (2016). Web 3.0 technologies and transformation of pedagogical activities. In Mobile Computing and Wireless Networks: Concepts, Methodologies, Tools, and Applications (pp. 728-748). IGI Global.

Noy, N. F., & McGuinness, D. L. (2001). *Ontology Development 101: A Guide to Creating Your First Ontology* (Stanford Knowledge Systems Laboratory Technical Report KSL-01-05 and Stanford Medical Informatics Technical Report SMI-2001-0880). http://www.ksl.stanford.edu/people/dlm/papers/ontology-tutorial-noy-mcguinness-abstract.html

Noy, N. F., & Musen, M. A. (2009). Traversing Ontologies to Extract Views. In *Modular Ontologies: Concepts, Theories and Techniques for Knowledge Modularization* (pp. 245–260). Springer Berlin Heidelberg. doi:10.1007/978-3-642-01907-4_11

Noy, N. F. (2004). Semantic integration: A survey of ontology-based approaches. *SIGMOD Record*, *33*(4), 65–70. doi:10.1145/1041410.1041421

Noy, N. F., & Musen, M. A. (2000). {PROMPT}: Algorithm and Tool for Automated Ontology Merging and Alignment. *Seventeenth National Conference on Artificial Intelligence and Twelfth Conference on on Innovative Applications of Artificial Intelligence (AAAI/IAAI)*, 450–455.

Noy, N. F., & Musen, M. A. (2004). Specifying Ontology Views by Traversal. In *The Semantic Web - ISWC 2004: Third International Semantic Web Conference, Hiroshima, Japan*, November 7-11, 2004. *Proceedings* (pp. 713–725). 10.1007/978-3-540-30475-3_49

Nuno, L., Seyma, N. S., & Jorge, B. (2015). A Survey on Data Quality: *Classifying Poor Data. Conference Paper.* 10.1109/PRDC.2015.41

O'Brien, H. L., Kampen, A., Cole, A. W., & Brennan, K. (2020). The role of domain knowledge in search as learning. In *Proceedings of the 2020 Conference on Human Information Interaction and Retrieval* (pp. 313-317). 10.1145/3343413.3377989

O'Mahony, N., Campbell, S., Carvalho, A., Harapanahalli, S., Hernandez, G. V., Krpalkova, L., ... Walsh, J. (2019l). Deep learning vs. traditional computer vision. In *Science and Information Conference* (pp. 128-144). Springer.

O'Reilly, T. (2006). *Web 2.0 Compact Definition: Trying Again.* http://radar.oreilly.com/2006/12/web-20-compact-definition-tryi.html

Ocker, F., Kovalenko, I., Barton, K., Tilbury, D., & VogelHeuser, B. (2019). A Framework for Automatic Initialization of Multi-Agent Production Systems Using Semantic Web Technologies. IEEE Robotics and Automation Letters, 4(4), 4330–4337.

Olawande, D., & Segun, F. (2009). Developing Ontology Support for Human Malaria Control Initiatives. *Nature Precedings*, 1–1. doi:10.1038/npre.2009.3591.1

Oldenziel, R. (2006). Introduction: Signifying semantics for a history of technology. *Technology and Culture, 47*(3), 477–485. doi:10.1353/tech.2006.0194

Open Data Portal Council of Madrid. (2020). https://datos.madrid.es/portal/site/egob/

Open Data Portal Madrid Government. (2020). http://gestiona.madrid.org

Open Data Portal Meteorology Service. (2020). http://www.aemet.es/es/datos_abiertos

Open Data Portal of EMT. (2020). https://opendata.emtmadrid.es/Home

Orłowski, C., Ziółkowski, A., & Czarnecki, A. (2010). Validation of an Agent and Ontology-Based Information Technology Assessment System. *Cybernetics and Systems, 41*(1), 62–74. doi:10.1080/01969720903408805

Ouf, S., Ellatif, M. A., Salama, S. E., & Helmy, Y. (2018). A proposed paradigm for smart learning environment based on semantic web. *Computers in Human Behavior, 72*, 796–818. doi:10.1016/j.chb.2016.08.030

Oviatt, S., & Soulier, L. (2020). *Conversational search for learning technologies. Dagstuhl Report on Conversational Search.* arXiv:2001.02912v1.

Pal, K. (2018). A Big Data Framework for Decision Making in Supply Chain. IGI Global.

Pal, K. (2020). Information Sharing for Manufacturing Supply Chain Management Based on Blockchain Technology. In Cross-Industry Use of Blockchain Technology and Opportunities for the Future. IGI Global.

Pal, K. (2020). Information Sharing for Manufacturing Supply Chain Management Based on Blockchain Technology. In Cross-Industry Use of Blockchain Technology and Opportunities for the Future. IGI Global. doi:10.4018/978-1-7998-3632-2.ch001

Pal, K., & Ul-Haque, A. (2000). Internet of Things and Blockchain Technology in Apparel Manufacturing Supply Chain Data Management. *Procedia Computer Science*, 450-457.

Pal, K. (2017). Supply Chain Coordination Based on Web Services. In H. K. Chan, N. Subramanian, & M. D. Abdulrahman (Eds.), *Supply Chain Management in the Big Data Era* (pp. 137–171). IGI Global Publication.

Pal, K. (2019). Algorithmic Solutions for RFID Tag Anti-Collision Problem in Supply Chain Management. *Procedia Computer Science, 151*, 929–934.

Pan, J., & Jain, R. (2008). *A survey of network simulation tools: Current status and future developments.* https://scholar.google.co.za/scholar?oi=bibs&cluster=6577555124204483644&btnI=1&hl=en

Pandurang Nayak, P., & Levy, Y., A. (1995). A Semantic Theory of Abstractions. *Proceedings of IJCAI-95.*

Paneva-Marinova, D., Pavlova-Draganova, L., Draganov, L., & Georgiev, V. (2012). Ontological presentation of analysis method for technology-enhanced learning. *Proceedings of the 13th International Conference on Computer Systems and Technologies - CompSysTech '12*, 384. 10.1145/2383276.2383332

Pang, B., & Lee, L. (2008). Opinion mining and sentiment analysis. *Foundations and Trends in Information Retrieval, 2*(1–2), 1–135. doi:10.1561/1500000011

Pan, J. Z., Staab, S., Aßmann, U., Ebert, J., & Zhao, Y. (Eds.). (2013). *Ontology-Driven Software Development.* Springer Berlin Heidelberg., doi:10.1007/978-3-642-31226-7

Paulheim, H. (2011). Ontologies in User Interface Development. In *Ontology-based Application Integration* (pp. 61–75). Springer. doi:10.1007/978-1-4614-1430-8_4

Pauwels, P., McGlinn, K., Törmä, S., & Beetz, J. (2018). Linked Data. Building Information Modeling, 181-197.

Perera, C., Zaslavsky, A., Christen, P., & Georgakopoulos, D. (2014). Context Aware Computing for The Internet of Things: A Survey. *IEEE Communications Surveys and Tutorials, 16*, 414–454.

Perera, C., Zaslavsky, A., Christen, P., & Georgakopoulos, D. CA4IOT: Context Awareness for Internet of Things. In *Proceedings of the 2012 IEEE International Conference on Green Computing and Communications.* Besancon, France: IEEE Computer Society.

Person, P., & Angelsmark, O. (2015). Calvin-Merging Cloud and IoT. *Procedia Computer Science, 52*, 210–217.

Phillips, W., & Fleming, D. (2009, September-October). Ethical Concerns in the Use of Electronic Medical Records. *Missouri Medicine, 106*(5), 328–333. PMID:19902711

Pilkington, M. (2016). 11 Blockchain technology: principles and applications. *Research handbook on digital transformations*, 225.

Pirolli, P. (2007). *Information foraging theory: Adaptive interaction with information.* Oxford University Press. doi:10.1093/acprof:oso/9780195173321.001.0001

Pirolli, P., & Card, S. (1999). Information foraging. *Psychological Review, 106*(4), 643–675. doi:10.1037/0033-295X.106.4.643

Poria, S., Gelbukh, A., Hussain, A., Howard, N., Das, D., & Bandyopadhyay, S. (2013). Enhanced SenticNet with affective labels for concept-based opinion mining. *IEEE Intelligent Systems, 28*(2), 31–38.

Prabhu, D. (2017). *Application of web 2.0 and web 3.0: an overview.* LAP LAMBERT Academic Publishing.

Prableen, B. (2016). *Bitcoin Vs Ethereum: Driven by Different Purposes.* https://www.investopedia.com/articles/investing/031416/bitcoin-vs-ethereum-driven-different-purposes.asp

Pradhan, A. M., & Varde, A. S. (2016, October). Ontology-based meta knowledge extraction with semantic web tools for ubiquitous computing. In *2016 IEEE 7th Annual Ubiquitous Computing, Electronics & Mobile Communication Conference (UEMCON)* (pp. 1-6). IEEE.

Privacy Subcommittee. (2017). *Blockchain Technology and Privacy.* https://www.americanbar.org/content/dam/aba/events/business_law/2017/04/spring/materials/blockchain-tech-201704.authcheckdam.pdf

Puttonen, J., Lobov, A., & Lastra, J. L. M. (2013). Semantics-Based Composition of Factory Automation Processes Encapsulated by Web Services. *IEEE TII, 9*(4), 2349–2359. doi:10.1109/TII.2012.2220554

Puttonen, J., Lobov, A., Soto, M. A. C., & Lastra, J. L. M. (2010). A Semantic Web Services-based approach for production systems control. *Advanced Engineering Informatics*, *24*(3), 285–299. doi:10.1016/j.aei.2010.05.012

Quilitz, B., & Leser, U. (2008). Querying distributed RDF data sources with SPARQL. *Proceedings of European Semantic Web Conference*, 524-538 10.1007/978-3-540-68234-9_39

Ragnedda, M., & Destefanis, G. (Eds.). (2019). *Blockchain and Web 3.0: Social, Economic, and Technological Challenges*. Routledge. doi:10.4324/9780429029530

Rajpurkar, P., Irvin, J., Ball, R. L., Zhu, K., Yang, B., Mehta, H., ... Patel, B. N. (2018). Deep learning for chest radiograph diagnosis: A retrospective comparison of the CheXNeXt algorithm to practicing radiologists. *PLoS Medicine*, *15*(11), e1002686. doi:10.1371/journal.pmed.1002686 PMID:30457988

Razzak, M. I., Naz, S., & Zaib, A. (2018). Deep learning for medical image processing: Overview, challenges and the future. In *Classification in BioApps* (pp. 323–350). Springer. doi:10.1007/978-3-319-65981-7_12

Redd, C. B., & Bamberg, S. J. M. (2012). A wireless sensory feedback device for real-time gait feedback and training. *IEEE/ASME Transactions on Mechatronics*, *17*(3), 425–433. doi:10.1109/TMECH.2012.2189014

Reis, R. L. D. P. (2016). *O jornalismo em Portugal e os desafios da Web 3.0* (Doctoral dissertation).

Rhayem, A., Mhiri, M. B. A., & Gargouri, F. (2020). Semantic Web Technologies for the Internet of Things: Systematic Literature Review. *Internet of Things,* 1 - 22.

Richey, R. C., & Klein, J. D. (2014). Design and development research. In J. M. Spector, M. D. Merrill, J. Elen, & M. J. Bishop (Eds.), *Handbook of Research on Educational Communications and Technology* (4th ed., pp. 141–150). Springer. doi:10.1007/978-1-4614-3185-5_12

Rico, M., Vila-Suero, D., Botezan, I., & Gómez-Pérez, A. (2019). Evaluating the impact of semantic technologies on bibliographic systems: A user-centred and comparative approach. *Journal of Web Semantics*, *59*, 100500. doi:10.1016/j.websem.2019.03.001

Rieger, O.Y. (2010). Framing digital humanities: The role of new media in humanities scholarship. *First Monday, 15*(10-4), 1-21. Available at: http://firstmonday.org/ojs/ index.php/fm/article/ view/3198/2628

Rinaldi, A. M., & Russo, C. (2018). User-centered information retrieval using semantic multimedia big data. In *2018 IEEE International Conference on Big Data (Big Data)* (pp. 2304-2313). IEEE. 10.1109/BigData.2018.8622613

Ristoski, P., & Paulheim, H. (2016). Semantic Web in data mining and knowledge discovery: A comprehensive survey. *Journal of Web Semantics*, *36*, 1–22. doi:10.1016/j.websem.2016.01.001

Rodger, M. W., Young, W. R., & Craig, C. M. (2013). Synthesis of walking sounds for alleviating gait disturbances in Parkinson's disease. *IEEE Transactions on Neural Systems and Rehabilitation Engineering*, *22*(3), 543–548. doi:10.1109/TNSRE.2013.2285410 PMID:24235275

Rodriguez-Mier, P., Pedrinaci, C., Lama, M., & Mucientes, M. (2016). An integrated semantic web service discovery and composition framework. *IEEE Transactions on Services Computing*, *9*(4), 537–550. doi:10.1109/TSC.2015.2402679

Romero, L., Gutierrez, M., & Caliusco, L. (2014). Towards Semantically Enriched E-learning Assessment: Ontology-Based Description of Learning Objects. *2014 IEEE 14th International Conference on Advanced Learning Technologies*, 336–338. 10.1109/ICALT.2014.236

Romero, L., Gutiérrez, M., & Caliusco, M. L. (2012). Conceptualizing the e-Learning Assessment Domain using an Ontology Network. *International Journal of Interactive Multimedia and Artificial Intelligence, 1*(6), 20–28. doi:10.9781/ijimai.2012.163

Romero, L., North, M., Gutiérrez, M., & Caliusco, L. (2015). Pedagogically-Driven Ontology Network for Conceptualizing the e-Learning Assessment Domain. *Journal of Educational Technology & Society, 18*(4), 312–330. doi:10.2307/jeductechsoci.18.4.312

Rosse, C., & Mejino, J. L. V. Jr. (2003). A reference ontology for biomedical informatics: The Foundational Model of Anatomy. *Journal of Biomedical Informatics, 36*(6), 478–500. doi:10.1016/j.jbi.2003.11.007 PMID:14759820

Rudman, R., & Bruwer, R. (2016). Defining Web 3.0: Opportunities and challenges. *The Electronic Library, 34*(1), 132–154. doi:10.1108/EL-08-2014-0140

Ruixiang, O., Yao, H., Feng, P., & Hui, P. (2019). Research on information retrieval model under scarcity theory and user cognition. *Computers & Electrical Engineering, 76*, 353–363. doi:10.1016/j.compeleceng.2019.04.008

Russell, M. A. (2013). *Mining the Social Web: Data Mining Facebook, Twitter, LinkedIn, Google+, GitHub, and More.* O'Reilly Media, Inc.

Russomanno, D. J., Kothari, C. R., & Thomas, O. A. (2005). Building a Sensor Ontology: A Practical Approach Leveraging ISO and OGC Models. *2005 International Conference on Artificial Intelligence*, 637-643.

Russo, V. (2017). Urban media activism in web 3.0. Case analysis: the city of Chieti. In *Recent Trends in Social Systems: Quantitative Theories and Quantitative Models* (pp. 303–313). Springer. doi:10.1007/978-3-319-40585-8_27

Rust, C. (2011). The Unscholarly Use of Numbers in Our Assessment Practices: What Will Make Us Change? *International Journal for the Scholarship of Teaching and Learning, 5*(1), 1–6. doi:10.20429/ijsotl.2011.050104

Ruta, M., Colucci, S., Scioscia, F., Di Sciascio, E., & Donini, F. M. (2011). Finding commonalities in RFID semantic streams. *Procedia Computer Science, 5*, 857–864. doi:10.1016/j.procs.2011.07.118

Ryan, R. M., Mims, V., & Koestner, R. (1983). Relation of reward contingency and interpersonal context to intrinsic motivation: A review and test using cognitive evaluation theory. *Journal of Personality and Social Psychology, 45*(4), 736–750. doi:10.1037/0022-3514.45.4.736

Sa De Souza, L. M., Spiess, P., Guinard, D., Kohler, M., Karnouskos, S., & Savio, D. (2008). SOCRADES: A Web Service Based Shop Floor Integration Infrastructure, The Internet of Things. Lecture Notes in Computer Science, 50-67.

Saboor, A., Kask, T., Kuusik, A., Alam, M. M., Le Moullec, Y., Niazi, I. K., Zoha, A., & Ahmad, R. (2020). Latest Research Trends in Gait Analysis Using Wearable Sensors and Machine Learning: A Systematic Review. *IEEE Access: Practical Innovations, Open Solutions, 8*, 167830–167864. doi:10.1109/ACCESS.2020.3022818

Salmeron, L., Kammerer, Y., & Delgado, P. (2018). Non-academic multiple source use on the Internet. In J. L. G. Braasch, I. Braten, & M. T. McCrudden (Eds.), *Handbook of mult-source use* (pp. 285–302). Routledge. doi:10.4324/9781315627496-17

Samek, W., Wiegand, T., & Muller, T. (2017). *Explainable Artificial Intelligence: Understanding, Visualizing And Interpreting Deep Learning Models.* arXiv:1708.08296v1 [cs.AI] 28.

Sarasa-Cabezuelo, A. (2019). Exploitation of Open Data Repositories for the Creation of Value-Added Services. *Proceedings of International Symposium on Distributed Computing and Artificial Intelligence*, 134-141.

Sarasa-Cabezuelo, A., & Fernández-Vindel, J. L. (2019). Merging Open Data Sources to Plan Learning Activities for Online Students. *Proceedings of 23rd International Conference Information Visualisation (IV)*, 306-311. 10.1109/IV.2019.00058

Sarkar, S., Mitsui, M., Liu, J., & Shah, C. (2019). Implicit information need as explicit problems, help, and behavioural signals. *Information Processing & Management*. Advance online publication. doi:10.1016/j.ipm.2019.102069

Sarker, M. K., Krisnadhi, A. A., & Hitzler, P. (2018). OWLAx: A Protege Plugin to Support Ontology Axiomatization through Diagramming. *Proceedings of the ISWC, 2016*, 1690. https://arxiv.org/abs/1808.10105

Satti, F. A., Ali, T., Hussain, J., Khan, W. A., Khattak, A. M., & Lee, S. (2020). Ubiquitous Health Profile (UHPr): A big data curation platform for supporting health data interoperability. *Computing, 102*(11), 2409–2444. doi:10.100700607-020-00837-2

Sauermann, L., Cyganiak, R., & Völkel, M. (2007). *Cool URIs for the semantic web*. Academic Press.

Savolainen, R. (2012). Conceptualizing information need in context. *Information Research, 17*(4), paper 534. Available at http://InformationR.net/ir/17-4/paper534.html

Schaal, M., Smyth, B., Mueller, R. M., & MacLean, R. (2012). Information Quality Dimensions for the Social Web. In *Proceedings of the International Conference on Management of Emergent Digital EcoSystems, ser. MEDES '12*. New York, NY: ACM. 10.1145/2457276.2457287

Schlicht, A., & Stuckenschmidt, H. (2006). Towards Structural Criteria for Ontology Modularization. *Proceedings of the 1st International Workshop on Modular Ontologies, WoMO'06, co-located with the International Semantic Web Conference, ISWC'06*. http://ceur-ws.org/Vol-232/paper7.pdf

Schoefegger, K., Tammet, T., & Granitzer, M. (2013). A survey on socio-semantic information retrieval. *Computer Science Review, 8*, 25–46. doi:10.1016/j.cosrev.2013.03.001

Schulz, S., & Boeker, M. (2013). BioTopLite: An Upper Level Ontology for the Life SciencesEvolution, Design and Application. In *Informatik 2013, 43. Jahrestagung der Gesellschaft für Informatik e.V. (GI), Informatik angepasst an Mensch, Organisation und Umwelt, 16.-20. September 2013*, (pp. 1889–1899). https://dl.gi.de/20.500.12116/20620

SEAIC (Sociedad Española de Alergología e Inmunología Clínica). (2020). https://www.polenes.com/

Seiger, R., Huber, S., & Schlegel, T. (2018). Toward an execution system for self-healing workflows in cyberphysical systems. *Software & Systems Modeling, 17*(2), 551–572. doi:10.100710270-016-0551-z

Sein-Echaluce, M. L., Fidalgo-Blanco, Á., & Esteban-Escaño, J. (2018). Technological ecosystems and ontologies for an educational model based on Web 3.0. *Universal Access in the Information Society, 18*(3), 645–658. doi:10.100710209-019-00684-9

Seltzer, W. (2016). World Wide Web Consortium (W3C) standards for the open web platform. *Open Source, Open Standards, Open Minds Conference Proceedings*.

Selvalakshmi, B., & Subramaniam, M. (2019). Intelligent ontology-based semantic information retrieval using feature selection and classification. *Cluster Computing, 22*(5), 12871–12881. doi:10.100710586-018-1789-8

Seyler, D., Dembelova, T., Del Corro, L., Hoffart, J., & Weikum, G. (2018, July). A study of the importance of external knowledge in the named entity recognition task. In *Proceedings of the 56th Annual Meeting of the Association for Computational Linguistics* (vol. 2, pp. 241-246). 10.18653/v1/P18-2039

Shadbolt, N., Berners-Lee, T., & Hall, W. (2006). The semantic web revisited. *IEEE Intelligent Systems, 21*(3), 96–101. doi:10.1109/MIS.2006.62

Shahzad, S. K. (2011). Ontology-based User Interface Development: User Experience Elements Pattern. *Journal of Universal Computer Science, 17*(7), 1078–1088. doi:10.3217/jucs-017-07-1078

Sha, W. (2017). Examining the construct validities and influence of affective risk in B2C e-commerce. *Issues in Information Systems*, *18*(4), 46–56.

Sheridan, T. B. (2016). Human-robot interaction: Status and challenges. *Human Factors*, *58*(4), 525–532. doi:10.1177/0018720816644364 PMID:27098262

Sheu, P. (2017). Semantic computing and cognitive computing/informatics. In *2017 IEEE 16th International Conference on Cognitive Informatics & Cognitive Computing (ICCI* CC)* (pp. 4-4). IEEE.

Sheu, P. C. Y., Wang, S., Wang, Q., Hao, K., & Paul, R. (2009). Semantic computing, cloud computing, and semantic search engine. In *2009 IEEE International Conference on Semantic Computing* (pp. 654-657). IEEE. 10.1109/ICSC.2009.51

Shi, L., Li, S., Yang, X., Qi, J., Pan, G., & Zhou, B. (2017). Semantic health knowledge graph: Semantic integration of heterogeneous medical knowledge and services. *BioMed Research International*, *2017*, 2017. doi:10.1155/2017/2858423 PMID:28299322

Shimizu, C., Eberhart, A., Karima, N., Hirt, Q., Krisnadhi, A., & Hitzler, P. (2019). A Method for Automatically Generating Schema Diagrams for OWL Ontologies. In B. Villazón-Terrazas & Y. Hidalgo-Delgado (Eds.), *Knowledge Graphs and Semantic Web. KGSWC 2019* (Vol. 1029, pp. 149–161). Springer. doi:10.1007/978-3-030-21395-4_11

Shivalingaiah, D., & Naik, U. (2008). *Comparative study of web 1.0, web 2.0 and web 3.0*. Academic Press.

Shi, W., Connelly, B. L., & Hoskisson, R. E. (2017). External corporate governance and financial fraud: Cognitive evaluation theory insights on agency theory prescriptions. *Strategic Management Journal*, *38*(6), 1268–1286. doi:10.1002mj.2560

Shuen, A. (2018). *Web 2.0: A Strategy Guide: Business thinking and strategies behind successful Web 2.0 implementations*. O'Reilly Media.

Shung, K. K., Smith, M. B., & Tsui, B. M. W. (1992). *Principles of Medical Imaging*. Academic Press.

Shute, V. J., Leighton, J. P., Jang, E. E., & Chu, M.-W. (2016). Advances in the Science of Assessment. *Educational Assessment*, *21*(1), 34–59. doi:10.1080/10627197.2015.1127752

Silva, M. S. (2018). *Fundamentos de HTML5 e CSS3*. Novatec Editora.

Silvello, G., Bordea, G., Ferro, N., Buitelaar, P., & Bogers, T. (2017). Semantic representation and enrichment of information retrieval experimental data. *International Journal on Digital Libraries*, *18*(2), 145–172. doi:10.100700799-016-0172-8

Siow, W. T., Liew, M. F., Shrestha, B. R., Muchtar, F., & See, K. C. (2020). *Managing COVID-19 in resource-limited settings: critical care considerations*. Academic Press.

Solanki, M. R., & Dongaonkar, A. (2016). A Journey of human comfort: Web 1.0 to web 4.0. *International Journal of Research and Scientific Innovation*, *3*(IX), 75–78.

Sołtysik-Piorunkiewicz, A. (2015). The evaluation method of Web 2.0/3.0 usability in e-health knowledge management system. *Online Journal of Applied Knowledge Management, A Publication of the International Institute for Applied Knowledge Management*, *3*(2).

Spiro, R. J., Collins, B. P., Thota, J. J., & Feltovich, P. J. (2003). Cognitive flexibility theory: Hypermedia for complex learning, adaptive knowledge application, and experience acceleration. *Educational Technology*, *43*(5), 5–10.

Steiner, C. M., Albert, D., & Wang, S. (2017). Validating domain ontologies: A methodology exemplified for concept maps. *Cogent Education*, *4*(1), 1263006. Advance online publication. doi:10.1080/2331186X.2016.1263006

Stephen, O., Sain, M., Maduh, U. J., & Jeong, D. U. (2019). An efficient deep learning approach to pneumonia classification in healthcare. *Journal of Healthcare Engineering, 2019*, 2019. doi:10.1155/2019/4180949 PMID:31049186

Steven, V. (2008). *Accessibility and clarity: The most neglected dimensions of quality? Committee for the Coordination of Statistical Activities. Conference on Data Quality for International Organizations*, Rome, Italy.

Stockdale, R., Standing, C., Love, P. E. D., & Irani, Z. (2008). Revisiting the content, context and process of IS evaluation. In Z. Irani & P. Love (Eds.), *Evaluating Information Systems: Public and Private Sector*. Butterworth-Heinemann & Elsevier. doi:10.1016/B978-0-7506-8587-0.50006-8

Stonebraker, M., Bruckner, D., Ilyas, I. F., Beskales, G., Cherniack, M., Zdonik, S. B., . . . Xu, S. (2013, January). Data Curation at Scale: The Data Tamer System. In Cidr (Vol. 2013). Academic Press.

Stuckenschmidt, H., & Schlicht, A. (2009). *Structure-Based Partitioning of Large Ontologies. BT - Modular Ontologies: Concepts*. Theories and Techniques for Knowledge Modularization., doi:10.1007/978-3-642-01907-4_9

Studer, T. (2010). *Privacy Preserving Modules for Ontologies*. In A. Pnueli, I. Virbitskaite, & A. Voronkov (Eds.), *Perspectives of Systems Informatics* (pp. 380–387). Springer Berlin Heidelberg. doi:10.1007/978-3-642-11486-1_32

Sutcliffe, A. (2002). *User-centred requirements engineering*. Springer. doi:10.1007/978-1-4471-0217-5

Swaminathan, J. M. (2000). *Supply chain management*. In *International Encyclopedia of the Social and Behavioural Sciences*. Elsevier Sciences.

Taibouni, N., & Chalal, R. (2019). A toolbox for information system evaluation. In *Proceedings of the 2nd ACM International Conference on Big Data Technologies*, (pp. 283-290). 10.1145/3358528.3358537

Tajbakhsh, N., Shin, J. Y., Gurudu, S. R., Hurst, R. T., Kendall, C. B., Gotway, M. B., & Liang, J. (2016). Convolutional neural networks for medical image analysis: Full training or fine tuning? *IEEE Transactions on Medical Imaging, 35*(5), 1299–1312. doi:10.1109/TMI.2016.2535302 PMID:26978662

Tako, A. A., & Kotiadis, K. (2015). PartiSim: A multi-methodology framework to support facilitated simulation modelling in healthcare. *European Journal of Operational Research, 244*(2), 555–564. doi:10.1016/j.ejor.2015.01.046

Tamine, L., & Daoud, M. (2018). Evaluation in Contextual Information Retrieval: Foundations and Recent Advances within the Challenges of Context Dynamicity and Data Privacy. *ACM Computing Surveys, 51*(4), 1–36. doi:10.1145/3204940

Tang, W., & Su, D. (2013). Locomotion analysis and its applications in neurological disorders detection: State-of-art review. *Network Modeling and Analysis in Health Informatics and Bioinformatics, 2*(1), 1–12. doi:10.100713721-012-0020-8

Taouli, A., Bensaber, D. A., Keskes, N., Bencherif, K., & Badir, H. (2018). Semantic for Big Data Analysis: A survey. In *Proceedings of the 7th Innovation and New Trends in Information Systems conference* (pp. 163 – 177). Academic Press.

Taouli, A., Bensaber, D. A., Keskes, N., Bencherif, K., & Badir, H. (2018). Semantic for Big Data Analysis: A survey. In *Proceedings of the 7th Innovation and New Trends in Information Systems conference, 21-22, December, 2018 in Marrakech Morocco, Algeria* (pp. 163 – 177). Academic Press.

Tawfeq, J. F., & Mohammed, S. M. (2015). Resource Description Framework Schemas for E-Library. *Journal of Madenat Alelem College, 7*(2), 27–35.

Thang, N. X., Zapf, M., & Geihs, K. (2011). Model driven development for data-centric sensor. In Conference on Advances in Mobile Computing and Multimedia. ACM.

Tsai, A. C. R., Wu, C. E., Tsai, R. T. H., & Hsu, J. Y. J. (2013). Building a concept-level sentiment dictionary based on commonsense knowledge. *IEEE Intelligent Systems, 28*(2), 22–30.

Tsarkov, D., & Horrocks, I. (2006). FaCT++ Description Logic Reasoner: System Description. In U. Furbach & N. Shankar (Eds.), Lecture Notes in Computer Science: Vol. 4130. *Automated Reasoning. IJCAR 2006* (pp. 292–297). Springer. doi:10.1007/11814771_26

Tsou, M. H. (2015). Research challenges and opportunities in mapping social media and Big Data. *Cartography and Geographic Information Science, 42*(1), 70–74. doi:10.1080/15230406.2015.1059251

Ugarte, H. E. (2017). *A more pragmatic Web 3.0: Linked Blockchain Data.* https://semanticblocks.files.wordpress.com/2017/03/linked_blockchain_paper3.pdf

Upadhyay, P. (2020). Comparing non-visual and visual information foraging on the web. In Extended abstracts of the 2020 CHI conference on human factors in computing systems extended abstracts (pp. 1-8). doi:10.1145/3334480.3383025

Vandenbussche, P. Y., Atemezing, G. A., Poveda-Villalón, M., & Vatant, B. (2017). Linked Open Vocabularies (LOV): A gateway to reusable semantic vocabularies on the Web. *Semantic Web, 8*(3), 437–452. doi:10.3233/SW-160213

Varde, A., Rundensteiner, E., & Fahrenholz, S. (2010). XML based markup languages for specific domains. In *Web-based Support Systems* (pp. 215–238). Springer. doi:10.1007/978-1-84882-628-1_11

Varelas, G., Voutsakist, E., Raftopoulout, P., Petrakis, E. G. M., & Milios, E. (2005). Semantic Similarity methods in WordNet and their application to information retrieval on the Web. In *Proceedings of the 7th annual ACM international workshop on web information and data management.* Bremen, Germany: ACM. 10.1145/1097047.1097051

Varghese, A., Varde, A. S., Peng, J., & Fitzpatrick, E. (2015). A framework for collocation error correction in web pages and text documents. *SIGKDD Explorations, 17*(1), 14–23. doi:10.1145/2830544.2830548

Vasek, M. (2015). *The age of cryptocurrency.* Academic Press.

Veli, N. S., Dipak, K., Pierre, L., Alan, R., Jean, M. R., Karl, A. S., Gyorgy, S., Bedirhan, U., Martti, V., & Pieter, E. Z. (2009). Semantic Interoperability for Better Health and Safer Healthcare. *Deployment and Research Roadmap for Europe.* doi:10.2759/38514

Verma, A. (2017, January 18). An abstract framework for ontology evaluation. *Proceedings of the 2016 International Conference on Data Science and Engineering, ICDSE 2016.* 10.1109/ICDSE.2016.7823945

Vidal, M. E., Endris, K. M., Jozashoori, S., Karim, F., & Palma, G. (2019). Semantic data integration of big biomedical data for supporting personalised medicine. In Current Trends in Semantic Web Technologies: Theory and Practice (pp. 25-56). Springer.

Vinu, E. V., & Kumar, P. S. (2015). Improving Large-Scale Assessment Tests by Ontology Based Approach. *Proceedings of the Twenty-Eighth International Florida Artificial Intelligence Research Society Conference,* 457–462. https://www.aaai.org/ocs/index.php/FLAIRS/FLAIRS15/paper/view/10359

Vinu, E. V., & Kumar, P. S. (2017). Automated generation of assessment tests from domain ontologies. *Semantic Web, 8*(6), 1023–1047. doi:10.3233/SW-170252

Vogt, L., Baum, R., Köhler, C., Meid, S., Quast, B., & Grobe, P. (2018). Using Semantic Programming for Developing a Web Content Management System for Semantic Phenotype Data. In *International Conference on Data Integration in the Life Sciences* (pp. 200-206). Springer.

von Wendland, M. (2018). *Semantic Blockchain - A Review of Sematic Blockchain and Distributed Ledger Technology Approaches.* DLT. doi:10.13140/RG.2.2.33005.90088

Voorhees, E. M., & Harman, D. K. (2005). TREC: Experiment and evaluation in inform. retrieval. MIT Press.

Vrandečić, D. (2012). Wikidata: A new platform for collaborative data collection. *Proceedings of the 21st International Conference on World Wide Web*, 1063-1064. 10.1145/2187980.2188242

Wang, P., Xu, B., Wu, Y., & Zhou, X. (2015). Link prediction in social networks: The state-of-the-art. *Science China. Information Sciences*, *58*(1), 1–38. doi:10.100711432-014-5237-y

Wang, Y., Zhong, Z., Yang, A., & Jing, N. (2018). Review Rating Prediction on Location-Based Social Networks Using Text, Social Links, and Geolocations. *IEICE Transactions on Information and Systems*, *101*(9), 2298–2306. doi:10.1587/transinf.2017EDP7180

Webb, D. C. (2010). Troubleshooting assessment: An authentic problem solving activity for IT education. *Procedia: Social and Behavioral Sciences*, *9*, 903–907. doi:10.1016/j.sbspro.2010.12.256

Webber, W. E. (2010). *Measurement in Information Retrieval Evaluation* (Unpublished PhD Thesis). University of Melbourne, Australia.

Weyrich, M., & Ebert, C. (2016). Reference Architectures for the Internet of Things. *IEEE Software*, *33*, 112–116.

White, R. W. (2016). *Interactions with search systems*. Cambridge University Press. doi:10.1017/CBO9781139525305

Whittle, M. W. (2014). *Gait analysis: an introduction*. Butterworth-Heinemann.

WHO. (2020). *Coronavirus disease 2019 (COVID-19) situation report*. World Health Organisation. https://www.who.int/emergencies/diseases/novel-coronavirus-2019/situation-reports

Williams, B., Onsman, A., & Brown, T. (2010). Exploratory factor analysis: A five-step guide for novices. *Journal of Emergency Primary Health Care*, *8*(3), 1–13. doi:10.33151/ajp.8.3.93

Williams, M. T. (2014). *Virtual Currencies—Bitcoin Risk. World Bank Conference*, Washington, DC.

Wood, G. (2016). *Polkadot: Vision for a heterogeneous multi-chain framework draft 1*. Available: https://github.com/polkadot-io/polkadotpape/raw/master/PolkaDotPaper

Wood, D., Zaidman, M., Ruth, L., & Hausenblas, M. (2014). *Linked Data*. Manning Publications Co.

Wu, X., Zhu, X., Wu, G. Q., & Ding, W. (2014). Data mining with big data. *Knowl Data Eng. IEEE Trans.*, *26*(1), 97–107.

Xu, J., Yuan, C., Cheng, Y., Zeng, C., & Xu, K. (2018). A classification of polarimetric SAR images based on active deep learning. *Remote Sensing Land Resource*, *30*(01), 72–77.

Xu, X., Jiang, X., Ma, C., Du, P., Li, X., Lv, S., ... Lang, G. (2020). A deep learning system to screen novel coronavirus disease 2019 pneumonia. *Engineering.*, *6*(10), 1122–1129. doi:10.1016/j.eng.2020.04.010 PMID:32837749

Xu, Y., Liu, A., & Huang, L. (2019). Adaptive scale segmentation algorithm for polarimetric SAR image. *Journal of Engineering (Stevenage, England)*, *2019*(19), 6072–6076. doi:10.1049/joe.2019.0408

Xu, Y., Nguyen, H., & Li, Y. (2020). A Semantic Based Approach for Topic Evaluation in Information Filtering. *IEEE Access: Practical Innovations, Open Solutions*, *8*, 66977–66988. doi:10.1109/ACCESS.2020.2985079

Yan, Y., Xu-Cheng, Y., Bo-Wen, Z., Chun, Y., & Hong-Wei, H. (2016). *Semantic indexing with deep learning: a case study*. doi:10.118641044-016-0007-z

Yaqoob, I., Ahmed, E., Hashem, I. A. T., Ahmed, A. I. A., Gani, A., Imran, M., & Guizani, M. (2017). Internet of Things Architecture: Recent Advances, Taxonomy, Requirements, and Open Challenges. *IEEE Wireless Communications*, *24*, 10–16.

Ye, Q., Zhang, Z., & Law, R. (2009). Sentiment classification of online reviews to travel destinations by supervised machine learning approaches. *Expert Systems with Applications*, *36*(3), 6527–6535.

Yim, Y. B., & Ceder, A. (2006). Smart feeder/shuttle bus service: Consumer research and design. *Journal of Public Transportation*, *9*(1), 5. doi:10.5038/2375-0901.9.1.5

Ying, J. (2017). U.S. *Patent Application No. 29/556,275*. Washington, DC: US Patent Office.

Yuan, F. G., Zargar, S. A., Chen, Q., & Wang, S. (2020). Machine learning for structural health monitoring: challenges and opportunities. In *Sensors and Smart Structures Technologies for Civil* (Vol. 11379, p. 1137903). Mechanical, and Aerospace Systems. doi:10.1117/12.2561610

Yue-ting, Z., Fei, W., Chun, C., & Yun-he, P. (2017). *Challenges and opportunities: from big data to knowledge in AI 2.0*. doi:10.1631/FITEE.1601883

Yue, W. S., Chye, K. K., & Hoy, C. W. (2017). Towards smart mobility in urban spaces: Bus tracking and information application. *AIP Conference Proceedings*, *1891*(1), 020145. doi:10.1063/1.5005478

Zafari, F., Gkelias, A., & Leung, K. K. (2019). A survey of indoor localization systems and technologies. *IEEE Communications Surveys and Tutorials*, *21*(3), 2568–2599. doi:10.1109/COMST.2019.2911558

Zan, T., Pacheco, H., Ko, H. S., & Hu, Z. (2017). BiFluX: A Bidirectional Functional Update Language for XML. *Information and Media Technologies*, *12*, 1–23.

Zargaran, E., Schuurman, N., Nicol, A. J., Matzopoulos, R., Cinnamon, J., Taulu, T., Ricker, B., Garbutt Brown, D. R., Navsaria, P., & Hameed, S. M. (2014). The electronic Trauma Health Record: Design and usability of a novel tablet-based tool for trauma care and injury surveillance in low resource settings. *Journal of the American College of Surgeons*, *218*(1), 41–50. doi:10.1016/j.jamcollsurg.2013.10.001 PMID:24355875

Zhang, R., Pakhomov, S., McInnes, B. T., & Melton, G. B. (2011). Evaluating Measures of Redundancy in Clinical Texts. *Proc AMIA*, 1612–1620.

Zhang, W., Doi, K., Giger, M. L., Wu, Y., Nishikawa, R. M., & Schmidt, R. A. (1994). Computerized detection of clustered microcalcifications in digital mammograms using shift-invariant artificial neural network. *Medical Physics*, *21*(4), 517–524. doi:10.1118/1.597177 PMID:8058017

Zhang, X.-D. (2020). Machine Learning. In *A Matrix Algebra Approach to Artificial Intelligence* (pp. 223–440). Springer Nature Singapore Pte Ltd., doi:10.1007/978-981-15-2770-8_6

Zhao, D., & Weng, C. (2011). Combining PubMed knowledge and EHR data to develop a weighted Bayesian network for pancreatic cancer prediction. *Journal of Biomedical Informatics*, *44*(5), 859–868. doi:10.1016/j.jbi.2011.05.004 PMID:21642013

Zhao, Z., Han, S. K., & So, I. M. (2018). Architecture of knowledge graph construction techniques. *International Journal of Pure and Applied Mathematics*, *118*(19), 1869–1883.

Zheng, Z., Xie, S., Dai, H., Chen, X., & Wang, H. (2017). An overview of blockchain technology: Architecture, consensus, and future trends. In *2017 IEEE International Congress on Big Data (BigData Congress)* (pp. 557-564). IEEE.

Zhou, P., Zheng, Y., & Li, M. (2012). How long to wait? Predicting bus arrival time with mobile phone based participatory sensing. *Proceedings of the 10th international conference on Mobile systems, applications, and services*, 379-392. 10.1145/2307636.2307671

Zhou, Y., Qureshi, R., & Sacan, A. (2012). Data simulation and regulatory network reconstruction from time-series microarray data using stepwise multiple linear regression. *Network Modeling and Analysis in Health Informatics and Bioinformatics*, *1*(1-2), 3–17. doi:10.100713721-012-0008-4

Zillner, S., & Sonntag, D. (2012). Image metadata reasoning for improved clinical decision support. *Network Modeling and Analysis in Health Informatics and Bioinformatics*, *1*(1-2), 37–46. doi:10.100713721-012-0003-9

About the Contributors

Olawande Daramola is currently a senior academic with the Cape Peninsula University of Technology, South Africa. He received his Bachelors, Masters and PhD degrees in Computer Science in 1997, 2004, and 2009 respectively. He has authored several scientific publications in reputable journals, book chapters, and conference proceedings in the fields of software engineering and artificial Intelligence (AI). His research interests include semantic computing, ontologies, machine learning, big data analytics, knowledge-based systems, and software engineering. He serves on the programme committee of several prestigious international conferences in Computing, and as reviewer for several top journals in the fields of Computer Science, and Information Technology.

Thomas Moser is working as the head of the research group Digital Technologies at St. Pölten University of Applied Sciences in Austria. He received his master and PhD degrees from Vienna University of Technology in 2006 and 2010, and since then authored a number of scientific publications and was involved in several research projects on national and international levels. His main research interested are data integration, knowledge graphs and digitalization in industry ("Industrie 4.0").

* * *

A. Kayode Adesemowo is Sr. lecturer at the Nelson Mandela University, South Africa. His research interests are - Information Assurance and Risk, Information Security, Asset, e-Assessment, Technology enhanced learning. A Kayode is a consummate Information Assurance Consultant, Chartered Engineer, Project Manager and Researcher. He undertakes and consults on information assurance, strategy and project management. He has an excellent blend of educational research and extensive industry exposure. Further, A Kayode is conversant with and employs best-practices and international standard. A. Kayode is experienced in making representations on labour matters and technology policy related issues across board. When not consulting, he is active in Audio-Visual solutions especially live visual projection. He had published in journals and conference proceedings and also a reviewer for journals.

Babajide Samuel Afolabi is a Professor in the Department of Computer Science and Engineering, Obafemi Awolowo University, Nigeria, who holds a Ph.D. from Université Nancy 2, Nancy, France. He is focused on developing applications for enhanced Living. He is currently the Director of the Obafemi Awolowo University Computer Centre. He researches in Information system and Software engineering. He is well published and has attended learned conferences both locally and internationally. He is a member of ISRG, ISKO France, NCS and CPN.

Rashmi Agrawal is Professor, Faculty of Computer Applications, Manav Rachna International Institute of Research and Studies, Faridabad.

Bernard Ijesunor Akhigbe holds a PhD in computer science and he is a Senior Lecturer in the Department of Computer Science and Engineering, Obafemi Awolowo University, Nigeria. He researches generally in Information system and Software engineering. He has published widely and attended learned conferences both locally and internationally. He is a member of ISRG, ISKO France, NCS and CPN.

Oluwasefunmi T. Arogundade holds a doctoral degree in computer software and theory, from Graduate University of Chinese Academy of Sciences (GUCAS), Beijing China in 2012. She had the M.Sc. degree and BSc. Degree in computer science from the Federal University of Agriculture, Abeokuta, and University of Ado Ekiti, Nigeria in 1997 and 2003 respectively. She is currently an associate professor and works as a researcher and lecturer in Federal University of Agriculture, Abeokuta, Nigeria. She has benefited both local and international awards and fellowships including Federal Government of Nigeria Postgraduate Fellowship (2001/2002), IFUW fellowship (2011-2012), OWSDW postgraduate fellowship (2009-2012). She is a member of many international organizations including ACM, IAENG, IFUW, and OWSDW. Her current research interests include software engineering, security modeling and ICT4D. She had published many articles in journals and conference proceedings.

Rangel Arthur. He holds a degree in Electrical Engineering from the Paulista State University Júlio de Mesquita Filho (1999), a Master's degree in Electrical Engineering (2002) and a Ph.D. in Electrical Engineering (2007) from the State University of Campinas. Over the years from 2011 to 2014 he was Coordinator and Associate Coordinator of Technology Courses in Telecommunication Systems and Telecommunication Engineering of FT, which was created in its management. From 2015 to 2016 he was Associate Director of the Technology (FT) of Unicamp. He is currently a lecturer and advisor to the Innovation Agency (Inova) of Unicamp. He has experience in the area of Electrical Engineering, with emphasis on Telecommunications Systems, working mainly on the following topics: computer vision, embedded systems and control systems.

Reinaldo França has a B.Sc. in Computer Engineering in 2014. Currently, he is an Ph.D. degree candidate by Department of Semiconductors, Instruments and Photonics, Faculty of Electrical and Computer Engineering at the LCV-UNICAMP working with technological and scientific research as well as in programming and development in C / C ++, Java and .NET languages. His main topics of interest are simulation, operating systems, software engineering, wireless networks, internet of things, broadcasting and telecommunications systems.

Neha Gupta is currently working as an Associate professor, Faculty of Computer Applications at Manav Rachna International Institute of Research and Studies, Faridabad campus. She has completed her PhD from Manav Rachna International University and has done R&D Project in CDAC-Noida. She has total of 12+ year of experience in teaching and research. She is a Life Member of ACM CSTA, Tech Republic and Professional Member of IEEE. She has authored and coauthored 30 research papers in SCI/SCOPUS/Peer Reviewed Journals (Scopus indexed) and IEEE/IET Conference proceedings in areas of Web Content Mining, Mobile Computing, and Web Content Adaptation. She is a technical programme committee (TPC) member in various conferences across globe. She is an active reviewer for

International Journal of Computer and Information Technology and in various IEEE Conferences around the world. She is one of the Editorial and review board members in International Journal of Research in Engineering and Technology.

Yuzo Iano received B.Sc. (1972), M.Sc. (1974) and Ph.D. degrees (1986) in Electrical Eng. at UNICAMP, Brazil. Since then he has been working in the technological production field, with 1 patent granted, 8 filed patent applications and 36 projects completed with research and development agencies. He has supervised 29 doctoral theses, 49 master's dissertations, 74 undergraduate and 48 scientific initiation works. He has participated in 100 master's examination boards, 50 doctoral degrees, author of 2 books and more than 250 published articles. He is currently Professor at UNICAMP, Editor-in-Chief of the SET International Journal of Broadcast Engineering and General Chair of the Brazilian Symposium on Technology (BTSym). He has experience in Electrical Engineering, with knowledge in Telecommunications, Electronics and Information Technology, mainly in the field of audio-visual communications and multimedia.

C. Maria Keet (PhD, MSc, MA, BSc(hons)) is an Associate Professor with the Department of Computer Science, University of Cape Town. She focuses on logic-based knowledge representation, ontology and Ontology, and conceptual data modelling, which has resulted in over 90 peer-reviewed publications, most of them as main author, at venues including KR, EKAW, ESWC, ER, CIKM, Applied Ontology, Data and Knowledge Engineering, and the Journal of Biomedical Informatics. She is PI on a NRF-funded (CPRR-grant) project on a grammar engine for Nguni languages, and was PI on an DST/MINCyT-funded bi-lateral project with Argentina on ontology-driven conceptual modelling and on a UKZN-funded project on crowdsourcing an isiZulu terminology. She was involved in the EU FET FP6 TONES, EU IRSES FP7 Net2, and EU FP7 e-Lico projects, coordinated the development of the WONDER system for intelligent access to biological data, and has served in over 25 Program Committees of international workshops and conferences and reviewed for 14 journals. She is a NRF-rated researcher (C1). Before her employment at UCT, Maria was Senior lecturer at the School of Computer Science, University of KwaZulu-Natal, South Africa and before that, a non-tenured Assistant Professor (ricercatore a tempo determinato) at the KRDB Research Centre, Free University of Bozen-Bolzano, Italy. She obtained a PhD in Computer Science at the KRDB Research Centre in 2008, following a BSc(honours) 1st class in IT & Computing from the Open University UK in 2004, and 3.5 years work experience as systems engineer in the IT industry with its vocational training (MSCE, ASE, ITIL). In addition to computer science, she obtained an MSc in Food Science (Microbiology) from Wageningen University and Research Centre, the Netherlands, in 1998, and an MA 1st class in Peace & Development Studies from the University of Limerick, Ireland, in 2003.

Zubeida C. Khan is a senior researcher at the Council for Scientific and Industrial Research (CSIR). Her research interests include Semantic Web technologies and tools such as ontologies, and cyber security. She has over 20 peer-reviewed publications on ontology and cyber-security related research.

Ana Carolina Monteiro is a Ph.D. student at the Faculty of Electrical and Computer Engineering (FEEC) at the State University of Campinas - UNICAMP, where she develops research projects regarding health software with emphasis on the development of algorithms for the detection and counting of blood cells through processing techniques. digital images. These projects led in 2019 to a computer program registration issued by the INPI (National Institute of Industrial Property). She holds a Master's degree in Electrical Engineering from the State University of Campinas - UNICAMP (2019) and graduated in Biomedicine from the University Center Amparense - UNIFIA with a degree in Clinical Pathology - Clinical Analysis (2015). In 2019, he acquired a degree in Health Informatics. Has experience in the areas of Molecular Biology and management with research animals. Since 2017, she has been a researcher at the FEEC/UNICAMP Visual Communications Laboratory (LCV) and has worked at the Brazilian Technology Symposium (BTSym) as a member of the Organizational and Executive Committee and as a member of the Technical Reviewers Committee. In addition, she works as a reviewer at the Health magazines of the Federal University of Santa Maria (UFSM - Brazil), Medical Technology Journal MTJ (Algeria) and Production Planning & Control (Taylor & Francis). Interested in: digital image processing, hematology, clinical analysis, cell biology, medical informatics, Matlab and teaching.

Attoh Okine is Professor and Interim Academic Director (Cybersecurity Initiative), University of Delaware.

Joy Olawuyi holds B.Sc and M.Sc in Computer Science, currently a PhD student. research interests are deep learning algorithms, medical image analysis, big data, blockchain technology.

Kamalendu Pal is with the Department of Computer Science, School of Mathematics, Computer Science and Engineering, City, University of London. Kamalendu received his BSc (Hons) degree in Physics from Calcutta University, India, Postgraduate Diploma in Computer Science from Pune, India, MSc degree in Software Systems Technology from Sheffield University, Postgraduate Diploma in Artificial Intelligence from Kingston University, MPhil degree in Computer Science from University College London, and MBA degree from University of Hull, United Kingdom. He has published widely in the scientific community with research articles in the ACM SIGMIS Database, Expert Systems with Applications, Decision Support Systems, and conferences. His research interests include knowledge-based systems, decision support systems, blockchain technology, software engineering, and service-oriented computing. He is a member of the British Computer Society, the Institution of Engineering and Technology, and the IEEE Computer Society.

Padma Priya received her B.Tech degree from Regency institute of technology in 2010 and M.Tech degree in the field of network and internet engineering from Pondicherry University in 2012, India. She is doing research in the area of Wireless sensor network at Anna University, Chennai, India. Her area of interest includes Wireless sensor network, Internet of Things and Bio inspired computing. She has also published 6 papers in International journal, 6 in International Conference. She is currently working as an Associate Professor in IFET College of Engineering for the department of Computer Science and Engineering.

Aswini Raja has completed her bachelor of Engineering at Kalasalingam Institute of Technology in 2013 and her masters at Sathyabama University as gold medallist in 2015. Her main areas of research interest are Internet of Things, Blockchain, Cybersecurity and Datamining. She has published five papers in international journals and four papers in SCI and Scopus Indexed Journal and three in IEEE conference. She is currently working as an Assistant Professor in IFET College of Engineering for the department of Computer Science and Engineering.

A Kader Saiod is working as the head of the IT Department at HUME International. He received his PhD from Nelson Mandala University (NMU), Port Elizabeth, South Africa in 2019 and MASTER WITH HONORS from Donetsk National Technical University Donetsk, Ukraine in 2008. Since then authored a number of scientific book chapter publications and conference paper. His main research interested are artificial intelligence, machine learning language and deep learning and data integration."

Antonio Sarasa-Cabezuelo has a MS. degree on Mathematics of Computer Sciences from the Complutense University of Madrid, BS. degree on Computer Sciences from the National University of Distance Education, MS. degree on Computer Sciences from the Open University of Catalonia and CS PhD from the Complutense University of Madrid. Currently, he is an associate professor in the Computer Science School at Complutense University of Madrid, and a member of the research group ILSA (Implementation of Language-Driven Software and Applications,, http://ilsa.fdi.ucm.es). His research is focused on e-Learning, markup languages and Domain-specific languages. He was one of the developers of the Agrega project on digital repositories. He has published over 50 research papers in national and international conferences. Likewise, he is a member of the 36 Subcommittee of AENOR.

Darelle van Greunen leads a research, engagement and innovation group at Nelson Mandela University, namely the Centre for Community Technologies (CCT). The CCT integrates transdisciplinary research and innovation with community engagement through the development and implementation of apps and other smart technologies that enable the advancement of education, health, rural and social development, particularly in low income communities. This is combined with training, networking and policy analysis and advice. She is recognised as one of a handful of innovators for the people and is affectionately known as "the people's professor" who has managed to introduce smart technologies to the man in the street. She was the first joint-appointment as a senior researcher between a South African University and the German multinational software corporation SAP AG in 2006. Over the past five years, Prof Van Greunen and her team of change-maker researchers have won various awards and international acknowledgement for their ground-breaking research and application development within the African context and thus realising her vision of "ICT solutions for Africa, by Africans, in Africa". Prof Van Greunen has published a number of well-cited scientific papers and also acts as an external reviewer for a number of international journals and actively assists with the formulation of policy for the South African Government. As such, she is then recognised as one of the leading academics in the space of advancing the 4th Industrial Revolution in Education. Qualifications Ph.D Computer Science (UNISA) M.A Computer Aided Learning (UPE) Further Diploma Educational Computing (UPE) Higher Education Diploma (UPE).

Index

4IR 166-169, 171, 175, 182

A

abstraction 22, 72-80, 83, 85, 87-89, 121-123, 131, 136, 182, 222
API REST WEB SERVICES 147
application layer 117, 121, 126
artificial intelligence (AI) 22, 130, 223, 237, 251
auto-grading 166, 170, 174, 180-182, 184

B

big data (BD) 22
blockchain 11-12, 18-19, 50-62, 64-71, 125, 220, 233
Bloom's taxonomy 170, 175, 183, 189

C

Cognitive Computing 3, 16-17, 21, 144-145
Communication Layer 126
COVID-19/nCov-19 189
cryptocurrency 11, 19, 50, 62-63

D

Data Quality (DQ) 23, 27
Data Service Layer 126
decision support 64, 211-212, 220, 236-238, 242, 247, 249, 256
deep CNN 128, 135, 138-139, 141-142
Deep learning (DL) 22
Description Logics 75, 89-90, 218, 225-226, 234, 240
Digital Repository 165
digital signature 50, 56-57
disease diagnosis 137, 236-237, 239-240, 252
distributed ledger technology (DLT) 50, 58

E

Electronic Health Records (EHRs) 236, 238-240, 246, 251-255
EPC 222, 234

G

gait analysis 236-243, 249, 252-256
geolocation 149, 152-157

H

Hand-crafted ML Algorithms 128
Hash Key 50
HCI 204, 209

I

ICT networking 166-171, 174, 176, 182-183
information 1-15, 17-21, 23-24, 26-35, 37-39, 45, 47-48, 50-51, 53-57, 59, 61-62, 64-67, 69, 80, 89, 93-99, 103, 111-118, 120-126, 129, 131, 134, 137-140, 142-143, 145, 147-158, 160, 162-167, 171, 183-187, 190-192, 194-197, 199-202, 204, 208-215, 218-225, 227, 231, 233-234, 237, 239-240, 244, 246, 249, 251-254
Internet of Things 11, 16, 113, 123-126, 163, 190, 208-209, 213, 218, 220-221, 230, 232-234, 237, 242, 253

K

knowledge graph 20, 147, 237, 242-243, 245-250, 255-256
Knowledge Management 8, 19, 90, 111, 243

L

lexicon adaptation 93, 103
linked data 10, 14, 19, 64, 147-150, 161-163, 165, 204, 238, 242, 244, 246, 248

M

manufacturing business 115, 119, 218, 222, 231
medical image analysis 128-130, 132, 135-136, 145
Microservice 113, 115, 126

N

networks engineering 166
NreASAM 166, 169, 175-182, 189

O

Object Layer 126
online submission 166, 175, 178, 180-183, 185
ontologies 2-3, 6-10, 14-15, 18, 23, 32, 51, 72-78, 80-81, 83-95, 97, 99, 110, 117, 126, 144, 147-148, 168, 171, 180, 183, 186-188, 209, 221-222, 224, 231, 234-238, 246
ontology modularisation 72, 74, 76, 88, 90
ontology modularity 72, 85
Ontology Module 72, 84
open data 9, 147-154, 158, 161-165, 237-238, 240, 243
Opinion Mining 93, 96-97, 111-112

P

Packet Tracer 166, 170-171, 178, 180, 182-183, 185

R

RDF 3, 6-8, 13, 17, 50, 64, 95, 126, 147-148, 163-165, 235, 245, 248
recommender 147, 162, 175, 182, 185, 249
resource-limited settings 236, 238, 244, 247, 250-252, 255
RFID Reader 126, 234
RFID tag 125-126, 234

S

Science 1, 15-16, 19-20, 48, 72, 125, 128, 143-145, 163-164, 185-186, 188, 190, 210-212, 214, 232-234, 243, 253-254
Semantic Computing 3, 19, 21, 88, 129-130, 133-134, 136, 140, 143, 145, 182, 199
semantic data integration 236-239, 241-243, 245, 250, 253, 256
Semantic IR 190-191
semantic machine learning representations (SMLR) 22
Semantic Medical Image Analysis 128-129
Semantic Search Computing 190, 194
Semantic Web 1-3, 5-10, 12-21, 42, 50-52, 54, 64, 70, 72, 89, 91, 93-96, 117, 147, 162-163, 165, 181, 184, 186, 188, 191, 198-200, 209-210, 212-213, 218, 221, 223, 232-235, 245, 248, 256
Semantic Web service 9, 18, 218, 223, 235
sentiment analysis 45-46, 93-94, 96-99, 101-102, 104, 107, 109-112
Service-Oriented Architecture 54, 113, 115, 120, 123-124, 126
simulator 166, 169-170, 174, 177, 180
smart contract 51-52, 58, 61-62, 70
SPARQL 64, 147-148, 150, 161, 163, 165, 224, 245, 248
Supply Chain Management 113-114, 116, 125-126, 218-219, 231, 233-235
sustainable assessment 168-171, 174, 178, 183-184, 189

T

transfer learning 22, 128, 131-133, 136-139

U

user-centred evaluative framework and theories 190
users' requirement 190, 199

W

Web 3.0 1-5, 8-13, 15-19, 21, 70-71
Web Ontology Language (OWL) 126, 235
web service 9, 18, 119, 125, 150, 152-153, 163, 165, 218, 222-223, 232, 235
Wikidata 149-151, 164-165

Printed in the United States
By Bookmasters